Man: The Image of God

BOOKS BY G. C. BERKOUWER

MODERN UNCERTAINTY AND CHRISTIAN FAITH

THE TRIUMPH OF GRACE IN THE THEOLOGY OF KARL BARTH

STUDIES IN DOGMATICS SERIES —

THE PROVIDENCE OF GOD

FAITH AND SANCTIFICATION

FAITH AND JUSTIFICATION

FAITH AND PERSEVERANCE

THE PERSON OF CHRIST

GENERAL REVELATION

DIVINE ELECTION

Studies in Dogmatics

Man: The Image of God

BY

G. C. BERKOUWER

PROFESSOR OF SYSTEMATIC THEOLOGY
FREE UNIVERSITY OF AMSTERDAM

WM. B. EERDMANS PUBLISHING COMPANY
GRAND RAPIDS, MICHIGAN

ISBN 0-8028-3035-8

First printing, April 1962
Second printing, June 1968
Third printing, March 1969
Fourth printing, May 1972

Translated by Dirk W. Jellema
from the Dutch edition, *De Mens het Beeld Gods,*
published by J. H. Kok N.V., Kampen, The Netherlands

Printed in the United States of America

Contents

ABBREVIATIONS

BC   — Belgic Confession

CD   — Canons of Dort

ET   — English Translation

HC   — Heidelberg Catechism

Inst.   — *Institutes of the Christian Religion* by John Calvin

K.D.   — *Kirchliche Dogmatik* by Karl Barth

TWZNT — *Theologisches Worterbuch zum Neuen Testament* ed. by G. Kittel

CHAPTER ONE

THE MYSTERY OF MAN

TODAY, more than at any time, the question "What is man?" is at the center of theological and philosophical concern. The number of studies that have taken this problem as their theme is almost innumerable. And yet, the fact that this problem has forced itself to the attention of contemporary thought does not take away a rather puzzling aspect of the problem itself; namely, Why should this be a *problem?* It would seem that there is nothing so widely and generally "known" in everyday experience as is man. Is not the problem of the "nature" of man an abstract problem, a strange, reflexive, obvious problem? Is not this "nature" experienced by all of us, in ourselves and in others, in countless relationships, in the heights of human happiness and the depths of grief? Who does not "know" man, whom we daily encounter, and the man that we ourselves are?

There can be only one answer to such questions; namely, that this almost irresistible problem appears to many a mind *not* to have found a clear and obviously irrefutable answer, and that this apparently general "knowledge" of the nature of man is not so obvious after all. Its obviousness is indeed drastically relativized as soon as we discover that man's reflection on the nature of man has produced an astonishing variety of views. Hence it does not appear, on second thought, to be at all clear and obvious *who* and *what* man *really* is, and there is thus every reason to pose the problem.

Indeed, there is scarcely another theme dealt with by human consciousness which has aroused so much controversy as this theme — the nature of man, which is the subject of this book. There is, nevertheless, a generally dominant feeling or intuition that man, in one way or another, occupies a central position in the whole of reality; although there are great differences of opinion as to the nature of this central position, and although there are some views of man which tend to play down the uniqueness of his nature. Nor, generally, does this feeling of man's central position imply a

10   MAN: THE IMAGE OF GOD

one-sidedly anthropocentric view which neglects non-human reality. It is with a certain *naturalness*, evidently, that we direct our attention first and foremost to man, and bring in non-human reality in connection with man.[1] We are forcibly reminded here of the Biblical narrative of creation, which describes the creation of all of reality, but which unmistakably culminates in the creation of man. And we generally find a similar relationship posed between center and periphery — whether or not it is related to the Biblical account — wherever the uniqueness of man, *"der Mensch in seiner Eigenart,"* in Sombart's phrase, is investigated in connection with the world which surrounds him.[2] There is for most people strong evidence for this centrality of man. Nor can we say, on Biblical grounds, that this attention given to man is in itself evidence of a dangerous over-evaluation which proudly places man in a central position and judges him to be the most important thing in reality. It is true that the term "anthropocentric" has usually been used, in the historical development of theology, to describe an error which understood this centrality in illegitimate ways; but we can certainly not deny this centrality on Biblical grounds, and indeed we may not do so.[3]

When, however, we go beyond this general agreement on the centrality of man, and inquire as to the specific nature of man, we are immediately confronted with an impressive variety of answers. We may feel that this large number of conflicting views is strange and paradoxical, when seen against the general experience we all have of the nature of man; but, nevertheless, it is a fact, and one

1. Cf. H. U. von Balthasar: "Philosophy has become anthropology; not as though there were no reality outside men, but in the sense that all natural reality is oriented to man" (*Die Gottesfrage des heutigen Menschen*, 1956, p. 46).
2. The phrase is the title of the first volume of Werner Sombart's *Vom Menschen. Versuch einer geisteswissenschaftliche Anthropologie* (1938). This also has a chapter on "animalism," in the context of "doubts concerning man's uniqueness in the cosmos." Sombart contrasts "hominism" with "animalism." The "human form of existence in its uniqueness" as a bridge between biology and anthropology is treated by A. Portmann in *Zoologie und das neue Bild des Menschen* (1956), p. 12. Cf. also Max Scheler, *Die Stellung des Menschen im Kosmos.*
3. A contrast is sometimes drawn between "anthropocentric" and "theocentric" theology, as by, e.g., E. Schaeder in his critique of nineteenth-century theology; see Chapter 10. Actually, illegitimacy occurs in anthropocentrism when the latter is understood as being in competition with theocentrism — something which is completely ruled out in the narrative of creation, as in the rest of the Bible.

which raises a new problem. What is the cause of these striking divergences in outlook?

We need only read a contemporary symposium on the problem to be struck by the far-reaching differences in outlook. In the Netherlands, for example, the recent *Gesprekken op Drakenburgh* (edited by J. Peters) might be cited. It includes a chapter on man as "the witness of the mystery of being." We might indeed be inclined to raise the question whether perhaps man is a mystery to himself, and whether desperate confusion of views regarding the "nature of man" might not be due to man's groping after something which is hidden, which is an unknowable mystery, a hopeless riddle.[4] Does what Paul says about the heathen and their search for God (Acts 17:27) — "that they might feel after him and find him" — apply also to our search for man?[5] Or is the confusion and hesitation, the doubt and uncertainty, only the self-alienation of man, who has lost a true understanding of himself and others?

It is clear, in any case, that thought in general has not been content to rest with man as "mystery" or "riddle." There is no real parallel to religious agnosticism, which affirms the unknowability of God, in man's search for man's nature; there is no real agnosticism about man. Alexis Carrel, to be sure, wrote a book on *Man, the Unknown*; but the whole book treats of our knowledge of man; and in any case the problem of the *nature* of man has been raised time and time again since then. It is a problem which, as soon as it is posed, raises a host of further problems, as our attention is directed to the origin of man, the future of man, his soul, his body, his freedom, his responsibility, and, most importantly, his relations to his fellow man. These are problems which have been discussed almost endlessly, and indeed there has been no generation which has heedlessly passed them by. Man has always been concerned, in scholarly fashion as well as in the popular consciousness, with the many aspects of man's humanity, and thus with man

---

4. Cf. Max Scheler's remarks on indefinability as an attribute of man's nature, in *Vom Umsturz der Werte* (1919), I, 296.
5. Some notion of the many variations and divergences in man's idea of God can be gained from such a book as C. J. Bleeker *et al., Anthropologie religieuse* (1955), which among other things, takes up primitive anthropology and also the anthropology of Babylonia, Greece, Persia, India, Buddhism, and Gnosticism. Compare Werner Sombart (*op. cit.*, pp. 3-5), who gives a long list of definitions of the "nature" or "essence" of man, and ends by judging them all either erroneous or one-sided.

himself.[6] And yet we can scarcely deny that in our time the
attention given to this problem has a new urgency, seriousness,
and concentration. This intensive contemporary interest is closely
tied in with the actual manifestations of man's nature in the
events of the twentieth century. Our concern with the nature
of man does not grow from a purely abstract and theoretical interest, but is related to the fact that we have learned to "know"
man, in our age, in direct and often alarming or catastrophic
manner. "Real life" has recently produced experiences which have
powerfully stimulated the consideration of the question, What
is man? We are faced with an increased interest in the nature
of man; not an interest in the abstract idea of man, but in the
concrete actual man in all his acts and omissions. The problem is
indeed frequently posed in a very specific and realistic manner as
follows: What hopes may we have for the future of man and
humanity?

The searchlight of contemporary interest concentrates on man —
living man, in all his striving and acting, his love and hate, his
potentialities and limitations, his struggles and tensions.[7] This
interest is not a merely ontological interest in the nature of man,
or in the manner in which he is "composed" of different "parts"
(body, soul, spirit). It is an interest in the concrete man with his
power and capacity, his motives and passions, his race and national-
ity — in man, who in our century has revealed himself in so
many ways as a *danger* to his fellow man.[8] A "disinterested" ontological investigation seems to have become nearly impossible. The
experiences of our century have suddenly given a new urgency
and an oppressive seriousness to the old words of Jeremiah: "The
heart is deceitful above all things, and desperately corrupt: who
can understand it?" (Jer. 17:19).

---

6. According to Max Scheler (*ibid.*, p. 274), all the problems of philosophy
   go back to the basic question, What is man? Cf. N. Berdyaev, *Von
   der Bestimmung des Menschen* (1935), p. 68; ET, *The Destiny of Man*
   (1937): "The problem of man is the basic theme of philosophy."
7. Cf. the titles of the works of Emil Brunner; e.g., *Der Mensch im
   Widerspruch* (1937); ET, *Man in Revolt* (1947); or G. J. Hoenderdaal, *De
   Mens in Tweestrijd;* ET, *Man in Conflict* (1956).
8. Any collection of definitions reveals that on the one hand many are
   ontological — e.g., Schiller's "that nature which is able to will," or
   Waitz's "that animated being which experiences"; and many are *qualify-
   ing* — e.g., Rousseau's "depraved animal," Freud's "suppressor of instincts," Klages's "thinking animal," and so forth. Sombart (*op. cit.*,
   p. 4) says that he did not find among these the "very important definition: man is that creature who bores himself."

Whenever we reflect on the nature of man, we cannot escape considering *evil*, which man does and lives and experiences in his everyday life. It is not possible to distance ourselves from this serious problem by a simple relativizing of human evil. Nor is it possible to escape it by stressing the anonymity of evil, since it stands constantly before us in concrete and localized form. Once again our attention is directed to man as unique and central — but this time in his manifestations *in malam partem*, in his appearance as an evil force. We can hear, in this century, many voices that appear to display a certain receptivity to Jeremiah's stress on the *unique* in man's evil: "deceitful *above all things*." Perhaps, instead of being an overly pessimistic view of man, Jeremiah's judgment is simply realistic. "*Man's* heart" — that appears to be a universal judgment which allows no exceptions and no distinctions between groups of men. Such are the questions which again constantly occupy our minds; specifically whether such an "abysmal" view of man is, after all, not an extreme exaggeration brought about by bitter and disappointing experiences, but rather a genuine description of the *real* man in these depths and in this ruin. And if this be the true picture, again and again it is asked, Is there no future perspective, no hope for restoration and renewal? Must man be on his guard only against "man," that "inventor of evil" (Rom. 1:30)? Is not the answer to the problem of the nature of man really found in the experience of thousands in our century who have known, often irrevocably, what man is and what can be expected of him? Has not man become identifiable in the figure of Cain, who hated and murdered his brother? Is he not the man of danger, the man who has embarked on a course which marks him as "full of envy, murder, strife," "faithless, heartless, ruthless," the egocentric man, untrustworthy in his fickleness, the man who — when all his masks fall away — becomes *known* to us with inescapable clarity?[9] Is man, then, really the *un*known?

It is well to remember, once again, that we are not dealing with an abstract *idea* of man, but with actual man. Reflection which thinks it can ignore the darker aspects of man's nature is occupied with an abstraction and will never acquire the right view of the actual problems of man's life. And, indeed, this fact is now generally recognized and applied. In various ways we are attempting to

9. Rom. 1:29-31. We are not forgetting the relation between this description and God's judgment which "gave them up in the lusts of their hearts" (Rom. 1:24, 26, 28), but we are here dealing with possibilities, which become actualities in human nature.

reach a sound analysis of the darker depths of man's nature and of the very abysses of his soul. And this attempt at a "phenomenology" of evil immediately raises a further question: Is it possible to find behind man's nature in its darker and more horrible aspects the *real* man, of whom we can say better and nobler things? This problem, the possibility of finding a hidden center, of going beyond the actuality of man's evil aspects to the real man, the essential man, is the basic problem of all humanism. Humanism, in whatever form, can never remain satisfied with our empirical understanding of the darker aspects of man; it believes there are reasons to seek beyond this for the real man. It is thus understandable enough that in times when our more optimistic views of man's nature are drastically disturbed, specific crisis phenomena always appear. Is such a reduction, such a search for the real man, still possible, or even meaningful? A. V. A. Röling remarked recently, in the course of a discussion of man and the law, that man's position is steadily becoming more precarious, and that hence there arises the need to "preserve essential human values."[10] And what he noted in connection with the legal profession has a much wider application. Indeed, whenever we view man — whether through scholarly eyes or not — our empirical observation forces such "existential" approaches to the fore.

In the light of experience, how can the search for "essential human values" still be justified? And whence comes still the *courage* to continue to posit any contrast whatever between the "actual" man and the "real" man?

As a partial answer to this question, we should first note that the impression made by contemporary humanism is complex. On the one hand, it is frequently critical of exaggerated optimism about man, and on the other hand, it remains unwilling to give up the humanistic transition from the "actual" man to the "real" man. It is not willing to accept the idea that search for the deeper resources of human life has been proven illusory through inescapable facts. Indeed, quite the contrary — humanism has not been willing to give ground on this point, but has rather been driven by contemporary experiences to search even more earnestly for the "real" man. It would once more appeal to the *deepest* aspects of man's nature, to potentialities that lie still deeper, to springs of power that had been neglected and blocked up previously but which

10. A. V. A. Röling, "De Mens in het Recht," *Scripta Academica Groningiana*, VI (1955), pp. 71ff.

now — in a time of crisis — must be tapped. Confidence in humanity, faith in man, is not completely lost.

It is striking that contemporary humanism in its various forms has more than once insisted that it does not want to be identified with the earlier, naively optimistic faith in man. Rather, the more mature and realistic contemporary versions of humanism wish to include elements of quite another sort, which make for wide differentiation from earlier humanism's trust in man's nature and from the related belief in progress. The nature of this change is rather complicated. There can, for example, be reference to a recognition of the *tragic* aspects of man's life — a recognition which greatly relativizes earlier humanistic optimism — accompanied by a candid recognition of the *demonic* aspects of man's nature.[11] But, despite the sometimes striking differences from earlier humanism which such developments may produce, we still must reckon with the fact that in the last analysis humanism's outlook as regards the "real" man still remains. Despite all the allowances it makes for the reality of the "un-human" in man, contemporary humanism still refuses to yield its affirmation of the inviolability and indestructibility of the *humanum* in man, of the "real" man. It is prepared to speak of man's badness and even of his "inhumanity"; it is prepared to picture man in the unfathomable depths of hate and envy, in the abysses of egoism and angry menace, both in his conscious and unconscious aggressiveness towards his fellow man, in his pitiless hardness of heart. It is prepared for a *démasqué*, a ripping off of the masks, which will break through the illusions of bourgeois morality and show man for what he "actually" is. But this unmasking does not mean that humanism has accepted defeatism or hopelessness. For in and beyond this unmasking a further goal is visible: the "nevertheless," the continuing search for transcending the alarming empirical data, the reaching towards a deeper and more basic aspect of human nature which cannot be denied, however much it may seem to be hidden behind the "actual" man.

11. For Berdyaev, Marxist humanism, with its optimistic belief in progress, is the one remaining form of rationalistic humanism. The change in the nature of humanism, says Berdyaev, came in the second half of the last century, when recognition of the tragic principle in human life led to an inner crisis (cf. Nietzsche, Kierkegaard, Dostoievski). See N. Berdyaev, "Alte und neue Wege des Humanismus," *Theologische Zeitschrift*, II (1946), pp. 124f. Cf. also Jacques Maritain, *Towards a New Christendom* (1936); H. R. Hoetink, *Humanisme en Socialisme* (1946), especially pp. 27ff. and 181ff.; and also my *De algemene Openbaring* (1951), pp. 181ff. (ET, *General Revelation*, 1955).

It takes no great insight to detect in all this a new optimism, which breaks through all experience and empirical data.[12] Humanism may be prepared for discounting the "actual" man, but sooner or later there comes an end to this discounting, and a new trust in man, which results in a new appeal. It is a trust which still, in one way or another, appeals to the *humanum* in man, the "greatness" of man. It might well be asked to what extent such a concept is parallel to Pascal's well-known phrase regarding the greatness and misery of man, *"misère et grandeur de l'âme."* As it strikes us, this phrase is in our day often quoted to emphasize that man's "greatness" has revealed itself in astonishing ways in this century and, on the other hand, man's misery and evil, his destructive capacities, have become just as obvious. A variety of views about man, the secret of his nature, his mysterious and riddle-filled nature, often circle around these two words — greatness and misery. Precisely this alienating contrast has been referred to as man's "unique paradoxicality."[13]

12. Cf. J. P. van Praag, *Modern Humanisme: Een Renaissance?* (1947), p. 241: "Our course does indeed lie across a treacherous sea of demonic technical skills, massive anxiety and egoism, cynicism and discouragement — but seamanship and bravery have often accomplished the apparently impossible." Van Praag recognizes the "demonic" character of the "actual" man, but his appeal is *still* to the creative powers of man and the tasks which they imply "even though every specific realization of these powers should again crumble in our hands like chalk." The "nevertheless" is the strong diapason here; that is, even if the "actual" man is demonic, we must "nevertheless" strive to saturate all of life with humanness. Even though, strictly speaking, "it is very well possible that the realization of this aim will remain a dream even in the future," still, "that does not lessen its inner reality in the present." We can see clearly in Van Praag the problems of a humanism which has been shocked and arrested, but which still strives towards rebuilding and a viable future. Humanism is generally less pessimistic than Van Praag's words here are. Cf. G. J. Hoenderdaal, *De Mens in Tweestrijd* (1956), pp. 72ff.; Paul Tillich, *De Moed om te zijn* (1955), pp. 150ff. (ET: *The Courage to Be*), on "the courage to take on one's self the fear of meaninglessness" — here meaninglessness is integrated into courage. For another discussion of the renewed "optimism" of contemporary humanism, see H. de Vos, *De Christelijk Idee der Humaniteit* (1947), p. 13.

13. For man's "unique paradoxicality," see K. H. A. Hidding, *Hoe zien wij de Mens van philosophisch Standpunt beschouwd?* (1951), p. 23. For the passage in Pascal, cf. C. Serrurier, *De Pensées van Pascal* (1955, 3rd. ed.), pp. 106ff.; Leo Sjestov, "De Nacht van Gethsemane," "De Philosophie van Pascal," *Crisis der Zekerheden* (1931); P. Brunner, "Pascals Anschauung vom Menschen," *Imago Dei* (1932); Emil Brunner, *Der Mensch im Widerspruch*, p. 169 (ET: *Man in Revolt*); A. Béguin, *Pascal par lui-même* (1952), pp. 146ff. For Pascal's idea of the close relation

It is actually clear enough, however, that Pascal's words in any event have nothing to do with any relativizing or "reduction" of man's misery along humanistic lines. He is not concerned with a "greatness" which is the hidden center of man, which is "left over" from man's apparent evil, and which finally lessens the seriousness and range of the misery. He is not speaking of a "remainder" which shows that the damage is after all not so catastrophic. For Pascal, on the contrary, man's "greatness" and "misery" are closely related to each other. Man's misery is "the misery of a nobleman, the misery of a dethroned king." The greatness of man, created by God, is reflected in the depth of his fall. It is clear enough that Pascal is not speaking of any hidden center in man. This is a different view of greatness and misery than that given by humanism, where the greatness is sought behind the misery as the hidden center, the "real" man in his true humanity.

When we reflect on this new trust in man — rising above the many disillusionments of our age — then we can understand why the conflict regarding the nature of man constantly finds its point of concentration in the Christian confession regarding man's corruption and fall. We shall later examine this idea of *corruptio totalis* more closely, but it should be noted here that this Reformation doctrine has been attacked from many sides as a seriously erroneous presentation of man's nature, an attack on his human worth, a strange and untenable pessimism. The religious description of man as "corrupt" is always an impassable stumbling-block for humanism, whatever its variety. When humanists speak of man's corruption, inhumanity, and demonic qualities, they do *not* mean thereby to give a complete and final description. When Ernst Cassirer speaks of the basic point at issue between humanism and the Reformation, he speaks of the "radically different presentation of the problem of original sin," in that humanism and the

---

between man's greatness and misery, see P. Brunner, *op. cit.*, p. 145: "Man's greatness and misery are not isolated from each other, but are reciprocally related"; cf. A. Stöcker, *Das Bild vom Menschen bei Pascal* (1939), pp. 66ff.: "not two parallel conditions, but an 'état complexe' . . . the misery is direct evidence for the grandeur." Cf. also H. Kraemer, *Kerk en Humanisme*, p. 30. The analogy of the "dethroned king" is from Pascal, *Pénsees*, No. 364. Pascal, in his noted *Mémorial*, uses the expression "the grandeur of the human soul," but the context makes it very clear that these words cannot be used in isolated form. Cf., e.g., R. Guardini, *Christliches Bewusstsein. Versuche über Pascal* (1935), pp. 23, 45.

Enlightenment, while not denying a fall, tried to some extent to "weaken this dogma and sap its force."[14] In all reflection on human nature we shall constantly encounter the reality of evil, and shall always find ourselves eventually confronted by the attempt to find the hidden center, an attempt which appears to dominate every view of man's nature which man himself forms.

It is clear enough that any search for a hidden center in man's nature which turns from the actual man to look for the "real" man must face the question whether this shift is justified. Just how are we able to search so hopefully and trustingly for, and to appeal so expectantly to, this "real" man, who is and must be so different from man as we experience him? Is there some kind of a priori intuition at the basis of this search, or is it — even partially — based on experience, on some light which cuts through the apparent darkness of human life?

These questions are urgent, for the man who engages in the search is a man and is thus not merely evaluating others but speaks of himself as a man who participates in man's nature. Every view of man's nature affects not only others, but also the man doing the viewing. No man can abstract himself from his own nature, and it is precisely this fact which gives such an existential character to every judgment about "man" and to every view of man's nature. When we inquire as to the source of our knowledge about man, we are asking about the source of our knowledge about *ourselves*. And, while it appears at first glance simple enough to include both under the same word "knowledge," on closer examination we are faced with a rather strange situation — a man may sometimes obtain a good insight into the lives of others without ever coming to a true self-knowledge. There is no guarantee at all that a scholar or scientist who has done all sorts of research on the nature of man has gained thereby true knowledge about himself. We may even say that there is often a wide gulf between our

14. Ernst Cassirer, *Die Philosophie der Aufklärung* (1932), p. 185. In 1926 Max Scheler in his study of Judeo-Christian anthropology as the first. major view of man, spoke of the anxiety which this view (cf. the fall, original sin) produced, and the consequent feeling of alienation which even today "powerfully influences Western man, including the non-believer." We have not yet seen, he said, the "great psychoanalyst of history" who might free us from this anxiety, "the emotional root of the specifically Judeo-Christian world of ideas." (See Scheler's "Mensch und Geschichte," *Philosophische Weltanschauung*, 1954, p. 67.)

analysis and knowledge of others and of ourselves. "Know yourself!" said the oracle of Delphi, and there already was implied that such self-knowledge was not a simple and obvious thing which everyone possessed.

It is often apparent that man's self-knowledge is extremely limited and incomplete, and that man's picture of himself does not correspond at all with the actuality of his nature. It seems undeniable that "our eyes become clouded" more quickly in examining ourselves than in examining others.[15] The Bible often calls to our attention examples of illusory and unsubstantial self-portraits. Thus, Isaiah ridicules the king of Babylon, the morning-star, the son of the dawn, who said, "I will ascend into heaven; I will exalt my throne above the stars of God; and I will sit also on the mount of the congregation, in the uttermost parts of the north; I will ascend above the heights of the clouds; I will make myself like the most High" (Isa. 14:13-14). On the contrary! So Isaiah pricks the conceit of this self-"knowledge" and exposes its unreality and perversity, which are so blatant as to approach the ludicrous and invite judgment.

Elsewhere we hear Nebuchadnezzar boasting in praise of himself: "Is this not great Babylon, which I have built for the royal dwelling place, by the might of my power and for the glory of my majesty?" (Dan. 4:30). And then a voice from heaven answers and brands all of this "knowledge" as illusion and *non-sense*. So much for the the king's "self-knowledge"!

But we should not limit this radical misinterpretation of man's nature to a few spectacular historical extremes. This misinterpretation (at least as self-interpretation) occurs everywhere in man's life. We see it not only in the Biblical portrayal of Antichrist (e.g., II Thess. 2:4), who turns himself against everything which can be called divine or an object of adoration, and who puts himself in the temple of God in the pretense that he is a god; we see it also in the "self-knowledge" of the Pharisees (e.g., Luke 18:9-11, Acts 8:9-10), who trusted in themselves that they were righteous, but who were actually filled with the many works of their own ego. With what norms, and from what perspectives is this "view of man" drawn! And how clearly it appears here that this "self-knowledge" occupies a very basic position, and directly

15. Cf. M. Landmann, "Menschliche Selbstdeutung in Geschichte und Gegenwart," *Philosophisch Anthropologie* (1955), p. 55: "As long as we are thinking of man in general, we can say, with Democritus: Man is something we all know. But if we consider our own self, then we must say: what man is, no one knows."

influences our judgment of others. It is certainly no accident that
the Pharisees thought themselves righteous and others not so.
Ernst Cassirer calls self-knowledge "the Archimedian point, the
fixed and immovable center of all thought."[16] And the *problem*
of gaining true self-knowledge lies not only in the difficulty of
inner perception, but also in the "idols of self-knowledge" which
can cloud our view of others.[17] Self-knowledge, because of these
idols, becomes an illusion, and God's judgment of the Pharisee and
the publican is quite different than man's; the publican, not the
Pharisee, is justified.[18]

Thus man appears to be — not in his own judgment, but in
actuality — always *homo absconditus,* hidden man. He can indeed
obtain all sorts of theoretical knowledge, and work up various views
on the ontological "composition" of man's nature — but this does
not answer the question, What is man?. The way to self-knowledge
appears blocked, closed with impassable barricades. And hence
we need not wonder that the question again and again arises
whether it is possible either by way of science or of inner examination to acquire knowledge of man, or whether it is not religion
alone which furnishes the most profound source of self-knowledge.[19]

This last point is stressed especially by John Calvin. In his
treatment of the nature and origin of self-knowledge, he says that
man's self-knowledge can never be isolated from his knowledge
of God.[20]

It is clear, according to him, "that man never attains to a true
self-knowledge until he has previously contemplated the face of
God and come down after such contemplation to look into him-

---

16. *An Essay on Man* (1953), p. 15.
17. Max Scheler, "Idole der Selbsterkenntnis," in *Vom Umsturz der
    Werte* (1919), II, 5-140.
18. Luke 18:14, to which is added "for every one that exalteth himself
    shall be humbled; but he that humbleth himself shall be exalted." Cf.
    Mark 9:35, regarding those who "would be first" — a desire which always
    arises from a certain type of self-evaluation. Cf. also Mark 10:43 and
    Luke 14:8-10.
19. See Cassirer on Pascal, *An Essay on Man,* p. 28; cf. also L. Onvlee,
    Wij Mensen (1956), p. 22.
20. In Gustave Corcao's novel *Cursus van de Dood* (1951), the protagonist
    answers a question from his doctor regarding his religious belief: "I
    have arrived at the point where I now am without knowing who I am
    and who God is." The statement is all the more striking here in that
    the rest of the novel concerns an attempt to gain this knowledge in
    the months remaining to him: the "curriculum of death."

self."[21] Man cannot truly know himself if he ignores the light of God's revelation, which falls over his life, and which unveils the true nature of man, of actual, concrete man.

In this connection, Calvin points out the perverted self-knowledge and self-evaluation which arise from pride, and in which we evaluate ourselves as righteous. The standard for true self-evaluation is lacking, and we take satisfaction in an idle and vain picture of self-righteousness. Calvin does not deny that we may then still have a certain experiential knowledge of others' lives, and even of our own; we may know a miscellany of facts about human nature; but Calvin's concern is with the total, the actual man; he is thinking of a trustworthy picture of man which will conform to reality. Such a picture will always be lacking as long as man does not examine and identify himself in the light of revelation. And as we see ourselves in that light, then "what formerly delighted us by its false show of righteousness, will become polluted with the greatest iniquity."

Man then becomes visible to himself in his true actuality, and no longer in a self-generated illusory picture which does not conform with reality as God sees it and as it actually is.[22] It is clear that Calvin is not here concerned with some particular "ontological" structure of man's nature (such as body, soul, spirit); rather he speaks of man's self-knowledge in his relation to God, from which man in his self-knowledge cannot abstract himself.

Thus, anyone who tries to construct a picture of man or of himself without the light of divine revelation can never obtain anything except a picture in which the unique nature of man

21. Calvin, *Institutes*, I, I, 2. He also writes that "we cannot clearly and properly know God unless the knowledge of ourselves be added" (I, XV, 1). For the close relation between our knowledge of God and knowledge of self, see also I, I, 1ff. The chapter heading of I, I (1953 ed.), reads: "The Knowledge of God and of Ourselves Mutually Connected. — Nature of the Connection."

22. Thus Job confesses himself to have been without insight and is repentant (Job 42:3, 6). Cf. also the exposure of David's guilt by Nathan's "Thou art the man!" (II Sam. 12:5-9). Even though David's "moral" feelings functioned well enough with regard to man in general (the man that hath "done this is worthy to die"), he was lacking in self-knowledge, because of his contempt for the Word of God in this instance. What David did in secret is contrasted with what God shall do in judgment, "before all Israel, and before the sun" (II Sam. 12:12). Cf. Ps. 51:6, "thou desirest truth in the inward parts and in the hidden part thou wilt make me to know wisdom." As man comes to self-knowledge, he can also make his guilt known to God. Cf. also Psalm 32:5.

does not appear[23] — quite apart from the further question of whether such a picture will be a more optimistic or a more pessimistic one.

Man's self-knowledge can become actual only in the light of God's revelation, and Calvin expresses this by saying that man can obtain true knowledge of himself only after he has contemplated the nature of God. And by this he does not mean only that man is shown to be a sinner by God's revelation. The light of God's revelation reveals not only guilt, but also grace, as Calvin points out in a citation from St. Bernard (*Inst.*, III, II, 25): "Man doubtless has been made subject to vanity — man has been reduced to nothing — man is nothing. And yet how is he whom God exalts utterly nothing? How is he nothing, to whom a divine heart has been given? Let us breathe again, brethren. Although we are nothing in our hearts, perhaps something of us may lurk in the heart of God. O Father of mercies! O Father of the miserable! how plantest thou thy heart in us? Where thy heart is, there is thy treasure also. But how are we thy treasure if we are nothing?" Calvin is concerned with the twofold portrayal of man, in his guilt and in the grace of God. How should man truly know himself without this revelation?

This close bond between self-knowledge and knowledge of God we must not try to dissolve, because every view of man which sees him as an isolated unity is incorrect. There have frequently been attempts to draw a picture of man through an elaborate and detailed analysis of man *an sich*, in himself, whereby man's relation to God was necessarily thought of as something added to man's self-enclosed nature, a *donum superadditum*, a "plus factor." But the light of revelation, when dealing with man's nature, is not concerned with information about such a self-enclosed nature; it is concerned with a nature which is not self-enclosed, and which can never be understood outside of its relation to God, since such a self-enclosed nature, an isolated nature, is nothing but an ab-

23. Compare the prayer of Psalm 139:23: "Search me, O God, and know my heart: try me, and know my thoughts." This prayer for divine examination is related to hating those whom God hates (vv. 21-22); it is while *in* that positive attitude that the writer feels the need for such examination and protection from unholy ways (v. 24). The *Heidelberg Catechism* (Q. 3) asks, "Whence do you know your misery?" and answers, "Out of the law of God." The same applies to true self-knowledge. Cf. Q. 115; the ten commandments should be preached in relation to increasing our understanding of our sinful nature.

straction.[24] The relation of man's nature to God is not something which is added to an already complete, self-enclosed, isolated nature; it is essential and constitutive for man's nature, and man cannot be understood apart from this relation.[25] Only an abstract view of man, which ignores this relationship, can abstract or separate the knowledge of man from the knowledge of God — with the unavoidable result that such "knowledge" becomes abstract, and no longer refers to actual man, real man, man as he really is. And many of the answers given to the question, What is man? give an unmistakable impression of such abstractness. They bear the mark of an abstract ontology, and lack the Biblical accent with which the question has been put for all time in the Word of God: "What is man, that thou art mindful of him? And the son of man, that thou visitest him?" (Ps. 8:4).

It is not at all surprising that Calvin's strong insistence on the bond between self-knowledge and knowledge of God has always evoked opposition. It has been regarded as too radical, and the question is raised whether it is not possible to speak of self-knowledge and knowledge of man outside the light of divine revelation. This question has gained additional force in our time, now that man is no longer naively idealized and glorified but is frequently discussed in a very critical manner, even by humanists. The existentialist picture of man appears, in its darker aspects, to denigrate rather than to idealize him, and delivers many an annihilating judgment on his actual nature. Is there not here — so it is often asked nowadays — at least a point of contact with the Biblical picture of man with his guileful heart? Is there not in existentialism, with its often black and non-idealistic picture of man — even though it has no intention of being religious, much less Christian — is there not an important preparation for true knowledge of self and

24. Compare Karl Barth's criticism of this abstraction — this view of man as an isolated entity — in his *Kirchliche Dogmatik*, III, II, 83ff. Barth rightly says that, on the contrary, man's nature "must from the very beginning be understood as a nature standing *in some kind of relation to God.*" Man does not exist as "a self-enclosed area of reality" but as related to God. This relation is not "coincidental, contingent, transitory, but a necessary and constant determination of his nature."

25. A. D. R. Polman rightly says (*Christelijke Encyclopedie*, 1956, I, 247, *s.v.*, "Anthropologie") that "the relation to God is essential for delimiting the nature of man." Our reference to *donum superadditum* concerns the term in its literal sense rather than its technical meaning in Roman Catholic teaching.

man, perhaps even more than in the idealistic view of man, which portrayed him in unbroken power, and sometimes even as divine?[26]

The problem is raised by statements similar to Van Niftrik's:[27] "Existential thought on man exhibits a close formal and structural relationship with the Biblical witness, even though Christianity must oppose it on many material points." He refers elsewhere to the "affinity" between Biblical and existentialist thought,[28] and believes that "existentialism has rediscovered and brought to light many important phenomena of man's nature." If we now ask just what this affinity or structural similarity means, then it appears, to begin with, that Van Niftrik does not want to overestimate it. He feels that although it can throw light on many human phenomena, existentialism nevertheless remains "vague and formal." We should not deny it all value, since existentialism does provide "a better understanding which man can now have of himself." Existentialism has rejected the idealistic view of man, and hence a real dialogue is now again possible, he says.

It would appear, however, that the important question is just what we are to understand by this "better understanding," this transition from the idealistic to the existentialist view of man. On closer examination, the question can hardly be answered in a simplistic manner. It is not enough to speak of an affinity that lies in a shared stress on the unity of man, since everything depends on how this unity is understood; materialism and psychic monism also deny idealism's "dualism" and talk of man's "unity." Besides, it is possible for all sorts of idealistic motifs to play a role within this existentialist "unity"; the existentialist emphasis on human freedom is an example. The same is true regarding the existentialist stress on evil in man, since in the phenomenology of evil the problem of the search for the hidden center, the search for the "real" man, again becomes acute. Indeed, in our opinion, it can hardly be

26. The problem is generally raised in connection with existentialist thought, but it is not at all limited to that. Cf. Max Scheler, "Mensch und Geschichte," *Philosophische Weltanschauung* (1954), p. 78, on the anthropology of the *necessary* "decadence" of man, in "strong opposition to the common faith all previous Western anthropology and historical theory"; a decadence which presumably lies "in the nature and origin of man himself." Cf. also Werner Sombart, *op. cit.*, pp. 92ff.
27. G. C. van Niftrik, "Hoe ziet de moderne Mens zichzelf en hoe ziet de Bijbel de Mens?" *Kerk en Theologie* (1952), p. 164.
28. See Van Niftrik, *op. cit.*, and also *De Boodschap van Sartre* (1953), pp. 61, 158, 160 and *Zie de Mens* (1951), pp. 39, 41. G. van der Leeuw also uses the term "affinity" in his *Sacramentstheologie* (1949), p. 6: "close affinity to Biblical thought" (in contrast to idealism).

denied that some previous philosophies have spoken at least as gloomily about man (cf. man as decadent) as does existentialism.

Furthermore, in existentialism generally, the search for the hidden center, the "real man," is strikingly evident. This is surely true in the atheistic existentialism of Sartre (with which Van Niftrik is concerned); and we might thus seriously question whether the break with idealism is indeed really so radical that we can speak of an affinity and structural relationship between existentialism and the Biblical view of man. As Van Peursen rightly remarks, "It surely is an illusion to see existentialism as some sort of translation of the Heidelberg Catechism's section on human misery,"[29] since existentialism does not continue its concentration on man's misery, but points to his (self-produced) salvation. It is, of course, characteristic of existentialism that it wishes to be anti-bourgeois and anti-romantic and that it therefore emphasizes a critical evaluation of man, an unmasking of his faults; but that is not in itself enough to comprise an affinity with Biblical thought. There is actually no thought of a radical unmasking, since at the critical moment the search for the hidden center of man reappears, which results in finding man, in his freedom, as self-choosing subject. Van Niftrik himself calls this Sartre's "idealistic heritage."[30] When he then goes on to speak of an objective affinity and a structural relationship with Biblical thought, we can only ask, in some surprise, whether Sartre's idea of freedom must now be thought of as only peripheral, and not something which dominates his whole view of man. The antithesis to a Biblical view of man lies in idealistic anthropology — even if it incorporates within itself a certain amount of realism and unmasking of man's evil. No one would think of denying that there are many existentialist criticisms of various *modi* of man's nature,[31] but this criticism does not at all imply a necessary affinity to Biblical thought.

Van Niftrik's view that existentialism gives "a better understanding" of man raises the question whether its rather gloomy judgment on man is really a sign of true self-knowledge. It is striking that

29. C. A. van Peursen, "Existentie-Philosophie en Christelijke Verkondiging," *Kerk en Theologie* (1952), p. 114.
30. Van Niftrik, *De Boodschap van Sartre*, p. 161.
31. Cf., e.g., Sartre's strong attack on the Russian invasion of Hungary in the autumn of 1956 ("Après Budapest: Sartre parle," *L'express* of Paris, November 4, 1956, pp. 14-16): "this crime . . . for which Stalinism is entirely responsible." Stalinism is "totally and irremediably responsible" for "the massacres of Budapest."

this judgment refers generally to the other, or to others. St. Paul, in Romans 2:1, passes judgment not on an idealism which glorifies man, but on the man who judges others unfavorably: "Therefore thou art without excuse, O man, whosoever thou art that judgest: for wherein thou judgest another, thou condemnest thyself; for thou that judgest dost practice the same things." God's judgment is unbiased, and corresponds with reality. But man's judgment does not conform to reality — even if it recognizes something of the vast power of evil — because it constantly separates knowledge of man from self-knowledge. Note that "the other" does no evil (Paul does not deny that — "thou . . . dost practice the same things"); but this judgment condemning the other is — when not joined with a knowledge of self — untrue. It is an abstract judgment; and it is that because a condemnatory judgment of the other can be paired with an idealistic vision of man's "freedom." And hence Paul can so admonishingly tear off his mask also: "And reckonest thou this, O man, who judgest them that practice such things and doest the same, that thou shalt escape the judgment of God?" (Rom. 2:3). For this reason, in our opinion, we can hardly ascribe to the "realistic," non-idealistic view of man given by existentialism any basic structural relationship with Biblical thought. The critical, Biblical question is not whether we are influenced by those undeniable facts which reveal life as ravaged and defaced; it is not whether we react to these facts in a condemnatory judgment of the other man; but it is whether our picture of man has brought us to a better understanding of *ourselves.*

It is also true that one can reach a "self-knowledge" which condemns oneself, as with Judas, who no longer condemned the other, but himself: "I have sinned in that I betrayed innocent blood" (Matt. 27:4).[32] A man's own life, as well as that of others, can crumble under the overwhelming power of spreading evil, so that even a blind man could sense the looming chaos. But the important question is, In what relationships is this misery seen and acknowledged when we have true self-knowledge? This "better understanding" is thus by no means an easily understood magnitude whose dimensions can be ascertained with little trouble. Is there really a better understanding of ourselves? Is there a "better understand-

---

32. The Bible mentions Judas' repentance when he saw that Jesus was condemned, and Judas speaks at the same time of "innocent blood." We note this Biblical reference to Judas especially since here there is no judgment of *the other*, which is precisely the case in most condemnatory judgments.

ing" of man in the Jew, who condemned the heathen?[33] Given the Biblical witness regarding self-knowledge, we are forced to inquire more closely into the nature of this "better understanding." The Jew did not have a better understanding *because* he was able to judge the heathen. In the sphere of *abstract* morality this could possibly be said, but this is not Biblical morality — O man, who judgest others!

Nor is it clear how we can escape this conclusion by speaking of a "formal" similarity of structure and a "formal" affinity, since it is precisely the structure which is essentially and wholly delimited by the relationship between the knowledge of man and the knowledge of self *in the eyes of God.* We can hardly say that the Pharisees had an accurate "knowledge" of man when they pointed to the sins (the *real* sins) of publicans and sinners. This judgment, which separated knowledge of man from self-knowledge, was as nothing in God's eyes. The "knowledge" of the Pharisees was of a wholly different sort than that of the publican Zacchaeus, who both recognized the same obvious facts that the Pharisees saw, and confessed: "If I have wrongfully exacted aught of any man I restore fourfold" (Luke 19:8). A realistic condemnation of man and a critical unmasking of his evil can never lead to a really new picture of man, since they can so easily be coupled with a practically or theoretically *idealistic* view of man. And thus it is difficult to see how we can speak of a real "point of contact" between existentialism and Christianity. The idealistic view of man may see the gospel as a *skandalon*, a stumbling block; but a "realistic" view of man can also completely ignore the secret of the gospel message when it takes its rise from an abstract morality and a neutral phenomenology of "evil," and in its final definitions still manifestly refuses to accept the indissoluble Biblical relation between knowledge of man and knowledge of self.

33. Cf. also Christ's use of the mote and the beam: "Why beholdest thou the mote that is in thy brother's eye, but considerest not the beam that is in thine own eye?" (Matt. 7:3), and the following question, "Or how wilt thou say to thy brother, Let me cast out the mote out of thine eye; and lo, the beam is in thine own eye?" And then the sharp, "Thou hypocrite, cast out first the beam out of thine own eye, and then you will see clearly to take the mote out of your brother's eye." The admonition begins with: "Judge not, that ye be not judged. For with what judgment ye judge, ye shall be judged; and with what measure ye mete, it shall be measured unto you." Kittel (*Theologisches Wörterbuch*, s.v., *metron*, p. 637), in commenting, relates this to eschatological seriousness; and also (s.v., *krino*, III, 940) to the "subordination" of man's judgment on man to the "certainty that God's judgment will judge the judgers."

A similar kind of formal relationship in structure is often spoken of in connection with Martin Heidegger's use of the terms anxiety, guilt, and conscience. Again we must ask just what the word "formal" means here; especially since Heidegger himself has warned against encasing his thought in contexts essentially alien to it. "The existential-ontological interpretation as such makes no statements regarding the 'corruption of man's nature'; not because the necessary evidence is lacking, but because its dialectic *precedes* any statements about corruption or non-corruption. Decay is an ontological 'concept of movement' [*Bewegungsbegriff*]," and he clarifies his use of the term "guilt" thus: "The 'being-guilty' which pertained originally to the ontical composition of the '*Dasein*,' the 'being' of man, is to be clearly distinguished from the theologically understood concept of *status corruptionis*, the state of corruption."[34] The understanding of man's "*Dasein*" is ontological in nature, and reveals man's existence to be doubtful and threatened. There is little affinity here with Biblical thought, as appears clearly enough when we consider that this threat does not lead to nihilism and despair *because*, in this "doubtfulness" a "heroism" of trust and courage leads us on the way to a new form of humanism.[35]

34. For the quotations, see M. Heidegger, *Sein und Zeit* (4th ed., 1935), pp. 179, 306. Cf. also p. 306: "The existential analysis of 'being-guilty' implies nothing either for or against the possibility of sin. Strictly speaking, one cannot even say that it leaves the possibility open, since the ontology of man's being [*Dasein*] is a philosophical problem which does not take into account the concept of sin." R. F. Beerling, *Moderne Doodsproblematiek* (1945), p. 46, speaks in the context of Heidegger of a "tragic-heroic" attitude; the "heroic" manifests itself wherever there is an attempt in one way or another to come to terms with death, and which is given an interpretation that eventually takes away its terror. Cf. J. Wach, *Das Problem des Todes in der Philosophie unserer Zeit* (1934). For the interpretation of death in its metaphysical sense in Schopenhauer, and the concept of "freedom to die" (*Freiheit zum Tode*) in Feuerbach, Simmel, and Heidegger, see Wach, *op. cit.*, p. 46; cf. Heidegger, *op. cit.*, pp. 248, 265ff. on "antecedent ontological interpretations of death"; cf. Beerling, *op. cit.*, pp. 243ff. Beerling rightly raises the question, in connection with Heidegger's statement that an ontological analysis of being-at-an-end does not anticipate an existential taking position with regard to death, whether such an analysis does not really *presuppose* such a position already taken (Beerling, *op. cit.*, p. 245). Cf. also my *De Voorzienigheid Gods*, pp. 300ff. (ET, *The Providence of God.*)

35. Cf. A. Delp, *Tragische Existenz. Zur Philosophie Heideggers* (1935), p. 103, and especially N. Berdiaev, "Alte und neue Wege des Humanismus," *Theologische Zeitschrift*, II (1946), pp. 134ff. regarding existentialism in the context of "the contradiction": "This terror before the abyss of not-being, the anxiety for the absurdity of the world, is

This problem of a possible affinity cannot be seen correctly as long as the affinity is viewed as "formal," since this form itself is nothing more than an abstraction, particularly when in a given view of man the essential religious aspect of man's being is lost in a _horizontal_ type of analysis.[36] The procedure, which Heidegger follows makes his whole view of man precarious, since he wants to deal with man as he actually is; and the way to self-knowledge is impossible to traverse with this kind of horizontal analysis, since the decisive dimension of man's nature, his relation to God, remains outside the analysis. The key to true self-knowledge is lacking, since man is seen and analyzed _outside_ of this basic dimension. And that is the reason that man can judge the other, his fellow man; that a bitterly serious _j'accuse_ can be hurled as part of a heroic "phenomenology" which admits the existence of evil and stresses the _Fragwürdigheit_, the constant "being-threatened" of man's being; and that — despite all this — there is still, from a Biblical point of view, no true knowledge of man's nature, no real evaluation of the actual man.

If man's relation to God is not merely something _added to_ man's nature, then it is clear enough that any view which abstracts man from this relation can never penetrate the mystery of man. And nowadays, indeed, it is often emphasized that the sciences which deal with certain aspects of man can make no more than a partial contribution towards our understanding of man, and cannot unveil the secret of the whole man.

In this context the problem arises as to the significance of theological or dogmatic reflection on man. After all, theology as a science does not command some sort of special methodology which can reach that which other sciences, dealing with aspects of man's nature, cannot reach. Nor can its aim be merely to repeat what

---

a new form of godlessness, which one is none the less to take on heroically; it is Nietzche's _amor fati,_" (acceptance of fate). Man will "save himself the while he relies only on himself; he will create, and only therein find relief from the nausea inspired by not-being and emptiness." There is for Berdiaev only one way towards a new Christian humanism — as opposed to this defunct humanism — in this "anti-human age"; namely, by the way of a religiously inspired social personalism. Cf. also Berdiaev's remarks on Russian Communism in the same passage.

36. Cf. W. J. Aalders, _Het Woord Existentie in het moderne weten-schappelijke Spraakgebruik_ (1933), p. 4. Cf. also Heidegger's comments (_op. cit._ p. 272) on H. G. Stoker's _Das Gewissen. Erscheinungsformen und Theorien_ (Bonn, 1925), in which Heidegger sees a confusion between phenomenology and theology.

philosophy and the special sciences have already discovered about
man. Nor can we say that theology, as queen of the sciences, deals
with some kind of arcane knowledge about man, or with the key
to this knowledge. Rather, there is justification for a theological
approach only when theology deals with man as he appears in
the light of the *normative* divine revelation, and then not with
man in one or more of his aspects, but with the whole man. Thus
theology can hardly say it treats a special *aspect* of man, the
"religious" aspect, which is *added to* other aspects. The words
"religion" or "religious" carry the implication, indeed, that they
do *not* concern a "point of view," but deal with man in his relation
to God. And hence, in the *locus de homine* in theology, man
is treated *in this relationship*. And this is taken to imply a Biblical
view of man, within which further distinctions can be made between
the view of man presented, for instance, by Isaiah and that presented by Paul or John. These distinctions are not always seen
in the same way; sometimes they are seen as deep-seated divergences
between different Biblical views of man, and sometimes as merely
nuances within a unified Biblical view of man. Without investi-
gating closely the merits of the term "Biblical view of man" at
this point,[37] we can say that the whole Bible continually sheds
light on man in all his numberless relations, and that it does not
concern itself simply with a way of approaching the nature of
man, but with the *actual* man, who stands outlined in the searching
light of the revelation of God.

There is a growing consensus among theologians that the
Scriptural data on man do not render superfluous research directed
at the various aspects of man. Or, in other words, the theological
investigation of man cannot seek a solution along the lines of a
scientific anthropology, or a Biblical psychology and physiology, as
if the intention of Scripture were to give us information about the
various *aspects* of man, or the details of the composition of man.[38]
It has often been thought that this was indeed the case, and
theologians have thought to find specific "data" which they could

---

37. G. C. van Niftrik, *De Boodschap van Sartre,* p. 169, is of the opinion
    that the Bible gives us no "view of man." All depends, actually, on
    how this term is defined. There is more reason to speak of a Biblical
    view of man than to speak of a Biblical anthropology. When Beek
    maintains that it is impossible to write an Old Testament anthropology,
    he does not deny that there is a Biblical view of man.

38. We shall come to the problem of whether man's nature is dichotomous
    or trichotomous in another connection (see Chapter VI), that is, in
    examining why trichotimism was rejected by the Church.

force the various sciences dealing with man to accept. In this way, a conflict arose between theology and the growing sciences dealing with man (such as psychology) — much in the same way that conflicts broke out when theologians made Scripture into a source of data regarding the natural sciences (physics, etc.). But such an interpretation does not realize that the real *scopus,* the real concern of revelation, is not the furnishing of such bits of information. It is clear enough from Scripture that its concern is with the whole man, the full man, the actual man as he stands in God's sight, in the religious bond between the totality of his being and God.

* The term "theological anthropology" has, in our day, gained general acceptance. Now what is the meaning of the term? It is used alongside of other terms such as "Biblical anthropology" and "Pauline anthropology;"[39] though primarily the word "anthropology," it would seem, has scholarly implications. On closer inquiry, however, it appears that "Biblical" or "Pauline" anthropology is used not to describe a systematic and scholarly anthropology, but rather a Biblical or Pauline "teaching" regarding man; and further, to describe it not as a closed system, but rather as a limited way of approaching and shedding light on the nature of man; so that a "picture of man" is all that is meant, rather than a scholarly discipline.[40] But "theological anthropology" is used more in the sense of such a discipline, frequently in contrast to philosophical anthropology.[41] Though it can hardly be denied that "anthropology" is a term used in many different contexts and meanings, it is usually

39. E.g., E. H. van Leeuwen, *Bijbelse Anthropologie* (1906); W. Gutbrod, *Die Paulinische Anthropologie* (1934).
40. J. N. Sevenster, "Die Anthropologie des N. T.," in *Anthropologie religieuse* (1956), pp. 166ff., even says that no "real anthropology" can be found in the New Testament or in the whole Bible; that is, a "unified view of man." Cf. the use of the term "anthropology" in *Waarheid, Wijsheid en Leven, Studien voor Prof. Dr. J. Severijn* (1956), which considers the concept in Calvin, the later Reformers, Barth, Kant, various Protestant Confessions, and Paul. It appears here also that the term is usually used in a very general sense to mean "picture of man" (cf. especially W. C. van Unnink's article on Pauline "Anthropology"). E. H. van Leeuwen (*op. cit.,* p. 1) begins his book by noting that he does not mean to use "anthropology" in "the scholarly sense of the word."
41. The *Christelijke Encyclopedie* (2d ed., 1956), includes separate articles on philosophical anthropology (C. A. van Peursen) and on theological anthropology (A. D. R. Polman).

clear enough what is meant, and this is surely true of contemporary use of the term "theological anthropology."[42]

Thus Gutbrod sees its task as determining "what man is, through his relation to God; or, better, through God's self-relation to man," and by Pauline anthropology he means that Paul "understood and described the actuality of man in the light of his faith in God and on the basis of the revelation of God." For Gutbrod, "only in a light so distinct can human existence be understood in its actuality." To view man in this light is the task of the theological anthropologist; not constructively to arrive at some inexact estimate of man.[43] Such remarks clearly establish that the relation of man to God is seen as *decisive* for the whole being of man.[44] At no time is man viewed as "neutral" or isolated, but always in relationship to God; that relationship which brings out not a *Teilaspekt*, a partial aspect, of his being, but his whole being.[45] "Theological anthropology" is thus concerned with the light thrown by revelation on that which is *central* and *integral* in man's being; it sees him not as *placed* in that light (as a previously defined entity), but as *seen* in that light.

Gogarten describes theological anthropology in a similar manner when he writes: "When it discusses man, it does not speak of man alone, man in and by himself; it always speaks equally of God." This does not mean that man and God are "correlate" or reciprocally dependent on each other; it means that when the Bible speaks about man it is not expressing some subjective estimate of man, but is speaking about the real actual nature of man, "who can simply not be thought of without God." And that is what the theological approach demands; it asks for the opposite of an abstract view of man which treats man as an isolated and self-enclosed unity which

42. Besides Biblical, Pauline, philosophical, and theological anthropology, we now have the term "religious anthropology"; cf., e.g., M. Landmann, *Philosophische Anthropologie* (1955), pp. 63ff., and the symposium *Anthropologie religieuse* (1956), edited by C. J. Bleeker. P. Althaus, interestingly, avoids the use of the term in the title of his book, *Paulus und Luther über den Menschen* (1937).

43. Gutbrod, *op. cit.*, pp. 5-7.

44. Cf. C. A. van Peursen, *Christelijke Encyclopedie* (2d ed., 1956), p. 245, on the picture of man as created in God's image, and also Polman, *ibid.*, pp. 246-248.

45. Gutbrod cites by way of illustration II Cor. 5:16: "Wherefore we henceforth know no man after the flesh." Paul indeed goes on to discuss our not regarding Christ "after the flesh," but he does also say we know "no man" in that way. Apart from the merits of Gutbrod's exegesis, his meaning is clear enough — the revelation of God places the actual man in full view.

can exist and which can be understood by itself.[46] This does not mean that the theological approach can boast of a specially given knowledge — a special *gnosis* — of man. It is well aware that the light of God's revelation concerning man is not the particular prerogative of learning and scholarship, of theological science. Theology is indeed itself concerned especially with that light which is withheld from the wise and which is revealed to children. But it does pay special attention to *man* as he stands revealed before us, in the depths and contexts of Scripture; that is, in his religious relationship to God. That light — it can be said without hesitation — streams through the whole of Scripture, and in it the mystery of man is made clear. It is not concerned with a formal analysis of man's nature, which latter is then held to consist of a certain "openness," a non-isolation, which distinguishes man from the animals.[47] Without in any way underestimating the value of various anthropological analyses of the *Eigenart*, the unique characteristics, of man, it must be said that the light of Scripture reveals not a formal relationship, but a wholly real relationship to God, without which man in his essence and his actuality can never be understood.

Man is presented in many different ways in Scripture. He is shown in numerous contexts, with many facets; but in all this variation we meet again and again the one central and essential dimension of man, that in which he stands *not* as an isolated entity, but in the light and the presence of God. This does not mean, of course, that we cannot speak of man's "isolation" or of his unreceptiveness to God's revelation. These, too, are pointed out with unmistakable clarity in the Bible. Nor can we use the term "openness" without explanation. For this non-isolation, this being-in-relation, does not concern the start of a way for man to reach God; it means, rather, the overwhelming actuality of God in man's life, and man's dependent relationship to Him, from which he can never escape.

Scripture uses various ways to picture man in this inescapable

46. F. Gogarten, "Das Problem einer theologischen Anthropologie," *Zwischen den Zeiten*, XIX, p. 493. Cf. Herrade Mehl-Koehnlein, *L'homme selon l'apôtre Paul* (1951), p. 6; Paul, "like all the authors of the N.T., does not consider man in himself; he sees him only and always in his relation to God," and "man is really only in his existence before God, for or against God."

47. Cf. the view of A. Portmann, *Zoologie und das neue Bild des Menschen* (1956), pp. 12ff., on the uniqueness of this "openness," ("*die Eigenart der Offenheit*"); and cf. also Van Peursen, (*Christelijke Encyclopedie* (2d ed., 1956), I, 245) on the contrast between the views of man as an independent entity and man as a peripheral entity.

relationship. When Israel speaks about "man," it knows of God's fathoming the depths of man's heart (Jer. 17:9ff.; cf. Ps. 139:23). And man's being is related to and made dependent on God in a prayer (Jer. 10:23): "O Jehovah, I know that the way of man is not in himself; it is not in man that walketh to direct his steps." The Bible never speaks of man in himself, as isolated, but always in terms of his relationship to God, in a special light: in his creatureliness (Gen. 12:27, Prov. 7:29), his fall (Gen. 3, Rom. 5), his vanity (Ps. 60:13, 108:13, James 2:20, Ps. 144:4), his superficiality (I Sam. 16:7), his being different from God (Job 33:12; Ezek. 28:2, 9; Hos. 11:9), his mortality (Ps. 39, 90), and so forth. So universal in application are these descriptions that Scripture can speak merely of "man," without there being any exceptions to the general statements. We often carelessly speak in general terms of "men" without analyzing what we mean (cf. Ps. 116:11), but it is not that sort of careless generality which is used by Scripture; it can speak in generalities because it is the light of God which falls on man-in-general (cf. Gen. 6:6, Prov. 7:29), just as the law of God affects man-in-general, *all* men (cf. Micah 6:8, Prov. 12:13). Man is never taken out of, nor can he flee, the searching light of the ever present God (Amos 9:1-4, Ps. 139:7) — even though he may prefer the darkness to the light.

This decisive dimension of man's being, which, far from being merely one "aspect" among other aspects, unites them and goes beyond them, thus does *not* define man in the manner frequently encountered in theology — "man's essential nature lies in his reason," or definitions of that sort. Such definitions are actually the contrary of what we call the Biblical view of man, since they make no mention of what Scripture presents as the essential and unique characteristic of man and man's nature — the relation to God.[48] We never encounter such a man — man-as-reason, or however he is distinguished from the animals — in Scripture. Indeed, if we follow Scripture, we must say that neither man-as-

48. Cf. Karl Barth's criticism, *Kirchliche Dogmatik,* III, 2, pp. 88ff., of Polanus' definition of man as *"animal ratione praeditum"* ("rational animal"), because such definition proceeds as though "there is no such thing as a relation of God to man." Polanus *later* goes on to speak of man's relation to God, of course, but not as integral to the "definition." Besides the definition of man as "rational animal," which is one frequently used to distinguish man from brute, there are many other definitions of similar nature, which do not include man's relation to God. These are usually aimed at defining man's nature or essence; cf. the *Helvetic Confession,* VII: man is composed of "two different and diverse substances"; cf. also Heppe, *Dogmatik* (1861), pp. 162ff.

essentially-reason (or some similar definition) nor man's nature-as-essentially-rational really exists at all. If man is defined in such a way — and it is sometimes done for apologetic reasons — man's relation to God can only be described as something which pre-supposes man and man's nature as already defined entities, basical-ly isolated actualities. If it is true that the relation to God is essen-tial in the definition of man,[49] than all such "neutral" or "non-religious" definitions of man-in-himself can throw no light at all on the true nature of man.

It is indeed true that the concept of relation has often been interpreted in ways which are erroneous. It can be interpreted to mean that man exists only in relation to God, and God only in relation to man; and thus God and man are related pantheistically or in some other unbiblical way. But such misuses of the concept may not deter us from giving due weight, great weight, to the Biblical concept of relation to God, the *coram Deo* in all of its Biblical power. Nor should this be seen as choosing relation over reality, or relational over ontological, or choosing one horn of any such dilemma; for such a dilemma, such a contrast, is not at all in line with the Biblical outlook, which does not sacrifice reality to relation, but shows us reality existing as reality, full created reality, only *in* this relation to God.[50]

We need not wonder that theological reflection on man has returned again and again to the emphasis which Scripture places on man's relation to God, and thus also to Scripture's designation of man as the image of God.[51] The often agitated and vehement discussion on this image of God reflects something of the serious-ness of what Scripture means by the relatedness of man in his totality to God. Once this is seen, the question naturally arises as to just what sort of relationship is meant; and the answer to this important problem is sought in examining the image of God. It is clear that the term "relation" can, by itself, throw little light on the

49. As, for instance, Polman says (*loc. cit.*).
50. J. J. Louët Feisser has recently warned against the danger of over-estimating the worth of the concept of the relation ("De Anthropologie van Karl Barth," in *Waarheid, Wijsheid en Leven* [1956]; cf. pp. 105-106). This is understandable enough as a warning against false dilemmas — though just how one can "over-estimate" the worth of the relation is not too clear — but even then, full appreciation must be given to what Louët Feisser calls "the Biblical correction to the increasingly secularized picture of man as a rational animal."
51. Sombart (*op. cit.*, p. 3), in the midst of a long list of definitions of man, gives "Christianity's definition" of man as "the image of God."

uniqueness of the actuality of man's being and nature, since there are so many "relations" in which man is placed. Hence the intensive investigation of the Scriptural references to the image of God; and even the many tiring aspects of the conflicts regarding it should never make us forget that the Word of God itself calls us to the search for what we may term, in all seriousness, *the secret of man.*

The image of God . . . the mysterious character of the Biblical expression has often been noted. The wish is often expressed in one way or another that Scripture had given us a precise definition of the image of God, a description of what it means. Does it not seem, as it is, that the search for the "secret of man" will again prove fruitless because of the variety of opinions as to the meaning of the image of God, and the heat of the quarrels about this meaning?

The image of God — what is it? The questions have multiplied. Is the term applicable to the man whom we meet in the street, apart from the *modus* of his existence as man? Or is it a reminder of a "paradise lost" which makes us acutely conscious that we no longer have this image? Or is the expression analogous to the picture of man given by idealism, in which man is praised as *mikrotheos,* somehow divine, a characteristic which can never, despite all appearances, be lost?[52]

---

52. Cf. Karl Jaspers on the impossibility of "ultimately despairing" of man: "Symbolically: Man is created by God in His image — that can never wholly vanish, even in the depths of alienation," "Möglichkeiten eines neuen Humanismus," *Rechenschaft und Ausblick* (1951), p. 272.

CHAPTER TWO

A PRELIMINARY ORIENTATION

W HEN we use the phrase, "image of God," most of us think immediately (and perhaps only) of the original creation of man. In the development of the doctrine, however, theologians have not restricted their discussion of the image of God to man before the Fall. In the context they have also constantly concerned themselves with the further question: What about man after the Fall? Can we still speak of him as in the image of God; and if so, in what sense?

In the order used by systematic exposition of doctrine, one may indeed find the subject of the image of God treated before the discussion of the Fall, in direct connection with the creation narrative of Genesis 1, but this fact does not, of course, imply that man's sin is excluded from consideration. Theologians evidently are not satisfied to regard the image of God merely as a remembrance of something which was once existent but has now been lost. It is evidently not possible, at least for most of them, to liken the image of God to a beautiful city which, being the target of annihilating violence in time of war, was razed to the ground, and now lives only in memory. Rather, the relation between the image of God and sin continually injects itself, and more specifically as the question of the relation between _homo creatus_ and _homo peccator_, man before and after the Fall. Can _homo peccator_ also be called the image of God — in spite of sin — or can the term be meaningfully employed only in relation to man as originally created, and to man after the restoration of the original image through grace?

The type of answer given to these questions is indeed noteworthy. The answer often gives the impression of a "dialectic," since it is not given in terms of a simple "yes" or "no," but is given with many explications and qualifications, which at first hearing may produce an impression of hesitation and uncertainty. The very fact that in the answer the making of all sorts of distinctions is deemed necessary already seems to indicate that we feel incapable of a direct, clear, and unequivocal answer.

We can make a beginning towards orienting ourselves in this rather unusual situation by calling to mind a well-known distinction in Reformed theology, namely, that between the image of God in the broader and in the narrower sense.[1] It is understandable that this distinction arouses a certain aversion in many; they protest that it is difficult to hear an echo of the Biblical witness in such complexity, and that we are in danger of wandering into the quagmires of scholasticism with such a procedure. And besides they contend — and not without justification — the terms "broader" and "narrower" are vague and meaningless, and shed no light on the real meaning and content of the image of God.

Though such objections are understandable enough, there is nevertheless every reason for us to look at this distinction more closely in the effort to get at the idea behind it. For the distinction has played such a dominant role in the history of discussions of the image of God that it seems likely to be more than a useless bit of hairsplitting which ignores the simplicity of Scripture. This seems all the more the case when we consider that this distinction has found favor not only in Reformed theology, but can be observed far outside those boundaries, now here and now there, playing its role in investigations regarding the image of God in man.

Without giving a priori approval to the distinction, as some traditionalists might wish to do, we do feel that it is hardly a meaningless question to ask whether we may not here be touching on a real problem, at least a real question, which led to this distinction.

The intention of the distinction between the broader and narrower sense of the image of God can be described thus. The broader sense of the image is used to stress the idea that man, despite his fall into sin and corruption, was not bestialized or demonized, but remained man. The narrow sense of the image is used to stress the idea that man lost his communion with God — his religious knowledge, his righteousness, his holiness, his conformity (conformitas) to God's will. This latter was a radical change in man's nature, which originally was wholly turned towards God, and now after the Fall is turned completely away. Man was "good, righteous, and holy, capable in all things to will agreeably to the will of God" (BC, Art. XIV); man was created by God "good, and after His own image; that is, in true righteousness and holiness" (HC, Q. 6). Man was "originally formed after the

1. Herman Bavinck, *Gereformeerde Dogmatiek*, II, 490.

A PRELIMINARY ORIENTATION

image of God. His understanding was adorned with a true and saving knowledge of his Creator, and of spiritual things; his heart and will were upright, all his affections pure, and the whole man was holy" (CD, III-IV, 1). But all this wealth vanished with the Fall.

It is understandable that the real debate in connection with this distinction centered not on the image of God as used in the narrower sense but rather as used in the broader sense. The question of the extent of sin's ravages in relation to the original conformity to God, the original *conformitas*, was indeed discussed in the conflicts with the Pelagians and semi-Pelagians, with synergism and Arminianism. Nevertheless, in the discussions as to the validity of this distinction between the broader and narrower sense of the term "image of God," it was the broader sense which received the lion's share of attention. For it was this broader sense which was to remind us of what was not lost through sin and corruption. Inasmuch, now, as what had not been lost of the image was identified with the specifically human in man, the question was unavoidable what, concretely, was then to be understood by the specifically human. By way of reply, the specifically human was designated at that in man's being which forever makes man different on the one hand from angels and on the other from animals. And thereupon followed attempts to define exactly just what this specific difference in the being of man was, attempts which led, for example, to distinguishing between the essence and the nature of man; "essence" designating the image of God in its broader sense, "nature" referring to it in its narrower sense. The way was then open for Reformed theologians to ascribe various specific characteristics to the *imago essentialis*, the essence of man.[2] Thus A. Kuyper, Jr., says that man as such (that is, in essence) is "a reasonable and spiritual being, or, a being with an individual ego which has two faculties, namely, to know and to will." And herein — in possessing this essence — man then still possesses the image of God in the broader sense. A variation on this kind of summary is given by James Orr, who speaks of the specific quality distinguishing man, and goes on to find this not in the body but "in that higher constitution of his being which makes him spiritual," and then describes man's essence more closely in such terms as "person, spiritual, self-conscious being, rationality and capacity for moral life, self-determining freedom and social affections, highest of all in his capacity for fellowship with God."

2. A. G. Honig, *Handboek van de Gereformeerde Dogmatiek* (1938), p. 341.

He calls the *imago essentialis*, the image kept after the Fall, "an indestructible element in man's constitution [comprising] reason, conscience, freedom, etc."[3]

Thus, in delimiting the image of God in the broader sense, we meet various anthropological differentiations and descriptions against the background of the earlier distinction between man's essence and nature. A Kuyper, Jr., even says that theologians, using philosophical modes of approach, realized that the essence of man is something other than his nature, and only then realized that the image of God in the wider sense is revealed in man's essence; so that the restoration of the original image in the saved man refers only and exclusively to his nature, which "is once again, after being unholy, made holy." Kuyper's idea here could also be expressed in terms of a distinction between *imago essentialis* and *imago existentialis*, the latter referring to existence, to the manner of being, the quality of being. In any case, the purpose of all such distinctions is to differentiate between that which remains in man even in sin (man's essence), and that which is lost through sin — his orientation towards God.[4] We can hardly avoid an impression of a certain arbitrariness, however, when we consider the way in which the characteristics of man's essence are often described. Orr, for example, places moral capacity and conscience on the same level with reason and freedom. We are reminded of Brunner's idea of a formal image, which he describes in terms that can hardly be called merely formal. Indeed, that the distinction between the broader and narrower meanings of the image of God is often criticized because of the arbitrariness and uncertainty of the delimitation of the image in the broader sense is quite understandable.[5] Nor is the distinction less suspect when it is based on the philosophical distinction between essence and nature. Can we say that man's essence was not affected at all by sin, that it remained fully intact? Is it possible to separate essence and nature in the way A. Kuyper, Jr., does, for whom the permanent essence becomes embodied in a holy or unholy nature? He compares fallen man's essence, his "I," his ego, to "a picture without color"; the adornment, man's right-

3. A. Kuyper, Jr., *Het Beeld Gods* (1929), p. 64; J. Orr, *God's Image in Man* (1948), pp. 56-59.

4. See A. Kuyper, Jr., *op. cit.*, pp. 61-66. The image of God in the narrower sense then lies in man's nature, that is, in his holy nature. Man's nature is inseparably tied to his essence. The essence remains: "Man is and remains man, quite apart from the question of whether he remains true to God and fulfills the covenant, or departs from God and sells his soul to Satan."

5. Cf. K. Schilder, *De Heidelbergse Catechismus*, I, 292.

eous nature, is gone.[6] It is clear that such a view of man's essence is made possible only by abstracting from man's unique relationship to God, thus preparing the way for the strange inference that man's essence is not affected by sin. This is a conclusion rather different from that of Bavinck, who speaks not only of sin's destruction of the image of God in the narrower sense, but also of the "destruction and corruption" it caused in the image in the wider sense. He shows more understanding of the defects of the distinction between a permanent essence and a changeable nature than A. Kuyper, Jr., exhibits.

Besides this, the further working out of this distinction reveals various difficulties, as for example when capacity, conscience and freedom are treated as unchanging "givens" belonging to the "indestructible element" in man — which arouses some acute problems, especially in relation to the question of "free will." We can hardly escape the conclusion that the use of the distinction between being and nature or between essence and existence does little to clarify our insight into the loss of the image.

It remains true, however, that we can see in the background of such a distinction a motif which deserves our full attention. Without legitimatizing the distinction thereby,[7] we may say that the desire to emphasize the truth that sinful man is still man led to calling this humanity the image of God in the broader sense, which was untouched by sin.[8]

Now we face an important question, which again and again dominates discussions of our problem: whether the idea of the image of God in the broader sense does not lose all sense when we consider fallen man, "totus peccator," of whom Scripture speaks in such radical terms as children of wrath (Eph. 2:3), wandering in the vanity of their mind, having the understanding darkened, being alienated from the life of God (Eph. 4:17-18). Does not the term image of God — however it is further delimited — ascribe too much, far too much, to the worth of fallen men, who although "knowing God, they glorified him not as God,

6. See A. Kuyper, Jr., op. cit., pp. 68, 72, 130.
7. Cf. A. Kuyper, Jr., op. cit., p. 130. He even says that whatever was lost through Adam's sin, "man retained the image of God as such." Man exhibits the image, however, in an unholy and sinful nature. Cf. also A. Kuyper, Sr., "Locus de homine," Loci, p. 119. He says that the "substance" of man is not affected by sin, but his "nature" is.
8. Cf. Bavinck, op. cit., II, 511ff. He clearly expresses the view that sin also affected the image as used in the wider sense, but he still values the distinction.

neither gave thanks . . . and exchanged the glory of the incorruptible God for the likeness of an image of corruptible man" (Rom. 1:21, 23)?

Does not the image of God, according to the testimony of Scripture, refer only to the richness and glory of man as created in the image of God, to man as the child of God? And is it not then a strange and unlikely usage to speak of fallen, corrupt, and perverted man, who has rebelled against God as the image of God? These are serious questions. In reply to these questions, it was said that the distinction between essence and nature was not generally meant or used to underestimate the seriousness of sin and corruption. To employ the notion of an "ontic" image, an image not yet definite in relation to good and evil or obedience and disobedience, an image as man neither animalized nor demonized, is not necessarily to excuse evil nor to relativize it. Avowedly, the intention is to honor the Word of God, which employs the word "man" when calling attention to our guilt ("Therefore thou art without excuse, O man, whosoever thou art," Rom 2:1). Though no longer exhibiting the image of God in the narrower sense, the *conformitas*, man is still man; just as the prodigal son, alienated from the glory of his father's house, is still son, even when sojourning in the land of sin. The continual recurrence of ideas such as these is evidence enough that when the distinction is employed, it is not with the purpose of limiting the extent of sin's effect in man, but to emphasize the serious character of sin. It is man who has sinned, the son who was alienated, *homo peccator*.

There is no doubt that this distinction, at least in its intent, is much closer to Pascal's outlook than it is to humanism (cf. our remarks above in Chapter 1). And it is clear that a refusal to give a simple "yes" or "no" to the question of whether the image of God has been destroyed by sin, was considered justified by the fact that however strongly we picture the alienation and corruption brought about by sin, still this continuing guilt and destruction (Brunner's *Dauerrevolution*) goes on within the limits of man's man-ness.[9]

The distinction between the ontic image and the actual image, or between essence and nature, thus understandably raised the

9. It does not, of course, follow that this distinction, if misused, can not easily lead to an idealistic interpretation of man. The point is that the intent of the distinction was clearly not to glorify man or to make sin relative.

further question of whether this twofold aspect of the image of God could be justified in the light of Scripture.

Does Scripture give us any reason for seeing the image of God ▬ as anything else than communion with God, sonship of God? Can this be applied to "children of wrath," which we are "by nature" (Eph. 2:3)? Can we, after such a radical judgment on the darkness of our nature, still postulate an essence different from our nature and apply the term "image of God" to it?

In the history of dogmatic theology, the two aspects of the image of God have often been related to the double usage of words in Genesis 1 (*tselem* and *demuth*) and in the New Testament (*eikoōn* and *homoiōosis*). Indeed, this double usage has played a rather curious role in the history of theology, since it was viewed as a basis for the two aspects of the image of God. It was thought that "*tselem*" and "*eikoōn*" referred to man's essence, which did not change, and "*demuth*" and "*homooosis*" to the changeable aspect of man. The first usage of image thus lay in the area of man's essence, while the *similitudo,* or nature, or likeness, could be lost. Thus the distinction between the two uses of "image" became "an enduring element of theological anthropology."[10]

We do not at this point propose to examine these Scriptural terms more closely, but it can be stated as generally held today that this supposed Scriptural basis for the double usage of the term "image of God" is not convincing, and that the conclusions drawn from the dual terminology used in the Old and New Testaments are invalid.[11]

The fact remains, however, that this dual terminology was certainly not the only reason for the idea of the double usage of the term "image of God." It was especially the way Scripture spoke of fallen man which stimulated the development of the idea. Even those who did not accept the supposed dual terminology used regarding the image still held that various Scriptural passages dealing with post-lapsarian man give occasion for reflection and differentiation, supporting their distinction between essence and nature. The texts particularly referred to are the well-known passages in Genesis

---

10. Cf. O. Weber, *Grundlagen der Dogmatik* (1955), I, 624.

11. Greek Orthodox theology is an exception here. Its view of the image of God remains defined by this distinction. "It remains, in our age also, fundamental for Orthodox theology," B. Vyscheslavzew, "Das Ebenbild Gottes in dem Sündenfall," *Kirche, Staat und Mensch* (1937), p. 298. There is said to be a "wholly clear contrast between the ontological and the normative meanings of image" (B. Vyscheslavzew, "Das Ebenbild Gottes im Wesen des Menschen," *ibid.,* pp. 316ff.).

9:6, James 3:9 and I Corinthians 11:7. Genesis 9:6, speaking of protection against the taking of man's life, says, "Whoso sheddeth man's blood, by man shall his blood be shed; for in the image of God made he man." This last clause was generally understood not as a reference to man's lofty origin in the distant past, but as an appeal to human inviolability *because* man is created after God's image, presumably indicating a truth about man also *after* the Fall. Thus Bavinck understands the sentence as meaning, "Man after the Fall is still called image of God and as such must be reverenced";[12] and others also regard this implication as inescapable.

The image of God is taken up in Genesis 9 as an important matter which is directly related to the ban on killing one's fellow man; in James 3:9 it is mentioned only casually and in passing. James criticizes the sins of the tongue, a restless evil, full of deadly poison. To point up the horror of such sins, he goes on: "Therewith bless we the Lord and Father; and therewith curse we men, who are made after the likeness of God." This passage also is generally understood to refer to something more than a mere reminder of man's original creation in God's image; especially since the point of James's complaint is that *man* is cursed by the tongue — *God* is praised, and His *image* is cursed.[13]

And, finally, Paul's words in I Corinthians 11:7, where he speaks of the image very generally and in a context of admonition: man is "the image and glory of God." These terms make sense in the context only if applied to man as he is now, since the Fall.

It is especially on the grounds of these texts that it was held to be unfair to Scripture to say without qualification that the image of God is lost through sin.

---

12. Bavinck, *op. cit.*, II, 511. Cf. M. A. Beek, "Anthropologische Notities bij het O.T.," *Anthropologische Verkenningen*, pp. 37-38. He denies that "man according to Genesis has lost the image of God, because of his disobedience to God's command." Important in his estimate is also Gen. 9:6 as showing that the image is "thus clearly not yet lost." Cf. also Kittel, TWZNT, II, 389, 390, *s.v.*, *eikoon*. He writes about the Biblical witness to an actually existing image, referring to Gen. 9:6 and 5:3 — "A reference to long-past creation of man's essence would be as such of little concern to the O.T. faith." And hence "the O.T. gives no indication that the image has now been lost."

13. Cf. Grosheide, *Commentaar*, p. 473. He says, "thus it is all the worse, since it directs itself against beings who can be described in the words which follow." Cf. F. Hauck, *Die Kirchenbriefe*, p. 23. *re* "unnaturalness". Cf. H. Windisch, *Die Katholische Briefe*, p. 24. He contrasts *Urbild* with *Abbild*, original image and present representation, praising God and cursing man.

But this leaves us with a difficult question: How must we understand the image of God in fallen man, and what do we mean by it concretely? We surely do not want to minimize at all the radicality and absoluteness of the break in man's life, the alienation and lost condition, the darkness and vanity. Besides, the object of the New Testament treatment is not an image which is obviously and as a matter of course present in all men, but is rather the renewing of the image through the grace of God, a new *conformitas cum Deo* by way of an image that had been lost. When Paul treats the putting away of the old man and the taking on of the new, which "hath been created in righteousness and holiness of truth" (Eph. 4:24), "renewed unto knowledge after the image of him that created him" (Col. 3:10), his concern is with an *eikoon*, image, nature of man, as something which is to be established — or, better, re-established.[14]

Thus here we are confronted with a miracle of restoration, the renewal of man's nature as a salvation, in eschatological and Christological perspective, from being lost, and a destining to be "conformed to the image of his Son" (Rom. 8:29). This renewal of the image of God is a gift of grace, made against the somber background of man's lost wealth. It is the grace of sonship, it is the being "wholly other" than before (cf. Eph. 4:20), it is being the new man as over against the old (cf. Eph. 4:22). Grace brings about a historical transition from the old to the new man, to that man who is created after God's image in true righteousness and holiness. Does this transition, therefore, afford occasion for contemplating any duality other than the duality old and new? May it not be that the distinction between the wider and narrower sense of the image ignores this transition which is so decisive in the *Heilsgeschichte*, the history of salvation? Does not that distinction imply other categories than those which Scripture seems so clearly to indicate?

Before examining this very important question more closely, we might well remind ourselves that the distinction between the wider and narrower meaning of the image does not deal with a peculiarly Reformed problem, but with a problem which in various ways also appears elsewhere. The contemporary Lutheran theologian Paul Althaus, for example, has called attention to the twofold aspect of the image; he sees it as a feature of the Biblical witness which, though it had already caught the eye of Luther and Calvin, has been treated adequately only in very recent theological anthro-

14. Kittel, *op. cit.,* II, 395.

46 MAN: THE IMAGE OF GOD

pology. He uses the term *Gedankenreihen,* orders of thought, but in a manner in which we can easily recognize the ontic and the actual image (essence and nature).[15]

And, indeed, already in Lutheran theology of an earlier day we come upon the double aspect of the image of God. The Lutheran view, true enough, is generally presented as one which identifies the image of God with man's *justitia originalis,* and concludes that the image of God was wholly lost through the Fall. Nor is this common interpretation of the Lutheran view without plausibility; the identification is found in the Lutheran *Formula of Concord.*[16] But especially in view of this latter fact, it is striking to note that this identification was not consistently maintained, as is especially clear in the Lutheran theologian John Gerhard. He takes up the question of whether the image of God should be understood as active (that is, as *conformitas*) or ontic (as man's essence). On reading Gerhard, one's first impression is that he admits only the active image, the conformity to God, as he deals with man's perfection, righteousness, integrity and *conformitas.*[17]

Schumann correctly describes Gerhard's idea of the image as "man's actual state of righteousness before God."[18] It is not concerned with a general, ontic image which all men possess, but with a concrete and active conformity to God's will, with positive righteousness and holiness.

But having interpreted this active *conformitas* as being the image of God (i.e., the image lost through the Fall and restored in Christ), Gerhard suddenly becomes entangled in the general and ontic aspect of the image, when he poses the question whether the image was wholly lost through the Fall. One would certainly expect, having noted the *Formula of Concord's* identification of the image with

---

15. See Paul Althaus, "Das Bild Gottes bei Paulus," *Theologische Blätter,* XX (1941), pp. 81-92. He says, "The Bible uses the concept of the image of God in a double sense." Cf. also Althaus, *Die Christliche Wahrheit* (1948), II, 32.

16. See *Formula Concordiae* (in *Die lutherischen Bekenntnisschriften,* p. 576). It says, *"defectus . . . justitiae originalis seu imaginis Dei,"* in which man had been created, *"in veritate, sanctitate atque justitia."*

17. See Gerhard, *Loci,* F. Frank, ed. (1885), II, 141. He says that the image of God in the first man includes *"summa perfectio . . . rectitudo, integritas, et cum Deo archetypo conformitas."* He also says that the Apostle defines the image of God *"per veram sapientiam atque justitiam."* (p. 125; cf. also pp. 115-16).

18. F. K. Schumann, "Imago Dei," *Imago Dei. Beiträge zur theologischen Anthropologie* (1932), pp. 170ff.

original righteousness, that Gerhard would unequivocally answer in the affirmative. But at first he seems to leave room for an image that has not been lost. If the image could be thought of as man's essence, as will and intellect, then indeed it was not lost; but, he argues, if we think of it supernaturally, as righteousness and holiness, then the image is radically and totally lost: The restoration of the image in Christ presupposes that it has been lost. But Gerhard then unexpectedly adds that there are indeed "remnants" (*reliquiae*) of the image even in fallen man,[19] which leads Schumann to ask the pointed question: "Gerhard speaks here of remnants of the image; can he also speak of remnants of original righteousness?"[20] If this is not the case — because of man's total corruption and his complete loss of *conformitas* — then it would appear that the image of God and *justitia originalis* can not be simply identified. And then the concept of *conformitas* suddenly becomes inadequate to explain Gerhard's idea of the image. This means a shifting of position which in succeeding Lutheran descriptions of the image of God occasions all sorts of distinctions; and all of them, even if using different words, are exactly the same as the Reformed distinction between the wider and narrower meanings of the image. This can be seen clearly, for example, in Baier, who speaks of an "*imago divina* generaliter *et* specialiter *accepta*" — a general and a special image.

Thus it would seem that for some reason it was very difficult also for Lutheran theology to maintain clearly and unequivocally the identification of the image of God with man's original righteousness. The actual, active image (i.e., man's *conformitas*, or his original righteousness), though posited at first in opposition to every metaphysical or ontic definition of the image, receives as a "supplement" the remnants of the image which even fallen man possesses — and this despite continued emphasis on man's total corruption. This is a clear enough indication that theologians had to make distinctions in struggling with the problem of defining the image of God — in Lutheran as well as in Reformed theology.

Schumann, in discussing the development of Lutheran ideas on this point, notes the "broadening of the idea of the image," which was motivated by "the desire to stress the existence of

19. Gerhard, *op. cit.*, pp. 138-140. He says that nothing (*"nihil"*) remains of the original righteousness and sanctity; but there are remnants (*"reliquiae"*) even though these are obscured by sin (*"per peccatum obscuratae"*) .
20. Schumann, *op. cit.*, pp. 170, 172.

remnants of the image of God even in fallen man." In his opinion, there is no question here of "a semi-Pelagian softening of the idea of original sin," which would aim at weakening the idea of total corruption. The concept of "remnants" is not the result from a more optimistic view of man. He concludes that "it may well be asked whether it is not a real and basic dogmatic necessity, dimly sensed rather than clearly understood by these theologians, which produced the broader concept of the image of God." This is a question of incisive importance not only for Lutheran theology but also for Reformed theology, and indeed for the entire doctrine of the image of God.[21]

In the present context we should also not fail to mention the problems arising from the treatment of the image of God in Eastern Orthodox theology. We are struck, in examining this treatment, by the constant emphasis on what we may call the ontic (essential) content of the image. Lutheran and Reformed theology were willing only with great caution and not without careful qualifications to state that man "in some sense" kept God's image after the Fall: but this statement receives arresting emphasis in Eastern theology. This is already apparent in its critique of Protestant views. It notes that the early Protestant theologians thought of the image as lost in the Fall, but finding this position untenable, were led to admit the idea of "remnants" (reliquiae). But even with this

21. Cf. H. Schmid, *Die Dogmatik der evangelisch-lutherischen Kirche* (7th ed., 1893), pp. 157ff. He discusses not so much the distinction between the *imago accidentalis* (prelapsarian man) and the *imago substantialis* (here referring to Christ, as in Hollaz), but the distinction between *imago accidentalis* as *generaliter* and as *specialiter*. The general image refers to man's general "likeness to God," as shown, e.g., by man's soul (*substantia animae*) which is related to the divine (*quaedam divina exprimit*) — with an appeal here also to Gen. 9:6 and Jas. 3:9. Cf. also W. Elert, *Der Christliche Glaube* (1940), p. 339. He writes about *"imago stricte et late dicta"* — in a broader and narrower sense. Cf. also K. Hase, *Dogmatik der evangelisch-lutherischen Kirche* (12th ed., 1883), pp. 161ff. He discusses the *imago* as *generaliter-specialiter, improprie-proprie*. Cf. also Quensted. He says "the image of God and original righteousness are related as whole and part," and the image has "a part which remains — see Genesis, Corinthians, James — and a part which is lost and must be restored — see Ephesians and Colossians." Quensted distinguishes further between two kinds of *conformitas*, a primary and a secondary, the latter possessing *impassibilitas* and *immortalitas* and *dominium*. All of this shows clearly enough the shift away from the *Formula of Concord* and also from, e.g., Melanchthon's views (*Apologie*, I, 17) on the image as consisting of wisdom and righteousness. Cf. also, in general, Paul Althaus, *Die Christliche Wahrheit* (1948), II, 194.

admission, the Protestant view is considered, e.g., by Zenkowsky, as a "monstrous perversion" of Biblical teaching concerning man. How is it possible, he asks, that the thesis of the loss of the image was even considered, when it is clear that "the nature of man is completely different from that of all other living things"? He sees in the Orthodox view of man an assured intuition, and "an imperishable, because primary, truth, which is grasped intuitively." For in this intuition there is preserved the possibility of viewing the image of God as the actuality of man's being, "the whole reality of his humanity."[22] It is possible, therefore, without prejudice to speak descriptively of the "ontological realism" of Eastern theology, and to describe the image of God as in its view "the *ens realissimum* of man, the basic essence, the permanent and indestructible divine ground of his existence."[23]

The emphasis here is, of course, quite different from that in Lutheran or Reformed theology. It is directed especially at preserving the ontic image, the quality and structure of humanness, which is concentrated in man's reason and freedom, or in his personality.[24] Bratsiotis, for example, gives various illustrations of the major role played by this ontic element; thus "it is not the image of God in man, but rather his nature, which is corrupt." Not that the active image (*conformitas*) is neglected; love is "the essential primary element in the image." But it remains true that the emphasis is on the ontic image, via the distinction between *eikoon* and *homoioosis*. From this distinction far-reaching conclusions are drawn regarding the preservation of the image in sinful man; the image may include not only reason or freedom of spirit but also "those traces of a yearning for God and a striving for the good which remain in man."[25] This stress on the ontic also affects the view of the extent of sin's effects in man, and there

22. Basilius Zenkowsky, *Das Bild des Menschen in der Ost-Kirche, Grundlagen der orthodoxen Anthropologie*, p. 19. (Zenkowsky teaches at the Russian Orthodox Theological Institute in Paris.) Cf. also J. de Graaf, *De Anthropologie in de moderne Russische Wijsbegeerte* (1949), p. 56. He cites another book by Zenkowsky which he describes as stating the "boundless confidence in man, the consciousness that nothing can obliterate the image of God in man."

23. S. Bulgakov, "Die Christliche Anthropologie," *Kirche, Staat und Mensch. Russisch-orthodoxe Studiën* (1937), p. 223.

24. Cf. *ibid.* Bulgakow says that the personality is the "heart of man's being."

25. Panayotis Bratsiotis, "Genesis 1:26 in der orthodoxen Theologie," *Evangelische Theologie*, XI (1951), 289-297. Cf. especially pp. 295-297, where Androutsos ("the best of our theologians") and Zenkowsky are treated.

is a much more positive evaluation of the "remnants," since "the power of evil and the extent of man's corruption are viewed as only relative." Man remains man. And this involves man's retaining his freedom (however weakened it may be); "man is capable, despite the darkening of his understanding, of seeking the truth and partially finding it."[26] Thus the image of God, is both ontic and actual, and it is viewed in a manner which relates it closely to a semi-Pelagian view of man's will.[27]

The Orthodox stress on the ontic aspect of the image,[28] then, produces a "broadening" of the image which also has consequences for the *conformitas* or actual aspect of the image. And Orthodox indignation at Protestant teaching is then understandable enough. This all shows clearly enough, in our opinion, the dangers that continually threaten the doctrine of the image. Appealing to the ontic aspect of the image can almost automatically lead to a relativizing of man's corruption. Consider how such appeal involves pleading in behalf of the *ens realissimum* of man's ontological structure, and pleading on the basis of the empirical evidence (man differs from the brute). This ontic conception of the image tends next to become imperialistic and to encroach on the domain of the active aspect of the image, man's *conformitas* to God! If one listens attentively to the recurrent theme of the plea, one cannot avoid the impression that we are being carried far away from the witness of Scripture. It, too, speaks of man and beast. "The ox knoweth his owner, and the ass his master's crib; but Israel doth not know, my people doth not consider" (Isa. 1:3). Isaiah is not unaware of the difference between man and beast — the point lies precisely in the difference — he views man not in his isolated

26. S. Verkhowsky, "Die Lehre von Menschen im Lichte der orthodoxen Theologie," *Evangelische Theologie*, XI (1951), 321, 323.

27. Cf. Bratsiotis, "Das Menschenverständnis in der Griechisch-Orthodoxen Kirche," *Theologische Zeitschrift*, VI (1950), 382. He sees the Orthodox view of man as midway between the Pelagianizing Roman Catholic position and the Protestant position. This is certainly not fair to the Roman Catholic view.

28. We often meet strong expressions of this view in Eastern theology. Thus, man is in some sense *"mikrotheos,* a miniature god" (Vyscheslavzew, *op. cit.,* p. 313). Cf. also N. Berdyaev, who reproaches humanistic anthropology, not because it places man too high, but because it does not place him high enough, since the secret, the core, of man also implies a "perfecting of divine life," even though this is not clearly stated in Scripture. He is referring to the creative nature of man as creator (see his "Das Problem des Menschen," *Kirche, Staat und Mensch,* pp. 206-208, and *Von der Bestimmung des Menschen. Versuch einer paradoxalen Ethik* [1935], pp. 51ff.).

"ontic structure" but in his guilt, and this gives Isaiah's comparison its accusing power. This is a serious warning against any treatment of the ontic aspect of the image in isolation, and a warning also against any over-evaluation of that aspect. The Word of God never presents man in this isolated ontic aspect; man, together with all his human capacities, always stands in the light of God's judgment.

When we hear Eastern theology sing its hymn of praise for man's personality or freedom or reason, we remind ourselves that Scripture speaks of "brutal men, skillful to destroy" (Ezek. 21:31). These words do not imply that men do not still think; but it is not this thinking as such which is the central point of Biblical interest, but rather that which these thinking men, in the totality of their existence, are and do. And thus, viewing the image as treated in Eastern theology, we may conclude that we should always be alert for the dangers of stressing the image of God in fallen man. There is always the possibility that such accentuation is the result of a kind of thinking in which emphasis on man's reason, freedom, and personality surely seriously weakens, if it does not destroy, the reality of sin and corruption.[29]

We encounter questions similar to those treated above when we next consider the thought of Emil Brunner, who also employs a double aspect of the image of God, and speaks of a formal and a material image.[30] The formal image is that which cannot be lost, which is not affected by "the contrast between sin and faith."[31]

---

29. For the Protestant-Eastern controversy on the image, see especially E. Schlink, "Der Mensch als Sünder, "*Evangelische Theologie* (1955), pp. 325ff.; S. Verkhowsky, "Der neue Mensch in Christus," *ibid.*, pp. 332ff.; Ivan Tschetwerikov, "Ssobornostj," *ibid.*, pp. 351ff.; and the *Protokoll des Gesprächs zwischen evangelischen und orthodoxen Theologen in Frankfurt-am-Main* (1951). The latter is a very interesting discussion.

30. Bratsiotis concludes his evaluation of the Orthodox teaching on the image as occupying a place midway between Roman Catholic and Protestant views with the remark: "It appears to me that among Protestants Emil Brunner's view is closest to the Orthodox." See his "Das Menschenverständnis in der Griechisch-orthodoxen Kirche," *Theologische Zeitschrift* (1950), p. 382. This article was originally meant for the *Festschrift* for Brunner, *Das Menschenbild im Lichte des Evangeliums* (1950). The distinction between formal and material aspects of the image, "not only formal, but also according to its contents," is already used by H. de Vos, *Christelijk Humanisme in het Licht der nieuwere Wijsbegeerte* (1939), p. 12.

31. E. Brunner, *Dogmatik*, II, 91. Cf. also Brunner, *Der Mensch im Widerspruch*, p. 521; cf. also p. 86. He refers to Van Oetinger's earlier use of the concept of a formal image.

While the material image is no longer possessed by fallen man, and can be restored to him only through Jesus Christ. This distinction reminds us strongly of Reformed theology's distinction between the wider aspect of the image (which is retained) and the narrower aspect (which is lost). The term "material image" patently refers to man's *conformitas*, his "obedience to the Word of God in the sense of original righteousness, renewed for men by Jesus Christ, and achieved through salvation." The meaning of the term "formal image" for Brunner is more difficult to describe. He views it as a "special characteristic of human nature, which is also possessed by sinful man: personality, lordship over other creatures, rational choice in the moral sense." This image remains, and Brunner protests against the "making light of and profaning man's humanity" inherent in ignoring it. Brunner's concept here approaches closely that of the view of the image of God in the wider sense, which has indeed often been described as man's *humanitas*, and he refuses to under-evaluate man's continuing *humanum*. Apart from the question of the orientation of man's being, his being man is *in itself* entitled to be called image of God, and Brunner consequently speaks of "two basically different aspects of the image."[32]

It is not the intention at this point to engage in extensive treatment of Brunner's concept of the image. Were such our intention, the question we should have to consider would be this: Does not Brunner's concept of a formal image tend to color his view of the lost material image, the *conformitas* — just as is the case in Eastern Orthodox theology?[33] But our present concern is merely to exhibit how problems similar to those raised in earlier Lutheran and Reformed theology are encountered everywhere in treatments of the image of God. One cannot escape the important conclusion that in every instance the main point at issue is the problem of man's *humanitas*, that which makes even fallen man still man, together with the problem of the meaning of this *humanum* in relation to the image of God.

This being the case, it is fully understandable that all sorts of questions were raised in connection with the double aspect of

32. Brunner, *ibid.*
33. This appears to me to be unmistakable, especially considering the way in which Brunner explains the meaning of the formal image. Cf. further A. Szekeres, *De Structuur van Emil Brunners Theologie* (1952), pp. 69-78; H. G. Hubbeling, *Natuur en Genade bij Emil Brunner* (1956), pp. 15ff., 65.

the image, and that much uncertainty and hesitation may be observed in the attempts to work out this concept more clearly. Do we not, then, in dealing with an image which is both kept and lost, have to do with a strange paradox, or a dialectic, or a mysterious antinomy, which invites confusion?[34] It must be said that, in general, theologians have not been satisfied with any such answer, and have tried to avoid confusion in terminology. We detect this attempt, for example, in Herman Bavinck. He says that too often in distinguishing the image in the wider and narrower senses the two "images" are placed alongside each other, as related merely mechanically, and that the concepts must be related organically, so that they will not be seen merely as dualistic co-ordinate concepts.[35] But Bavinck never explains exactly what he means by such an organic relationship. On the one hand, he speaks of the two concepts as elements which together describe the complete image of God and, on the other hand, he says that sin not only caused the loss of the image in the narrower sense but also caused corruption and destruction of the image in the wider sense. These statements point up the difficulty, since the image in the wider sense is always understood as that element which is not lost because of sin. It is clear enough that the problems here center around the nature of this (preserved) humanity — not understood in a humanistic sense as some moral and inviolate hidden essence of man, but understood as man's structure, the structure of his being human. But then, is there, using the concepts of the wider and narrower meaning of the image, any way to escape from the danger of dualism, of antinomy, of letting the two concepts stand unreconciled?[36] Or is the tenacity with which theologians have time and again held to this duality in the image a clear indication of a very real problem which arises in connection with man's nature, his "humanness"?

34. Cf. E. Schlink, op. cit., p. 331. He speaks of a "true antinomy," involving "both this — that the image of God can be wholly lost in man's sin; and this — that the image of God can never be lost even in the greatest sin."
35. Bavinck, op. cit., II, 215.
36. See Brunner, Der Mensch im Widerspruch, p. 521. He speaks of "a contrast between the O.T. and N.T. presentations," but on the other hand asserts that this contrast between formal and material is not wholly absent even in the N.T. Cf. Brunner, Dogmatik, II, 91. He discusses O.T. formal and structural as contrasted with N.T. substantial and material.

One possible way to escape from the "antinomy" involved in a dualistic understanding of the image is to acknowledge that fallen man is indeed man; maintaining, however, that this humanness is not related to the image of God. This approach can be seen clearly in Klaas Schilder. He begins with a denial of the distinction between "wider" and "narrower," which he says cannot be supported from Scripture.[37] The appeal to Genesis 9 and James 3 must be rejected, since such passages refer to man's lofty origin, to what he once was; they do not imply at all that fallen man *now* retains the image of God.[38] Acts 17:28 and I Corinthians 11:7 also refer to man in his original state. Hence Schilder wishes to distinguish between creation and image. Man's creation is indeed the precondition for the image, but it is not the image itself. The actual image lies in the office, the *officium*, created man received. We should not describe the image of God in terms of nature or qualities, but in terms of calling. The image of God does not refer to a static, ontic state, but to man's service, man's fulfilling his calling. The image is expressed in a dynamic and close fellowship with the God of the Covenant. And — says Schilder — the image exists only when that close contact, that communication, that loving relationship exists. For "not in static possessions of abstract adornments but only in dynamic discharge of his calling can man reflect God in His world here below." The word "image" implies "making visible." God has given man the task of "representing Him on earth through being in His image." Naturally, the image has some relation to man's human qualities. God established this relation in His work of creation; it is *created* man who must represent God, and in the nature of the case all his attributes play an important role in his fulfilling this representation. They are to function in accord with man's official calling. But these qualities are not in themselves the image. Such an idea abstracts the qualities from the calling, and makes "image" that which is actually only a necessary condition for the development of the image.

When Schilder thus contrasts the static and ontic with the dynamic of a vital communion with God, a vital service in man's calling, it is not difficult to detect a stress on the narrower sense of the image, man's *conformitas* to God, the actualized and active image of God as mirrored and made visible in deeds. This should

---

37. See K. Schilder, *Heidelbergse Catechismus*, I, 300. Cf. E. Schlink, *Der Mensch in der Verkündigung der Kirche* (1936), pp. 182ff.

38. Cf. also Schlink, *op. cit.*, p. 188. He says, "These passages do not say that man 'has' the image of God, but rather that he was *originally* like God." Cf. further C. Vonk, *De voorzeide Leer*, IIIa (1955), 346.

be qualified somewhat, for Schilder accuses the Arminians of making the image too dynamic. But there is actually no contradiction. Schilder's complaint is that the Arminians did not relate the image to the actual state of man in Paradise but, rather, to that which can develop in man, so that the image of God referred not so much to the peace of Paradise as to the struggle for civilization. This is the same objection he directs against Barth, who sees the image of God primarily in terms of man's destiny. "Barth makes the image a *future* thing; Calvinists make it so also, but primarily a thing of the *present.*" Thus Schilder does not protest against a dynamic view of the image as such; indeed, he himself supports it as over against a static and ontic view. His own concept of the image connotes nothing if not dynamic *conformitas,* service, active representation — the image exists only when this is present. As against the Arminians, he wants only to maintain that this dynamic image was already realized in Paradise. The fault of the Arminians lay not in their idea of the dynamic, but in their denial of the existence of a dynamic *conformitas* in Paradise.[39]

Schilder's concept of the image is thus clear enough. The creation of man, his whole created existence, is the background and presupposition for the image. But the actual image is found in the *use* of these created qualities in an active and dynamic service of God. Thus and only thus can man reflect God, mirror God, be in God's image. The image of God does not consist of qualities in themselves, but in created man's life *in actu,* in action, and in functioning.

Thus Schilder's main concern is to reject an abstract and metaphysical view of the image, which would see it as consisting of man's ontic structure as such. His own concept of the image might at first glance seem to imply that man's ontic qualities are wholly excluded, but this is not his meaning. "Our description of the image does not exclude the qualities; it makes them secondary." Man's qualities are essential to man's imaging of God, and the actual image exists *in* and *with* these qualities. Schilder indeed stresses the active *conformitas* of man to God as basic for the image, but it is the *conformitas* of the whole man, with all his

39. For the foregoing, see Schilder, *op. cit.,* pp. 236-241, 254-255, 263-265, 272, 293-295, 300-306, 312. In dealing with the Arminians, Schilder comments that Episcopius did not want to overestimate the abilities of the first man, and indeed left room for a kind of theory of evolution; and remarks that Scripture in speaking of the image makes mention *first* of the created actuality of man (*ibid.,* pp. 215ff., 237, 250) .

qualities. Thus Schilder holds that it is unreasonable "to *separate* the image from the qualities," for these qualities serve man in his functioning, and man represents God *in* and *with* these qualities. But we must also avoid the error of "seeing in these qualities, abstracted from man's actions and service and sacrifice and calling, a 'part' of the image." If this service changes to rebellion, this obedience to disobedience, then we can no longer speak of the image of God.

One might therefore say that Schilder agrees with the original Lutheran formula in the *Apology* and the *Formula of Concord*: the image is original righteousness, *imago est justitia originalis*; it is man's dynamic reflecting and representing God in earthly reality, a representing which becomes once again actual when the image is renewed in Christ. The glory of the image shines forth only in the service of God, the true mirroring of God, the imaging of God. How can fallen man, using his qualities in rebellion, reflect or image God? "Can man's humanness as such be the image?" asks Schilder. If the image of God means the active service of God, then it vanishes when man rebels against God. It exists only in the believer, as it existed once in Paradise, in man's *status integritatis*.[40]

Summarizing our discussion so far, we may conclude that theological concern with the image of God has concentrated on the so-called dual character of the image, and especially on the question of whether we can correctly speak of the image when man's conformity to God's will has vanished. Some would say that man's humanness, his humanity — however this is defined — as such is part of the image; and others would stress man's *conformitas* as the essence and the structure of the image. The point at issue is thus the relationship between the *humanum*, man's humanness, and the image of God. For even those who, like Schilder, deny that fallen man has the image of God, do not deny that man is still man, even after the Fall. They only emphasize that fallen man is turned away from God, no longer serves God, is no longer righteous and holy, and that therefore he no longer bears the image of God. They would thus emphasize not the ontic qualities of man, but what he *does* with these qualities. For if the image of God should lie in such ontic qualities, then Satan himself would exhibit the image of God. Thus Luther attacks Augustine's view that the image consists of memory, understanding

40. For the foregoing material, see Schilder, *op. cit.*, pp. 255, 273, 294, 306.

and will.[41] Luther – like Schilder – would view man's response to God, by loving and glorifying Him, as the essential component of the image.

It is not justifiable to object that this view denies that fallen man is human or annihilates the distinction between fallen man and beast. That was Bavinck's objection to the Lutheran definition of the image in terms of man's original righteousness: the distinction then "has so little religious and theological meaning that it hardly receives attention." He held, on the contrary, that the image consisted not only of knowledge of God, righteousness and holiness, but also of "everything that is human in man," so that man "always and forever remains man, and to that extent always and forever remains image of God." This thesis Bavinck then, in connection with man's origin, relates to creationism, which maintains the specifically human characteristics of man and respects the boundary between man and beast.[42]

Actually, however, a denial that fallen man bears the image of God does not necessarily involve a wish to deny or underestimate the fact that man remains man. This is understandable enough when we consider the view of the image implied – that it lies in man's representing God in earthly reality. Decisive is always what content is put into the term, image of God. In any case we can begin to discern the real issues involved in the conflicts over the existence or non-existence of two aspects to the image only if we recognize that those who see the image as consisting in the active service of God in no respect deny the humanity of fallen man, in all his sinfulness.

The importance of this insight of Schilder's, in agreement with Luther, can hardly be denied. Does not Scripture's treatment of the image – which we examine more closely in the following chapter – deal with wealth and glory, and is not the image of God in man related to the likeness of a child to his father? Does it not refer to man's activity, his response to God, his imaging of God, his serving God? Have not theologians discussing image in the narrower sense almost unanimously pointed to these also in their attempts to delimit the image? And then is it possible to talk meaningfully of a loss of the image in the narrower sense, and a retention of the image in a broader sense? Doesn't the concept of two aspects of the image of God actually involve the postulating of two very different things, two separate images? Such

41. See D. Cairns, *The Image of God* (1953), p. 4.
42. See Bavinck, *op. cit.*, pp. 547-548.

are the questions which arise even in our preliminary examination, and which lead directly to the problem of the meaning and the content of the image of God in man.

The problem is not this, that some affirm and some deny that man remained man even after the Fall, but rather in this, whether or not fallen man's humanness is part of the image of God. A decisive point then is this, whether the Biblical witness gives us any basis for relating man's *humanum*, his manness, the ontic structure of man, to the image of God — regardless of whether this ontic structure is used in the service of God. Does Scripture give us any reason to see in man's humanness as such, apart from the service of God and the richness of sonship, an analogy, an *analogia entis*, an analogy of being, an analogy between the being of God and the being of man, an analogy which can never be annihilated or destroyed, an analogy which on man's side expresses itself in, say, man's person, or his reason, or his freedom?

Thus we are faced again with Schumann's question as to the meaning and legitimacy of the "widening" of the concept of the image of God. The discussion as to the legitimacy of such a wider use has naturally centered around the well-known Scriptural passages in Genesis, James, and I Corinthians. Are these passages intended to call our attention to a permanent "analogy" in respect to the wider aspects of the image, even though every other analogy, every other resemblance, has disappeared in man's alienation from the life of God (Eph. 4:18)?

Not only Schilder but also Schlink has vigorously denied this, and has seen in these passages merely a reminder of man's origin. Man is so referred to, in relation to his lofty origin, because "God from the very beginning intended something glorious for him."[43] Schlink, too, sees the reference to the creation of man in the image of God not as implying a permanent and inviolate *analogia entis*, but rather as indicating God's remaining faithful to the creation of man in God's image: "this original similarity is for Him the basis for His plan of salvation, which begins with the law, and this lost similarity again appears by way of the law as a demand made of man." Man thus no longer is the image of God because of some permanent analogy, but God has thoughts about man "in His mindfulness of the act of creation and in His objective for the new creation." Schumann goes even further: "God has impressed in the structure of man's being the divine intention that man shall find the fulfillment of his existence only from God, in God

43. Schilder, *op. cit.*, p. 312.

and through God," and even talks of man's *Wesensmöglichkeit*, his potentiality for gaining essence, gaining real being.[44]

These views of Schilder, Schlink and Schumann are all concerned, despite various nuances in expression, with the same basic point in their understanding of the Biblical references to the creation of man in the image of God. And with this, they are, we feel, indeed on the track of some very important Biblical concepts; for the Biblical language implies an unmistakable perspective. The reference is not to some purely "historical" reminder of a lost Paradise. The term "reminder" can be used here only if we bear in mind that it means reminder of the divine act of creation. It is in connection with this act of creation that Scripture refers to man's inviolable humanity, and earnestly proclaims that no one may offend against this humanity, and shows why this may not be done (Gen. 9:6, James 3:9). That the creation of man in God's image is thus spoken of, in the midst of a world of fallen man, indicates that we may never think of man apart from the original aim of his creation. Such passages do not mean to turn our attention to some abstract thesis of the image of God as an *analogia entis*; they deal with a humanness, a being human, in a context of God's plan of salvation. Thus anyone who attacks his fellow man, or curses him, violates the mysterious essence of man, not because man is *mikrotheos*, or demi-god, but because he is *man*. In all his relations and acts, he is never man-in-himself, but always man-in-relation, in relation to this history of God's deeds in creation, to this origin of an inalienable relation to his Creator. And this man is protected and maintained in his relation to God by Him. And thus the distinction between the image in the wider and narrower sense does contain an important element of truth. It is noteworthy that the image in the wider sense has been almost without exception described in such a way that man, even when fallen, remains man. And this faithfully reflects the witness of Scripture. But Scripture does not intend to focus our interest on an *analogia entis* derived more or less directly from what God and man have in common, and in which fallen man retains his likeness to God.

It is regrettable that the valid emphasis in the dogma of the image of God in the wider sense has often taken on the form of an analysis of the ontic structure of man, e.g., as defined by person, reason and freedom. For it is undeniable that Scripture does not support such an interpretation. Scripture is concerned with

44. See Schlink, *op. cit.*, p. 189; Schumann, *Imago Dei*, p. 177.

man in his relation to God, in which he can never be seen as
man-in-himself, and surely not with man's "essence" described as
self or person. Thus it is understandable that Scripture speaks of
man's lost glory and of what is restored in Christ. It witnesses to
man as he actually is, man in his guilt and rebellion, but still man.
But this approach to man is hardly one which would encourage
us to dwell on ontic qualities that in themselves establish a likeness
between God and man. If we try to find the image of God in
such ontic qualities, and define the image in the wider sense in terms
of such qualities, we soon are involved in speculations which have
no support from Scripture. This can be clearly seen, for example,
in such a theologian as Daubanton. He understood the image in
an ontic sense, and worked this out so that man imaged God in
the sense that God thinks and wills, and man does; that God is
a person, and so is man. Thus the image of God lies in the modality
of man's existence; it is an ontic image. Hence Daubanton rejected
all attempts to relate the image to man's goodness, righteousness
and holiness, since man's *conformitas* is not part of his bearing
the image of God.

But it soon becomes all too apparent that such an exclusively
ontological concept of the image leads to insoluble difficulties.
Daubanton condemns any attempt to pass from the formal to the
material, from the modal to the qualitative, and describes the image
only in terms of the self, the person, thinking and willing, and
"the pneumatic soul"; but even this does not help him. For when
he attempts to synthesize the various modal components of the
image, he soon is describing man as a "religious-moral creature,"
upholding an analogy between "God is love" and "man has love,"
and concluding that man, created in God's image, is a religious
being and thus also a moral being.[45] It is clear enough that
Daubanton has gone far beyond his "ontological image" here. And
it is also clear that such an exclusively ontological approach involves the use of various analogies which lead us in directions
quite different from that indicated by the Biblical witness, which
does not stress such ontological qualities — though they may indeed

---

45. See F. E. Daubanton, "De Mensch geschapen naar Gods Beeld volgens
Zijn Gelijkenis," *Theologische Studiën*, IX (1891), 236ff. He speaks
specifically of modal components of man's being, and sees "the image
of God as the modality of man's existence as man." The term "image
of God" implies nothing at all as to the quality of man's moral existence.
Thus he sees Article 14 of the (Calvinist) *Belgic Confession* as unbiblical,
since it describes the image as good, righteous and holy; while he
approves of the formulation of the *Heidelberg Catechism*, Q. 6: "created
good and after His own image."

exist — but rather emphasizes the concepts of *conformitas* and child-father relation to God as basic to the image.

The same sort of difficulties appears also if the image is understood as both ontological and active (i.e., as wider and narrower). It has proved impossible to bring any real clarity to this duality in the image, this ontic structure on the one hand, and man's *conformitas* on the other. Despite all attempts to overcome the "antinomy" involved and to develop a unified view of the image, the "twofold image" remains stubbornly dualistic, because the image understood in the wider sense has a very different content than the image understood in the narrower sense. This is the problem, and it is one which Bavinck sensed when he called for an "organic" view of the relation between the two aspects to replace our faulty "mechanistic" concept.[46] But he did little to develop this idea, beyond suggesting that the image in the narrower sense was "very closely related" to the image in the wider sense. We can perhaps see why he was unable to go further: a synthesis between the ontic and active image is impossible when the attempt is made using such concepts as "essence" and "nature." For when we try and delimit the meaning of man's "essence" or "being," man's relation to God is not considered, and it can only be added later, after we have described man's essence; and it is then impossible to develop any "organic relationship" between the two. A duality remains, and must remain: *conformitas*, which is lost through sin, and some sort of permanent analogy between God and man, an analogy of person or reason or freedom. This analogy then becomes an independent theme, and it soon becomes difficult to see how any synthesis between the two aspects of the image can possibly be worked out.

This can also be seen clearly enough in A. Kuyper, Jr., whose image in the wider sense is the same as Daubanton's image as the modality of man's being. He sees the image in man's self (his "I"), his person, and his reason. But in a later chapter on the Antichrist, the "terrifying counter-image," he sees him as "the complete opposite of man, who bears the image of God." It is perhaps surprising that the younger Kuyper holds that remnants of the image remain in fallen man, because of God's common grace, but sees in the Antichrist the absence of common grace. Hence he views him as man's opposite — a strange view, since II Thessalonians 2:3 speaks of him as "the *man* of lawlessness." Further, it is difficult to see why the image should be expected to vanish in the Antichrist, the "man of sin," if Kuyper, Jr., is correct in seeing the

46. See Bavinck, *op. cit.*, p. 515.

image in the wider sense as an *analogia entis*. The difficulties he encounters are clear enough here; in the extreme case, the ontic and the active images are completely separate and unrelated. The problems raised by this approach are insoluble.[47] A synthesis is not possible because the two aspects of the image are tied in with two very different concepts.

Attempts have been made to find Scriptural support for the ontological image, the *analogia entis*, the permanent similarity between man and God. Thus Psalm 94:7, 9 is appealed to: "he who planted the ear, does he not hear? He who formed the eye, does he not see?" (Cf. also Exod. 4:11 and Prov. 20:12). It is clear enough, however, that this is a strange sort of exegesis. The passage gives no evidence for *analogia entis* at all; its concern is to evidence apostasy and arrogance of man towards his Creator (cf. also Ps. 94:10), and the Creator's grandeur and majesty in relation to the creature dependent on Him. Hubbeling[48] has also attempted to appeal to Luke 11:9-13, the analogy of the father's good gifts to his children. He notes correctly that the passage is concerned with the acts of God, not with His being, but adds that the two can never be separated. This is indeed true; how could we ever separate God's acts from His being? But such defenses of the *analogia entis* are based on an independent and non-Scriptural interest in finding ontological analogies between man and God which would define the sense in which man is the image-bearer. When we say that Scripture gives us no basis for this interest in ontological analogies, we are not saying that all uses of the concept of analogy are illegitimate; we shall consider the matter further later. But if theologians attempt to equate the image in the wider sense with the *analogia entis*, and further define it in terms of self, person and reason, then they are using concepts which are notably not used in Scripture with reference to the image. We are not then helped at all in our attempt to understand the meaning of the image of God in man.

With such concepts, the essence of man is defined in terms of his ontic qualities, and man is viewed formally and abstractly, as if it were possible to define the essence of man without reference to his relation to God. And it helps such theologians little if they attempt to delimit the "analogy" more closely, and stress the discontinuities also involved, and even speak of God as "wholly other," *totaliter aliter*, and pay their respects to the infinite qualitative

47. See A. Kuyper, Jr., *Het Beeld Gods*, pp. 131, 318-325.
48. H. G. Hubbeling, *Natuur en Genade bij Emil Brunner* (1956), pp. 70-73.

difference between man and God: for in doing this they have abandoned their original concept of analogy. This is evident enough in Hubbeling, who speaks of such analogies as "vague forms, empty contours, which point towards God," and then goes on to conclude that man's being is "formally analogous" to God's being.[49]

The real nature of the problems which supporters of the image of God in the *wider* sense encounter becomes apparent in these closer delimitations and interpretations of analogy in the ontological sphere. Viewing man apart from his orientation towards or away from God, they consider in what respects man as such can be thought of as analogous to God, an image of God. They reach the conclusion (which we shall examine more carefully later) that the body of man is not included in the image; and this conclusion in itself is indicative of the problems inherent in the distinction between the wider and narrower aspect of the image, for Scripture always speaks simply of *man* as created in the image of God, and gives no warrant for considering only a part of man as partaking of the image.

We are not forgetting that the basic motive underlying employment of such terms as "image in the wider sense," "ontic image," "man's being as such," is the desire to do justice to the fact that even in the state of sin man remains man. In the "widening" of the image, this motive indeed continually comes to the fore. None the less it is remarkable how frequently elucidation of the concept does not get beyond reference to the reality of the humanness of sinful man, and never arrives at a serious attempt to expound the *analogia entis* (analogy of being) as an *analogia rationis et voluntatis* (analogy of reason and will). To the extent that they call attention to this humanness, these efforts are undeniably in line with Scripture, which constantly presupposes precisely this humanness of the sinner. But for Scripture it is the humanness of man in his apostasy, his rebellion, his enslavement in sin; it is man — *in* his *humanitas* — before the eyes of God. And this man,

---

49. Cf. M. Matthys, *Theologisch Woordenboek* (1952), *s.v.,* "Beeld Gods." He says that man is endowed with intelligence, and this gives him "a very special resemblance to God." Man is *therefore* the image of God, while other creatures are only *vestigia Dei* and do not have the image. Cf. also his remarks on man's spiritual characteristics, and on Augustine's attempt to show that man is not only in the image of God, but indeed in the image of the Triune God. This is followed by an attempt to support Augustine, though it cannot be stated with certainty "exactly what the likeness to the divine Persons includes." Cf. also the remarks on thinking, willing and loving which follow.

sinful man, is not referred to in Scripture in terms of his ontological qualities, but in terms of his loss and his guilt. Only thus can he be placed in the perspective of the promise of salvation.[50]

When theologians direct their attention to the humanness of the sinner, his being human, and view it as an important aspect of the image of God, it should be clear enough that they are not at all thinking of a "moral" humanity in the sense in which we customarily speak of "humane" and "humaneness." And yet they constantly speak of a *humanitas,* a humanness, which is retained by sinful man. It is understandable that such usage can easily lead to misunderstanding, and give the impression that this *humanitas* refers to some remnants of goodness which survive in fallen man. This shift of meaning, once accepted, leaves the way open for the entrance of all sorts of Pelagian and humanistic views. And indeed, the history of theology shows that this danger has always been acute, and has often led to a more or less far-reaching relativizing of human depravity, a de-emphasizing of the effects of sin, on the ground of the *humanitas* retained by the sinner.

This is evidence enough that the term *humanitas* can be used as a starting point for either of two paths, and that it should be made clear which path the theologian who uses the term intends to take. The Biblical use of the term is clear enough. The Vulgate uses *humanitas* in its translation of the Greek *philanthropia* in Titus 3:4, which reads: "the goodness [*benignitas*] and loving kindness [*humanitas*] of God our Savior"; the word *humanitas* translates the Greek *philanthropia,* the "love of man" of our Savior and God. Here there is no ambiguity in the word *humanitas;* clear, and free of all dialectio, *humanitas* is directly linked with God's goodness (*benignitas; chrēstotēs*). The series of problems which produces the careful distinction between "humanness" and "true humanity" is a series which does not apply to God. The

---

50. It seems to me that in this respect the Lutheran and Calvinistic views of the image of God are much closer than most theologians recognize (e.g., Bavinck, *op. cit.,* II, 547ff.). Cf. also Polman, *Christelijke Encyclopedie,* I (2d ed., 1956), *s.v.,* "Anthropologie." This seems borne out also by careful reading of this Calvinist theologian's sympathetic description of Luther's view on the image as "not a collection of static qualities, but a complete orientation towards God." Polman also views this orientation as central, and will not accept the image in the wider sense (with appeals to Gen. 9 and Jas. 3:9) or the image "as man's essence in distinction from his nature." Cf. also, on "essence" and on religious orientation, J. Waterink, *De Mens als religieus Wezen en de hedendaagse Psychologie* (1954), pp. 5, 14, 21, 23.

divine *humanitas* of Titus 3:4 refers clearly and unmistakably to God's pity for man and His salvation of man.

But when we examine man, we must make distinctions between man's actual being and his "true humanity." It is not man's tragedy but rather his guilt that he, in his humanness, must face God's judgement on his inhumanity. Scripture gives us no rational synthesis of this frightful duality. Rather, it issues a call to man, and at the same time proclaims the *kerygma* of the salvation of man through that other *humanitas,* that unambiguous and unspotted *humanitas* of God, which comes to us in Jesus Christ.

How this warns us against using man's "humanity" as a means of excusing ourselves! Scripture does not picture man's "humanness" as a starting point for speculations about the *analogia entis* between man and God, and its witness can hardly be misunderstood. For Scripture, in the context of this *humanitas,* speaks of the darkness, apostasy, rebellion of man, his opposition to everything God intended in creating man in His image. Hence man, in his rebellion, precisely in his insistence on autonomy, is in inescapable and deep-seated conflict with himself, with his "essence," his true humanity. There is no need to be surprised when man, speaking about man, distinguishes between man's "true humanity" and that "humanity" which characterizes man as he actually is. This is not meant (not even in speaking of fallen man's "inhumanity") to deny the "humanity" of sinful man, *homo peccator,* but rather to emphasize the darkness and unnaturalness of sin, sin which does not merely affect man's "nature," as some abstract distinctions imply, but also his "essence."[51] And thus the separation between "essence" (inviolate) and "nature" (corrupt) can never satisfy us. For man as sinner is alienated not only from God but also from himself.

At this point we might raise a further question: What was meant by those many theologians in the history of the doctrine of the image of God who made use of the concept of the remnants or traces of the image in fallen man? We need not wonder that this concept was the center of heated controversy, for at first hearing the term does not make much sense. What is meant by remnants? This question comes up especially in the course of the constant discussions on the "humanity" of fallen man. Does this notion of "remnants" of the image refer to the so-called ontic image (in

---

51. Cf. Polman, *op. cit.,* p. 247. He speaks of an ontological definition or delimiting of the "image of God," but it is clear from the context of the article that he is concerned not with an isolated ontic image, but with the reality of the whole man, the actual man, as the image of God, as appears from his contrasting ontological and actual.

some sense retained) or to the active image (*conformitas*, which is lost)?

Such questions, which necessarily arose in the course of the development of the problems surrounding the whole concept of the image, are very closely related to two basic questions. First, what is the meaning of the Biblical expression "image of God"? And second, just what power or effect do sin and corruption have in man's life? Our preliminary orientation in this chapter has shown us the way to get at these questions. We shall first attempt to understand the sense in which the Word of God uses the term "image of God," and then direct our attention to the problem of the relation between the image of God and man's corruption.

CHAPTER THREE

THE MEANING OF THE IMAGE

I F WE examine the Biblical witness regarding man, we soon discover that it never gives us any kind of systematic theory about man as the image of God. It is indeed rather striking that the term is not used often at all, and that it is far less "central" in the Bible than it has been in the history of Christian thought.[1] This apparent discrepancy vanishes, however, when we note that Scripture's references to the image of God, whenever there are such, have a special urgency and importance. Furthermore, there is the possibility that Scripture often deals with the concept of the image of God without using those exact words, so that we surely should not a priori limit our investigation of the concept to considering only those places where the term itself is used.

It is understandable enough, however, that attention has always been directed first of all to those Biblical passages where the creation of man in God's image and the restoration of the image in Christ are dealt with specifically, or where Christ as the image of God is directly considered.

We shall begin, then, with an examination of the passage which speaks of God's original decision (Gen. 1:26) to "make man in our likeness, after our image," and the following passage: "God created man in his own image, in the image of God he created them; male and female he created them." These passages are shortly followed by Genesis 5:1, "When God created man, he made him in the likeness of God," and Genesis 9:6, where the shedding of man's blood is forbidden "*for* God made man in his own image."

Special note has always been taken of the fact that in Genesis 1:26 two words are used; "image" and "likeness," "*tselem*" and "*demuth*." This has led to various views of the image of God which

---

1. Cf. H. Gunkel, *Genesis* (1902), pp. 99ff. He says, "The primary difference between the O.T. and Christian dogmatics as regards this point is that in the latter it plays an important role — it has sometimes served as occasion for developing a complete anthropology — while in the former it has no special importance; in the Prophets and the Psalms, for example, it is wholly absent."

were based on a fairly strong distinction between *"tselem"* and *"demuth."* Bavinck refers to a naturalistic view and a supernatural-istic view which both appeal to the distinction between image and likeness. The former sees man as created only in God's image, and as gradually evolving into God's likeness. The latter sees in the likeness something added to the image, a *donum superadditum.*[2]

We have already noted the fact that it is today generally agreed that earlier theologians who drew far-reaching conclusions from this dual terminology in Genesis were on the wrong track. There are not many today who would follow Origen, for example, when he writes that Genesis mentions man's creation in the image but is silent about any creation in the likeness, in order to indicate that man in creation received the dignity of the image, but that its fulfillment in the likeness was reserved for the future, and is reached through works and exertion.[3]

There has been a long tradition of such ideas,[4] related to the Septuagint translation *"eikona kai homoioosin"* (Vulgate *imaginem et similitudinem*), i.e., image *and* likeness. This tradition was broken with by both Luther and Calvin[5] and today there is a strong convergence of opinion which rejects this tradition, in exegetical as well as in dogmatic literature.[6]

2. See Bavinck, *Gereformeerde Dogmatiek*, II, 494, 499. The supernatural view, says Bavinck, actually did not derive from the distinction, but was later tied in with it.

3. See Origen, "De Principiis," III, IV, 1, *Opera Omnia*, ed. De la Rue, p. 375. Note the passage *"indicat quod imaginis quidem dignitatem in prima conditione percepit, similitudinis vero perfecto in consummatione servata est; scilicet. . . ."* Cf. further H. Crouzel, *Théologie de l'image de Dieu chez Origène* (1955), pp. 217ff.; A. Struker, *Die Gottebenbildlichkeit des Menschen in der Christliche Literatur der ersten zwei Jahrhunderte* (1913) ; R. Bernard, *L'image de Dieu d'après St Athanase* (1952) .

4. Emil Brunner, *Der Mensch im Widerspruch* (1937), p. 523. He speaks of "the standard distinction, from Irenaeus on, between image and likeness." Cf. also the *Theologisch Woordenboek*, I (1952), s.v., "Beeld Gods." It says that the Fathers distinguished between image and likeness and that "this may have also been the intent of the sacred writer, who wrote these words under God's guidance," and then follows with a distinction between natural and supernatural image.

5. See Calvin, *Institutes*, I, XV, 3. He says that the traditional commentators sought a distinction between the two words which is not really there, since "likeness" is added to "image" simply for purposes of clarification, and he refers to the Hebrew use of parallelism. Cf. also his *Commentary on the Pentateuch*, s.v., Gen. 1:26. Here he also denies the distinction. Brunner notes Luther's similar views.

6. For exegetical literature, see the following; e.g., O. Procksch, *Die Genesis* (1913) , p. 432; E. König, *Die Genesis* (1919) , p. 156; J. Skinner, "Genesis," *International Critical Commentary* (1930) , p. 32; B. Jacob, *Das erste*

This convergence of opinion[7] is closely related to the increased appreciation of the variety of ways in which Genesis speaks of the image. Genesis 1:26 uses both *"tselem"* and *"demuth,"* "image" and "likeness"; Genesis 1:27 and Genesis 9:6 use only *"tselem."* And if God's plan for man (that man should have both image and likeness) was only partially realized by man's creation in His image (as Origen and others claimed), then it is difficult to explain Genesis 5, which speaks of man's creation in God's likeness (*demuth*). And it goes on to speak of Adam's begetting a son "in his own likeness (*demuth*) and after his image (*tselem*)." Because of the variable usage of the two terms in Genesis, it is difficult to escape the conclusion that it is impossible to hold that *"tselem"* and *"demuth"* refer to two different things. As Bavinck says, the two terms "are used promiscuously and one is used in place of the other for no special reason."[8]

Both terms, obviously, refer to a relation between man and his Creator; a "likeness" between man and God, with no explanation given as to exactly what this likeness consists of or implies. When, for example, Von Rad speaks of man's "similarity, re-

---

Buch der Tora, Genesis (1934), p. 58; G. von Rad, *Das erste Buch Mose* (1953), p. 45; Th. C. Vriezen, "La création de l'homme d'après l'image de Dieu," *Oud Testamentische Studiën*, II (1943), 92; W. Eichrodt, *Theologie des Alten Testaments*, II/III, p. 60. The Septuagint, the Greek translation of the Hebrew, uses a copula to connect the two terms, while the Hebrew does not. Eichrodt comments that the Hebrew shows that there are not two separate terms expressed here, but one. All the authors cited above see "image" and "likeness" either as referring to the same thing, or see "likeness" as further explaining "image."

For works in dogmatics, see, e.g., Bavinck, *op. cit.*, p. 492; O. Weber, *Grundlagen der Dogmatik*, I (1955), 625; E. Brunner, *Dogmatik*, II, 90. The creedal *Synopsis* (Disp. 13, 27) already makes the same point, following Calvin.

7. Cf. E. Osterloh, "Die Gottebenbildlichkeit des Menschen," *Theologia viatorum* (1939), pp. 9-32. He is one of the exceptions; he even speaks of the "contrast" between the two terms, and further feels that there are grounds for holding to the two aspects of the image, as earlier theologians felt. Osterloh's view is a fairly isolated one in contemporary theology, and, in our opinion, his argument is not valid.

8. Bavinck, *op. cit.*, pp. 492-493. It should also be noted that the prepositions involved are used indifferently: after His image, in His image, after His likeness, in His likeness. Cf. Gen. 1:26, Gen. 5:3. Cf. also Ch. Aalders, *Genesis*, 2nd ed., I, 178. It is interesting to note that this point came up in the discussions of the Neo-Kohlbruggian interpretation of the image of God. Cf. also Böhl, *Dogmatik* (1887), p. 154; Böhl saw this preposition as showing the "various spheres in which and for which man was created." Cf. Bavinck, *loc. cit.*

semblance, correspondence" to God, this still does not explain in what the likeness lies.[9] It is clear enough that the likeness does not remove the difference between man and God, and that the insistence on this likeness at the same time witnesses to the uniqueness of man in comparison with other creatures. This last is clear enough from the story in Genesis, which refers to God's decision, His plan, in creating man: "let us make *man*. . . ." This creation, this creative act of God, is the high point of the whole creation, the aim, the purpose of the creation described in the preceding verses of Genesis.[10] And it is thus understandable that the image of God in man has been equated with that which makes man unique among created things. In this connection, attempts have sometimes been made to find some evidence as to the content of the image of God in man in the Scriptural text itself: e.g., by reference to Genesis 1:26, where God's making man "in our image, after our likeness" is directly related (some say) to the following words, "let them have dominion over the fish of the sea, and over the birds of the air, and over the cattle, and over all the earth, and over every creeping thing that creeps upon the earth." Some would conclude from this that Genesis itself clearly indicates that the image of God consists in man's _dominium,_ his lordship over the other creatures which surround him, and which are subject to him. This view, which we find, for example, in the Socinian *Catechismus Racoviensis*,[11] has aroused a great deal of opposition,

---

9. Bavinck, *loc. cit.* Cf. L. Köhler, "Die Grundstelle der Imago Dei-Lehre, Gen. 1:26," *Theologische Zeitschrift*, IV (1948), 21. Köhler sees in *demuth* (likeness) a weakening sort of qualification; "similarity" as contrasted to "representation or close similarity." Köhler does not, however, support a double aspect of the image. Cf. also K. L. Schmidt, "Homo imago Dei im Alten und Neuen Testament," *Eranos-Jahrbuch*, XV (1948), 165ff. He stresses the indifferent use of the two prepositions (*hendiadyoin*), but does not see the two terms as tautological; he agrees with Köhler in seeing *"demuth"* as added in order to clarify the possibly ambiguous connotation of *"tselem"* as implying very close similarity. Cf. also P. Humbert, *Etudes sur le récit du paradis et de la chute dans le Genèse* (1940), pp. 160, 172. He refers to Ezek. 1:26 — a likeness (*demuth*) which appeared as a man — as helping to clarify the sense of Gen. 1:26, i.e., as stressing that "likeness" does not imply substantial identity.

10. Von Rad, *op. cit.*, p. 45. Cf. Vriezen, *loc. cit.* He says "the author does not say where this image shows itself."

11. *Catechismus Racoviensis*, ed. G. L. Oederus (1739), p. 48. It says that the image consists of man's *"potestas et dominium in omnes res a Deo conditas supra terram"*, as Gen. 1:26 patently affirms. Cf. also regarding the remonstrant Arminians' views on the image, K. Schilder, *Heidelbergse Catechismus*, I, 233.

which also appeals to the very text to which this view looks for support. It is true that Genesis 1:26 does indicate that man, who is to be created in God's image, is intended for a unique status and task in the created world (his *dominium*). But this does not imply that the content of the image of God should be sought in this lordship, or that Genesis 1 is concerned with this *dominium* over other creatures as an image or representation of the complete and absolute sovereignty of God. It can be objected, and rightly so, that Genesis 1:28, in a special word from God, endows created man with this mandate (i.e., *dominium*): "fill the earth and subdue it," which is in itself a strong argument against equating image and *dominium*.[12]

To support this equation of image and *dominium*, an appeal is often made to Psalm 8:6-7 as illuminating what is the place occupied by man in the cosmos. And, indeed, the passage does refer in emphatic terms to the lordship of man: "Thou hast made him little less than God, and dost crown him with glory and honor. Thou hast given him dominion [*dominium*] over the works of thy hands; thou hast put all things under his feet." This indicates clearly enough the unique position of man in the created cosmos, but this in no sense implies that this *dominium* especially reveals the content of the image of God. To begin with, the term "image" is not used in Psalm 8, and this should be enough to arouse some caution. Ridderbos discerns an echo of Genesis 1 here, but still will not equate Psalm 8's *dominium* with the image of Genesis 1. He sees the passage as meaning "thou has created him a little lower than a god," not God, in distinction from *God*, in whose image man according to Genesis 1 was created.[13] In any event, Psalm 8 gives no support to an identification of *dominium* and image, even though the meaning of man's *dominium* and the special place

12. Cf. Skinner, *op. cit.*, p. 32; Köning, *op. cit.*, p. 159; Gunkel, *op. cit.*, p. 99; Vriezen, *op. cit.*, p. 98; Schmidt, *op. cit.*, p. 174; Humbert, *op. cit.*, p. 164. All these see the image as the basis for the *dominium*.

13. J. Ridderbos, *De Psalmen*, I (1955), 68, 75. The Hebrew of Psalm 8 refers to man as made a little lower than *Elohim*. The Septuagint translates this as *aggelous*, angels; cf. Heb. 2:7, "lower than the angels." Cf. also Heb. 2:9, taken over from the Septuagint, which, according to Ridderbos, is not thereby authenticated. The problems involved here are, in our opinion, not simple. In Hebrews 2, the "a little lower than" of vs. 7 becomes "for a little while" in v. 9, with reference to the temporary humiliation of Christ. Cf. besides the usual commentaries on Hebrews, G. Harder, "Die Septuaginta-zitate des Hebräerbriefs," *Theologia viatorum* (1939), p. 35.

which man occupies in the created world are strongly expressed.[14]
And thus our question as to the specific meaning of the image
remains unanswered, a fact which reminds us of Bavinck's remark:
"the full meaning of the image of God is nowhere unfolded for
us."[15]

Besides this view of the Socinians and others, which holds that
the meaning of the image is directly expressed in Genesis as *dominium*, we must consider the view of Karl Barth, who also holds that
Genesis describes the content of the image, but who relies on
exegesis. He attacks the Socinian position because he sees man's
dominium as a consequence of the image, rather than the image
itself, but feels that there can be no doubt that the passage does
tell us in what image consists. The image refers to man's creation
and being *as man and woman.* "God created man in his own
image, in the image of God he created him; male and female he
created them" (Gen. 1:27). Barth sees this as a "clear statement";
"the text says that the image consists of the difference and the
relation between man and fellow man, and with that we should
rest." Why, asks Barth, why have theologians resorted to speculations and neglected the importance of the difference between man
and woman, which is basic for the Scriptural picture of man?
The similarity, the analogy between man and God is here, not an
analogia entis (analogy of being), but an *analogia relationis* (analogy
of relation). The relation between "I" and "thou," which is already present in God ("let *us* make man in *our image*"), finds
its creaturely analogue in the relationship between man and woman.
Just as there is an "I — thou" relationship in God, "a community
of disposition and act in the divine essence," says Barth, so also
is there in man an "I — thou" relation, a "face-to-face" relation;
and thus the pattern of human life is analogous to that of the
divine life. This is the analogy, the *tertium comparationis,* we
have been seeking, and this is God's "image and likeness" in man.
We need seek no further for additional analogies in which to find
the real meaning or content of the image of God.[16]

Even though Barth is convinced that the text gives us a "well-nigh
definitive statement" of the content of the image, it is not un-

14. Eichrodt, *op. cit.,* p. 63; Calvin, *Institutes,* I, XV, 4.

15. Bavinck, *op. cit.,* p. 494.

16. For the foregoing, see Barth, *Kirchliche Dogmatik,* III, 1, 207-220. Note
p. 214, where Barth, in connection with the text's "let us make," rejects
the idea that this refers to a plurality of majesty, or to a heavenly court
(cf. G. Von Rad), and upholds the older orthodox view that the reference
is to the Trinity.

reasonable to ask whether this is actually the case. It is true that "God created man in his own image" is followed immediately by "male and female he created them." But this does not necessarily mean that the second clause gives a definition of the first; it does not necessarily imply that the image of God lies in the relationship between man and woman. It is extremely noteworthy that Barth sees the image lying in the' distinction between man and woman (I — thou; partnership) and at the same time says that it lies in the distinction and relation between man and fellow man (I — thou; community). Barth's whole point of view here sets up a series of problems rising from this lack of clarification on the man — woman relation and the man — fellow-man relation. When Barth speaks of the "definitive statement" of Genesis, the former is emphasized.[17] When he speaks more generally about the *analogia relationis,* the latter is stressed; "as God is for man, *so* is man for men; just as, namely, God is for him," and thus "man is as little solitary as God." Sometimes Barth speaks of both I — thou relations at once: "In human life, 'I' is related to 'thou,' man to fellow man, man to woman, in the same way that in the divine essence the *'anrufende Ich,'* the calling 'I,' which arouses the response of the divine 'Thou,' is related to that 'Thou.'" This ambiguity in Barth can hardly be resolved merely by his statement that the man — woman relation is simply the man — fellow-man relation "in its most original and concrete form." Barth holds, then, to *both* constructions: the man — woman relation because the text demands it, and the man — fellow-man relation because it is implied in an *analogia relationis.*[18]

We are of the opinion that what Barth calls his "straight forward defining explanation of the text" actually involves constructive interpretation, and that the ambiguities Barth soon becomes involved in show this. He is right in pointing to the unique importance of the man — woman relation in creation; but he is wrong in further concluding that this relation is the specific content of the image of God, and all the more so in that other Scriptural

17. Barth, *loc. cit.,* pp. 219-220. He refers also to various Scriptural passages which use the man-woman relation as analogous to God's relation with His people: Hos. 1:2, Isa. 54:5, Eph. 5:23, etc.
18. Barth, *loc. cit.* Barth says that the image was not lost through sin. His defense of this view also involves the ambiguity noted above, for it rests not on the man-woman relation but is supported "from the history of the community and traffic of God with man," which does not vanish with sin (p. 225).

declarations concerning the image make no direct reference to this relation.[19]

If the image of God cannot be satisfactorily defined as *dominium,* nor as an *analogia relationis,* we can easily enough see why theologians have often spoken of the "riddle" of the content of the image. Is not the content of the image of God an unfathomable mystery for us? J. C. Sikkel, for example, spoke of Genesis 1:26 as "one of the most mysterious passages in all of Scripture,"[20] one which is "for man, since the Fall, a deep secret." But he could not remain satisfied with this: "we can not analyze it, but we must understand it and respond to it in adoration."

Attempts to understand the riddle of the image of God have produced numerous proposed solutions. Most of these do not depend primarily — as did the interpretation of the image as *dominium* or *analogia relationis* — on certain Scriptural passages, but are attempts on more general grounds to arrive at the specific differentia of man. We can hardly say that the methods employed by most of these varied attempts arouse much confidence. One line of approach, for example, is to seek the content of the image in various anthropological categories. Thus Eichrodt sees it as lying in man's "spiritual superiority," which manifests itself in man's "self-consciousness and . . . personality," though the writer of Genesis could hardly be expected to use such abstract terminology to explain his meaning. Such approaches are opposed by those theologians, e.g., Von Rad, who would stress the real, the concrete meaning of the image. He considers it unfaithful to the Old Testament intention to read the texts in the light of the categories of a particular anthropology, and to use such concepts as spiritual

19. Cf. J. J. Stamm, "Die Imago-lehre von Karl Barth," *Antwort* (1956), p. 94. He cites Psalm 8 and Jesus Sirach, which he sees as showing that man as such is the image bearer. Cf. also O. Weber, *Grundlagen der Dogmatik,* I (1955), 634. His attempt to refer to I Cor. 11:7 hardly bears scrutiny, however, since it is clear that Paul does not support the Barthian view in that passage. The text, as well as the context, does relate to Genesis, and does concern itself with man, woman, and image. But Paul's concern here is merely to stress the distinction between man and woman, a difference rooted in creation. Cf. the remarks of Grosheide, *Commentaar* (*loc. cit.*) and also Robertson and Plummer, I.C.C., p. 231, who point out that it is not the woman's relation to God, but rather to man, which is emphasized. The text does not support Barth; the image is not seen in the man-woman relation. Paul's point is a different one.
20. J. C. Sikkel, *Het Boek der Geboorten* (2nd ed., 1923), p. 96.

being or essence, personality, ability to will. Von Rad would not rule out man's body as part of the image in man; quite to the contrary, he thinks that the idea of the image sets out from corporeality as something *visible*. According to the story in Genesis, the whole man is made in the image of God, and Genesis certainly does not imply that certain "higher" qualities exclusively make up the content of the image.[21]

We can say that contemporary theologians rather generally lean more to this line of approach, which is related to a strong consciousness of the integral unity of man, producing an opposition to any "division" of man into "spiritual" and "bodily" aspects and viewing the content of the image as lying exclusively in the former aspect.[22] It is very noteworthy, in this connection, that there has been increasing reluctance to exclude man's body from the image of God — an exclusion generally supported previously, when theologians sought the content of the image in man's "higher" qualities, in contrast to the "lower" bodily qualities, which should not be considered in connection with the image. It is clear enough that involved in this change of attitude is not merely some subtle nuance of meaning, but a change which raises questions of decisive importance for our whole notion of the content of the image.

Theologians, in their search for the meaning of the image, often sought various similarities or analogies between God and man, without thereby giving up the difference between God and man. In the search for such analogies, it often happened that man's body was excluded from the image of God (since man's body could hardly be similar to God's body!). The image was sought in the higher aspects of man, the spiritual, since it was thought that these could be thought of as being similar to qualities possessed by God. This "division also has in its background the stress on the incorporeality of God, *incorporalitas Dei*, which seemed for many to imply that man could resemble or image God in his spirit,

21. See Eichrodt, *op. cit.*, p. 62, and Von Rad's demurrer in Kittel's *Theologisches Wörterbuch*, II, 388-389: "the image of God does *not* lie in man's 'personality,' nor in his 'free ego,' nor in his 'human worth,' nor in his 'free use of moral tendencies.' " He sees arguments as to whether the image relates to the spiritual or the bodily aspect of man as "unpromising." Cf. also his *Das erste Buch Mose* (1953), p. 45. Here he attacks views "based on one or another set of anthropological concepts alien to the O.T. writer," which define the image limitedly and one-sidedly in terms of the "spiritual essence" of man.

22. See, e.g., E. König, *Die Genesis*, p. 158. He lists man's capability for abstract thinking, his ability to form religions and world-outlooks, his ego-consciousness, his moral aspect, and his freedom to will.

but not in his body. Man's body was excluded from the image, and it was believed that if this exclusion was not firmly upheld, the theologian would be supporting the naive *anthropomorphism* of earlier eccentric sects.[23]

This dualism between body and soul played a not unimportant role in the delimitation of the image of God. In this connection, we are always struck by a remark of Calvin's. He acknowledges that the image lies primarily in the understanding or in the heart, in the soul and its powers; but there is nevertheless "no part of man, not even his body, which is not adorned with some rays of its glory." But Calvin is really concerned here more with a general reflection of God's majesty in all the works of His hand than with the image of God as including man's body specifically. And thus he does not hesitate to attack Osiander on this point: ". . . [who,] extending the image of God promiscuously to the body as well as the soul, confounds heaven and earth together."[24] This is a reaction similar to that of Ursinus, who opposed any thought of the materiality of God, and for this reason excluded man's body from the image.[25] Man can be analogous to God, resemble God, only in his "spiritual" and "rational" attributes. Neither Ursinus nor Calvin denied the importance of the body, but they did deny that it could be part of the image of God; they did not deny that the body showed *vestigia*, vestiges, of God's power, but they denied that the body could be in any way analogous to God.

The opposition against the exclusion of man's body from the image of God arises, again and again, from the Scripture's reference to the image of God as in man, not in man's higher or spiritual

23. Cf. any theological dictionary *s.v.*, Anthropomorphism.
24. Calvin, *Institutes*, I, XV, 3. It is no more than fair to bear in mind that Calvin is directing his attacks especially at the strange ideas of Osiander. Cf. also, however, his remarks on Gen. 1:26, where, without mentioning Osiander, he attacks not only the "Anthropomorphites" who think of God as having human form, but also others who see the body of man as the image of God because it reflects His glory; this is an unscriptural opinion. Cf. A. D. R. Polman, *Christelijke Encyclopedie*, I, (2d ed., 1956), 246. He remarks that Calvin hardly knew how to handle the question of how the body was related to the image, and that Luther handled the problem better.
25. M. J. Arntzen, *Mystieke Rechtvaardigingsleer* (1956), p. 47. He takes Ursinus as an example of the reaction against Osiander. Cf. also K. Schilder, *Heidelbergse Catechismus*, I, 222-229. Cf. also James Orr, *God's Image in Man*, pp. 54-56, 1948 edition. Here reaction against Mormons and Swedenborgians also plays a role. He recognizes vestiges of God's glory in the body, but the image lies (and must lie) in "that higher constitution of his being, which makes him spiritual."

attributes, his self-consciousness or his person. Such opposition was especially marked in periods when the dualism between soul and body was rejected, but the decisive factor was that with reference to the image, not the least Scriptural warrant could be found for the division of man into soul and body. And thus the traditional view, which was surely not without its dangers, slowly crumbled, and the feeling grew that the older view did not do justice to the image of God. Thus in Bavinck, we have a clear statement that the body is part of the image. And Bavinck means not merely that the body is "an amazing work of almighty God's art" — for Ursinus also admitted that — but is rather thinking of the body as an organ which serves us, and of an incomprehensible union of body and soul, "far closer than that postulated by occasionalism."[26] Bavinck also opposes Osiander, but his reaction is different from that of Ursinus, and there are also others who have denied the necessity of concluding, from the incorporeality of God, that body must be excluded from the image of God.

Scripture's emphasis on the whole man as the image of God has triumphed time and time again over all objections and opposing principles. Scripture never makes a distinction between man's spiritual and bodily attributes in order to limit the image of God to the spiritual, as furnishing the only possible analogy between man and God.[27]

Gunkel refers to various objections that modern man brings against any bodily "analogy" between man and God, such as "God can have no form, since He is a spirit," and replies to such objections that the concept of the incorporeality of God is an abstract concept of which there is absolutely no trace in the earlier Old Testament, as is shown (he says) by the anthropomorphic ways in which God is described in the Old Testament. This explains, he says, why early Israel took no offense at the idea that man was created in God's image. But, in contrast, says Gunkel, the prophets deemed it blasphemy to picture God, an idea which grew stronger as the God-concept became more transcendent.[28]

Clearly, such a view as Gunkel's introduces an unwarranted contrast in suggesting that there was a conflict between Israel's

26. Bavinck, *op. cit.*, II, 521.
27. Cf. *Synopsis* (XII, XXXVI). Already the image is *"et anima et corpore."* Cf. Schilder, *op. cit.*, I, 263. He says we "should stop racking our brains trying to analyze how an incorporeal God can be imaged through a bodily man." Cf. also L. van der Zanden, *De Mens als Beeld Gods*, p. 60.
28. Gunkel, *op. cit.*, p. 99.

idea of man as the image of God and the sharp criticism levelled by the prophets against making images of God, against picturing God. The real question which might be asked here, however, is a quite different one. Are the two not in harmony? Does not the criticism depend on the *exclusive* way in which man images God? A relation has constantly been sought, and understandably so, between man as the image of God and the Old Testament forbidding of images.[29] This search is of little interest, obviously, if it is denied that man is actually the image of God. Wolmarans, for example, views it as impossible that Genesis 1 can actually mean this, since if man images God there must be a continuity of being between man and God, and this is completely excluded in Old Testament anthropology.[30] If such a priori views as Wolmarans' are rejected, however, we are faced with an interesting problem in trying to describe the relationship between the image of God and the forbidding of image-making; the more so in that the latter command is so all-inclusive. It is forbidden to make any image of any created thing (Ex. 20:4).

Jehovah's jealousy will be aroused and He will punish this iniquity to the third and fourth generation. As Kittel says,[31] it is "absurd to seek a figure in the created world which could adequately represent Jahwe." When Moses and the elders of Israel ascended the mountain, they saw God, but "there was under his feet as it were a pavement of sapphire stone, like the very heaven

---

29. Cf. F. Michaeli, *Dieu à l'image de l'homme* (1950), p. 72, and also Kittel, *op. cit.*, II, 378-379.

30. H. P. Wolmarans, *God en Mens*, I. *Die Mens naar die Beeld van God* (1932), pp. 181-184, 198. He sees the image of God as the Word of God which became incarnate in Christ. "It is not man who is the image of God. . . . The transcendent God-concept of Israel rules out our viewing man as the image of God," since man is "not similar in being" with God. Wolmarans' whole view of the image and his attack on the "anthropological" interpretation of the image derives from his equating "being the image of" and "being similar in being or essence," which is an a priori approach.

31. P. Volz, *Mose und sein Werk* (1932), p. 40. He sees the prohibition as based on God's spiritual nature, and designed to lift man into the realm of the spiritual, that "wholly other world." W. Zimmerli's remarks are in his "Das zweite Gebot," *Festschrift für A. Bertholet* (1950), p. 559. See also W. H. Gispen, *Exodus*, II, 66. The same emphasis can be seen in H. Schrade, *Der verborgene Gott. Gottesbild und Gottesvorstellung in Israel und das Alten Orient* (1949), p. 26. Cf. also O. Weber, *Jahwe "der Gott" und Jahwe "der Götze"* (1933), pp. 10ff. Cf. also G. Ch. Aalders, *Christelijke Encyclopedie*, I, (2d ed., 1956), *s.v., beeldendienst.* He saw the motive for the prohibition in "God's spiritual essence; He is a Spirit, and therefore invisible."

for clearness" (Ex. 24:9-10). If we would seek for an image or likeness of Jahwe, we must listen to Isaiah's question, "To whom then will you liken God, or what likeness compare with him?" (Isa. 40:18), and "To whom then will you compare me, that I should be like him, says the Holy One" (Isa. 40:25). An image is impossible and is forbidden because it is a violation of Jahwe's incomparability. "Therefore take good heed to yourselves. Since you saw no form on the day that the Lord spoke to you at Horeb out of the midst of the fire, beware lest you act corruptly by making a graven image for yourselves" (Deut. 4:15-16, cf. 4:25).

This emphatic prohibition has often been interpreted against a background of a supposed contrast between material and non-material, and of Jahwe as "spirit." Volz, for example, understands it thus; he is opposed, and rightly so, by Zimmerli, who pointed out that the stress on Jahwe's "sublime spirituality" goes hand in hand with anthropomorphic references to Jahwe and His real acts in visible history. Zimmerli correctly judges that the contrast between "spiritual and invisible" and "material and visible" is a contrast not drawn from the Biblical outlook but rather from idealistic philosophy. Gispen notes the significant fact that Exodus 20:5 gives as the motive for the prohibition not "I am Spirit," but rather "I the Lord thy God am a jealous God." This is not in conflict with Jer. 23:23, as its context makes clear.

The second commandment deals with a prohibition against the arbitrariness with which man tries to have God at his beck and call, tries high-handedly to control God's presence in the visible world. It is undeniable, for the Old Testament, that God through His revelation is present in this created world, and does not show Himself only as a God from afar. There is thus no contradiction between the second commandment and the theophanies in which God "appeared" to Israel, and Israel could speak of God in innumerable anthropomorphic ways without having the idea that the majesty of God was thereby in any way violated. In all such anthropomorphisms, Israel carefully respected the boundary beyond which God would be "humanized," subject to all the ambiguous, capricious, dark and changeable aspects of man. Anthropomorphism is useful in speaking about God, and useful in God's revelation in the world. By means of it we can almost immediately intuit and understand what God's revelation has to say to us. Meanwhile we hardly notice the "anthropomorphism" as such; as for example, when Mary says, in her song of praise, "He has shown strength with his arm" (Luke 1:51). God's revelation is made understandable to us not only through such striking anthropomorphisms as God's organs and feelings, but also in connection with God's speaking, seeing, and hearing (He who hears prayers!). Of central importance is what Scripture says to us regarding the living and active God, in the forms and images of active men.[32]

Thus we can hardly see anthropomorphism as something which clouds our view of God, which should be conquered and surpassed, in order to gain a more "spiritual" view of God.[33] We should rather see it as a manner of speaking which gives full perspective to our view of the living and active God, though we must never forget that this manner of speaking is and must always be inadequate.[34] And hence it is not the danger that God will be anthropomorphically compared to some part of man (e.g., his body) which produced the limitations on anthropomorphism, but rather the danger that unlimited use of it might be wrongly understood in the context of the religious ideas of the heathen world surrounding Israel. In any case, the point of the second commandment is not a spiritualistic point, a protection of Jahwe's spirituality and transcendence, against anthropomorphism, in which, actually, we are shown God in His acts and dealings, in His mighty acts, through use of the forms of living and acting — and to us familiar — man. This is an annoyance and a scandal only to those who think in the categories of an abstract idea of God, of an "unqualifiable and pure spirituality of God."[35] Anthropomorphism

32. See extensively J. De Groot and A. R. Hulst, *Macht en Wil. De Verkondiging van het O.T. aangaande God* (1952), pp. 189-208; E. Jacob, *Théologie de l'Ancien Testament* (1955), pp. 30ff.; F. Michaeli, *op. cit.*
33. See *Theologisch Woordenboek*, H. Brink, *et al.*, ed., I (1952), 157. It says that anthropomorphism devaluates the idea of God; and it perennially threatens theology. Cf. A. Chollet, *Dictionnaire de Théologie Catholique*, I, 1369-70. He is much more careful. H. G. Groenewoud, *Christelijke Encyclopedie*, I (2d ed., 1956), 249. He attacks the idea that anthropomorphism devaluates the idea of God. Cf. also Vriezen, *Hoofdlijnen der Theologie van het Oude Testament* (2d ed., 1954), pp. 183ff.
34. Scriptural anthropomorphism goes hand in hand with frequent specific references to the difference between God and man, e.g., Hos. 11:9, Num. 23:19, Prov. 5:1, Job 10:4-5; and for the further listings, see Michaeli, *op. cit.*, p. 115.
35. Cf. De Groot and Hulst, *op. cit.*, p. 201. They refer to the important article by Hempel; "Die Grenzen der Anthropomorphismus im A.T.," *Z.A.W.* (1939), pp. 75-85. For theriomorphism, see De Groot and Hulst, *loc. cit.;* and Jacob, *op. cit.* p. 30. Both note the sobriety of theriomorphic imagery. In our opinion, the structures of theriomorphism and anthropomorphism are different, since the former always contains a comparison, a *tertium comparationis.*

finds a meaningful place in Biblical religion, which finds its expression in the personal relations between God and man, in which He comes and goes, sees and hears and speaks, and in which He reveals Himself to His people as the living God. It is in and by means of this Biblical anthropomorphism that His "spirituality," freedom and sovereignty, His mercy and compassion, are shown. And it is this which makes it impossible for man to seek in man-made things that which he cannot find in man, and which comes to him only through God's activities, in a constant presence which is vouchsafed to him by God through various human analogies, in anthropomorphic manner, as an irrefutable and comforting reality.[36]

Reflecting on all this, we can understand why opposition to an abstract transcendent and idealistic interpretation of the second commandment has constantly turned for support to the anthropomorphic language of the Old Testament. And furthermore, it is not easy to see how such an idealistic interpretation can escape grave difficulty in doing full justice to Genesis' description of the creation of man in the image of God. If, on the contrary, the second commandment is understood as a prohibition of man's attempts to control arbitrarily the presence of God, then it is apparent that there is a basic connection between the prohibition of images and the creation of man in God's image. There lies, in any human attempt to make an image of God, an attempt to control Him, to bring Him close by. And it is this which is prohibited in the second commandment. As Zimmerli says, "Jahwe does not scorn the visible; He deals with Israel through it; but He does scorn those who would attempt to hold God captive, in images in this visible world."[37] The high-handed attempt to control the image of God is *per se* illegitimate, and is in its very origin

36. See also De Groot and Hulst, and Jacob, as cited above. Cf. Zimmerli, *op. cit.*, p. 561.
37. A relationship has often been seen between the anthropomorphic language of the Old Testament and the Incarnation. Cf. Michaeli, *op. cit.*, p. 166. He sees in it "a prelude to the fundamental doctrine of the Incarnation," which in turn is "extension of anthropomorphism." Cf. M. A. Beek, "De Vraag naar de Mens in de Godsdienst van Israel," *Vox Theologica* (1939), pp. 69ff. He sees a close parallel between the two, though he does not see the incarnation as the only possible consequence of the Old Testament. He agrees with Michaeli's remark that the doctrine of the Incarnation is unintelligible if one does not start with the Old Testament anthropomorphic idea of God. Cf., Vriezen, *op. cit.*, pp. 185. He hesitates — and in our opinion rightly — to make this connection, and sees Old Testament anthropomorphism as a result of the close relation between God and man.

an act of unmistakable alienation from God. And it is, simultaneously, an act of extreme self-alienation, since man thereby seeks to construct an "image of God," although he himself, in communion with God, should *be* that image in all of his being. Hence the worship of idols is not only illegitimate, but also senseless, and is in itself a sign of loss and alienation. Man now no longer knows either God or himself, and the problem of God's "absence," which man wished to "solve" by worshipping idols, becomes instead truly insoluble. Seeking the presence of God in such a manner involves a misunderstanding of man's own calling and destiny. It is only when man's communion with God is broken that there can arise such confused and aimless attempts to find the "image" by filling the vacuum with an artificially constructed divine "presence."[38]

A clear illustration of all this can be seen in Exodus 32. Moses was absent, and Israel turned to gods rather than God. Something was needed to fill the "vacuum." As Aaron carried out their wishes, there was once more a "presence," an altar, and their hearts were filled with joy. We read that Aaron interpreted Israel's new course as one which was still concerned with Jahwe: "Tomorrow," he said, "shall be a feast unto the Lord." And a remembrance of Israel's past history was included in the new ritual: "These are your gods, O Israel, who brought you up out of the land of Egypt." The narrative in Exodus 32 has always raised the question of the relation between the first and second commandments. Does it deal with "another god" or with another way, an arbitrary way, of honoring Jahwe, through an image? Gispen supports the former alternative,[39] and supposes that Aaron perhaps wished to prevent a sin against the first commandment by violating the second commandment; that is, that he transformed the worship of heathen gods which the people wished into a worship of Jahwe through images, in a celebration for the Lord. If this was indeed Aaron's wish, his attempt can be seen only as a misunderstanding. For the "worse evil" which Aaron wanted to prevent could hardly be avoided merely by relating the celebration to Jahwe and using Jahwe's name, by building an altar to Him and sacrificing to Him. The paganism which was expressed here was not made any better.

38. Cf. A. Kuyper, Jr., *Het Beeld Gods* (1929), pp. 223, 230, 245; also Karl Barth, *op. cit.*, III, 227. On Christ as the true image of God he says: "Christ makes images — of God and of man — and the prohibition of images, superflous"; "He is *the* image, so that the problem of the original is finally and absolutely answered."
39. Gispen, *op. cit.*, (2d ed.), II, 186.

when it is related to the name and presence of Jahwe, but indeed
became even more evil and dangerous, despite Aaron's "good intentions." Aaron merely "ornamented the ritual with the name of
Jahwe." Both the first and second commandments were broken
in this one act of dark and perverse evil. And this illustrates the
illegitimacy of such attempts to fill the vacuum of alienation, the
"absence" of God (in this case, in Moses' absence) — though
Israel was to be threatened again and again by the temptation to
use such illegitimate means. As Hellbardt correctly notes, the
struggle to serve the one God (the first commandment) is "determined and decided in this-struggle over the true or false image
of God."[40] For this false image is the work of the Israelites: it
is their gold; their construction, their projection of their ideas.
And this is a corruption (Exod. 32:7), a turning away, which does
not become less corrupt but rather more corrupt when this is linked
with the name of Jahwe.[41] For the name cannot conceal the
fact that this "god" which now stands before the Israelites is nothing

40. H. Hellbardt, *Das Bild Gottes. Eine Auslegung von II Mose 32* (1939),
p. 36; cf. also pp. 33, 67, 95.

41. H. Th. Obbink, "Jahwebilder," *Keur uit de verspreide Geschriften*
(1939), pp. 122-138. He attempts to show that there were no images of
Jahwe used by the Israelites, and that consequently these were not
referred to by the second commandment: "that which was not there
needed not to be forbidden." The second commandment, he says, is
indeed directed to the cultus of Jahwe, but against the heathen idols
used therein rather than against images of Jahwe. The prohibition
against "images" in Ex. 20 is motivated by Jahwe's "jealousy," and is
directed against the worship of heathen gods. Obbink sees a decisive
argument in this question: "How can Jahwe be 'jealous' when Israel
makes an image of Him and worships it?" But this view of Obbink is
difficult to reconcile with Ex. 20 and especially Deut. 4:15 though it
is true enough that the violation of either of the first two commandments can easily involve a violation of the other, as the Old Testament
makes clear in various passages (cf. Deut. 4:18-19, regarding worshipping the sun, moon and stars). Cf. Obbink (p. 137) on the
"mixtum quid" in connection with Ex. 32:4 and I Kings 12:28, and also
J. Ridderbos, *Deuteronomium I*, pp. 91-92. It seems to me invalid to
suppose that Jahwe's "jealousy" necessarily is directed only at images of
other gods, since *any* image used in Israel's cultus would imply competition
with Jahwe and awaken His jealousy. It is also understandable that
His "jealousy" is generally associated with other gods (cf. Deut. 32:21,
etc.). Cf. also Jean Daniélou, "La jalousie de Dieu," *Dieu vivant*, XXVI,
63-73. There is indeed reason to connect the first and second commandments closely; and this applies also to the third, since any image "which
man makes for himself violates Jahwe's freedom" (Zimmerli, *op. cit.*,
pp. 560-561).

else than "their own wishes and dreams." Such image worship can evoke only divine wrath (Ex. 32:10, 11, 12; cf. 19) at this "great sin" (Ex. 32:21, 30). For God views the worship of images most seriously — regardless of the view of the worshippers! This is nowhere more clearly expressed than in Jahwe's answer to Moses' pleas, "Whoever has sinned against me, him will I blot out of my book" (Ex. 32:33), and in the pulverizing of the golden calf to show its worthlessness. The golden glitter of this image did not lead Moses astray; the prohibition of images is earnest, basic, and final. The divine wrath against those who refuse to obey is not arbitrary anger, though it is indeed burning anger; God is concerned to maintain His holy intentions with the divine image, the image of God on earth.

Hellbardt's discussion of this incident continually emphasizes the contrast between the images which men make and the image of God in Jesus Christ. He reminds us of the New Testament passages in which Christ is referred to as *the* image of the invisible God: "in Him, as the final spiritual summit, all the power of God's image is concentrated." But it is difficult to understand why Hellbardt, in his otherwise excellent discussion, does not make mention of the creation of *man* in God's image. We should not, of course, isolate the creation of man from Christ as the image-bearer; but there is reason to point out that the creation of man in God's image is very directly related to the prohibition of images, and that this creation of man in God's image produces the prohibition of image worship. For in worshipping images, man completely misunderstands God's intentions and no longer realizes the meaning of his humanity in his communion with God.

This denunciation of all image-worship — whether of images of Jahwe or images of heathen gods — as improper and meaningless gives us some impression of the witness of Scripture regarding man as the image of God. The uniqueness of this image, its glory and honor, is already constantly emphasized for us in Genesis, as the creation account culminates in the creation of man in God's image. It is indeed noteworthy that Scripture nowhere says that all of created reality is the image of God, but uses the term only for man. And this brings us to an important point in our consideration of the meaning of the image of God, since the image has often been treated in some sort of "universal" sense. All the works of God's hand are then viewed as being, in some general sense, the "image of God." This idea is derived, rather unclearly, from an intuitive and vague idea of the image as a "reflection" of God. With such derivation, cannot the whole of created reality be called the image of God in a certain sense? Does not the *Belgic Confession* (Article II) tell us that the whole world is "before our eyes as a most elegant book, wherein all creatures, great and small, are so many characters leading us to see clearly the invisible things of God"? And with this, we naturally turn to the song of praise for nature given in many of the Psalms (see, e.g., Ps. 19:2), and it seems obvious to combine the idea of the image of God with the heavens telling the glory of God, and the firmament proclaiming His handiwork.

Actually, however, it may well be asked whether it is legitimate to link the idea of the image of God with the "nature Psalms" in this way. We feel that such a procedure makes the idea of the image of God general — without any warrant from Scripture; and man is then seen merely as an illustration — however special a one — of creation's general "reflection" of God. But the witness of Scripture opposes such a view. In Genesis 1, the works of God's hands are pronounced by God to be very good; but it is said of man, and only of man, that he was made in the image of God. Once the image is viewed in a general manner, it is impossible to treat man as the image of God, even by way of viewing him as a special illustration of the general principle, without introducing a vagueness into the idea of the image which is bound to lead us into error.

We come across this same problem in another connection when we consider the question, so often discussed, of whether the angels are made in the image of God. When Calvin says that "the lineaments of the Divine glory are conspicuous in every part of the world," he adds that "it is not to be denied that the angels were created in the similitude of God."[42] Having made this statement, he none the less considers it significant that Moses, in speaking of man in the image of God, "celebrates the favor of God towards us" by using that unique title; the angels' possession of the image then receiving no further special treatment.

---

42. Calvin cites Matt. 22:30, "in the resurrection . . . they are like angels in heaven," which seems to imply that man's fulfillment is to become like the angels. But this is very dubious evidence for the creation of the angels in God's image. The text is concerned with the eschatological perspectives of the resurrection in connection with "neither marrying nor being given in marriage," so that Calvin's conclusion hardly follows from the *hos aggelloi* of the text. See Calvin, *Institutes*, I, XV, 3. Cf. also L. van der Zanden, *De Mens als Beeld Gods*, p. 58.

A clearer treatment of the problem is given by Bavinck.[43] He speaks of the world as a beautiful and rich revelation of God, in which all creatures show forth vestiges of God's glory. But he sees man as the unique creature, and points out that the sharp distinction between men and angels is carefully maintained in Scripture, and that "men indeed, but never the angels, are spoken of as created in the image of God." He warns against the view often expressed by theologians, that the angels, because they are pure spirit, are higher than man, and "hence have more right, or at least equal right, to the title of image-bearers," and emphasizes that only man is the image of God.

[END
NOTES]

Kuyper, also, criticizes earlier Reformed theologians for their "confusion" on this point in teaching that angels as well as men were created in the image of God. He sees such a view as destroying the distinction between the two.[44]

It is clear that Scripture does not support the creation of the angels in God's image. This is doubtless the chief objection to such a view, and also the reason why attention has constantly returned to man. When such a view was used, it was used in connection with the idea of vestiges of God's glory in creation, and this soon involved a generalizing of the idea of the image which was more speculative than Biblical. And it was often tied in with a general concept of analogy; so that the "spiritual" nature of the

43. Bavinck, *Gereformeerde Dogmatiek,* II, 421-423, 516, 523. He reproaches both Reformed and Lutheran theologians for calling the angels image-bearers, and refers to Calvin and to the Lutheran *Synopsis,* XII, 7: "*creatos . . . ad imaginem Dei.*" Bavinck's view is not wholly clear since he elsewhere speaks of man as the summation and juncture of all of creation's *vestigia,* which in man are so combined as to become the image and likeness of God (II, 523). In addition, his argumentation begins from metaphysical grounds, i.e., from a consideration of the nature of angels and man, and concludes with an examination of their different relationships to Christ. But he again puts the nature of the angels in a different light when — despite his criticism of Calvin — he says that the angels do show various traits of the image (II, 422-423). But Bavinck's main idea is clear enough: "All creatures manifest the *vestigia Dei;* but man is the *imago Dei*" (II, 516).

44. A. Kuyper, *De Engelen Gods,* pp. 52-54. Kuyper argues that man's *dominium* is one of the characteristics of the image which the angels do not have. Cf. Ps. 8 and Heb. 2. Kuyper emphasizes the contrast between man's ruling and the angels' serving. Kuyper further (without specifically mentioning his name) attacks Calvin's reference to Luke 20:36. Kuyper, too, shows a certain hesitation in his argument, as when he says (in connection with the angels' spiritual being) that the angels do not fully express the content of the image, and that man has something more, which the angels lack.

angels was related to the "spirit" of man (as the seat of the image in man) and both were subsumed under the concept of "image." A systematic view of the image was built up from such analogies, from the *vestigia Dei* in creation, and from nature's "reflection" of God's glory. Further analogies were sought in created reality as a whole; and the result was that the specific meaning of the Biblical witness regarding man was lost.[45]

We have already noted that while the account in Genesis does say that man was created in the image of God, it does not give us any further details. As Kuyper remarked, the picture given is "not very clear." It is indeed evident that Scripture sees man as a creature in a certain relationship to God, his Creator, and that it speaks of a "likeness" of some sort between man and God; but always the question arose wherein this likeness consists. Though dismissing the attempts to delineate the image by means of various anthropological distinctions such as ego, personality, self-consciousness, and the like, we must not fail to notice a certain "method" for answering the question, one which is frequently encountered. We refer to the attempt to give more clarity to our picture of the image by paying special attention to the witness of the New Testament regarding the image. Perhaps we may might gain a clearer insight, some said, with this approach; not so much because the New Testament might add something to what the Old Testament has said, but rather because the New Testament speaks of the restoration of the image of God. Perhaps we could, by examining this restoration, arrive at a deeper understanding of the mystery of the image of God.

This "method" is used already by Calvin. He notes that it appears we can give no complete description of the image of God unless it becomes clearer which are the characteristics by which man excels and wherein he reflects the glory of God. In this connection, he arrives at what we might call a "hermeneutic method,"

45. For the use of analogy between men and angels, cf. Bavinck's remarks (see footnote 43) on the characteristics of the image possessed by the angels, and L. van der Zanden's accurate comment that this seems to contradict Bavinck's previous statements. Cf. also A. Kuyper, Jr., *Het Beeld Gods*, pp. 104-105. He says that the angels do not have the image, but do have characteristics of the image. For the "generalizing" of the idea of the image, see further Berkouwer, *De Triomf der Genade in de Theologie van Karl Barth* (1954), p. 178; and on "creation and humanity" as image and likeness: J. J. Louët Feisser, "Misverstand rondom Barths Leer over de Schepping," *Nederlands Theologisch Tijdschrift* (1952), pp. 252ff.

operating along the following line: the image "cannot be better known from anything, than from the reparation of his corrupted nature." Calvin is concerned with our knowledge of the image of God, and thus he refers to its restoration, which is treated in the New Testament. He has in mind the words of Paul (Eph. 4:24) in this context on "the new nature, created after the likeness of God in true righteousness and holiness," and (Col. 3:10) "being renewed in knowledge after the image of its creator," words which obviously refer back to the original creation of man in God's image.[46]

This line of approach is encountered in Reformed theology when the image of God is described as knowledge, righteousness and holiness. This triad may give the impression of a combination of words from Eph. 4:24 (righteousness and holiness) and Col. 3:10 (knowledge), but this summation is not intended to be exclusive. Calvin (in his *Commentary* on Gen. 1:26) points out that setting this triad forth as principal characteristics does not mean that they are the sum total of characteristics. In any case, the triad refers to man's new *conformitas, his conforming* to God.[47] We are concerned here primarily with the method used: it assumes that treating the restoration and renewal of the image will throw light upon the meaning and content of the original creation of

46. See Calvin, *Institutes*, I, XV, 4; and Calvin, *Commentary* on Gen. 1:26, *Opera*, Cunitz-Reuss, XXIII, 26. He says, *"Quoniam deleta est imago Dei in nobis per lapsum Adae, ex reparatione iudicandum est, qualis fuerit"*; i.e., the nature of the lost image is to be judged by that which is restored, citing Col. 3:10 and Eph. 4:24. Cf. J. Dupont, *Gnosis. La connaissance religieuse dans les épitres de Saint Paul* (1949), p. 33; and P. Althaus, "Das Bild Gottes," *Theologische Blätter* (1941), pp. 81ff. He has opposed the idea of a relation between original image and image in Ephesians and Colossians; this idea is related to his view of various stages in the Biblical view of the image. See Althaus, *Die Christliche Wahrheit*, II (1948), 96. He does not reckon enough with the words *ton anakainounon* and *tou ktisantos auton* in Col. 3:10. Cf. Kümmel, *Das Bild des Menschen im N.T.* (1948), p. 39. He correctly states that the words "doubtless" refer to man's original creation. Cf. Kittel, *Theologisches Wörterbuch*, II, 395, s.v., *eikon* on the being of man which is again to be restored. Cf. also E. F. Scott, *The Epistle of Paul to the Colossians* (1948), p. 69; E. Lohmeyer, *Die Briefe an die Philipper, an die Kolosser und an Philemon* (1953, 9th ed.), pp. 141-147; earlier, Ewald (Zahn) on Col. 3:10, p. 420; he rightly notes that this relation is not implied only in "renewed" (cf. Kittel, *op. cit.*, s.v., *anakainoo*), but in "the whole phrase" (*tou ktisantos auton*).
47. Lohmeyer, *op. cit.*, p. 142. He ties in the "knowledge" of Col. 3:10 with "knowledge" as "the decisive motif of the Genesis narrative."

man in the image of God. The same kind of approach is used by Bavinck, who says that Genesis 1 does express something, and indeed calls up further impressions (the reflecting image in connection with the parallel between Gen. 1:26 and Gen. 5:1, e.g.); but to understand what the complete image implies, we must also examine the restoration, the renewal, of the image.[48] Actually, however, Bavinck does not limit his attention to this renewal, but feels also that the meaning of the image is made even more clear in Christ, who is called the image of God in a unique sense. Thus Bavinck really stresses not only the theme of renewal of the image but also places next to this soteriological-pneumatological emphasis a Christological emphasis; and although the two are closely related for Bavinck, we should not confuse the two. In the stress on renewal — which is predominant in Calvin — we are, so to speak, projecting backwards from the renewal image to the original image; whereas a stress on the Christological emphasis involves dealing with the original image in terms of Christ, who Himself is the image of God (cf. II Cor. 4:4, Col. 1:15). Our diffuse impression of the image is, says Bavinck, thus more sharply defined, since we are confronted in Christ with the full actuality of the image.

And this brings us to consideration of an approach which has come more and more to the fore recently, and which has taken the form of trying to base anthropology on Christology. Karl Barth, for example, views this basis for anthropology as the only possible basis.[49] Bavinck speaks of a *further* understanding of the meaning of the image in Christ: Barth speaks of our knowledge regarding man as based *only* on Christ, on Jesus of Nazareth as

48. Bavinck, *op. cit.*, 492-494.
49. Cf. S. Greijdanus, *Toerekeningsgrond van het Peccatum Originans* (1906). He suggested this approach in the Netherlands a half century ago. He made a plea for Christology as the basis for anthropology, but in connection with what he considered the unsatisfactory character of explanations of original sin on the basis of creationism or traducianism. He felt himself thus driven to an anthropology in which "Christology would be the starting point or perhaps be central" (p. 49). He saw a satisfactory explanation for his problem (original sin) in a consideration of the distinction between person and nature (i.e., impersonal human nature) in Christ. Cf. J. Waterink, *De Oorsprong en het Wezen der Ziel* (1930). He also uses a relationship between anthropology and Christology, but with more of an anthropological accent, to help in defining the concept of person. It is clear that Barth's context of problems is quite different from either of these: see his *Kirchliche Dogmatik* (K.D.), III, 2. See more extensively my "Christologie en Anthropologie," *Feestbundel voor J. Waterink*.

man, as true man in the complete sense of the word.[50] He is the
revealed Word of God, and as such "is the source of our knowledge of the God-created being and nature of man." *Ecce homo!*
Behold the man, true man.

In this *vere homo,* this true man, "born in the likeness of
man" (Phil. 2:7; cf. Heb. 2:14, 17), which has always been
affirmed by the Church against every sort of docetism — in this,
says Barth, is the only way to true knowledge of man, in contrast
with attempts at an autonomous "self-understanding" without regard for Christ.[51] He does not wish to underestimate the attempts
made by scientific anthropology to obtain knowledge of the
physiological, biological, psychological and sociological aspects of
man; but these are only of relative value, and indeed — unless
they enter the realm of speculation rather than science — make
no claim to absoluteness. In such "phenomena" of man's being
we can gain but little help in our search for the true man; "the
real man is not brought to view through such procedures."[52]

Barth attacks not only those who feel that they can learn to
know the real man through some kind of neutral anthropology,
but also traditional orthodoxy insofar as it claims to establish who
man is through some independent "*locus de homine,*" some theological treatment of man in himself. Such "understanding of man

50. Barth, *Kirchliche Dogmatik* (K.D.), III, 2, 47: "Die Begründung der
Anthropologie auf die Christologie." He is conscious that this approach
breaks new ground, and that at this point he is further from the
traditional dogmatic teaching than was the case in his view of election
(see *K.D.,* III, 2, VII). Cf. H. Vogel, "Das Menschenbild im N.T.," *Vox
Theologica* (1952); *Christologie,* I (1949); and *Gott in Christo. Ein
Erkenntnisgang durch die Grundprobleme der Dogmatik* (1952), pp.
440ff. He calls it a "radical rethinking of the whole tradition" and agrees,
despite this, that the answer to the problem of man can be found only
in exegesis of the human nature of Christ. *True* man was revealed in
Christ, who put Himself in the place of *actual* man.
51. Cf. R. Prenter, "Die Lehre vom Menschen bei Karl Barth," *Theologische Zeitschrift* (1950), p. 211. Cf. also Barth, *K.D.,* III, 2, 23ff.
52. Barth, *K.D.,* III, 2, 143. Cf. the critique of H. van Oyen, *Theologische
Erkenntnislehre. Versuch dogmatischer Prolegomena,* (1955), p. 176.
He agrees that Christ is uniquely man, but says that "if we also call
Him the 'real' man, then man as known to us, actual man, is reduced
to a mere phenomenon of possibility." It appears to us, however, that
Barth's remarks on the "phenomena" of man's being intend precisely
not to imply that such phenomena are not real, but rather to point out
that they do not reveal the essential man, the real man, since a consideration of them alone excludes man's relation to God. Van Oyen perhaps
would agree, for he adds that "Barth certainly did not mean to say
that" — i.e., that man is merely a phenomenon.

is an illusion; for example, when we feel we understand man when we classify him as a rational animal, (*animal ratione praeditum*), a being endowed with *reason* in distinction from the beasts, "as if he had no special relation to God, as if he did not exist in a history based on this relation, as if everything implied for him in this relation was something which could be taken up later." Such an approach can not deal with real man, but gives us only a "shadow," says Barth, and it does not realize that "the relation to God is essential to man's very being. And even when man is defined in a more complex fashion — as a person, for example — there still remains the objection that man is defined apart from his relation to God, and hence the definition still misses man's essence. Indeed, says Barth, how could we know man apart from divine revelation? Apart from it would we not conclude that what we experience of man — that which is actually not his nature — is his real essence? Only from the revelation of the man Jesus can we seize the real meaning of the Word of God, which does indeed reveal man to be totally corrupt, but which also forbids us to stop there, for man is the object of God's grace, and man's corruption is not the final word.[53] Man indeed carries a load of guilt and shame, but his created nature is not destroyed, for "precisely that which God — in the freedom of His grace, over and beyond man's sins, relativizing and seeing through and overlooking those sins — knows man to be is man's original created nature: that which we are seeking." This verified human nature is revealed in Jesus of Nazareth; it is "God's relation and attitude towards sinful man." Man's being, man's nature, is to *stand in grace,* God's grace; this is the truth we discern in the election of the man Jesus Immanuel (God with us). Man is not essentially a "rational animal"; his essence is to be an object of God's grace. This essence is indeed covered and hidden by sin, but how can something which has its basis in God's grace be wholly destroyed? There is and remains a "continuum, an essence unchanged and unchangeable by sin."[54] Hence anthropology is based on Christology, and we can only know man's essence through the man Jesus of Nazareth.

In order to develop our view of man, then, according to Barth, we must "view, point for point, the essence of man as we en- counter it in the person of the man Jesus, and only from this vantage point view the essence of man as it is the essence of every

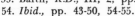

53. Barth, *K.D.*, III, 2, pp. 88-90, 109ff., 34-35.
54. *Ibid.*, pp. 43-50, 54-55.

man, of all other men." This does not imply a direct and simplistic parallelism between human nature and Jesus' human nature, nor that we can merely "read off" our anthropology from our Christology. We sinful men are different than Jesus; in Him human nature stands before us "without the self-conflicts and contradictions it suffers in us." His human nature is not ours, corrupted, disturbed by sin, and therefore hidden; but is "human nature preserved and maintained in its original form." He is sinless man and thus shows us "who and what the real man is." From these premises Barth arrives at the conclusion that we can not begin with a definition of human nature (as if we already knew what it is!) and then say that Jesus shared in this human nature: it is the other way around. Since Jesus is true man, we must say that "we possess human nature because Jesus first possessed it."

It is clear that we encounter in this last formulation a decisive phase of Barth's thought. So far we have been concerned with our knowledge of true man, but in these last words we are concerned not with the noetic aspect of Jesus' humanity, but with the ontic. The noetic aspect — having to do with our knowledge — was emphasized when Barth said that the "original and archetypal form" of human nature is revealed in Jesus.[55] But now Barth speaks not only of this knowledge, but speaks of our participating in or possessing human nature because Jesus first did this. We have here a unique turn in Barth's thought, one which we may call the Christological interpretation of man's nature. Barth is concerned not only with an answer to the noetic problem, but wishes to base the noetic on the ontic: Jesus of Nazareth as the source of all the ways of God. In Him we can therefore also see (noetically) who man is and what man's essence means: "to be related to God." That is man's inalienable essence, the "unchangeable original destiny of man, that he is related to God."

This essential nature of man can never be without God, and turning away from God is not a possibility for this nature: it is "the ontological impossibility of man's nature." It is not possible for man to turn away from God and still calmly retain his humanity: rather, ungodliness, since it is a renunciation of God, is also a renunciation of man's essence and nature, "an attack on the existence of his own creatureliness," through which his being man is "placed in question" — since man's very nature is "to be related to Jesus and to God." Thus turning away from God is not a possibility

55. *Ibid.,* pp. 58-60

within human nature, but is something which would (if it could) annihilate human nature. But the essence of man (his relation to God) is not annihilated by ungodliness — due to God. Since God maintains the relation, and since in this relation lies man's essence, it becomes impossible to "ascribe to man the possibility of destroying his nature." For God has here already intervened to save man; he has ruled out this "capacity" for annihilation and for becoming not-man. Man is man, and remains so; and Barth means this not as statement regarding some ontic structure (body, soul, spirit, person) in man, but as a reference to the a priori nature of grace, through which man's nature, man's being man, is preserved in grace. And it is in Jesus that we see revealed to us man's essence, which is His being related to God, being together with God. It is hearing the Word of God, being called, being obedient and thankful, being free. This is man's goodness, which sin cannot change. This goodness of man's true nature is not to be explained by a relativizing of the power of sin, but through the mystery of God's grace: Immanuel.[56]

It is clear that Barth's basing anthropology on Christology derives from the idea that we cannot understand "man" apart from his relation to God. In our opinion, this position is unassailable; man cannot be known with a true and reliable knowledge if he is abstracted from this relation to God. Man would then be, from a Scriptural viewpoint, nothing but an abstraction, and if we seek to define man merely in terms of various qualities and abilities, we are not giving a Biblical picture of man. The criticism of the definition of man as "rational animal," or in some more subtle version of such a definition, is completely correct.

But Barth goes beyond this, into Christology, and this fact raises all sorts of questions. They are questions which can be answered only after we examine how the attempt to base anthropology on Christology functions concretely. We can, as an example, take his treatment of the relation between body and soul. Barth takes up the "inner structure" of this created relation. His analysis first rejects the abstract and dualistic anthropology for which body and soul are two substances bound together, two substances which, as immortal soul and mortal body, are intrinsically alien to each other. He specifically attacks the immortality of the so-called *anima rationalis,* the rational spirit thought of as constitutive of man's essence, and also attacks the teaching that the soul is the *form*

56. *ibid.,* pp. 161-162, 167, 175, 195-197, 201ff., 213ff., 229, 235, 330.

of the body, which is nothing else than "trifling with or ignoring the problem of the body," or, elsewhere, "distancing the soul from the body, placing the soul higher than the body." Barth cannot see in this the Christian view of man. He also rejects just as strongly any monistic anthropology such as materialism or spiritualism, and states that man is completely soul and completely body, through the action of the living Creator.[57]

It is apparent that Barth here, like many others, is criticizing various forms of anthropology from earlier and later periods, and indeed various elements of his criticism show a striking relationship with the attacks of Stange, Althaus and Dooyeweerd on the substantial dichotomy of soul and body and the application of the form-matter relation to soul and body. We shall examine this question more closely in a later chapter.

Barth's critique emphasizes the unity of man, but he supports this by reference to man's creation, and it can hardly be said that this view of Barth's is specifically Christological. The relation to God in Christ does indeed play an important role, as for example when Barth says that if we consider man as an isolated whole "without remembering that he exists only because of God's favor towards him," then man can never be more than a mysterious duality, a "compositum" of two substances. ". . . Because of God's favor towards him . . . ." these words remind us of the Christological foundation, of "Immanuel" as the foundation of our knowledge of man. Over all, however, Barth's argument stresses primarily the dependence of the whole man in relation to his Creator; as, for example, when he says that the Bible gives us no theory about the relation between body and soul, and has no concern with the "composition" of man, but deals only with the whole man in his relation to God; or, when he in the course of this argument points to what Scripture says regarding the heart of man as the center of his whole mode of existence. "We must say of the heart that it is, in the sense of the Biblical texts, the kernel of the whole man; not only the center of his activity, but its total content."[58]

The undeniable value of many of Barth's anthropological views regarding the Biblical picture of man does give rise to some question regarding the Christological basis of this anthropology. We can put the matter thus: on the one hand, Barth builds his anthropology

57. *Ibid.*, pp. 440, 445-448, 471-472.
58. *Ibid.*, pp. 520-523.

on Jesus as archetype, *Urbild*, and on God's grace which preserves man's "essence"; on the other hand, the argument often stresses rather the creaturely dependence of the whole man on God, his Creator. It is clear, in my opinion, that we can not call this a consistent basing of anthropology on Christology. There is an inner tension in Barth's anthropology, one which cannot remain hidden when he develops his analyses. There is a constant interplay of the two motifs — the Christological and the motif of total dependence. This tension becomes understandable when we realize that from the Christological motif alone — Immanuel, God with us, as man's true nature — there is no way to arrive consistently at a critique of other forms of anthropology. Barth does indeed give us such a critique (as do Althaus, Dooyeweerd and others), but this is only possible for him because he uses another motif than the Christological as the basis for his critical argument: namely, the motif of the total dependence of the whole man on God. Nevertheless, Barth's own sympathies manifestly lean more to the Christological emphasis, and that taken not only noetically but also ontologically. We *participate* in Jesus' nature; not He in ours, but we in His.

The positiveness with which this is said is all the more striking when we consider that the Biblical reference to the Incarnation takes the form of saying that Jesus *became like* us. The starting point of the reference is in man, both in Philippians 2 and Hebrews 2. It is said that He became like man, that He "was made in the likeness of man," was "found in fashion like a man" (Phil. 2:7-8), that, like our children, He also "took part" in flesh and blood, that "He was made like" to His brethren; and this was done so that He might be a "merciful and faithful high priest in all things" (Heb. 2:14, 17). And this Biblical way of speaking is by no means accidental. It is man's real situation which determines the mode of expression; man's lost and fallen state; and it is *from this situation,* in which man's fallen condition is impressive reality, that Scripture points to the Word becoming flesh. Vogel cites Hebrews 2:14 in connection with "the full and complete consanguinity (*consanguinitas*) of the God-Man who is bodily delivered unto the bodily death into the curse of which his brethren had fallen."[59] The Incarnation is described as consanguinity *with us.* Barth, however, formulates the matter in the opposite way, so that Jesus does not participate in our nature, but *we in His.* Thus

59. H. Vogel, *Christologie,* I (1949), 321.

it is clear that Barth is concerned not only with a noetic problem
(cf. *"Ecce homo!"*) but also with an ontic problem. "We have our
human nature as such wholly from Jesus," he says.[60] He would
employ the aspect of grace to define man's essence. Hence, for
Barth, there is complete harmony between the Christological aspect
and the relational aspect, since he sees the latter as a relation of
grace, which *constitutes* man's essence. The essence of man must be
seen in the light of the a priori triumph of grace. It is through
grace that man remains man, and that the image of God in him
is indestructible, since it is in this *relation* that the image finds
expression.[61] The corollary of this triumph of grace is Barth's view
of Christology as the foundation of anthropology. The essence of
man is to stand in grace, and *therefore* Jesus does not participate
in our nature but we in His, since He is the Elected One of God.

We began this part of our exposition by recalling Calvin's
hermeneutic method in relation to the meaning of the image of
God, and with Bavinck's reference to the Son as the image of
God. However, when Barth speaks of "true man" and the essence
of human nature, he means something different (and indeed, he
himself realizes this clearly enough). The difference can be described as follows, that the viewpoint of Calvin and Bavinck is not
ontic, but rather noetic. They are convinced that we can never
discover the essence of man — that is, the image of God — through
empirical investigation. They thus refer to the Scriptural passages
in Genesis regarding the creation of man in God's image, and
refer further to the witness of the New Testament, which, in its
descriptions of the renewal of the image, sheds light on the meaning
of the image of God. And whenever Bavinck reminds us of the
"true man," the reference is noetic in character.

The reason that the ontic *motif*, which plays so decisive a role

---

60. See Barth, *K.D.*, III, 2, 58, 244-245. It is in this light also that his remarks
regarding the Biblical references to the "old" and "new" man are understandable. He says that "the Bible speaks relatively rarely in terms of
this contrast." Cf. Prenter, *op. cit.*, p. 222. In my opinion, he rightly
questions the truth of this statement, especially because of the import
and radicality of the Biblical references when they do occur. The context
of Barth's remarks clarifies his view on this matter: the "old" man, so
to speak, wandered outside "himself," and put on a "new" man, but
the "new" man is actually the (true and original) "old" man. Cf. his
remarks on the "good creation of God" (p. 245). In my opinion, Paul is
here not speaking explicitly of this contrast, but is thinking in terms
of the categories of old and new as used in *Heilsgeschichte*.

61. See my *Het Werk van Christus*, ch. 2 and *The Triumph of Grace in
the Theology of Karl Barth*, pp. 223ff.

in Barth's thought, plays no role in the thought of Calvin and Bavinck is not that they did not consider man's relation to God as it affects man's essence and our knowledge of it. The reason is rather that in their thinking they always approach the Incarnation from a consideration of man's fall and guilt. This method of approach does not make the Incarnation something arbitrary and contingent, unrelated to the decrees of God; on the contrary, it is a method which can never be relativized and this not only because it is an approach which Biblical thought shows is legitimate, but also because of the unity of the work of God, from the beginning of the world. Anyone who exchanges this approach for the reverse approach — beginning with Jesus of Nazareth — is driven, by inner necessity, to resort to speculation which can lead only to a striking modification of Biblical formulations, as is clear from Barth's formulation when compared with that of Hebrews 2:14. The intent of Barth's ontic viewpoint becomes especially clear when he posits the relation to God, constitutive of man's essence, as a relation of grace. Barth would surely not be satisfied with a formulation directed against previous ideas of man's essence as "rational animal" or the like which would merely stress man's relation to God as essential and which did not immediately add that this is a relationship of grace. It is this relationship of grace which forms the background to, and the content of, Barth's anthropology, and in it we see the same conception as that which appears in his views on Gospel and Law (i.e., the Law as a form of the Gospel) and on God's wrath and His love. And this makes it all the more understandable why Barth's basing anthropology on Christology does not mean a "reading off" of human nature from Christ's human nature, but that he is concerned exclusively to know ourselves and all human nature as the object of God's grace, which is revealed in the election of the man Jesus of Nazareth.[62]

62. Cf. Vogel, *Vox Theologica* (1952), p. 80ff. There is, I feel, a noticeable difference between Vogel and Barth within their common basing of anthropology on Christology. Vogel points to the mystery of man which is revealed "only when God as one of us, and indeed as one of us who as men are under the curse of our self-love and enmity towards God takes our place." It becomes evident that salvation concerns lost man. Though at this point there is no opposition to Barth, since Barth also says grace affects fallen man, yet Barth's accent on grace takes a much more aprioristic turn when he uses it to define man's nature; Vogel (p. 82) meanwhile says that "just in the judgment" and condemnation it remains true that the creature both in his origin and nature belongs to the Creator.

When we, with Calvin and Bavinck, refer to the significance
of the knowledge of man to be gained from considering man's
salvation in Christ, we do not mean to restore to honor the sort of
"reading off" which Barth condemns, but we do wish to emphasize
the importance of the Biblical witness to Christ as the image of
God and to the renewal, in communion with Christ, of man according to that image,[63] (spoken of in the New Testament.) We
shall begin with what the Bible tells us regarding this renewal.
Scripture pictures the new man in contrast to the old man, lost in
"the vanity of their mind, having the understanding darkened,
being alienated from the life of God." Replacing the dissoluteness
and impurity of the old man there now stands the new life, the
new man, who has put away the old man and who has learned to
know Christ, has been instructed in Him and has thus "put on
the new man" in righteousness and true holiness (Eph. 4:17-24). In
this life, the image of God becomes visible. The New Testament
sheds the fullness of its light on the newness of this life, and it
appears that this newness does not merely refer to a new aspect in
the life of an individual but that it includes and indeed brings about
the community. Thus Paul calls Christ "our peace, who hath made
both one, hath broken down the middle wall of partition between
us . . . to make in himself of twain, one new man, so making peace"
(Eph. 2:17; cf. 18-22). So deep is this community that it does not
arise from men who having individually been renewed now seek
each other out; it is a peace[64] which is proclaimed and which is
actuality in Christ, through the Cross.

In this newness, barriers are (not, will be) taken away, as two
are made into one. In this community and this peace, the wonderful
newness of man's humanness is manifested; thus Colossians 3:10,
directly after speaking of the renewal of man in God's image, goes
on to say that "there is no difference now between Greek and
Jew, circumcised and uncircumcised, barbarian and Scythian, slave
and free, but Christ is all, and all are in Christ." The remark that

63. Cf. R. Prenter, *op. cit.*, pp. 217-222. It is in this sense also that he
    accepts the basing of anthropology on Christology, and he says that
    this was already done by Luther and Irenaeus. When he places the
    Reformation (or at least Lutheran) contrast between "old" and "new"
    man over against Barth's "correspondence" and "likeness," the dilemma
    is not valid since, as we shall see, the New Testament uses "likeness" in
    very profound contexts.
64. Cf. on Eph. 2:14 also E. Best, *One Body in Christ* (1955), pp. 152ff.
    Cf. also in this connection Prov. 4:7-12, "two are better than one," which
    emphasizes the richness of community as over against solitariness.

the community referred to here and in Galatians 3:28 does not mean a giving up of differences is correct: this newness does not mean a leveling process, a removal of differences, but a community, which reveals its wonderful and hitherto unknown newness precisely in these differences. But the point of Paul's words is not the retention of differences, but the newness of the *community*, which may never be relativized or made secondary by the differences.

The new man — that is the mighty change which in Christ comes over human nature. It is not a change in the sense of a "transubstantiation," a change from one essence to another. Rather, man comes to his true nature, his nature as God intended it to be, a nature in which true community is no longer threatened, in which one man is no longer a danger for the other. No matter how deep-seated the differences between men may be, *in* Christ the tension and convulsiveness vanish before the new nature. Thus when we consider the image of God in man as it is restored in Christ, we are not concerned with some "analogy" of ego or personality or self-consciousness, but rather with the fullness of the new life, which can be described as a new relationship with God, and *in* this relationship as the reality of salvation."[65] It should not surprise us, therefore, that Paul treats sanctifying in the context of the renewal according to the image of the Creator: the new man is knowable in the new direction of his life as over against "evil concupiscence and covetousness," lies, "anger, wrath, blasphemy, filthy communication" (Col. 3:5, 8). These are the practices of the old man, which also affected his fellow man. Before the reference to "the new man which is renewed in knowledge" according to the image of God, Paul issues the warning: "Lie not one to another" (Col. 3:9). This disruption of the community in man's existence is the opposite of what the new creation in Christ is, in which the believers are God's "workmanship, created in Jesus Christ unto good works" (Eph. 2:10; cf. Jas. 1:18). There can be no doubt whatsoever as to the source of this renewal. Not only in general, but also in specific manifestations in human life, the source is clear: in Christ. The reality of renewal can be shown in various manners. Paul can say (Gal. 6:15), "neither circumcision availeth any thing, nor uncircumcision, but a new creature," and "neither circumcision availeth anything nor uncircumcision but faith which worketh by love," (Gal. 5:6), and in another context surprise us with the parallel "circumcision is nothing, and uncircumcision is

65. Cf. Kittel, *op. cit.*, III, 1033.

nothing, but the keeping of the commandments of God" (I Cor. 7:19).

Everywhere when Scripture discusses the new creation, God's gracious and mighty interference in the world of guilt and death, it clearly directs attention to man in his new *conformitas*, the conformity of holiness. When it deals with the renewal of the image of the Creator, it is concerned not with anthropological analogies — certainly not with partial analogies — but with *conformitas* as it is visible in man's existence. For it is precisely with the restoration of his communion, his community, with God, that man comes once more to his true self, and no longer threatens either his own humanity or that of his neighbor. This new life is a new birth, a birth from above (John 3:3), of God (I John 2:29), a living in love (I Cor. 13), a walking in truth (II John 4), a passing from death to life (I John 3:14). And this does not merely manifest itself in man's subjective feelings, but also in the concreteness and actuality of man's every-day life. Nothing is more contradictory than that someone should claim to be in the light and yet hate his brother; he walks in darkness, and knows not whither he goes (I John 2:9, 11). The new life responds, resonates, to the love and mercy of God. It is released from the convulsive tensions of autonomy, from the perversion of freedom. Man indeed finds himself, but this coming to himself is not in contradiction with a return to the Father's house — no more than it was with the prodigal son (Luke 15:17, 18).

In this new life, which can be described in very different ways — newness, community, peace, joy — man is re-created in the image of God. And the term "image" gives us every reason to ask ourselves, at this point, whether we cannot speak here of "analogy." There is indeed, even apart from the historical complications which have arisen from the use of such a term as "analogy of being" (*analogia entis*), every reason to be very careful in employment of the term "analogy." Further, one can not, in my opinion, place an *analogia relationis* over against the older *analogia entis*, as Barth wishes to do.[66] Even if one accepts the criticism given by

---

66. The many and varied additions to the concept of "analogy" have frequently given rise to much confusion. Besides *analogie entis* and *analogia relationis*, we now hear of *analogia existentialis*. See L. Feisser, "Misverstand rondom Barths Leer over de Schepping." *Nederlands Theologisch Tijdschrift* (1952), p. 300. Also see Van Oyen, *Theologische Erkenntnislehre* (1955), p. 177. He speaks of *"analogia verbi, ordinis et integritatis"* and further of *"analogia participationis"* rather than *"analogia entis,"* understanding *"participatio"* in the sense of *"einer*

Barth and Dooyeweerd against the *analogia entis,* one is not thereby compelled to choose for the other horn of a false dilemma — i.e., to accept an *analogia relationis.* For Scripture does not deal with a "relation," but with a relation *as it becomes visible* in and through the reality of salvation. The New Testament description of this renewal, if understood correctly, makes it completely impossible to hypostasize it as an actuality *in se,* since Scripture's "in Christ" and "through faith" so clearly determines it. But, nevertheless, we can speak of this reality, of the newness of life, in the most concrete and "everyday" sense. The believer is called, in this life, to the imitation of God.

One could perhaps make use of the word "analogy" — in its ordinary sense, with no metaphysical connotations, apart from the problems which have historically centered around the word — in connection with this marvelous demand that we imitate God; remembering, however, that this concept of "imitation" has also, historically, acquired a burden of connotation.[67] Our concern here, is to see clearly the *thing* to which Scripture alludes; and if we use "analogy" to refer, first, to the *reality* of this imitation, and, secondly, to the *creaturely* character of this imitation, we are in any case in the immediate context of what Scripture tells us regarding the "becoming like" and "similar" to Christ.[68] In any event, we should not shrink from using this Biblical language because of various incorrect interpretations given to it (form — matter; deification; etc.); for here, in this "imitation" of Christ, we come in contact with the deepest meaning of the renewal in God's image; a direct echo of the Biblical admonition which applies this "being like" to our daily lives: "Forbearing one another, and forgiving one another, if any man have a quarrel against any; *even as* Christ forgave you, *so also* do ye" (Col. 3:13).

This wonderful bond, this *similitudo,* is stressed time and again in the New Testament. "Be kind to one another, tender-hearted, mutually forgiving, *even as* God has in Christ forgiven you" — and because of this, Paul summons the Christian community to "pattern yourselves after God as his loved children, and live in loving ways,

---

ontisch personalen Teilhabe," or "koinoonia," or "analogia entis com-municantis." It is not clear why Van Oyen views the *analogia relationis* as too narrowly restricted to an ontical relation.

67. Cf. my *Geloof en Heiliging* (1949), ch. VII; S.C.W. Duvenage, *De Navolging van Christus* (1954); M. C. Slotemaker de Bruine, *Het Ideaal der Navolging van Christus ten Tijde van Bernhard van Clairvaux* (1926).

68. Bavinck, *Gereformeerde Dogmatiek,* II, 494.

just as Christ, too, loved you and surrendered himself for us" (Eph. 4:32ff.).[69]

This "imitation" of Christ thus is the imitation of Christ by His children; "as dear children" we must imitate Him. We are indeed now far from the idea of an *analogia entis,* since the Biblical presentation of the "being like God" has nothing to do with a "natural" state of affairs in the relation between God and man, but rather shows forth the wonder of the new birth (cf. I John 3:9), through which the life of the creature can once more exhibit God's image, and this "being like God" can shine forth as a light in the world. It is the light of good works: "Let *your* light shine among the people so that they may *observe* your lofty actions and give glory to your heavenly father" (Matt. 5:16). And that is the marvelous thing; that this human light does *not* result in the glorifying of men, but of the Father. This "imitation" or similitude, through which our life becomes transparent, and our "light" — of good works! — can shine through, finds its sharpest and most ineluctable expression in the summons of Jesus: "Be perfect, just as your Father in heaven is perfect" (Matt. 5:48).

This newness of life, this re-creation in the image of God, removes the obstacles for others gaining a correct view of God. Over against the slander of His name on our account there stands the praise of His name and the winning of our neighbor for Christ through our walk (*Heidelberg Catechism,* 86, 122). As Zechariah says, "In those days ten men of all tongues shall take hold, take hold of the skirt of a Jew, saying, We will go with you, for we have heard that God is with you" (Zech. 8:23); and not only that, but there is also praise of God through the *seeing* of the "likeness," the *seeing* of the light as the uncontradictable witness of the glory of God. The "imitation" of God forms the pendant of our witness in the world, in which word and deed are joined in an unbreakable unity. There is surely reason to remember that this likeness does not imply identity, but that it does not is already clear in the very meaning

69. Cf. my *Geloof en Heiliging* (1949), p. 147. It would be interesting to examine more closely the extent to which the imitation of Christ has been seen, in the history of theology, in relation to the Biblical meaning of the imitation of God. In any event, the imitation of *God* is referred to early, e.g., in the *Letter to Diognetus* (X, 4-6) : "imitator of Goodness"; we read that one must not wonder that this is possible: "Nor wonder whether man can become imitator of God." Continuing, this imitation is contrasted with the oppression of one's neighbor and the use of power against the weak: "Not in these things can one imitate God." Cf. also Ignatius, *Ad Trallum* 1.

of the comparison with "children." Any tendency in the direction of identity contradicts the reality of this filial relation.

In this context, says Michaelis,[70] "to take God as our example means exactly to remind ourselves without ceasing that as His children we live wholly out of His love and forgiveness." The statement is a fitting and necessary reminder of our complete filial dependence. But the statement equally reminds us to live, in and out of this love, in the likeness or image whereby man in the renewal of his life, in genuine sonship, *makes us think of God* in this creaturely likeness. Hence this likeness is the complete opposite of that which the Devil falsely placed before man in Paradise: "God knows that in the day you eat thereof your eyes will be opened and *you will be as gods*" (Gen. 3:5). *This* presentation of "being like God" is the opposite of the image of God.[71] It is the projection of autonomous existence through opened eyes which are no longer the eyes of children. Hence the word of judgment with which man was driven out of Paradise (Gen. 3:23):[72] "the man is become *like one of us,* to know good and evil" which in any event clearly shows the *rebelliousness* of this "being *like* God." This perversion is precisely the opposite of being a child of God and therein showing the image, since that involves the imitation of God in *His* love and mercy.

Such an imitation is not at all a usurpation, but rather God's

70. Michaelis, *Theologisches Wörterbuch.* Cf. J. A. C. van Leeuwen (*Commentaar op Efezen*) , p. 155. He says that the "patterning after God" (Eph. 5:1) is not an impossible exhortation and that the "as dear children" is a closer description and a restriction; the term "restriction" is not intended as a limitation on imitation, but as a defense against misunderstanding.

71. See Kittel, *op. cit.* III, 352. "This 'you shall be as God' now is made true by God." Hence to take this text as an introduction to the New Testament use of image is to play on words, since these words, of course, never did "become true" and the "likeness" of Gen. 3:5 is as far from the "likeness" of the New Testament as east is from west.

72. Cf. Aalders, *Genesis, ad hoc.* Even those who view an ironic interpretation of this text as untenable because of the expulsion from Paradise can hardly view this likeness as an identity, something which is clearly ruled out by the action of God. This is a "becoming like God" through destroying His authority (E. Konig, "Gehorsamsverletzung," *Genesis,* p. 252) ; a capitulation to temptation and an "analogia libertatis" reached thereby — a liberty which actually is nothing else than a fall and rebellion. Cf. the knowledge of good and evil (Gen. 3:22) ; that which forms the holiness and sovereignty of God is distortedly "imaged" in man as human autonomy. (Cf. Aalders and Konig, *loci cit.,* and, for a wholly different point of view, B. Jacob, *Das erste Buch der Thora,* 1934, p. 126) .

gift, restored in Christ. It is only possible and actual through the actuality referred to in Philippians 2:6, 7 where it is said that Christ became like man. This He did as one who did not treat the "being like God" as a thief might do, keeping it for Himself without considering others, but as one who walked to the bitter end the way of humiliation to free others. It is this "becoming like man" which in the New Testament brings into view the imitation of Christ and thereby the imitation of God.[73] And so this imitation takes its legitimate place. While the "you shall be as God" of Genesis was nothing but a call to rebellion, and to the fall from sonship, the New Testament uses our becoming like Him to mean the full *revelation* of this sonship (cf. Rom. 8:19ff.). And thus the numerous Biblical witnesses of the uniqueness of God[74] are indeed valid judgments against the "you shall be as God," but at the same time they do not shut out the wonderful perspectives of "being like Him" which are opened in the New Testament.

In the epistle of John, the eschatological perspective is in this connection especially noteworthy. When John speaks of our being children of God,[75] he sees this as an actuality — "Beloved, now we are children of God."

Such words "being like *Him*" have at various times in the history of the Church and of theology been watered down, as a reaction against any deification of man. Theologians were afraid to use such words, out of anxiety lest they be misunderstood, lest man be illegitimately raised above the limits placed on him as a creature.[76] In the light of history, such caution is indeed understandable.[77]

---

73. Cf. my *Het Werk van Christus,* ch. III, and D. Bonhoeffer, *Nachfolge* (1937); his last chapter ("Das Bild Christi") rightly emphasizes the point that the Incarnation is the basis for the imitation of Christ.

74. Cf., e.g., Isa. 44:7: "And who, as I, shall call, and shall declare it, and set it in order before me" and the positive denial in Jer. 10:6: "there is none like thee, Jehovah," and many other texts. Cf. also Kittel, *loc. cit.*

75. I John 3:2, and cf. also the preceding verse.

76. Was not the terrible picture of such self-exaltation outlined for us in Scripture? Thus, Isa. 14:14: "I will ascend above the heights of the clouds; I will make myself like the most High," cf. Ezek. 28:2. Cf. the self-exaltation of the man of sin, II Thess. 2:4: "he sitteth in the temple of God, setting himself forth as God."

77. Cf. E. Hendrikx, "De Leer van de Vergoddelijking in het Oud-Christelijk Geloofs-Bewustzijn," *Genade en Kerk* (1953), concerning the argument over the "deification" of man. He sees as the main theme of my *Conflict met Rome* the deep divergence existing between the Reformation and Catholicism regarding this "deification." Hendrikx himself gives some very strong formulations, not only for the *eschaton*, but also for this dispensation. Cf. the total re-creation of man, "also in his ontological

but does not justify our speaking about this eschatological perspective in embarrassed and barely audible tones. The emphasis
on this eschatological perspective is of the essence of this sonship,
no matter how difficult it may be to escape pagan parallels.[78]
The basic difference between Christian and pagan concepts is evident enough, even though difficult to pinpoint in exact terminology.
Thus it is said that John is not talking about "likeness in essence,"
while the pagan idea means a "qualititative likeness";[79] but all feel
how little such words actually say, in the final analysis. We can
indeed only describe the likeness in immediate relation to the
view of John himself: the relation is one of being children.

It is from this sonship, this being children, that the eschatological
perspective takes on color and form. The "likeness" is in no respect
removed from the contexts of salvation and the love of God, or
made into some metaphysical qualification. The likeness to God is
concerned with the likeness of loved children. It is not a deification
in one or another form, as in the gnostic mysteries, though the
same terminology is used by John to refer to the completion. In
the context of the term "likeness" it is *not yet revealed* what we
shall be, and this is still the context when John speaks of *knowing*
that we shall be like Him. In this paradox, probably, lies the
reason why, despite repeated attempts, theologians have not been
able, with the terminology employed, to supply a satisfactory explanation. John knows that he stands before God's eschatological
mystery and he looks with yearning toward what will someday
be revealed, but *in* this standing before the mystery he *knows* of
this "likeness," this being a child, which will be raised in complete
glory above every struggle and difficulty. In the context of John's
whole letter, there is in this knowing no giving up of the distinction
between child and Father, of creature and Creator. It is precisely

---

being, whereby he as a child of God here on earth becomes god in
expectation of his complete deification, also with respect to his body
in the Day of Judgement" (p. 146). Involved is the mystery of God's
almighty power and His love, about which the mystics could only
stammer (p. 114). Hendrikx acknowledges that the Catholic mystics,
for whom the "oneness with God" included an experienced partaking
of His nature, constantly had to avoid "the appearance of pantheism"
in describing this oneness.

78. For pagan parallels, cf. Kittel, *op. cit.*, pp. 351, 353, and R. Schnackenburg,
Die Johannesbriefe (1953), pp. 151ff. Cf. further H. Asmussen, *Wahrheit und Liebe* (1939), p. 73.

79. Schnackenburg, *op. cit.*, p. 150; F. Hauck, *Die Kirchenbriefe* (1953),
p. 133; C. H. Dodd, *The Johannine Epistles* (1947), p. 70.

the eschatological perspective which includes the "we shall see him as he is" (I John 3:2). Evidently the "being like him" does not at all annihilate the "being judged by him," but John rather sees being like Him as included in seeing Him as He is (cf. John 6:46, Heb. 12:14). Like John, we shall probably have to remain imprisoned in the Johannine stammering, in the knowing and not-knowing.

Every commentator attempts to escape, but appears in the attempt merely to participate in John's not-knowing; e.g., when Schnackenburg speaks of the "eschatological intensification and completion of being a child of God," or Hauck of "something much higher" than is actualized in our earthly life, or Dodd of "our mysterious but glorious destiny."[79] Indeed, almost every remark which goes beyond the text says strikingly little and is subject to various objections. The text refers to seeing God;[80] but what must one think of the explanation of this seeing as "unhindered intercourse on the same level of being"? (Hauck). In such formulations one sometimes gets the impression that there is an attempt to rise above the "not-knowing" of John. What he evidently only knew is that the seeing of God in immediate relation to being like Him will be the fulfillment in eschatological glory of that "being like Him" which is the privilege of believers already in this life as children of God. The full revelation of this *doxa*, this glory, is God's mystery.[81] This *docta ignorantia* (learned ignorance) is not a concession to agnosticism, but is the form taken by the most *intense* expectation, for

80. I John 3:2: "that we shall see him as he is." Cf. Matt. 5:8, I Cor. 13:12. Calvin's comment that "God gives himself to be seen by us not as he is but in such a manner as we can comprehend him" (*Commentary on I John*) is contrary to the literal text. Nor can we see why Greijdanus thinks he has avoided Calvin's difficulty by relating the text to the seeing of Christ. Cf. Dodd, *op. cit.*, p. 70.

81. Cf. P. Volz, *Die Eschatologie der jüdischen Gemeinde im N.T. Zeitalter* (1934), pp. 397ff. for other *doxa*-parallels in rabbinical, apocalyptic and apocryphal literature.

82. It should be noted that attention has been paid, especially in Roman Catholic theology, to the so-called *visio Dei beatifica*. This beatific vision is possible only in the future (as an eschatological fruit of salvation) through the *lumen gloriae*. Cf. the Council of Vienne's rejection (1311) of the teaching of the Beghards that the soul *"non indiget lumen gloriae"* (Denzinger, 475). The viewing of God is impossible for the human soul as such, so that a *habitus supernaturalis* is necessary. In 1336, Benedict XII spoke of an "intuitive vision" of the divine essence (Denzinger, 530), while the Council of Florence in 1439 added *"et intueri clare ipsum Deum trinum et unum, sicuti est"* (Denzinger, 693). The statement of Pope John XXII that the vision of God will first come to the believers *after*

it is bound up with the hope, which now calls us to imitation of God[82] (I John 3:3).

The whole Scriptural witness makes clear that our understanding of the image of God can be sound only when in unbreakable relation to the witness regarding Jesus Christ, who is called the image of God. Not only is the creation of the new man after the image of God spoken of in direct relation with Christ — *in* Christ — but He is Himself called the image, the *"eikoon"* of God. In II Corinthians 4:4, Paul writes of the "gospel of Christ, who is the image of God" and in Colossians 1:15 of Christ, who has delivered us from the power of darkness, as "the image of the invisible God."

Both texts deal with the visibility, the emanation, of God's glory in and through the glory of Jesus Christ. "In His speech and action and bearing, the splendor of God's glory has become knowable and tangible." The truth becomes visible in the gospel of Christ (II Cor. 4:2), comes to the light, over against practices which cannot see the light. "We have renounced the hidden things of shame, not walking in craftiness . . . but by the manifestation of the truth commending ourselves to every man's conscience in the sight of God. And even if our gospel is veiled, it is veiled in them that perish, in whom the god of this world hath blinded the minds of the unbelieving, that the light of the gospel of the glory of Christ, who is then image of God, should not dawn upon them" (II Cor. 4:2-4). But the light shines, as when God at Creation said, "Let there be light," and now light shines in the hearts of men, to enlighten them with the "knowledge of the glory of God *in the face of Jesus Christ*" (II Cor. 4:6).

Colossians 1:15 talks of Him who has saved us from the power of darkness. He is the image of the invisible God. Van Leeuwen rightly remarks that we may not here begin with the dilemma whether this refers to the Son in His pre-existence or in His incarnate form. Paul calls Christ the image of God (II Cor. 4:4) in a context (the light that streams forth in His Gospel) which

the Last Judgment has been much commented on (it was spoken as an individual, not *ex cathedra;* cf. Pohle, *Dogmatik*, III, 588) ; John expressly changed his mind before his death, however (Diekamp, *Dogmatik,* III, 394) . All views of the *visio Dei beatifica,* however, merely strengthen our impression that we can never advance beyond the "not-knowing" of I John 3:2; certainly not when a theologian speaks of the "accidental" joys of heaven in contrast to the "essential" good of the *visio Dei* (Bartmann, *Dogmatik,* II, 479) . To the "accidental" joys belong mingling with "Christ and his glorious Mother, with angels and saints."

goes beyond this dilemma,[83] and likewise in Colossians, where the deliverer from the power of darkness is He who is the image of God, the first born of all creatures. He is the son of His love, the head of the Church, and in Him we have our redemption, the forgiveness of sins (Col. 1:13, 18, 14).[84]

When the Jews of Jesus' day came in contact with Him — *God* revealed in the flesh — they opposed Him not only for His breaking the Sabbath, but also because He "called God his own Father, making himself equal with God" (John 5:18). The same criticism occurred when Jesus forgave sins (Mark 2:5). They saw in this a claim to a likeness between Christ and God, and said that He blasphemed God, for "who can forgive sins but one, even God?" (Mark 2:7). They were astonished and disturbed over this "analogy" which issues in identity, and they did not understand the mystery of this "authorization." We read in the Gospel of John that Jesus not only spoke of His unity with the Father but also said that the Father was greater than He (John 14:28). But, impressively, it is precisely *in* this subordination that the likeness, the "analogy," comes so strongly to the fore in His actions. After the complaint of the Jews that He made Himself equal with God, Christ said (John 5:19): "the Son can do nothing of himself, but what he seeth the Father doing." It is precisely *in* the humiliation that the "likeness" becomes visible, in this unique analogy or similarity, just as in the words which follow (John 5:21): "for as the Father raiseth the dead and giveth them life, even so the Son also giveth life to whom he will" with which corresponds the text which strongly accentuates the uniqueness of this likeness, that all must honor the Son *as* they honor the Father. "He that honoreth not the Son honoreth not the Father that sent him" (John 5:23).

---

83. Cf. J. A. C. van Leeuwen, *Commentary on Colossians*, 1:15. Cf. Grosheide, *Commentary* on II Corinthians, p. 146. See H. N. Ridderbos, *Paulus en Jezus* (1952), p. 73. He feels that Grosheide's exegesis of the text is untenable because of Col. 1:15; the question might be raised whether Paul's statement (Col. 1:15) about Christ as the image of the *invisible* God is evaluated enough in the light of the clear point of Paul's teaching in II Cor. 4:4, 6. Van Leeuwen rightly notes that our knowledge can make no distinction between the Son in His pre-existence and His revelation in the flesh (*op. cit.*, p. 161). Cf. also, in his discussion of "invisible," Van Leeuwen's reference to John 1:18. Calvin considers Col. 1:15 as a summary of Paul's letter to the Colossians: God exhibits in Christ His justice, goodness, wisdom, etc.; we must therefore beware of seeking Him apart from Christ.

84. Cf. also Heb. 1:3. In this text also, the dilemma does not fit. Cf. H. van Oyen, *Christus als Hogepriester* (1939), pp. 10ff. He refers, and justifiably, to John 14:9.

In this likeness, in all the heights and depths of His life, He was truly the image of God. The whole gospel is filled with this — and this is the most basic cause of the essential controversy over the deity of Christ through the centuries — as appears when Christ says to the disciples:[85] "If ye had known me, ye would have known my Father also; from henceforth ye know him, and have seen him (John 14:7). When Philip evidently did not in the least understand this mystery of the revelation of God, and said, "show us the Father, and it sufficeth" (John 14:8), Christ's answer is one of complete astonishment: "Have I been so long time with you, and dost thou not know *me*, Philip? He that hath seen me, hath seen the Father. . . ."

We stand here before an unsearchable mystery, the mystery of "God revealed in the flesh,"[86] but in that mystery is the revelation of God, "the only begotten Son, he hath declared him" (John 1:18) in His entire living and dying. He is the image of the invisible God, and there is actually no reason for the question of Philip, who wanted to know and see more than God's revelation in Christ, and more than the revelation in Christ Himself.

Anyone who notes and is impressed by the Biblical statements about Christ as the image of God would certainly hesitate to speak of the believer as also renewed after God's image, if Scripture itself did not so emphatically lead us in this direction. Do we not read that "whom he foreknew, he also foreordained to be conformed to the image of his Son, that he might be the first-born among many brethren" (Rom. 8:29)? And is there not therefore a likeness or similarity or analogy or however one will phrase it? Reality is always something more than words can portray, and the word "similarity," too, is useful only to direct our attention to the great mystery (cf. II Cor. 3:18, Phil. 3:21). It is not coincidental that the word "mirror" has often been used to refer to the mystery of

---

85. H. Crouzel, *Théologie de l'image de Dieu chez Origéne* (1955), p. 55. He says that we may well wonder why John does not know the theme of Christ as the image of God, and then explains his statement by saying that "the image appeared to John to be insufficient to express the communion of the two persons" because for John, Christ is not only *eikoon* but also *theos*. But this argument is difficult to maintain, for John 1:1 does not in the least oppose the idea of the image, and further-more, John does emphasize the "likeness" so clearly and places much emphasis on Christ as the Revelation of the Father (cf. John 17). Crouzel himself admits that the "theme of the resemblance" occurs explicitly in John (*op. cit.*, p. 62).

86. Origen already spoke of Christ as the image of the invisible God, emphasizing John 14 (Crouzel, *op. cit.*, p. 82).

the image; an expression which we encounter especially often in Calvin.[87]

This term deserves our attention all the more in that it is used in Scripture; e.g., in I Corinthians 13:12, "now we see as in a mirror," where it occurs in a context in which "image" (*eikoon*) is also used. In any event, it is necessary to pay attention to the manner in which the symbol of the mirror is employed in explaining the image of God, rather than following some vague intuition as to its meaning. We should consider especially the witness of II Corinthians 3:18,[88] where Paul, in dealing with the greater richness and glory of the new covenant as compared with the old, writes: "we all, with unveiled face beholding as in a mirror the glory of God, are transformed into the same image." This passage concerns itself especially with the meaning of this reflection, this *katoptrizoo*. It is clear that Paul refers to the dispensation of the Spirit (II Cor. 3:11ff.). It is the dispensation of freedom and liberty, wholly different from the case of Moses, who put a veil before his face when he approached the people. There is now an unveiling, an unconcealment, glory, radiating glory.

There is indeed, in the New Testament dispensation, still a covering over the hearts of the Jews, the hardness of their hearts, but this covering is no longer a necessary and fixed thing in the history of salvation (*Heilsgeschichte*), but is a correlate of the guilt which can be broken through only by conversion (II Cor. 3:14-16). And now the service of the Spirit is described as a "reflection" of the glory of God.

Grosheide points out that the word *"katoptrizoo"* appears only here, and that it can mean either "reflect" or "view as in a mirror." He chooses the latter meaning: "the context does not refer to a reflection of received glory, but it does refer to the possession of glory." And this "viewing as in a mirror," in his opinion, shows that even in the new dispensation this glory reveals itself as not

---

87. T. F. Torrance, *Calvin's Doctrine of Man* (1949), p. 36. He says "there is no doubt that Calvin always thinks of the image in terms of a mirror." But it is always necessary to examine in what sense the word "mirror" is used. Cf. Bavinck, *op. cit.*, II, 491. He begins his treatment of man's essence with a reference to the image of God, and then calls the world as revelation of God "a mirror of his qualities and perfections"; and later speaks of man as "the mirror of the *universum*" (II, 524).

88. Cf. D. Cairns, *The Image of God in Man* (1953), p. 131. In the Middle Ages, St. Bernard considered this text very intensively, as he did Rom. 8:29. Cf. M. Standaert, *La doctrine de l'image chez St. Bernard* (Louvain, 1947).

yet complete. He finds a parallel in I Cor. 13:12 (our *"seeing through a glass"*). It is clear that in Grosheide's exegesis there is no place for a "reflection," and if this exegesis is correct, then we can no longer place II Cor. 3:18 alongside the words of Calvin about the mirror symbol in connection with the image of God.[89]

But we encounter in other commentators, e.g., Zahn and Pop, the meaning of "reflection." And indeed, it appears to me that there are strong grounds for seeing Paul's words as implying a "reflection." We are reminded that in II Corinthians 3:18 it is said that there is no longer a covering on our faces in contrast to the veil on Moses' face, which kept back the brightness which Moses had from his nearness to God. The covering *now* is taken away, so that the streaming forth of this brightness is possible and actual. This happens in the transformation to the same image, so that Pop writes (correctly, in my opinion), "the man in whom the Spirit has begun the completion of this transformation, shows forth various characteristics which remind us of the perfections of the Lord . . . he begins to show the characteristics of the image of God, to reflect the glory of the Lord."[90] Thus Paul is concerned in his use of the figure of the mirror not to emphasize (as in I Cor. 13:12) the inadequateness of our present sharing in glory, but rather to emphasize this glory in its concrete outpouring and manifestation. This glory manifests itself in the now uncovered and receptive life, in the freedom and liberty of the believers, who are, says Paul, epistles which can be read by and known to all men (II Cor. 3:2).

In the New Testament community, the concern is most certainly not with remaining hidden but with becoming revealed, with that visibility, that knowability (II Cor. 3:3), in which it is "made manifest that ye are an epistle of Christ."

When reference is in fact made to a "reflection" of God's glory, it is clear that such reference is in the context of the transformation, the becoming similar to Christ, the continuous renewing of life. And if one interprets *"katoptrizoo"* as "reflecting," the context clearly reveals that the transformation into the *image* of God is intimately concerned with this reflection as the concrete and visible expression of this decisive transformation. This transformation is eschatologically oriented, but is nevertheless already

---

89. See Grosheide, *Commentary on II Corinthians, ad loc.* Cf. his summary (p. 46), where he translates "view as in a mirror" rather than "reflect."
90. Pop, *Apostolaat in Druk en Vertroosting. De tweede Brief aan de Corinthiërs,* p. 112.

actual in principle, and it becomes manifest in the community, which is a readable epistle of Christ. The relationship between the image of God and the newness of life, indeed the identity of the image and the concretely visible sanctification, in which the glory of the Lord becomes evident to all, is unmistakable.

It goes without saying that everything which the New Testament says about this reflection of God's glory is Christologically defined, and wholly so. Only through and in Him and through His Spirit is this visibility an actuality. The interest in showing forth the image is never abstractly or ontologically oriented. This does not mean that we do not have to do with an ontological reality; we are dealing precisely with the actual being of man in this restoration, this renewal, this re-orientation. Paul speaks elsewhere (Rom. 8:29) of our being destined to be similar to the image of His Son.[91] Here the goal of the ways of God becomes manifest. The "beforehand" of election realizes itself in the eschatological reality. The complete meaning of this similarity is beyond all doubt. The believers receive a participation in Christ, who is Himself the image of God. As Michel puts it, "Jesus Christ is not only the Son, but also the image of God. As this image of God, He is God made present, He is His representation, His truth, for man."[92] This becoming similar to Christ corresponds also to the relation between Christ as the first-born from the dead and the others; he is the first-born *among many brothers* (Col. 1:18, Rom. 8:29). There can be no question, therefore, that similarity to the image of Christ involves an "analogy," a "likeness," an "imitation" — but in Christ and in continuing communion with Him: the new reality, not merely future, though indeed eschatological. In this connection, we should consider not only those texts where the

91. For the interpretation of "reflection," see also Bachmann, *Commentary*, Zahn, ed., *ad. loc.* On what are in my opinion strong grounds he says that the text does not refer to "viewing" the glory, and is not drawing a parallel with the children of Israel but rather with Moses, "who did not see the brightness of God but it reflected from him." So also Crouzel, *op. cit.*, p. 60; J. Dupont, "Le chrétien, miroir de la gloire divine d'après II Cor. 3:18," *Révue Biblique* 56 (1949), pp. 392ff.; cf. also his *Gnosis* (1949), pp. 119ff., on the difference between I Cor. 13:12 and II Cor. 3:18. For the other exegesis, see W. Straub, *Die Bildersprache des Apostels Paulus* (1937), p. 24 (on I Cor. 13:12); Kittel, *op. cit.*, II, 693; and Calvin (*Commentary, ad loc.*), who, in spite of his interest in the symbol of the mirror, here does not choose for that translation, since the meaning of the word in Greek is "doubtful."

92. O. Michel, *Die Brief an die Römer* (1955), p. 182.

word "image" is specifically used, but also Paul's admonition:[93]
"I am again in travail until Christ be formed in you" (Gal. 4:19).

It is clear that even though the word "image" is not specifically
used in the passage quoted, we may well suspect that we are in
the same context of ideas. It is a text from the letter to the Galatians,
who were in danger of losing their Christian liberty and of again
taking on the yoke of the slave and returning to the righteousness
of the law (Gal. 5:1; 4:21-31;2:21). If that is righteousness, then
Christ has died in vain! In this dangerous and seductive situation,
Paul addresses them lovingly as "my children," for whom he
sustains new sorrows; he compares himself to a mother experiencing
the travail that will end as it were in a new birth. This new birth
is Paul's concern for the Galatians, in the midst of their dangers.
Their situation will again be good only when this new birth occurs,
that is, when Christ takes shape again in them. Paul is not thinking
of a mystic birth of Christ within them,[94] but of the form of
Christ becoming visible and apparent to those outside. The newly
born man, whom Paul has in mind here, "bears the comprehensible
and visible image of Christ in him."[95] This certainly is related to
a correct insight into the meaning of Christ for salvation, as
Hermann rightly emphasizes, but it deals particularly with the
lived knowledge of the Galatians, in the actuality of their life.
It is not concerned with a mystical secret, but with this form as
"perceptible and real." It is a change of form, a metamorphosis,
which affects the depths of man's whole existence, and which therefore becomes manifest in his whole existence. When Paul exhorts
the adoption of this new form, he directs this "re-forming" toward
discerning the will of God, and it stands in direct relationship with
not conforming to this world, and with the presenting of the body
a living and holy sacrifice acceptable to God (Rom 12:1-2). It
is impossible to separate the idea of concreteness and visibility from

---

93. Cf. R. Hermann, *Theologische Literatur Zeitung* (Dec., 1955), on
the significance of the Greek.

94. Cf. the article of Hermann, who extensively attacks the idea that Paul
is dealing with a sort of Christ-mysticism in connection with Christ
being born in us. Cf. also Kittel, *op. cit.*, IV, 761, on the "obtaining
of the image" as "becoming a new man." Behm (in Kittel, *loc. cit.*)
mentions Calvin's formulation: Christ *"nascitur in nobis, ut vivamus eius
vitam"* — Christ is born in us so that we may live His life. But the
passage really shows how far Calvin was from the mystics, who used
language much stronger than that of Calvin. The preceding sentence
in Calvin is *"Porro Christum in nobis formari et nos in Christo, idem
est."* This is hardly an emphasis like that of the mystics.

95. Kittel, *op. cit.*, IV, 753.

this new form. For, as Calvin writes on Galatians 4:19, this form becomes manifest, the figure of Christ becomes visible, when we lead His life.[96] Just as we read of the figure of a servant[97] in connection with Christ (Phil. 2:6ff.), and as we see in this the actuality and concreteness of His whole life from day to day and even unto death,[98] so also the "form" of the believer as "form" of Christ is the actuality of His day-to-day life in imitation of Him.

We frequently encounter, in various contemporary views of the meaning and content of the image of God, the word "representation."

If we examine what is meant by this concept, we must indeed admit that it has the essence of the image of God in view. This does not, of course, mean that the use of precisely this word will give us the key to an understanding of the image of God, but the content with which this concept is concerned is without a doubt central in Scripture. The idea of representation refers to man in the concreteness and visibility of his earthly life; to man, who was created in God's image and likeness and who is called to represent and portray this image here on earth, and after the Fall is again called away from the deformation of his entire life, and elected to become similar to the image of Christ. Being in the image of God refers to *this* representation, and therein to the reality of the creature's analogy — a word which, despite all the historical difficulties surrounding the *"analogia entis,"* we can here hardly do without. Analogy (as the analogy of the creature) is implied in representation.

This concept deals with man as he actually is, the non-autonomous and non-independent creature, unable to rely on himself alone; man, who can find and possess his riches and his glory precisely only in his dependence on and in his communion with God. It concerns man as the child of God, and there are perhaps no words in all of Scripture more apt to indicate the profound meaning of

96. Cf. Greijdanus, *Commentary,* p. 282, on this being re-formed to the image of Christ and on showing the form of Christ in all of life.

97. The term *"morphe theou"* (form of God) is also used, but Behm (in Kittel, *op. cit.,* IV, 758) rightly explains this as "a term used by Paul in contrast to *"morphe doulou"* (form of a servant), and should be understood in relation to the context."

98. See Kittel, *op. cit.,* II, 390 ("*Eikoon* and *Mandatar*"); E. Jacob, *Théologie de l'Ancient Testament* (1955), p. 136 ("*la fonction de re-presentation*"); B. Jacob, *Das erste Buch der Tora, Genesis* (1934), p. 59 ("*Stellvertreter*"); Pop, *op. cit.,* p. 127; K. Schilder, *Heid. Catechismus,* I, 255 ("*representative*").

the image of God than the words of Christ: "ye therefore shall be perfect, even as your heavenly Father is perfect" (Matt. 5:48). Similar are these other words, in the call to goodness and mercy: "love your enemies, and do them good, and lend, never despairing . . . and you will be *sons* of the Most High . . . . Be merciful even *as he is merciful*" (Luke 6:35-36). The image of God shines forth in His *children* in the analogy of their whole life with the life of God. This being a child of God, this analogy, is not subjectively shut up and invisible, but is directed precisely to becoming visible. This perceptibility does not refer to awe-inspiring and spectacular deeds, but to sanctification, to the doing of all things without murmuring or objection, to being blameless and spotless in order so to be "blameless and harmless, children of God without blemish in the midst of a crooked and perverse generation, among whom you shine as lights in the world" (Phil. 2:14-15).

If we find the word "representation" too cold and mechanical, and the word "analogy" too full of difficulties, let us in any case think on this similarity, this conforming, and on the perceptibility to others of this similarity. This does not mean any pomp or boasting, any theatrical holiness in public to show ourselves before men (Matt. 6:5, cf. 6:1). Whoever intends such display is simply reminded that the Father sees into the secret heart of man (Matt. 6:6). Such display of one's self before men is radically different from letting our light shine before men, even though there may not be much difference in the terminology used. They are distinguished from each other by what it is that other men see, and this is decisive; do men see ourselves or do they see the good works for the glory of God (Matt. 5:16). That is the difference between boasting and being children of God, between vainglory and the image of God.

We have already noted at various places in Scripture that the manifestation of the image of God in the similarity to Christ is not at all a reality which we can speak of in a purely individualistic way. Indeed, how could that be possible when we are dealing with the image of *God* and the becoming similar to *Christ,* and dealing with true imitation? How could we speak of such an imitation unless the image of God shows forth visibly a godly "philanthropy"? (Titus 3:4). It is certainly not coincidental that the calling to the imitation of God constantly concentrates on communion with others, a communion which finds its basis in the imperative reminder ". . . even as God" and ". . . even as Christ."

How could the image of God be renewed in the actuality of our existence if it did not become actual and visible for others? In the first Epistle of John, with its emphasis on the eschatological perspective of our being like *Him*, this communion with others is especially emphasized. These are not two polar opposites, but the same actuality, the actuality of our true human nature. The eschatological seriousness is felt in this earthly life in the opposition between love and hate. It is the children of God whom we here see sketched, not in a hidden and obscure existence, but "knowable" (I John 3:10) in that he who does not love his brother is not from God. John's letter strongly emphasizes this relationship. It deals with an indicative which is at the same time an imperative: "Hereby know we love, because he laid down his life for us; and we ought to lay down our lives for the brethren" (I John 3:16; cf. also 4:21 and John 13:14). The reality of this likeness is indissoluble: "Whoso . . . shutteth up his compassion, . . . how does the love of God abide in him?" (I John 3:17).

Nor will the word or the tongue be sufficient here, but only the act, in the midst of the actuality and visibility of human life (1 John 3:18). Let us love one another, *because* love is from God (I John 4:7), and "if God so loved us, we ought to love one another" (I John 4:11). Where this love is lacking and we hear the words "I love God," we are hearing lies (I John 4:20).

In all the various nuances of the New Testament witness, there is a deep harmony in this relationship. It is the harmony of the new commandment,[99] the commandment of love, the fulfilling of the law: "Owe no man anything, save to love one another, for he that loveth his neighbor hath fulfilled the law" (Rom. 13:8). Here are the same words about the one thing that is indispensable, the one thing we owe. It is commandment and freedom, in one. It is a conforming to Christ, to His mind which manifests itself in deeds. It is not coincidental that in the powerful Christological pericope of Philippians 2 on Christ's humiliation and His taking on the form of man, this renewal becomes actualized and visible in taking on the mind which was also Christ's. Thus this imitation is freed from all superficial meaning, and at the same time made highly concrete: "be of the same mind, having the same love . . '. do nothing from selfishness or conceit . . . have this mind in you which was also in Christ" (Phil. 2:2ff.).

This analogy of love (*analogia amoris*) has its strong foundation

---

99. Cf. John 13:24; I John 2:8, II John 5-6; I John 4:21. Cf. my *Geloof en Heiliging*, p. 157 (ET: *Faith and Sanctification*).

in the emptying, the kenosis, of Jesus Christ, who became like man: the renewal of the image of God.

And if now again we recall the eschatological perspective of being like Him, as in I John 3, we can understand something of the enrapturing vision of Isaiah: "They shall not hurt nor destroy in all my holy mountain; for the earth shall be full of the vision of Jehovah, as the waters cover the sea" (Isa. 11:9-10). Men shall do evil no more because of their *knowledge* of God, and "it shall come to pass in that day that the root of Jesse, that standeth for an ensign of the peoples, unto him shall the nations seek, and his resting place shall be glorious."

But it is not yet *revealed* what we shall be. . . .

If we listen to the Biblical witness regarding the image of God, we find it filled with actuality, and with earnestness. We can hear a note of eschatological earnestness which is evidently the earnestness of our ordinary life. The image of God stands before us in the contexts of guilt and restoration, of being lost and being found. The image of God is something which concerns the whole man, his place in this world and his future, his likeness *in* his being a child of a Father, of *this* Father in heaven. No erroneous speculation, no matter how serious the error, on man as *"microtheos"* or on man as "deified," may hold us back from letting the message of Scripture on this point have effect and resonance in our lives. It is on the one hand a reminder or remembrance — not in the psychological sense of remembering what is past, but in the indictment of the judgment of God. At the same time it is a calling to man's true destiny, in being conformed to Christ (Rom. 8:29).

Here man is assigned to his place in the plan of God. This true human nature is warned and protected with unmistakable clearness against man's over-evaluation and self-glorification. But in this protection there lies also a warning against under-evaluation of man's nature, such as reveals itself in a protest against "life" and against human nature. One could at this point speak not unjustifiably of the *critical function* of the Biblical witness regarding the image of God, for it stands in an undissoluble harmony with the law and the gospel, the *usus paedagogicus* and the *usus normativus*. And in all this, it shows us a way; not as a romantic ideal in which man can again project his own dignity, but as a call from darkness, a call which is and remains a call to freedom in Christ. This witness regarding the image of God places man once again centrally in the works of God; in the center of God's creation, which is subjected to vanity and which waits with longing for the revealing of the sons of God, for it, too, "shall be delivered from the bondage of corruption into the liberty of the glory of the children of God" (Rom. 8:19-21).

To be central in this manner can not be misunderstood or interpreted as anthropomorphism; it is too clearly described; it is full of warning and comfort both. "A new commandment write I unto you, which thing is true in him and in you; because the darkness is passing away and the true light already shineth" (1 John 2:8).

CHAPTER FOUR

THE CORRUPTION OF THE IMAGE

WHEN we treated the double aspect of the image of God, which constantly comes to the fore in the discussion of the image, we noted that theologians generally emphasized the image which was retained, the image in the wider sense, or the "*imago essentialis*," thereby meaning to say that man after the fall and indeed *in* his sinful turning away from God nevertheless remained man. Discussion was usually confined to this general statement and it was explicated so that Scripture could refer back in ringing admonitions to man's being created in the image of God. Thereupon some attention would be paid to that part of the image which was lost, *and* to its restoration in imitation of and conformity to God (*conformitas*). But this customary approach inevitably raises the question—what concretely is to be meant by this image which was retained, and whether this concept did not immediately introduce a dualism into the theology of the image. The unevenness of the terminology (wider, narrower; general, special; essential, existential) merely accentuates the urgency of this question; and all the more in that theologians, after noting the existence of a retained image, go on to speak of the "real" image, and a clear relation to the retained image is not always visible.[1]

Thus the idea of man remaining man has constantly come to the fore in dogmatic reflection, and even though we are not warranted in concluding a dual concept of the image, nevertheless we encounter here an important motif, which undoubtedly owes much of its influence to the Biblical witness to it. But the striking fact is that, even though man's being man is the continual interest

1. This applies, e.g., to various views of the Old Testament which emphasize that it knows nothing of a loss of the image. Cf. M.A. Beek, "De Vraag naar de Mens in de Godsdienst van Israel," *Vox Theologica* (1952), p. 71; also his "Anthropologische Notities bij het Oude Testament," *Anthropologische Verkenningen*, p. 38. Beek also says (p. 78) that man finds his destiny in the imitation of the example of God's acts.

of the whole of the Bible,[2] our attention is directed to what man
has done with and in his humanity, in his fall away from God,
which affected tremendously every nook and cranny of his being
and existence. And thus we encounter a theme which has constantly been under discussion in the doctrine of the image of God;
namely, to what extent man was corrupted by his apostasy and sin,
and whether this corruption should be viewed as total and radical,
or whether something was "left over" which must be seen as
an unmistakable limit to this corruption.

Some theologians made a distinction along these lines, that man's
nature was indeed totally corrupted, but not his essence; others are
not willing to go so far, even in their description of man's nature,
and they speak of a serious but not a total corruption. And when
we remember that the Reformation witnessed so emphatically to
total corruption, we must consider the question whether this
"totality" makes it impossible to accept any limits on corruption,
whether every idea of "remnants" of the image is not thereby
ruled out.

Such questions are all the more urgent since we encounter in
the same Reformation theology, and in the confessions, various
references to remnants, or traces, which cannot be denied to exist
in fallen man, traces and remnants of what originally had belonged
to the image of God. In this concept of "remnants," we encounter
an idea which has given rise to much discussion. While some
theologians saw no objection to speaking of remnants or seeds in
fallen man, others saw in such a concept a necessarily quantitative
idea which would inevitably lead to a relativizing of man's corruption. Would it not take away from sin its shocking and fearsome
effects? Would it not open the way for a evaluation of man which
would be unable to offer any real resistance to a humanistic or
semi-humanistic view of man? Does it not represent a last attempt
of man — manifesting itself in theology — to maintain the worth
of man against the judgment of God, an attempt to reaffirm the
worth of man by placing limits on the extent of his corruption?
Or, in summary: Are not "total corruption" and "remnants" contradictory concepts?

This question deserves serious consideration in an epoch in
which a new recognition of the evil in man appears to play an

2. E.g., Rom. 2:1, Mic. 6:8, and the many passages in which the difference
between God and *man* is emphasized; e.g., Ezek. 28:2, 9; Hos. 11:9, etc.

important role, and in which writers do not shrink from such terms as the "dehumanization" and "demonization" of man. True, such writers do not always intend these terms in their exact literal meaning — i.e., that man is no longer man and has become a demon — but the purpose is nevertheless to point to the loathsome, the horrible, the fearsome aspects of human behavior, through which the really human is threatened and unrecognizably mutilated in a frightful manner. Both terms suggest a change, a transformation, a perversion of the real human being which goes so far as "dehumanization."[3]

In such a denigration, various motives can play a role. Plessner speaks of tendencies in our epoch which "serve as an especially fertile soil for misanthropy," which can arise from feelings of "antipathy, bitterness, and all sorts of resentment. Men generalize, they no longer see the individual as despicable and an enemy, but rather mankind and human nature."[4] Or, behind the denigration may be disappointment in one's personal life; or again, the impression which man makes on the observer in a time of especial terror and egoism, the empirical phenomenology of evil, which the observer compresses into a metaphysical denigration. Thus there arise protests against romanticism and idealism, and a demand that man be unmasked, that his bourgeois morality be exposed as a superficiality, that he be seen without camouflage, even to the darkest depths of his heart.

In this context, we face the problem whether the Church, as over against such a denigration as a complete judgment, will put forth a plea for "remnants," for "seeds," of the original image of God. That a Voltaire should criticize a pessimistic view of man

3. The term is also used in another sense, as a dishonor which is done *to* man. The reference then is to the technization of life and to the rise of a mass society, through which man is dehumanized and becomes a robot; to the threat to the really human which is posed by the great power of super-personal economic and technical factors, through which man loses the status conformable with his dignity as human. Cf., e.g., F. L. Polak, *De Bedreiging der Menselijkheid in de Crisis der Moderne Cultuur, een Antwoord aan Virgil Gheorghiu* (1950, 3d ed.), pp. 67, 40: "modern mechanized culture threatens man," "technical civilization slays the living man of flesh and blood and prepares the modern sacrificial offering," "bureaucracy and statistics are replacing the stake and the auto-da-fé." Obviously the word "dehumanization" as used in the text refers rather to the evil of man, to a disqualification of moral worth which approaches "demonization."

4. H. Plessner, "Ueber die Menschenverachtung," *Offener Horizont, Festschrift für K. Jaspers* (1953), pp. 326, 321.

and call Pascal a misanthrope we can understand;[5] but what can the Church mean when it speaks of "remnants" and "vestiges" of the original image?

That is to say, is not any such context of ideas about "remnants" an unmistakable sign of what is, finally, an idealistic view of man? Is there not in the heart of man an ineradicable inclination towards making excuses for himself, at least to a relativizing of the divine judgment on guilty and depraved man? We see such tendencies, in various ways, arise also in the Church and in theology when the divine sentence on man is indeed pronounced, but nevertheless at the last moment attempts are made to withdraw from the radicalness of this guilt, and to set a limit on the extent of man's corruption. The purpose is not so much to excuse man as to return to a relative goodness in man which has remained despite the fall. It is true that in theory as well as in practice, an idealistic or semi-idealistic view of man emerges despite the acknowledgements of sin and imperfection, an interpretation of one's own essential nature and that of others which once more yields perspectives from man's point of view.

We can thus speak of a series of problems arising around the concept of "remnants," and we might well reckon with these before we go on and concern ourselves with the much-discussed use of the idea of "remnants" in the confessions and theology of the Reformation.

We can well illustrate the sort of problems which arise by considering the well-known views of Immanuel Kant regarding the "radical evil" in man. It has often been remarked that Kant appears here to come close to the Reformation confession of man's total corruption, which likewise emphasizes the radical nature of the evil in man, and locates its seat not in the periphery but in the very root, radix, of man's existence.

Kant's view on the radical nature of evil in man plays an important role in his philosophy. He held that man was evil *by nature* and had a corrupt "inclination towards evil."[6] Kant did not agree with "various philosophers" who held to the essential goodness of human nature. Evil in man is radical, so much so that it cannot be overcome by human power. It is a "perversion of the heart,"

5. Cf. E. Cassirer, *Die Philosophie der Aufklärung* (1932), pp. 192ff.; Voltaire "took up Pascal's challenge, and declared himself willing to fight for the cause of humanity against this 'sublime misanthrope.' "
6. Kant, *Die Religion innerhalb der Grenzen der bloszen Vernunft* (Reclam-Universität Bibliothek; 1793), pp. 35-38, 49-55.

a "congenital guilt." This radicality goes so deep that it is useless to expect any salvation from a gradual improvement in man. There is only one way, one possibility; a "revolution in the disposition of man." "A new man can emerge only through a sort of re-birth, a new creation and a transformation of the heart," he says, referring to John 3:5 and Gen. 1:2. Kant thus, in passing, mentions the Biblical idea of rebirth, but goes on to ask how then it would be possible for man to "bring this revolution to pass through his own powers and become a good man through himself." In answering this question, Kant suddenly sets a limit on the radicality of evil. For Kant is of the opinion that such a revolution is necessary and *therefore* must be possible for man to accomplish. It *is* possible through a "unique unalterable decision" in which the tendency of the heart is transformed. There is a way from the *"Sollen,"* the moral law, to the ability to conform to it. "When the moral law commands, we are obliged to be better men, and it follows that we must, and thus that we can."

Man may be corrupt to his very depths, says Kant, but *out of these depths,* too, must come the free act of revolution. Though under the power of radical and far-reaching evil, man must hope to accomplish this revolution through his own powers. In the depths of freedom lies our last unsearchable reserve. Kant indeed does not deny the help of a higher power, but this *Mitwirkung* does not alter the human character of the redeeming revolutionary act of freedom, and Kant in this connection sets himself against the idea that this transformation is not possible for *us* to accomplish: "God can make better men without having to add anything more to them." Man can hope for higher help only "when he has made use of the original tendency towards good."

We can thus — regardless of how this is all worked out further — speak of a concept of "remnants" in Kant, a concept of clearly affirmed idealistic character. The radicality of evil does not have as an unsuspected and wonderful correlate the radicality of divine salvation, but man's *own* deed, his own revolution — the idealistic interpretation of man's potentiality: It is this remnant — this intelligible freedom — which is not annihilated and which therefore can open new perspectives for man. In Kant's idea of the radicality of evil, we have a view in which the "remnant" relativizes the radicality and finally makes it less fearful and less radical. For this radical evil evidently does not pertain to the root, the radix, of human existence. For in the radix lies the possibility of a "revolution" in man's disposition, which remains *in spite of* and indeed *in* man's corruption. When Kant proposed his outlook on the radicality of evil in 1793, Goethe accused him of having bespotted and smeared his philosophical cloak with the stain of radical evil; Goethe appears to have suspected Kant of a radical break with humanism and idealism.[7] This is an interpretation which finds no support in Kant's own analysis of the problem.[8] For the radicality of evil is no sooner pointed to than it becomes speedily relativized. And the treatment of the concept of "remnant" in Kant is illustrative of the danger of sooner or later turning from an acknowledgement of evil back to some more basic remnant or human potentiality.

Thus we confront in this conception a typical illustration of a generally occurring reduction or simplification, which places a limit on the extent of corruption; and there is every reason for us to be conscious of the nature of this simplification, which has played such an important role, not only in humanism but also in Christian theology.[9]

This is especially necessary when we encounter a series of problems, a dialectic, regarding the "remnants" of the image, in the milieu of the theology of the Reformers. In general, there was not much attention paid to this point by Roman Catholics and humanists during the time of the Reformation (nor indeed since); the Reformation was generally accused of having a pessimistic view of man, of holding a view of *total* corruption which threatened man's being man.[10] There was, it is true, a consciousness that the

7. Cf. K. Jaspers, "Das radikal Böse bei Kant," *Rechenschaft und Ausblick* (1951), p. 90, and "Goethe's Menschlichkeit," pp. 50ff. He says, "Goethe, in contrast to Kant, stands in the line of such thinkers as Plotinus, Nicholas of Cusa, Spinoza and Hegel, for whom evil is nothing."
8. Cf. Kant's criticism of theological and philosophical chiliasm (*op. cit.*, p. 34). Cf. T. Hoekstra, *Immanente Kritik zur Kantischen Religionsphilosophie* (1906), p. 38. He says, "Kant paints the evil in the world with Schopenhauerian colors."
9. This is even more so because the discussion of "remnants" is often *combined* with the doctrine of the image of God. Cf. G. J. Heering, *Geloof en Openbaring* (1937), I, pp. 295ff. In his view of the image, he reminds us of what is often overlooked, that according to Calvin the image is not wholly darkened, and that the "remnants" of the image is the point of contact for grace. Apart from that, Heering attacks the one-sided hamartiological anthropology of the Reformers, and feels that at issue is the image: "in the doctrine of the image of God, the theological roads separate."
10. Such criticism from Roman Catholics was often in connection with a criticism of Augustine's too somber view of man.

praises of the worth of man had often been sung too exuberantly,[11] and that there could be no room for such an attitude in the Church, which lived from grace; but it was held nevertheless that the preaching of divine grace could not and should not lead to a belief in total corruption.

Actually, however, the Reformation's view of man cannot be summarized so simply, as it often was by Catholics and humanists. For we encounter its view of man in the immediate context of the confession of corruption, along with references to "remnants" of the original image.

It is an important question, then, whether if we honestly analyze this concept, we can discover a parallel with the concept of Kant, who likewise strongly emphasized the radicality of evil, but who then finally could not escape the attraction of a simplifying limitation which relativized this radicality. It can be said, of course, that this parallel, when viewed in the total context of the Reformation beliefs, is a priori unlikely; but even so, there is every reason to concern ourselves with the idea of "remnants" as found in the Reformation confessions.

Especially important is Article 14 of the Belgic Confession, which deals with man, created after God's image and likeness, turning to sin of his own will, and thus "having his whole nature corrupted" ("totamque naturam suam corrumpit"). In this confession, nearly all of the New Testament descriptions are brought forward; man is dead, cursed, cut off from God, penalized with spiritual and bodily death, nothing more than a slave to sin, in enmity against God; the *natural* man. But in this context the matter is put thus: man is godless, distorted, and corrupt in all his ways, and has lost all the wonderful gifts which he received from God, and he has retained only small remnants (*vestigia*) of them; these are, however, enough to deprive him of all guiltlessness, since that which was light has been turned to darkness. The noteworthy thing in this article of the Confession is that "remnants" are spoken of in a context which makes it clear that they do not make the situation of man less serious, or relativize total corruption, for closely related is the serious charge that therefore no man can plead innocence, for *all* that is light in us has been turned to darkness (cf. John 1:5).

11. Cf. *Giovanni Pico della Mirandola über 'Die Würdigkeit des Menschen'* (1940), and H. W. Russel's introductory remarks, pp. 7-8. For this type of thinking in connection with the uniqueness of man, see B. Groethuysen, *Philosophische Anthropologie*, pp. 111ff.

Thus reference to the "remnants"[12] does not relativize corruption, but underscores its extent, and places corruption in the light of these "remnants" to emphasize its darkness; while the mention of man's inexcusability is an unmistakable reference to Romans 1:20-21, where the heathen are spoken of as inexcusable, since their unwise hearts became darkened.

The Canons of Dort (III, 4) also speak of man's creation in God's image in the sense of conformity to God (conformitas cum Deo); possessing true and blessed knowledge of the Creator in will and heart, righteousness, purity in all his inclinations, complete holiness. Through sin, man robbed himself of all these wonderful gifts and replaced them with blindness, fearful darkness, vanity and perversity of judgment in his understanding, evil and disobedience in will and heart, impurity in all his inclinations. To this is added, however, that man after the Fall kept "some light of nature" through which he retains some knowledge of God and of natural things, and of the distinction between honorable and dishonorable, and some practice of virtue and external good. (Cf. Art. IX of the Gallic Confession.)

This appears to be a more positive description of the "remnants" than we find in the Belgic Confession; but again there is a qualification. We read not only that this light of man does not lead to saving knowledge of God and to conversion, but also, and especially, that man does not use this light correctly even in natural things and civil affairs, and indeed in various ways stains and suppresses this light, and in so doing takes away all his innocence before God. (A parallel is drawn between this light of nature and the Decalogue; the law, too, brings no power to escape from the power of sin, and leaves man under the curse.) There is an even clearer reference to Romans 1:18 here, since not only culpability but "suppressing" in unrighteousness is expressly mentioned.

We can say, in summary, that both the Belgic Confession and the Canons of Dort acknowledge that something is retained of the image (vestiges of gifts, some light of nature), but that at the same time both make clear that corruption manifests its *total* character precisely in relation to these "remnants." It is, moreover, striking that in other confessions total corruption is professed with no contextual mention of "remnants" or vestiges of the image. This fact would be inexplicable if the purpose of the idea of "remnants" was to relativize the totality of corruption. But if the

---

12. Cf. the French text in J. N. Bakhuizen van den Brink, *De Nederlandse Belijdenis Geschriften* (1940), p. 84: ". . . et ne luy est demeuré de reste sinon des petites traces d'iceux."

purpose is not to limit the extent of corruption, but to point to some other aspect of fallen man, then it is understandable that a confession in dealing with man's fall in other contexts would not mention these "remnants"; as is the case with the Heidelberg Catechism, which says (Q. 5-8) with no further qualification that man is prone by nature to hate God and his neighbor, and is wholly incapable of any good and inclined to every evil. Such words can be paralleled from many other confessions, and indeed it even appears sometimes that the concept of "remnants" is opposed in order to emphasize the totality of corruption.[13]

In the light of all this we can begin to obtain some insight into the unique nature of the series of problems surrounding the concept of "remnants." Above all it is clear that the confessions, when speaking of "remnants" or "seeds," are not referring to some last reserve in man, some untouched and untouchable "part" of man which has escaped the power of sin and corruption. To the question of the meaning of the concept of "remnants" as used in the confessions only one answer is possible: it is used to express the conviction that man through sin became wholly corrupt in his disobedience and enmity, his rebellion and alienation; but that *in* this turning away from God he still remained man and did not escape his relationship to God nor the endowments still bestowed on him. It is clear that the confessions did not attempt to give a philosophically formulated solution of the problem of man's concrete being. They speak of a light of nature, of some distinguishing between good and bad, of some cultivation of virtue and outward discipline. But this does not make man more innocent before God; on the contrary, it witnesses all the more to his guilt, since man, with all his endowments and with the surrounding light of nature, still clutches a totally apostate way of life, which stamps and defines fallen man in the total act of his whole life. Hence the appeal to

13. Thus, the Scottish Confession of 1560: the image in man *"penitus obliterata fuit"*; the Anglican Articles: "depraved nature"; the Westminster Confession: "wholly defiled," "wholly inclined to all evil"; the Later Helvetic Confession: "wholly disposed to evil," "able of themselves to do no good." See Müller, *Bekenntnis Schriften,* pp. 250, 508, 557, 178, 179. For opposition to an idea of "remnants," cf. the Gallic Confession: man is "wholly corrupt" and "has lost all his integrity, with no residue remaining." But here too, there is mention of "some distinguishing between good and evil"; but "that which he has of light is converted to darkness." Cf. also the Hungarian Confession, which speaks of the corruption of the whole man (Art. 13), but goes on (Art. 14) to say that he retains enough light to make him inexcusable. See Müller, op. cit., pp. 224, 380. Cf. also Polman, *Onze Nederlandse Geloofsbelijdenis,* II, 133.

John 1:5 and Romans 1. The "endowments," the "knowledge" and the "light of nature" are involved and included in man's apostasy. Man acts as apostate and inimical to God not without these endowments but with them. And thus the concept of "remnants" in the confessions does not connote a quantitative reduction of the power of sin, or an only partial corruption, which would correspond with a partial salvation, but rather an activity in and with these endowments; it connotes darkness against light. Man's life is not "relatively" good, so that we can fall back, with one or another subtle distinction, on man's essence as contrasted to his nature. For it is exactly man himself, in the fullness of his whole life, who with all his endowments, is involved in this alienation from God. And although the term "remnants" might lead to some misunderstanding, this should not hinder us from realizing its motivation which, in the confessions at least, is clear and apparent. And we might posit that the contemporary criticism of "solutions" which would "solve" by saying "part corrupt, part not" (*teils-teils-Lösung*) is justified; but that does not touch the confessions in their deepest meaning, since the accusation, that man is inexcusable, by which man is unmasked, too clearly implies the opposite.

It is understandable that difficulties have constantly arisen in connection with the use of "remnants," since this term always arouses associations of some sort of quantitative reduction of the extent of corruption which would make it peripheral and partial rather than basic and total. Not only is the term so used in ordinary speech, but also in Scripture, which in connection with Israel, speaks of a "remainder" or "remnant" in the judgment of God, implying that His judgment is not total (cf. Isa. 1:9, 4:3; Amos 3:12, 7:2). It is thus understandable that also in the doctrine of image "remnant" and "totality" are simply opposed as contraries. But however much the usage of the word may have led to this misunderstanding, it should be stated that the confessions clearly use the term in quite another way, and do not have a meaning of a simple "part corrupt, part not," a simple quantitative reduction. This is so clear from the context in which the confessions use the term that Gerstenmaier, in spite of his criticism of the "partly, partly" approach, writes that the concern which the idea of "remnant" represents cannot be given up,[14] though he rightly adds that

14. E. Gerstenmaier, *Die Kirche und die Schöpfung* (1938), p. 182. Cf. F. K. Schumann, *Imago Dei* (1932), p. 172, on the "expansion of the doctrine of the image," which in any event is not a semi-Pelagian weakening of the doctrine of original sin, since the total corruption of man

THE CORRUPTION OF THE IMAGE129

we neither can or may lift a part of man out of its relation with
sin, nor reduce the effect of sin through a distinction between
what is and what is not corrupted, through a distinction between
formal and material image.[15] It becomes possible to give full value
to and evaluate correctly the main themes of the Reformation's
doctrine of man only when we realize that Reformed theologians
did not isolate the concept of "remnants" of the image, but rather
held that these were included and involved in man's responding
to God by rebellion and alienation. Just as Pascal did not place
the greatness and misery of man next to each other as isolated
entities mutually limiting each other, so also the confessions did
not delimit the "remnants" of the image over against the effect of
corruption, but clearly held that it was precisely man's humanness
in his relation to God which made the seriousness of his guilt fully
manifest.

Now that we have examined the dangers inherent in the concept
of "remnants" and have seen the motive of the confessions in
employing this term, which in isolated form is an insufficient
one,[16] we can fruitfully turn our attention to the bitter struggle
which was carried on in the Lutheran church in connection with
total corruption, and in which we encounter a similar set of
problems. Total corruption was already emphasized strongly by
Luther; it forms the background of his fight with Erasmus over

---

continues to be confessed. Cf. E. Brunner, *Der Mensch in Widerspruch*,
p. 86. He also acknowledges that the Calvinistic use of "remnants" meant
to relate *humanitas* and *imago,* though he sees the term itself as an
illegitimate one, and sees here the point at which the Enlightenment
was able to attack and break through the position of the Reformation.
So too Gerstenmaier: "this small remnant became the bearer of great
things." It can hardly be denied, if we examine history, that there
is reason for caution.

15. Bachmann, *Commentaar*, p. 143. He rightly criticizes Brunner's distinction
between the formal and material image, remarking that it is illegitimate
from being-a-Person to abstract a sort of neutral thing (being-a-Subject),
which as formal decision-making lies above the antithesis between good
and evil and functions in both good and bad acts. Cf. Gerstenmaier,
op. cit., p. 182ff.

16. We encounter in Calvin the same motifs as in the confessions, with a
strong emphasis on the fact that the "remnants" do not relativize corruption. See his *Commentary* on Gen. 5:5 and 1:26: some remnants remain,
but they are so vitiated and mutilated that they are practically obliterated.
This should be remembered in reading, e.g., his comments on Ps. 8:5,
"*portio imaginis.*" Cf. A. D. R. Polman, *Onze Nederlandsche Geloofsbelijdenis*, II, pp. 103-106; and T. F. Torrance, *Calvin's Doctrine of
Man* (1940), pp. 83ff.

the freedom or enslavement of the will. In the Augustana Confession we see fallen man portrayed as lustful, untrustworthy, and without fear of God, while the Formula of Concord sharply sketches a radical and total corruption; just as in the Reformed confessions, we encounter words such as "complete" and "wholly" corrupt.[17]

In this connection, it is especially instructive to see how an especially bitter strife was waged in the Lutheran church on the nature and extent of corruption, a conflict which is especially associated with the name of Flacius, who wanted to retain a strong emphasis on the seriousness and radical character of total corruption in the face of a rising synergism. The struggle is of special interest to us because it was concerned with the central question of man's humanity *in* his sinfulness.

When the synergist Strigell taught that conversion did not mean a divine compulsion or a magical overpowering of man's will and that man cannot remain passive in the process but must work with God, Flacius replied that only after conversion can there be any possibility of such cooperation; it would be impossible and unthinkable before conversion, since man is wholly corrupt, dead in sin and evil, and thus life can come only from the divine act.

Flacius was motivated by the desire to remain in the Lutheran line with its emphasis on the sovereignty of grace, but the ways in which Flacius sought to strengthen his position gave rise to opposition. From the belief in total corruption, he soon came to the thesis that the image of God in man was transformed into the image of the devil, and he appealed to Scriptural references that speak of man's "stony" heart, from which nothing could be expected before God changed it to a heart of flesh (cf. Ezek. 11:19, 36:26). Sin has had such a distorting effect that we cannot describe it merely as a privation; it is, rather, an actual destructive power, a corruption. The original image as conformity with God, as original justice, was so completely and radically lost that Flacius could not be satisfied with describing sin as an "accident" of man's condition; he wanted to say that man had become essentially corrupt. Any "remnants" he retained could not change the situation. The term "accident," said Flacius, is far too weak to describe sin. It gives the impression that only the periphery of men's being was affected by sin, not his essence, while actually sin had touched and perverted man's essence; not his accidental characteristics, but his essence, his substance.

This passionate defense of the belief in total corruption by Flacius was thus concentrated in his emphasis on the corruption of

17. See, for example, Müller, *op. cit.,* p. 576.

man's human essence, his being-human, and it is indeed no wonder
that such a bitter struggle was waged around this matter.[18]

Though Flacius did not intend to uphold a Manichean sort of
psychic metamorphosis, he nevertheless, in his attack on the term
"accident," spoke of sin as man's essence, and he spoke of a transformation. It was difficult for his opponents to see how any meaning could then be given to fallen man's "human-ness." Strigell[19]
had a fairly easy time in replying to Flacius that man's human
nature was not destroyed by sin, nor was its way of acting (modus
agendi). But from this he then concluded that the corruption of
sin in man was merely an "accident," an accidental change. Man
remained man, and Strigell could say that his concern was with the
"relative integrity of man's essence and its powers." There was
indeed a tremendous change caused by sin, but through God's grace
the same man who had turned away from God could again serve
Him — and at this point one might for a moment receive the impression that Flacius and Strigell were both concerned to confess
the reality of corruption, and that their differences were merely
terminological. But on closer examination, this does not appear to
be the case. A real problem is being discussed, against the background of the arguments about "substance" and "accident." This
is evident not only from the bitterness of the struggle — Flacius
lost his position as leading Lutheran theologian and was by posterity
regarded as heretical in a certain sense — but also from the nature
of the problem itself. In any event, we should not forget that since
Melanchthon, synergism (the cooperation of man with God) had
again begun to play a role in Lutheran theology, and that Flacius
had seen the danger and fought against it. The Lutheran church
itself realized the seriousness of the controversy between Flacius
and Strigell, which led to a noteworthy statement on the matter
in the Formula of Concord.[20] Total corruption was expressly stated
and defended against those who would only speak of a weakening
of our nature and who taught that not all spiritual good was lost
in the Fall. The Formula denied that man retained anything good,
"no matter how small, little, and insignificant this might be"; e.g.,
man did not have the power to begin by himself any change in

18. See on Flacius especially L. Haikola, Gesetz und Evangelium bei Matthias
   Flacius Illyricus (Lund, 1952), pp. 111ff. Cf. also H. E. Weber,
   Reformation, Orthodoxie und Rationalismus, I, 2 (1940); G. Moldaenke,
   Schriftverständnis und Schriftdeutung im Zeitalter der Reformation, I,
   Matthias Flacius Illyricus (1936).
19. Haikola, op. cit., p. 111.
20. Müller, op. cit., pp. 578-583.

spiritual things. But the Formula also took a position against the
Manichean error, as if sin was something essential in man,
infused by the devil into our nature and mixed with it; the Fall
did not result in sin "coming into our nature, as the Manicheans
ravingly say, as if Satan created or made something essentially evil
and mixed it with our nature."

Human nature is indeed corrupt in all its powers, but there
is no transformation into another substance. This means, then,
that the Formula rejected the "part this, part that" solution, and
still protested against the annihilation of man's nature. The Epitome,
also, stresses that sin is not "essential and substantial," since the devil
cannot create a new substance, but only pervert those which
already exist.[21]

The terms "substance" and "accident" represent the dilemma
which was at the core of the conflict. Nor were the framers of the
Formula insensitive to the fact that to have formulated the conflict
in these terms was hardly to have solved it. The Formula points
out that the terms are not Scriptural and that -- since they are
not known to the ordinary man -- they might better be avoided
in preaching. But evidently it is difficult to escape using the
terms, since they can be used with precision and without misunderstanding in the schools, scholastically, to distinguish what
is essential to man from what is joined to him by accident
(*per accidens*). The terms continued to be used in the controversy,
so that on the one hand total corruption might be affirmed,
and on the other hand all substantializing of sin rejected. The
Formula takes pains to avoid any chance of misunderstanding by
denying that sin is only something superficial or affects only the
characteristics possessed by man, man's nature meanwhile retaining
something of its original goodness and integrity.

Thus the Formula, too, rejects any idea that sin is something
"accidental" if by that is meant that sin is something peripheral
and outward and relative, for sin affects man in all of his existence,
and in the depths of his nature.

We might now raise the question whether from such a position
an attack on Flacius could still be made, for he was concerned
precisely with attacking the idea that sin is "accidental." Did not
Flacius intend exactly what the Formula expresses when it rejects
the idea that sin is accidental?

In answer to this question, it must be said that the Formula
is also directed against the position of Flacius. Sin has indeed

21. Müller, *op. cit.*, pp. 522-523.

corrupted the whole of man's nature so that *we* in our corrupted nature can no longer distinguish between our "nature" and "original sin"; nevertheless we must distinguish between man's nature as created by God — in which original sin now dwells, — and original sin itself.

Further, Scripture even says that man's nature after the Fall is still the "work and creature of God" (see Deut. 32:6; Isa. 45:11, 54:5, 64:8; Acts 17:25; Rev. 4:11; Job 10:8-12; Ps. 139:14-16). God remains the Creator, and fallen man is not simply sin itself. Otherwise God would be the Creator of sin. Furthermore, Christ has partaken of our nature, which would not be possible if our nature was *essentially* sinful. Thus there is a difference between human nature and sin, and we can say with Augustine that original sin is not man's nature itself, but "accidental" (*accidens vitium in natura*). An accident, but such an accident that it leaves nothing actually good in any inner or outer power of man. This accident produces man's spiritual death, and therefore leaves no room for our minimizing the effect of corruption. But the work of God (our real nature) and that of the devil remain distinct from each other.

There can therefore be no doubt as to the intention of the Formula. *Its* use of the term "accident" is not to be interpreted in a synergistic sense. When Flacius encountered the term "accident," he saw in it only the superficial, the external, the relative, so that for him it implied that corruption could not be total. Moreover, it was clear that theologians on the synergistic side could easily use the term in order in some measure to lessen the mystery and miracle of conversion. So the struggle continued to be waged, without either side giving serious consideration to the fact that neither could reach full clarity as long as they used the terms "substance" and "accident."[22] For the term "substance" was surely unsuited to point to the far-reaching consequences of sin, and the term "accident" remained point of entry for synergism, despite all good intentions, especially those of the Formula of Concord.[23] As

22. Cf., e.g., what the Formula says on these terms, and on the complaint of Flacius that these were terms which Strigell had used (Haikola, *op. cit.*, p. 113); he added, however, that he himself was therefore also compelled to employ the term "substance."
23. Cf. H. Thielicke, *Theologische Ethik* (1951), I, 341. He remarks that Flacius indeed protested against the ontology of Strigell, but did this within the limits of the same schema: "protesting against the schema, he then inconsistently sought to make his ideas prevail within the limits of this schema."

Gerstenmaier says, the hope that by resorting to the scholastic terms "substance" and "accident," the Formula of Concord might succeed in disposing of the problem, was vain.[24]

At bottom, the problem when approached in this way was insoluble, since in the description of man's essence, his relation to God was left completely out of account. The argument presupposed man as a substance in himself, and it was *this* substance which Flacius held to be changed, and which Strigell said remained unchanged and intact as the modality of man's being. The relation of man to God remained outside the dilemma, and this is the reason that neither side could convince the other. In terms of this background, of man in himself isolated, as a substance, Flacius would have to see in Strigell's use of "accident" a denial of corruption, while Strigell naturally saw Flacius' idea of substantial transformation an attack on the mode of man's being man.

If we keep in mind this background, which made a resolution of the conflict impossible, we can also appreciate various motifs in the struggle, although they could not come to full expression against this background. Though the problem can not be settled by distinguishing between "essence" and "nature," or between "substance" and "accident," we can still appreciate the warning of the Formula of Concord against any substantializing of sin. And on the other hand, we can agree that the making of a distinction between sin and man as created by God, does not necessarily lead towards a relativizing of sin. Such a distinction can indeed be used illegitimately, as implying a quantitative reduction, but it is possible that protests against formulations such as Flacius' "horrible metamorphosis" are meant to protest against the danger of identifying man and sin, the danger of speaking of man, strictly taken, as "demonized" and "dehumanized." For such formulations may appear to point with special seriousness to the terrible effect of sin in the radical attack on and change in man's nature, his being, as resulting in a terrifying metamorphosis, so that man now portrays an image other than that of his Creator.[25] But involved in such formulations is the acute danger that we do not sufficiently reckon with fallen man's relation to God, with the fact that his humanness

24. Gerstenmaier, *op. cit.*, p. 130.
25. Cf. Weber, *op. cit.*, I, 2, 8. He sees the teaching of Flacius as a "forerunner of contemporary existential philosophy or theology," and then adds that it is merely "an application of the ideas of the Reformation." This latter remark strikes us as incorrect, since the Reformation denigration of man's worth is of an entirely different sort than that which occurs in existentialism."

is preserved, and he can not escape from this relationship to God into an area beyond humanness and responsibility.

That this truth was obscured by the dilemma of "substance" and "accident" does not alter the fact that the reason for distinguishing between, rather than identifying, man and sin, was not to excuse man or to relieve him of guilt, but to emphasize that man stands and remains standing in his human responsibility and in his human guilt over against God. This implies also that sin has no creative character and implies further that sin cannot "transubstantiate" man. Such statements do not at all imply that only the accidental characteristics of man, and not his nature or substance, were affected by sin; but only that we can never speak about man by himself and apart from his relation to God without falling into abstractions. We can rise above the dilemma of "substance" and "accident" only when we see man's nature, his being man, in his inescapable relation to God, which is the secret of his being-man. Only then can we avoid controversy and problems about "reducing the amount of evil," which always arise from a "part evil, part not" approach, an approach which is always accompanied by a relativizing of sin.[26] Such a reduction is indeed radically rejected by the Church in its confession of original sin; there is no limit or boundary within human nature beyond which we can find some last human reserve untouched by sin; it is man himself who is totally corrupt. Therein lies the worth of what Strigell called Flacius' "senseless protest" against the term "accident," which certainly is a term involving some danger, and one which, given the terminological formulation which both men accepted, cannot sharply be distinguished from an idea of reduction. But a warning against every attempt to find in fallen man some "remnant" which can escape the divine indictment should never minimize the reality of man's being human *in* his being sinner; something which in the eyes of God does not relativize sin, but emphasizes it.

The struggle that raged around the ideas of Flacius was not without drama. Once Flacius had gotten into the "substance-

---

26. Evidently this was the great danger Flacius envisaged, and rightly. He wished to emphasize that the whole man, man as human, was corrupted by sin, and that the idea of the reality of this "existential" guilt might be threatened by shifting from sin as "substance" to sin as (only) "accident," thus illegitimately emphasizing the distinction between man's nature and sin. Cf. Weber, *op. cit.*, pp. 8-9. For a balanced evaluation of both Flacius and the Formula, see Karl Barth, *K.D.* III, 2, 29ff.; IV, 1, 535.

accident" dilemma, he was accused of Manichaeism[27] and replied by accusing his opponents of violating the ninth commandment. This defense was understandable. He wanted to emphasize, as over against the idea of sin as "accident," the bottomless depth of the Fall as corruption and death, and to warn against any doctrine of sin which would make use of such concepts as privation (*privatio*), as in the Middle Ages, and in which man could still remain essentially man and keep his natural moral goodness even though losing some accidental characteristics (the *donum superadditum* of the image). Against such ideas, he posited the whole man as sinner to the very depths of his being, and cited Luther's "*totus homo peccator.*" But in this passionate defense, he made it impossible to follow out that other motif which plays a role in the Belgic Confession and the Canons of Dort — that we can speak of man's being man in his guilt, without necessarily involving ourselves in a reductive approach. In this possibility, which rules out all abstract views of man, lies the one way out of the conflict about "remnants" or "vestiges." And the conflict about Flacius' ideas makes it unmistakably clear how insoluble the problem is as long as attention is directed to man in himself, and as long as his relation to God becomes a mere *donum superadditum* which can be temporarily ignored in the discussion of man's corruption.

•   Let the extensiveness of our treatment of Flacius[28] be taken as an indication of the importance of the questions that cluster about the very basic belief of the Reformation concerning the totality of corruption. We should be warned by the controversy against an abstract anthropology, and also against the danger of humanizing the idea of "remnants." We must always measure every discussion of "remnants" against one standard — in what context and with what aim is the discussion carried on; that is, whether it is an attempt to escape from "*totus homo peccator*" (man as completely sinful) to

---

27. According to Frank in *Theologie der Konkordienformel*, pp. 1, 2, 64, the similarity was "*augenfällig*" (obvious) , since Augustine accused precisely the Manicheans that they did not consider sin as an *accidens vitium.* Cf. Haikola, *op. cit.*, pp. 155f.

28. Cf. Bavinck, *Gereformeerde Dogmatiek*, III, 76-77; IV, 47-48 on Flacius. He feels that Lutheran theologians, as over against Rome, sometimes expressed themselves too strongly regarding corruption. Bavinck refers to Luther's "*peccatum essentiale et essentia hominis.*" This was all perhaps well intentioned, but was nevertheless open to serious misunderstanding, and Calvinist theologians have in Bavinck's judgment guarded against such strong expressions. The expressions are not defensible, but "Luther's opponents have nevertheless taken them too literally."

some untouched human reserve, or whether the aim is to stress the seriousness of fallen man's humanity in the sight of God, his humanness *while* he is a sinner, so that his innocence is not vindicated, but rather is the force of the divine indictment.

It is understandable that later Lutheran theologians attempted to rise above the earlier dilemmas. And since we ourselves are of the opinion that the problem cannot be solved within the "substance-accident" framework, it is interesting to examine how it is posed today. One of the most instructive attempts to rise above the dilemma is undoubtedly that of Helmut Thielicke, who attempted to get at the real meaning of the Flacian controversy. The stumbling block in the controversy was, says Thielicke,[29] the use of ontological categories in dealing with the doctrine of the image. Over against this erroneous approach, he suggests personalism as the only solution, and it is important to examine whether this position perhaps affords a way out of the dilemma.

The basic point of the Reformation's controversy with Rome lay, says Thielicke, in "its opposition to an ontological framework." The Scholastics were concerned with the ontological status of man, first in his *status integritatis* and later in his fallen state. The Reformation (i.e., Luther) broke through this ontological approach and posited the image of God as a relation. Sin thus becomes not an abolition or a weakening of the original image relationship, but rather a shifting to a negative mode of that relation. This personalistic approach to the image of God actually did not long remain dominant in Reformation thought, however. Attention was once more directed to man's ontological characteristics, and soon an orthodox ontologism, a coordinate system of ontic structure, emerged. The ontology of man's original state naturally implied that man's fallen state also be treated ontologically, i.e., as a giving up of the original ontological characteristics of man. But this attempt to work out the doctrine of the Reformation with Scholastic tools brought on catastrophe. It produced a dramatic encounter of outlooks, a deadly dilemma, as is shown especially in the conflict between Flacius and Strigell. Flacius placed the *"corruptio essentialis"* of Luther in the ontological being of man, and so combined Reformation doctrine with an ontological view of the image; he transferred the radicalism of the Lutheran teaching on sin to an ontological terrain. He allowed himself to be forced by Strigell to carry on the struggle in this terrain, and thus came to

29. H. Thielicke, *Theologische Ethik*, I, 337-350.

an impossible combination of personal and ontological approaches to the image. Later Lutheran theologians — e.g., Gerhard — used the same ontological background to arrive at a concept of "remnants."

And thus the use of an ontological approach, continues Thielicke, again results in a reductive process, no longer one with respect to nature and supernatural, but within man's nature. The image of God is reduced, and some remnant is left over. Thus an ontological approach threatens Luther's personalistic insight into the meaning of the image; the ontological characteristics of man are discussed apart from his relation to God; and this is completely opposed to Luther's criticism of such an approach, as when he remarked that if the image was merely a matter of ontological characteristics, the devil too could be called the image of God, since he surely has all the characteristics of a "rational animal."

It is noteworthy that Thielicke holds that the image does have an ontological element, and that there can indeed be no doubt on that point; but fallen man is not defined by this element. On the contrary, his characterization is received from "the other" of God's grace, and can be described only in personalistic categories. Any approach which tries to go beyond this one defining characteristic of man and raises questions about the "ontological substratum of the ego" is doomed to failure. For such questions once again treat man in himself, as isolated, and imply some sort of substratum which remains the same, which is "unaffected by man's communion with God and the dissolution thereof, and which must therefore be considered essentially neutral." Though Thielicke does not wish to neglect the ontological structure of the image,[30] he evidently does recognize a tension between the purely personal relation in the image and its ontic qualification. "If we attempt to see man in the aspect of his relation to God, then the ontical characteristics become blurred; and conversely if we try to see man in his ontical characteristics, then his essence, his existence in a relation to God, becomes blurred. It is impossible to see both at once."

Here, then, we encounter a personalistic approach to the image which endeavors to rise above the dilemmas of the earlier Lutheran

---

30. Cf. Thielicke, "Die Subjekthaftigkeit des Menschen. Eine Studie zu einem Hauptproblem der Imago-Dei-Lehre," *Das Menschenbild im Lichte des Evangeliums. Festschrift E. Brunner* (1950), pp. 72ff. There is indeed an ontological structure to the image, but the question is whether we should emphasize it when there are more important characteristics which demand our attention. Thus, not a denial of the ontological structure, but rather putting it in its correct place in the order of our theological knowledge.

discussions, and in order to do this avoids all so-called "neutral ontology." Thielicke tries to ground his view on Ephesians 2:1-7, where "nature" and "grace" are spoken of; not a "neutral" nature however, not an "ethically neutral substratum of the ego," but a nature qualified by the Fall. Thielicke in citing Ephesians 2:3 evidently wishes to protest against any abstraction or neutralization of man's nature as an independent property, as man in himself, regardless of his relation to God.

It cannot be denied that the dangers which Thielicke is trying to avoid are real. He rightly wishes to avoid any abstracting of man from his relation to God. But in his very reaction he himself becomes entangled in a new dilemma. His personalism is directed against ontology because to his way of thinking the ontological approach always presupposes an interest solely in man in himself. And, indeed, if this were always presupposed by an ontological approach, all ontological thinking would pose a threat to the indissoluble relation between man and God. It should be clear, however, that such abstraction is not necessarily presupposed by the ontological approach. And we certainly cannot play off the "relational" against the "ontological," as though they were mutually exclusive. Thielicke claims to have discovered in the Reformers a view which saw the image exclusively as a relation, and this then forms the basis for his own personalism. But it is actually impossible to describe the image of God as a relation. It is one thing to say that the relation to God is of the essence of the image, but quite another to make the image itself consist merely of a relation. This latter approach would again pose a dilemma, this time between "relation" and "reality"; while the Reformation view is characterized by its idea that the reality and actuality of man's nature come to expression precisely in the relation to God.[31] It is not at all clear why the ontological characteristics of man necessarily become "blurred" when we consider man in his relation to God. It would seem more accurate to say that the full actuality of man's nature becomes visible *in* this relation, since in dealing with the image of God we are dealing with man in the fullness of his nature in temporal reality. Thus a personalistic approach will not provide us with an escape from the earlier dilemmas. The relation of man to God is indeed one which defines man's essence, but man's real being

31. Cf. J. Waterink, *De Mens als religieus Wezen en de hedendaagse Psychologie* (1954), concerning man's being religious, "created in relation," p. 21. Cf. the discussion of man in connection with the question whether the image of God is an *additum*, added to man's being (p. 15) and his rejection of the entire argument. Cf. chapter VIII.

is revealed precisely in his apostasy and rebellion. Total corruption can never be understood without bearing this relation in mind; man's guilt is indissolubly bound up with his being human, his being man; and at the same time it is clear that therefore there is no way out in an approach involving a reduction of corruption's effect. Any such reduction is an attempt to protect man from the gravity of the divine indictment, and is in flagrant conflict with the belief in total corruption. But when we reject such a reduction, man's ontological being is clearly outlined in the bright light of divine revelation — not as a neutral substratum, as Thielicke in his passionate rejection of ontology characterizes it, but as a radical and complete exclusion of such a neutrality.

Thus we can evaluate contemporary personalism when applied to the image as a reaction against the dangers of an abstract ontology. As such, it is a constant reminder of these dangers; but it should at the same time be stated that this personalism itself operates with a concept of relation which does not sufficiently recognize that a being in relation should not underemphasize reality, but rather becomes evidenced in reality. For although the abstract ontology of man *an sich,* in himself, did not do justice to man's relation to his Creator as constitutive of his essence, nevertheless, in this relation we do confront the actuality and reality of man's nature, which even in its corruption has not escaped from God's hand, but rather stands guilty in every corner of his being, while in this relation.

It is possible along these lines to uphold the profession of the Reformation regarding total corruption, and at the same time to reject every approach involving a quantitative reduction of the extent of this corruption. This serious view of sin's extent, which constantly forms an unconquerable *skandalon,* stumbling block, especially for humanism in its various forms, and which is constantly rejected as pessimism from the Roman Catholic side, was undoubtedly based, in the view of the Reformers, on the witness of the Bible, which with unmitigable seriousness brands man as "sinner." There appears to be every reason to speak of the "perspicuity" of the Holy Scripture especially on this point. Although we cannot here treat extensively of the doctrine of sin, we should nevertheless remember the way in which Scripture witnesses to the radical nature of sin. It never palliates, nor at the last and decisive moment relativizes sin, as for example did Kant in his concept of the radicality of evil. Scripture constantly makes it clear that sin is not something which corrupts relatively or partially, but a corruption which fully affects the radix, the root, of man's existence, and therefore man himself.

Scripture speaks of this radicality already in treating man before God's judgment in the Flood. Already then we read that the earth was corrupt in the eyes of God, and full of violence (Gen. 6:11-12), and this sin is referred to as *great*. All that which man's heart brought forth was evil (Gen. 6:5). And this finds its sharpest expression in God's repentance that He had placed man on the earth; "it repented Jehovah . . . and grieved him" (Gen. 6:6-7). The power of sin since the Fall is like an avalanche, and it results in the intervening judgment of God. The heart of guilty man stands over against the heart of God, which grieves, and in its grief thinks back to creation. Genesis 8, after the Flood, also refers to the heart of man, and in an unusual connection, for God says, "I will not curse the ground any more for man's sake, for that the imagination of man's heart is evil from his youth" (Gen. 8:21).

This text has always attracted attention,[32] since it is not immediately clear why the evil of man's heart is placed in connection with not cursing the earth. In Genesis 6, man's evil is the designated cause of God's judgment, while in Genesis 8 it appears to be the basis for not again cursing the earth. Aalders sees difficulty as an insoluble one so long as a causal relationship between the two is postulated. He exegetes the passage to mean that God will not again execute His judgment because of evil. Von Rad speaks of a voluntary self-limitation of His punishing holiness, as the light of grace breaking through the darkness of wrath. However this text is to be explained, that it points out the extent of human corruption, man's evil, both in and after the Flood, is clear enough. The continuance of life on earth finds its ground not in the relative nature of man's sin but rather in the divine "nevertheless," in the grace, the saving grace, of God as over against corruption. And this corruption appears to have continued unabated after the Flood, thus evidencing the power of sin's avalanche, which allows nothing to stand in its way, and through which man's heart, his perverse heart, showed its effects in all of life's relationships.

The Old Testament refers to corruption in various ways. It emphatically states that there is no one who has an understanding heart and who seeks God (Ps. 14:2-3; cf. Job 14:4, I Kings 8:46). To this sinfulness, which affects the whole man, corresponds the holy wrath of God, His burning wrath (I Sam. 28:18, Hos. 11:9). Man's sin is described in various ways in the Old Testament,

---

32. Ch. Aalders, *Korte Verklaring, Genesis,* I, 227; cf. also K. Schilder, *Heidelbergse Catechismus,* I, 665ff.; cf. G. von Rad, *Genesis,* p. 95.

but in all the variations there is a constant stress on the seriousness of this turning from the way, this rebellion, this transgression and this error, which lead far away from God.[33] The total and radical character of sin is constantly kept before us. It is a rebellion which finds its sole answer in divine judgment, an aberration which causes us to miss the goal of a living communion with God.

Just as man's expulsion from Paradise (Gen. 3) shows forth the seriousness of sin and the depth of man's Fall, so God's wrath at sin appears throughout the whole Old Testament. The terms "radical" and "total" can also be applied to this wrath. As Isaiah says, "he has stretched out his hand against them . . . . and his hand is stretched out still" (Isa. 5:25; cf. 9:11, 16, 20; and Jer. 25:15-29). And when it is nevertheless made clear (Isa. 12:1) that there is a limit to the wrath of God, and that it is turned away — as when we read that His wrath lasts but a moment, but His "favor is for a life time" (Ps. 30:6; cf. Isa. 40:1ff.) — this limit is not considered as implying that man's corruption is after all not so serious, but rather as due to divine grace, just as the "remnant" of Israel can only be explained through His compassion. Thus we hear, after a most serious threat of judgment, that nevertheless "I will not utterly destroy the house of Jacob" (Amos 9:8), and "I will not come in wrath" (Hos. 11:9). Thus, total corruption, but a limited curse; but the limit on the wrath of God is never derived from a limited corruption. God "is a righteous judge . . . that hath indignation every day; if a man turn not, he will whet his sword" (Ps. 7:11-12). If the light shines in this impenetrable darkness, it is the light which shines in man's total corruption as the light of mercy.

The New Testament also stresses the radicality of sin and its terrible effects in heart and life. Man can be described simply as "sinful," as Peter confessed himself to be (Luke 5:8), as man was objectively judged in the declaration that the Son of man must be delivered into the hands of sinful men (Luke 24:7). The whole preaching of Jesus presupposes this undeniable reality of sin. He tells His hearers that they are "evil" (Matt. 7:11), and He sat down with "publicans and sinners" (Matt. 9:11, Mark 2:15). A

33. Cf. G. Ubbink, *Het Zondebegrip in de Synoptische Evangelien* (1939), p. 81. Calvin refers to an "ironic concession" here, a view which is attacked, e.g., by Schlatter. In any case, we should compare the criticism which Jesus passes on the "hypocrites" (Matt. 6:2, 15:7, 23:28) and the Pharisees, who trusted in their own righteousness (Luke 18:9) and cursed the crowd which "knew not the law" (John 7:49). Cf. also J. Haas, "Die Stellung Jesu zu Sünde und Sünder nach den vier Evangelien," *Studia Friburgensia* (1953), pp. 84ff.

sinner: such is man, to whom the gospel of a radical forgiveness is directed. This being a sinner is not a peripheral and relative thing, and therefore bearable, but so radical and fatal that the conversion of a single sinner causes rejoicing among the angels of God (Luke 15:7, 10). There is no limit in all the length and breadth of sin where its effects come to a halt. Christ indeed says that He has not come to call the "righteous," but sinners to repentance (Luke 5:32), and that the sick rather than the healthy need to be cured (Luke 5:31; cf. Matt. 9:12 and Mark 2:17). But this clearly does not refer to some "elite" group who are raised above the general sinfulness by a righteousness acceptable to God;[33] it is rather a caustic criticism of the boundless overevaluation, the failure to recognize that one is a sinner before his God.

The Gospels describe this being a sinner as being lost, indeed a clear indication of the radical situation in which sinful man finds himself. Any relativizing of sin is excluded. There is no way for man to escape this condition of being lost, no perspective which shows a way, no open window. The lost can only be *sought* and found.[34]

This lostness is evident throughout all of life, and comes up from the depths of the lost heart, which is alienated from the life of God (Eph. 4:18; cf. 2:12, Col. 1:21). The apostolic Epistles picture this corruption in numerous places, and in the most radical terms. Life outside of Christ and His renewing is portrayed as a life in sin and guilt, under the wrath of God, as a life in the lusts of the flesh by children of disobedience (Eph. 2:3; cf. 2:2). It is a life of man's "hardness and impenitent heart" (Rom. 2:5), of "ungodliness and unrighteousness" (Rom. 1:18), of "vanity and darkness" (Rom. 1:21), of "foolishness and uncleanness" (Rom. 1:22, 24): manifestations all, of man's alienation from God. Man is characterized by these things "by nature" (Rom. 1:29), and this darkness is not something incidental, but something lasting, filling the whole heart to its utmost depths. The law can do no more than speak so that the "mouth may be stopped, and all the world may be brought under the judgment of God" (Rom. 3:19), so that *no* flesh is righteous before Him (Rom. 3:20). Man is flesh, darkness,

---

34. Luke 19:10, 15:11ff. Cf. the connection between leaving the true way and this condition of being lost in Ps. 119:176 with Luke 19:10, to *seek* and *save* the lost. Cf. R. Otto, *Die Christliche Idee der Verlorenheit, Sünde und Urschuld* (1929), p. 206, on "the judgment of the lost condition," "a retrospective judgement on everything up to this time, and then a judgment that all of it is fully lost as an existence and a standpoint completely opposed to the ideal, as a nature distorting the ideal."

a slave of sin, lawless, rebellious, full of error. And in all this, he shows his enmity to God — one of Scripture's sharpest and most radical characterizations of sin. The inclination of the flesh is enmity towards God (Rom. 8:7; cf. Col. 1:21), since it neither is nor can be obedient to the law of God (Rom. 8:7). Despite all God's glory, there are enemies of God. (Cf. II Sam. 12:14, Ps. 139:21, Jas. 4:4). And Paul is not referring to one individual, or to a group, but to the inclination of the flesh.

Finally, we employ the word which if possible expresses the gravity of sin still more strongly, when we consider man not as engaged in active enmity to God, but in his *death*, dead in transgression and sin (Eph. 2:1, 5; Col. 2:13). Man's sinful passions produce fruits unto death (Rom. 7:5; cf. 6:23). And Psalm 7:15, "he . . . has fallen into the ditch which he made," finds an echo in James, "the lust which he has conceived beareth sin; and the sin, when it is fullgrown, bringeth forth death" (Jas. 1:15; cf. Rom. 8:6).

In view of this unequivocal witness of Scripture, it should be clear that the jubilation of salvation corresponds to this very real condition of lostness. New vistas open for man only through salvation from this radical peril, and then he feels himself "compassed about with songs of deliverance" (Ps. 32:7). After the call from the depths comes the joyous song of salvation (Ps. 130:1, 7). There is a change from death to life, from a stone heart to a living heart (Ezek. 11:19), and this is the act of God's salvation, which transforms everything.

In all of this unanimous witness, there is never any mention of a relativizing of sin. Any such relativizing would also automatically relativize the unspeakably wonderful nature of salvation (cf. the Heidelberg Catechism, L.D. 11). There is no possible reduction of the extent of evil in man, no falling back on some last reserve of goodness which can serve as the basis for a restoration and renewal of life. In this, indeed, lies the danger of any discussion of "remnants" which in one or another way does not give proper emphasis to the completeness of man's lost condition. For there is no relativization possible of man's enmity to God, his death, his alienation from the Father's house, his being in the world "without God." No, the only way out is in terms of another perspective — the perspective of life, which triumphs, *in* this death and alienation, over death; of grace, which triumphs over sin and brings man back to God through the peace which destroys enmity (Eph. 2:16, 17; Col. 2:13-15).

In the history of the Church and of theology, men have in various ways distorted the witness of Scripture on this point. And this distortion concerns, basically, not some purely theoretical considerations; it concerns this radical and total accusation and indictment which humbles man before God's countenance: man, who actually contributes nothing at all to his own salvation and whose life can be described only as an apostate autonomy and disobedience. The opposition to the radicality of evil is not a theoretical opposition, but an opposition of religious nature against the stumbling block, the *skandalon*, of this indictment. This opposition can either be directed against the indictment as such, from a completely humanistic standpoint, or else — within the confines of the Church and of theology — against the completeness and radicality of this indictment; an opposition which obviously casts its shadow over the radicality and completeness of salvation, and this is the most striking characteristic of any synergistic view of salvation, which attacks the doctrine of total corruption.[35]

Thus the positing of some limit to the extent of the power of corruption is one of the most serious phenomena in the history of the Church and of theology, one which inevitably casts its shadow over the richness of salvation, the jubilation over the radical and total character of *sola gratia*. We might well ask why, in the light of such a clear Scriptural witness, this belief in *sola gratia* has so often been dismissed as too somber and too pessimistic.

It seems to us that we can point to two causes for this striking fact. The first and most basic is this, that man by nature is opposed to, and often remains opposed to, this deepest humiliation and this radical indictment. It is part of the seriousness of sin, and the extent of the Fall, that man does not see his guilt and therefore is also not prepared to take on its burden; so that his guilt manifests itself also and especially in his attempts at establishing his innocence. This tendency is so strong in sinful man that it makes itself

35. Note the important remarks of the Catholic writer P. Schoonenberg, "Aantekeningen over Natuur en Genade," *Katholicisme en geestelijke Vrijheid* (1951), p. 26. In his judgment the Protestant view of the position of man's fallen nature "must not be rejected so much as completed." Protestants "sometimes" forget that the essential continuance of human nature must be acknowledged. He himself acknowledges that the effects of sin extend as far as all of creation. "But throughout, the creature remains a creature; and man — it is precisely the tragedy of the sinner, that he remains man, and creature." Cf. Tromp, *Natuur en Genade* (Wending, 1948), "the power of sin does not extend to annihilation, and its seriousness lies precisely in this, that it dwells in a creature of God." This appears to me to be an important point of contact for the controversy between Catholics and Protestants.

felt even when the confession of guilt begins to break through the darkness of false innocence. Even in that case, there remains opposition to a real "cry from the depths," to a confession of guilt without reservation. This opposition is reflected in the history of the Church and of theology and has often taken the form of a relativizing of corruption. We do not mean that this danger threatens only in various forms of synergism, but is averted when total corruption is confessed; we can "confess" total corruption without actually realizing it and applying it in everyday life. But precisely because of the danger that vital realization of the totality of corruption will be stifled under the cover of relativization, there is all the more reason to acknowledge that this opposition to a thorough confession of guilt can also play a role — unconsciously — in theological ideas. Both for those who confess the doctrine of total corruption and for those who feel that it does not do justice to human nature, it remains true that the actual opposition to the radicality of this indictment of the whole man gradually breaks down only when the Holy Spirit convinces the individual of sin and righteousness and judgment; and the Reformation wished to do nothing else than call itself, and others, to this understanding of the meaning of *sola gratia.* It was concerned with the correlation between sin and forgiveness, between the call from the depths (Ps. 130), and divine forgiveness.

But along with this, and on another level, there is a second reason why total corruption has been so often relativized. We refer to the oft-cited fact that the doctrine of total corruption appears to be so little in agreement with the reality of human life. It is true that the powerful influence of evil manifests itself in actual life, but at the same time and everywhere there appears to be a visible limit, and there seem to be opposing powers at work, through which man's evil is restrained. Partly for this reason also, the doctrine of total corruption has often been attacked as unrealistic, since it is powerless to explain the facts of human life. Is not the doctrine in flagrant contradiction to all the manifestations of man's nature in which his humanity still shines forth in the world as a light in the darkness; and can we then really hold that man's lost condition implies *total* corruption?

We encounter here a question which goes deep, which everywhere forces itself on our consciousness: Does not the "phenomenology" of evil oppose the doctrine of total corruption? Is it not strange that men hold to it in spite of everything, and with it unceasingly condemn themselves and others?

In the context of such questions we encounter a very important problem related to the nature and being of man. There is every reason to give it our full attention, since it is concerned with the confrontation of doctrine with reality. Precisely because this doctrine of total corruption continually remains a stumbling block, a *skandalon,* we can not avoid facing this problem. For it cannot be denied that when the Reformation emphasized so strongly the total corruption of man, it had in mind the real and factual nature of man.

CHAPTER FIVE

CORRUPTION AND HUMANNESS

T HE QUESTION with which we concluded the previous
chapter deeply affects a number of theological problems, but
it concerns most of all the everyday life of man. For the question
concerns the harmony and consonancy of the Reformed doctrine
of total corruption with the actuality of human life, as it reveals
itself in everyday concreteness. The doctrine of corruption is in
deed a doctrine of *faith*, but it concerns the reality, the actuality,
of human life. And objections have constantly arisen, in numerous
and variant forms, against the radical nature of total corruption;
objections which claim to be based on the facts, and which point
out all the various sorts of goodness and humanity which are
still encountered in human life. And indeed all the problems regarding the loss of the image of God which have arisen in the
course of history take on here — in real life — their concrete form
and urgency. This is all the more so since theologians were generally
inclined to acknowledge some sort of "humanity" in man, and
besides that were most reluctant to give up the idea of "gradation"
in the manifestations of evil. The Reformation, though it fought
the Roman distinction between venial and mortal sins, was certainly
no exception in this respect, so that the question inevitably arose
as to how such a distinction was possible and how it could be
explained, within a context of total corruption.

We can perhaps best approach the problems which arise in this
connection by pointing out that Reformed theology has at various
times given an answer — a controversial answer — in the doctrine
of common grace. The closeness of the relationship between this
doctrine and the series of problems with which we are concerned
is shown clearly by the fact that not only the modern Calvinist
theologian Abraham Kuyper, but also Calvin himself, take up this
doctrine in immediate connection with the doctrine of total corruption. Calvin discusses it in a chapter (*Institutes,* II, III) in which
he tries to show that man's nature produces nothing but that which
is worthy of condemnation. The basis for this view is the unequivocal witness of Scripture, says Calvin, where Paul in flaming

language condemns (Rom. 3:10) not merely certain individual men, but man, the whole race of Adam. Even though not every sin is manifested in every individual's life, still every evil lies within the heart of each. And it is in connection with this radicality and universality of evil that Calvin takes up the problem arising from the fact that in all ages there are those who, following the light of nature, have devoted their entire lives to the pursuit of virtue, and have thereby shown that there was "some purity" in their nature. Such examples appear to show, says Calvin, that we should not view man's nature as *wholly* corrupt, since some have not only performed outstanding deeds, but have also lived their entire lives honorably (II, III, 3). In acknowledging this fact, Calvin finds himself on the horns of an apparent dilemma. Should he now deny these "virtues," or should he weaken his doctrine of total corruption? But his answer denies both horns of the dilemma; another solution is possible. Within the corruption of man's nature, there is still room for some kind of divine grace not to cleanse this corruption, but to hold it in check. If God would let men follow their own desires completely, then the world of evil would be wholly different from what it is. But even where there is no renewal and salvation, God is nevertheless still active in the world of men's hearts, active in dealing with evil; an activity which Calvin calls one of restraining, of holding in check. This activity is not carried on arbitrarily, but "to the degree that He determines serviceable in the preservation of creation, of all things."

In this context it is evident as well that Calvin does not have in mind a merely external restraining activity, for he refers also to the effects of shame and fear, through which God in His Providence bridles the corruption of man's nature lest it break out unto death; but He does not purify this nature within.

Calvin goes on to speak expressly of gifts of God (II, III, 4). We must not ascribe to human nature the power to seek good as long as it is imprisoned in corruption, but we must nevertheless consider the gifts which God has given, in definite measure, to man. The resultant variation among men and the manifestation of "virtue" should not rule out our including the "good" man as well as the "bad" in the universal description of man as evil. In this connection, Calvin denies all value to what appears praiseworthy in unholy man, but he means thereby that man in the very reception of these gifts contaminates them with his ambition, and that in all of life there can be found no passion to act to the glory of God. And "no worth" means for Calvin in this context no worth in meriting righteousness before the divine judgment (III, XIV, 2).

Meanwhile we continue to acknowledge the difference between the moderation and equity of a Titus or a Trajan and the rage and cruelty of a Nero, but the former do not lead to merit, since all the endowments of the unbeliever are given by God. Calvin unceasingly applies the religious norm to the "good works" of the world, and asks how these gifts were used, and whether they were directed to the eternal goal of righteousness, that is, the serving of God (III, XIV, 3).

If this is not the aim, then true righteousness is lacking in all these "virtues," since our obligation is weighed not according to deeds, but according to intention. Thus for Calvin, the acknowledgement of the difference between men does not affect the doctrine of total corruption, since corruption concerns the whole man before the face of God, man in the total orientation of his existence.

And therefore it was possible for Calvin also to portray corruption in radical terms. Man was indeed endowed with outstanding gifts, but these have been so corrupted by sin that "no trace of purity is left," and we must thus seek all righteousness *outside* ourselves (*Commentary* on Acts 15:9). But it does not follow from such statements (and their number could be multiplied) that Calvin fails to appreciate the gifts of God to man. He sees these endowments in man's reason, which is not annihilated; and in his will, which though shackled by his lusts, is not completely taken away (II, II, 12, 16). However, that which remains in man must be always recognized as the gift of God. There is no reason to wonder what sort of contact the godless, wholly alienated from God, have with the Spirit; for though the Spirit of sanctification dwells only in the believer, still God achieves and moves all things through the power of His Spirit, in accord with the uniqueness of each thing, given it by Him in the law of creation.

These endowments can thus not be credited to man. Rather, his corruption manifests itself precisely in and with these endowments; and Calvin (as does the Belgic Confession) refers here to John 1:5, "the light shineth in the darkness, and the darkness apprehended it not." Calvin is concerned with this relation, this *Verkehrung*, this turning around of man's nature with these gifts in the direction of a radical alienation from God. Thus when Calvin speaks of "surviving signs of the image" which distinguish men from other creatures (II, II, 17), or when he speaks of the image as "soiled and *nearly* eradicated" through the Fall (II, II, 9), in neither case does he mean to relativize man's corruption. Some sort of contradiction is often seen between Calvin's statements on corruption and on the "remnants" of the image in man: thus Torrance says, "It is difficult to see how there can be any ultimate reconciliation between Calvin's doctrine of total perversity and his doctrine of a remnant of the *imago Dei*, though the very fact that he can give them in the same breath seems to indicate that he had no difficulty in reconciling them."[1] But this reconciliation is possible for Calvin precisely because he is not speaking of a quantitative reduction, but of divine endowments which are misused by sinful man. Calvin does not want to judge these endowments as few or unimportant, for he who so judges the gifts of the Spirit also so judges, and thus defames, the Spirit Himself (II, II, 15).

But from a consideration of God's gifts we may never, by way of a quantitative reduction, deduce a *limit* to the extent of corruption. Calvin's remarks on Rom. 9:4 (*Comm. ad. loc.*) illustrate his view well; he says that we are there taught that the godless can never so defile the gifts of God that they lose their worthiness as gifts, but that those who misuse them thereby produce only greater shame for themselves. The total corruption of man (with all his endowments) thus refers to the *total* and *central* deed of man, his turning away and alienation from God in apostasy and rebellion; but this deed manifests itself in connection with and through the gifts with which the living God endowed him. These gifts place him in a relation to God. Such a view leaves no room for Deism; corruption manifests itself *in* this relation. And when man *in* his alienation reaches something which can be praised, this can never be explained from some limitation of corruption, but only from the action of God, the *act* of His *grace*.

It is not a simple matter to obtain a clear insight into Calvin's precise meaning when he speaks about divine grace and the divine gifts to man. He distinguishes between natural and supernatural gifts (II, II, 12);[2] man lost the latter (faith, love, righteousness) but kept the former (understanding, judgment, will), though these were disfigured and darkened. Yet this disfiguring does not go so far that we may judge man's understanding to be continually and completely blinded, for this contradicts common experience. Calvin cites man's desire to investigate truth, though this very search shows how unfit fallen man is to search for truth and to find it.

Thus the solution lies, for Calvin, in the distinction between

1. T. F. Torrance, *Calvin's Doctrine of Man* (1949), p. 93.
2. Cf. A. S. E. Talma, *De Anthropologie van Calvijn* (1882), pp. 63ff.

earthly and heavenly things (II, II, 13). As regards the former, he acknowledges the light of reason and sees in the works of pagan writers a "wonderful" shining forth of this light, from which it appears that man has been adorned by God with excellent endowments (II, II, 15).

Thus when Calvin speaks of "general grace," he uses the concept to refer to natural gifts. Man has "by nature" a general notion of reason and understanding. There is a "light of nature" which is present in everyone, in the sense that this is a gift of divine grace to each individual, because of God's mercy. These "natural" gifts are possessed by all, godly and ungodly alike (II, II, 14).

It is noteworthy that Calvin here emphasizes these gifts, without bringing in the corrupting influence of the apostate heart, while this corruption is strongly emphasized when he is dealing with the Kingdom of God and spiritual insights; in such matters, man is wholly blind, and human acuteness only complete darkness (II, II, 18).

From all this it follows that Calvin, when considering the reality and actuality of human life, relates corruption to the total act of man in his alienation from God, but acknowledges that man's natural endowments can bring him to important achievements so far as earthly things are concerned. But this does not lead Calvin to relativizing the extent of corruption, for he sees these natural endowments as a result of divine grace. They remain through God's permission, for if He had not spared us, the Fall would have swept away our whole nature (II, II, 17). Thus, total corruption — and general or common grace.

The Dutch Calvinistic theologian Abraham Kuyper follows in Calvin's footsteps in his view of God's general grace or common grace, especially in his *De Gemeene Gratie,* a three-volume work on general grace. According to Kuyper, this teaching can be found in Calvin's work, and indeed forms an indispensable part of Reformed doctrine.[3] It arises from the confession of the deadly character of sin, and not from an attempt to relativize the extent of corruption. Kuyper, like Calvin, is enthralled by the beautiful and imposing achievements of men outside the Church. This undeniable fact, says Kuyper, puts us before the apparent dilemma of either denying all these achievements or else viewing man as

3. A. Kuyper, *De Gemeene Gratie,* I, 11; II, 29-36. Kuyper strongly attacked what he called the "pseudo-dogma" of the respectability of human nature. He posed the critical question of whether anyone really believed in this dogma when applied not to himself but to others.

after all not completely fallen. But Reformed doctrine refuses to choose either horn of the dilemma. On the one hand, this good may not and can not be denied; and on the other hand, the completeness of corruption may not be diminished. There is only one solution; that grace is at work even in fallen man, to check the destruction which is inherent in sin.

This checking of corruption is central in the whole doctrine of common grace, says Kuyper, as the holding back of the immense powers which from out of and through sin exercise their influence on human life. Kuyper considers unmistakable the phenomenon of "goodness" in sinful man, more particularly in the inclination towards good things and uprightness, things of good report, in the voice of public conscience, and in acts of philanthropy and mercy, performed by godless man (sometimes even to the shame of believers).[4]

It is against the background of total corruption that Kuyper comes to common grace, which in innumerable instances checks the deadly working of sin. The history of the human race shows that "on the one hand the terrible *law of sin* held sway, but on the other hand there was also a *law of grace* which broke the power of sin." When the image of God in Adam stood on the verge of being wholly eradicated, divine grace intervened to "save the last remnants" of the image. Thus man was protected from becoming demonic, and common grace kept man human. And this means for Kuyper not merely an external checking and limiting, in the sense of the Belgic Confession's statement (Art. 13, 36) that God "bridles the devil and all our enemies" and ordains the state in order to check the licentiousness of men. Common grace, for Kuyper, refers not to a power from outside, an external holding back of an evil which is itself unlimited in man, but rather to a power which finds a basis *in man himself* — and Kuyper cites what the confessions say about the remnants of the image in man.[5]

This is not to be explained from man's life itself, but rather from God's action in man's life in order to subdue the madness of sin in us. Kuyper cites as an example Abimelech, who is "held back" from sinning against God — in Kuyper's view God's direct intervention in the very depths of his life, a "holding back" which is not ethical in nature, nor due to conscience, but an act of power

---

4. Kuyper, *ibid.*, I, 252, with references to Calvin. See also I, 253, "When Pharaoh's daughter rescued the infant Moses from the Nile, did she do good or evil?" Cf. also H. Bavinck, *De algemene Genade* (1894), p. 27, and S. J. Ridderbos, *Rondom het Gemene Gratie-Probleem* (1949), p. 40.
5. *Ibid.*, I, 253-257.

which reaches down *into* man and there limits the working out of sin, where God intervenes "in the turning of the wheel of sinful life."

This tempering of the effect of sin is thus due not to a relative and "remnant" goodness in man's nature, but to God's grace, which bridles sin both externally and internally.

And since this bridling can in no respect be explained from man's goodness, the Reformed church confesses man to be inclined to every evil and incapable of any good. When the evil of man's nature reveals itself in terrible ways, this can not be explained because of some set of exceptional circumstances, but rather out of man's nature itself. And when man performs civil good, this is due exclusively to the divine holding back of the powers of evil.

Kuyper wishes with such a view to remain within the limits of the Confession's references to remnants and to the light of nature. He further cites Paul's statements on the work of the law in the hearts of the heathen. That also does not mean, he says, a quantitative reduction of the effects of evil, or a simplistic distinction between what has been lost and what has remained, but means rather a witness of God in the soul, to which the heathens' witness corresponds. Thus they arrive at the things which are of the law, and they do this not from their own power, but through the power of general grace, common grace. Thus the Confession correctly refers to a light of nature, and Kuyper sees such a close relationship to Scripture that he feels that Paul himself refers to "common grace or the light of nature."[6]

It is this light which limits the working of evil, and it is thus to be explained that the world, despite total corruption, turns out better than might otherwise be expected. Without common grace, man would have become unlimitedly sinful, but common grace is constantly at work "to bend partially back in the right direction those human powers and endowments, which were man left to himself would be wholly perverted.'[7]

---

6. *Ibid.*, I, 253-257; II: 62, 67, 53-54, 20-21, for the foregoing material.
7. *Ibid.*, II, 306-307. For this "holding back," cf. also J. Murray, "Common Grace," *Westminster Theological Journal* (November, 1942), pp. 1-28. He sees this as (p. 10) "one of the most outstanding features of God's government of this world." Kuyper sees in the fact that the world turns out better than total corruption might lead us to expect, a noteworthy parallel with the fact that in the life of the believer we encounter much which we would not expect from his renewal and restoration; i.e., the remnants of sin. Both sin and grace are held back in their full revelation; sin by common grace, and grace through the after-effects of sinful nature (Kuyper, *op. cit.*, II, 23, 29). It is however clear, in my opinion, that

This happens, then, because of God's intervention between man and evil, so that his actions to a certain extent conform to God's will; man's sinful instincts would carry him directly into absolute sin, but common grace makes him swerve, so to speak, so that he ends up in civil goodness. Thus we see that Calvin as well as Kuyper not only hold to total corruption, but that both through the doctrine of common grace wish to acknowledge and honor *in* the corrupted life a sort of "goodness," or "conformity" to the will of God, so that the life of fallen man parallels in limited fashion the life of the believer in his sanctification, which is of course also revealed precisely in conformity to God, in obedience to His command, in the doing of His will.

This approach wished to acknowledge the fact that in real life we do not encounter an absolute antithesis between complete holiness and complete evil, but that we find, in the concrete experiences of our existence, deeds in the lives of unbelievers which are unmistakably similar to the good works of the believers. Calvin and Kuyper thus mean by "general grace" not the restorative grace of God in Jesus Christ, not the renewing of the image of the Creator, but rather a "common grace" which limits the powers of evil. This common grace may be brought into relation with the grace of Christ in this sense, that this protection of man's humanness provides *opportunity* for man to have salvation through Christ; but it is as such nevertheless not Christologically defined or limited.[8] It is a holding back of sin which can lead to a relative but nevertheless striking conformity, which surely is not without meaning in the light of God's intentions, but which can never in the least degree excuse man in the total alienation of his life from God.

Before we go into various basic problems which now arise to confront us, we might note that the issues stemming from the "common grace" approach came expressly to the fore in the criticism which Herman Hoeksema leveled at Kuyper's views, and at the decisions of the Christian Reformed Church (meeting at Kalamazoo in 1924) because, he said, they gave confessional support to Kuyper's

---

this parallel is not a legitimate one, and that we cannot subsume both of these phenomena under one general idea of "limitation." It is striking that Klaas Schilder, a Dutch Calvinist theologian who often attacks Kuyper's idea of common grace, follows Kuyper in using this parallel.

8. Cf. H. Kuiper, *Calvin on Common Grace* (1928). He deals with Calvin on this point ("he never treats this subject at any great length") pp. 212ff.; and in Appendix XII with Kuyper; Appendix XIV with Hepp, a follower of Kuyper.

approach. The second and third points of the synodical declaration
are what concern us here.[9]

The second point stated that according to Bible and Confession there is a bridling of sin in the life of the individual man
and in society; "God through the general working of His Spirit,
without renewing the heart, bridles sin in its unhindered outbreak,
whereby human society remains possible." The third point, regarding the performance of civil righteousness, added that unbelievers, however unqualified they might be to perform any *saving*
good, can perform acts of civil good, and again the Scriptures and
the Confession were cited, where "it is taught that God, without
renewing the heart, exerts such an influence on man that he is
made able to do civil good."[10]

Hoeksema since then has constantly and bitterly opposed these
points, as well as the teaching of Kuyper, and especially from this
standpoint, that he sees in them a serious and far-reaching weakening of the total corruption of man.[11] The synod did indeed declare
(following Kuyper) that common grace does not renew the heart
of man and that man is unable to do any good and is inclined to
all evil; but actually, says Hoeksema, the result is that man can
no longer be viewed as *totally* corrupt; implied, he says, is confession
of "improvement" in the sinner apart from Christ, a non-spiritual
bettering; in consequence, the radical antithesis between the Church
and the world is surrendered and the way to secularization is
wide open. He himself regards it as impossible to limit the effects
of sin in something which is already totally corrupt. And he does

---

9 For the first point, see my *De Voorzienigheid Gods,* p. 87, and my
De Verkiezing Gods (1955), pp. 245, 292 (E.T., *Divine Election*).

10. Articles 13 and 36 of the Belgic Confession are cited for the second
point, and the texts (see the *Acts of Synod,* 1924, p. 129) cited are Gen. 6:3;
Ps. 81:12, 13; Rom. 1:24, 26, 28; II Thess. 2:6-7. The texts stating that
God gave man over to sin were cited because of the implication that there
is a previous period in which the limitation of sin plays an important
role. Cf. L. Berkhof, *De drie Punten in alle Delen gereformeerd* (1925),
p. 44. For the third point, Article 36 of the Confession and Canons III
and IV, 4 of the Canons of Dordt are cited, and II Kings 10:29-30, 12:2,
14:3; Luke 6:33; Rom. 2:14. Cf. Berkhof, *op. cit.,* pp. 56ff. For the Three
Points in general, cf. also C. Van Til, *The Defense of the Faith* (1955),
pp. 399ff., and J. Daane, *A Theology of Grace* (1954).

11. Hoeksema for many years has carried on his polemic in his Protestant
Reformed Church paper, *The Standard Bearer;* e.g., see April 15, 1939;
April 15, 1937. See further H. Danhof and H. Hoeksema, *Van Zonde en
Genade;* H. Hoeksema, *The Protestant Reformed Churches in America*
(1936), pp. 346ff., and *Drie Scheuren in het Fundament der Gereformeerd
Waarheid,* and (since 1943) his commentary on the Catechism, *The
Triple Knowledge.*

not hesitate to accuse the synodical declarations of Pelagianism and to characterize them as a revival of the heresy of Arminius. He evidently discovers here a manifestation of the idea of "remnants," summarizing his criticism in these words: "there is *no* remnant of original righteousness."

Hoeksema was, of course, well aware that the Reformed confessions mention civil righteousness, and a certain *justitia*, though this was *civilis,* and he was in duty bound to reflect on this fact. And it is noteworthy that he never attacks the Canons nor what they say on the natural light and outward "goodness," but he does protest the explanation of these statements given in the idea of common grace. He does not deny civil goodness, but he denies that this may be brought into relationship with the influence of God. Another explanation is necessary, and possible. The sinner sees himself placed before the various relations, laws and means of community ordained by God; he discovers their usability and appropriateness; and he then makes use of them. If successful, he may achieve acts which show a *formal* conformity to the laws of God.

In this way Hoeksema finds a place for the idea of *conformitas.* It indeed already has a place in the Canons *"justitia"* — which are not attacked by Hoeksema — as well as in the Westminster Confession, where we read that works which are *conformable* to the divine precept and useful to the individual and to others are possible for non-believers. It is made clear that these are not works of regeneration nor indeed can they be pleasing to God, since their deepest motivation is not the love of God, but it would seem that one can speak of a certain sort of "conformity" here. Hoeksema does not hesitate to do the same, but feels that no reference to divine grace is necessary for this. After various clarifications and further discussion, he speaks of the absurdity of "restraining grace," and there is only one conclusion possible for him: "the second and third points of 1924 arrive at the conclusion that human nature is not really depraved." And after a sharp attack on Kuyper and on the "Three Points," he reminds us, as a decisive argument, of the confession of the Church: "Are we then so corrupt that we are wholly incapable of doing any good and inclined to all wickedness? Indeed we are, except we are regenerated by the Spirit of God."

He is here substantially quoting the *Heidelberg Catechism* (L.D. III), also referred to both by Kuyper and by the synod, but he feels that we take this part of the confession seriously only when we read it in the light of what follows in the next section:

sin "without restraint." He raises the same question as Calvin and
Kuyper, i.e., whether our experience of man does not contradict
man's total corruption; is there not visible alongside all of man's
perversity a "higher moral level," and "integrity and nobility"?
In order to make this experience explicable, Hoeksema does not
resort to common grace but rather to the *organic development*
of the human race in culture and civilization, to which propor-
tionately corresponds the growth of sin, and thus in spite of man's
total corruption, the complete effects of sin are not yet visible.
"Not every man commits all sin. Each individual is but a branch
in the organism of the human race, and he bears that particular
fruit of the root sin of Adam which is in harmony with his place
in the organism." But that does not mean at all that we can
speak of some sort of "restraining grace." To do such is a "very
evident denial of the total depravity of the natural man." And
against this, Hoeksema affirms that man since the Fall is "wholly
darkness and foolishness, corrupt before God in all his ways, incapable of doing anything that is pleasing to Him, always inclined
only to evil, until he is regenerated by the Spirit of Christ." This
becomes all the more noteworthy when we see that Hoeksema also
speaks of "a remnant of natural light," and that this "remnant"
idea in the nature of the case also influences his view of natural
man. For this, says Hoeksema, does not mean merely that man
has kept his reason and his will, but rather that man has remained
a "rational moral being" and can "distinguish between good and
evil."

It is not at all clear what Hoeksema supposes the basis of this
ability to distinguish between good and evil to be, and even less
clear what meaning this can have in relation to an *unlimited* evil
in man, who has consciously chosen against God, and continues to
do so. The idea that man is not only a rational and willing being
but also a "moral" being seems to slip unnoticed into Hoeksema's
thought, though presumably he certainly would couple corruption
and immorality. And his idea of the "organic growth" of the human
race also is wholly insufficient as an explanation of the facts of
human existence.

This "organic" development may make clear why the individual
does not always commit every sin, but that is already implied in
the individual's creaturely limitations of time and space. It certainly does not explain why, even within these spatial and temporal
limitations, the corruptness of corrupt mankind never attains con-
summate expression in every kind of excess. How does one account
for the fact that man still continues to distinguish between good

and evil and, as Hoeksema recognizes, to practice civil righteousness? Hoeksema, too, is confronted by the same facts which forced Calvin and Kuyper to reflect, and he also admits some sort of limitation; man is led by "various and often conflicting motives, such as fear and shame, ambition and vain-glory, natural love and carnal lusts, malice and envy, hatred and vengeance."

Hoeksema places these motives next to each other, but it is surprising that we find natural love and shame as part of the listing. The impossibility of Hoeksema's solution is clearly revealed here. That is: it is impossible to see why, in Hoeksema's conception of total corruption, it should not *always* and *consistently* manifest itself, insofar as it is not bridled by external intervention, in that complete shamelessness which, according to the Scriptures, it indeed *often* produces (cf., e.g., Zeph. 2:1).

Hoeksema's warning against the relativizing of evil and total corruption may be necessary and worthwhile; nevertheless his explanation of the facts operates with motifs and categories which are incidentally brought in, and which in view of his presuppositions can only be called illegitimate. The most basic cause of his protest against common grace would appear to be his "deistic" view of the endowments left to man; this view enables him in dealing with the problem of such conformity to God as man's life still exhibits to attempt explanation *from man's nature* in its contact with reality, without having recourse to any action from God's side.[12]

The Dutch theologian Klaas Schilder[13] has also spoken at length on the question at issue here, and sharply criticized Kuyper's views on common grace. He concerns himself extensively with the apparent *conformitas* of fallen man, which he describes as "actions

12. For the foregoing material, see Danhof and Hoeksema, *op. cit.*, p. 169; Hoeksema, *Catechism*, I, 145, 182, 206; Hoeksema, *The Protestant Reformed Churches*, pp. 353, 355, 356. Strikingly, Hoeksema's language in speaking of Calvin, is much more cautious: "He seems to teach a certain grace whereby corruption in the sinful nature of fallen man is somewhat restrained, so that it does not break forth in all possible sins and violence" (*ibid.*, pp. 175ff.) ; but this he judges to be something else than "the modern conception under that name," and exegetes Calvin so that there is no conflict with the idea of total corruption, while such a harmony in Kuyper and the Synod of 1924 — who wished to follow Calvin — is a priori denied.

13. For Schilder's views and the material which follows, see his *Heidelbergse Catechismus*, I, 175ff., 116-120, 278, 284, 295, 109-110. For some valuable remarks on the difference between "good" and "useful," see the critique of Herbert Spencer in Thielicke, *Theologische Ethik* (1951), I, 1464.

analogous to the law's demands," and faces the problem (as did Calvin, Kuyper and Hoeksema) of how to explain these actions. Schilder's answer places strong emphasis on the external curbing of evil in the Providence of God, and he also speaks of remnants of the original endowments of man. Man after the Fall remained endowed with understanding and with will, and through this nature he can attain to some virtue and external discipline. But Schilder warns against thereby relativizing the apostasy of man; such relativizing would lead to the Catholic doctrine of the *donum superadditum*, of a second gift of God added to and going beyond man's original nature, though, with only the latter, man can still be more or less acceptable to God. Rejecting this view, one can still leave the way open for "analogous" actions *within* the limits of corruption, to be explained from the remnants of man's original endowments. But Schilder does not make clear, any more than Hoeksema, how this nature, if it is totally corrupt, can produce a certain "conformity" — especially since it generally does quite the opposite, in unmistakable disobedience. Schilder creates the impression that this *conformitas* of fallen man comes naturally from the remnants of the original endowments. When he says that the sinful nature and the natural existence of the heathen is the basic cause of their "analogous" actions, he is only pointing up the problem inasmuch as this same sinful nature can also be the cause of wholly different deeds, against which God's judgment goes out (cf. Romans 1). Paul indeed says that in performing these "actions analogous to the law" the Gentiles are a law unto themselves, so that we can doubtless speak of a certain "autonomy" here, but the surprising fact is precisely that from this "autonomy" there can arise such "analogous" acts, and not only deeds which are completely at variance with God's commands. Is man's nature the cause? Yes, says Schilder; but when on the basis of this answer he attacks the idea that we can speak of a general grace or general revelation in the context of Romans 2, he adds the remark that "it is another question whether this nature is not itself also qualified by what is called general revelation. But this matter is irrelevant." It was, however, exactly this matter which concerned Calvin and Kuyper. Any emphasis, such as Schilder's, on the causative effect of man's nature in Romans 2 leads precisely to that question: What are the characteristics of that nature, which is a corrupt nature, turned away from God and His commandments? And herein Schilder's solution — just as Hoeksema's — is unsatisfactory; Schilder operates with the "remnants" of man's original nature and tries thus to clarify the *conformitas* of fallen man. That man's fallen nature as fallen can not serve as explanation is clear enough. But neither do the "remnants" of the non-fallen nature *of themselves* lead to *conformitas,* since they can be misused by corrupt man. Schilder does indeed try to show how "nature and "remnants" can produce good acts; to this end he brings in the concept of *utility;* i.e., corrupt man is impressed with the usefulness of God's laws and thus can arrive at a certain outward conformity to them in his own life. In this connection Schilder makes many valuable remarks on the ways in which man can come to a certain outward or legalistic conformity. But we would most strongly deny that this concept of utility explains everything. It is certainly inadequate when we consider the phenomena of love, mercy and sacrifice which we encounter in fallen man. Schilder's example of man's legalistic obedience to a police ordinance is not particularly fortunate if it is meant to explain all fallen man's acts "analogous to the law." It is too simple and too uncomplicated, and there are other acts of fallen man which cannot be explained in this way. The concept of utility does not bring us far when we consider the possibility that one fallen man may die for another (cf. Rom. 5:7), or may spend his life in service of another and surround him with mercy, or may put into practice the Golden Rule, "all things therefore whatsoever ye would that men should do unto you, even so do ye also unto them; for this is the law and the prophets" (Matt. 7:12). Even as regards the Golden Rule, there is a possibility of fallen man's acting "analogously to the law," and it is clear that especially such acts impressed Calvin. How can we explain such deeds, coming from a corrupt nature? Should not we have expected the whole of life to manifest the break with God? And should not social life have been utterly impossible? How can we account for the "good," for this restraint? Can it be explained by a simple reference to man's "nature," and is this nature the exclusive cause of the actions "analogous to the law"?

These questions are of decisive importance precisely in connection with those things which arouse our special admiration; actions of love and sacrifice, mercy and community. When the Church confesses (e.g., *Heidelberg Catechism,* 5, 8) that man is so corrupt that he is wholly unable to do any good and is inclined *by nature* to hate God and his neighbor, this is a confession of guilt with reference to total corruption; the Church is confessing that from the heart of man can come nothing but enmity and hate. And that profoundly, is why Calvin speaks of grace and even of divine mercy in the life of fallen man. And even though it must be admitted that the various views of common grace raise many unsolved problems, the fact remains that they all mean to point out that the living God concerns Himself with the life of man, and does not let him fall from His hand. It is truly not coincidental that we are constantly driven to consider the relation between God's restraining of evil and His grace in Christ, and that the second and third points of the Christian Reformed Synod of 1924 cannot be separated from its first point (God's favorable inclination). Thus Calvin spoke of common grace, but also of God's mercy; and the Synod speaks of "a certain favor or grace, which He shows to His creatures in general." But the problem of fallen man's *conformitas* was posited and constantly pointed toward God's saving intervention in the world, which He loved. In this intervention, He concerns Himself with man, and protects his humanness in his impenetrable relation to Him.

We need not be surprised that this problem of "conformity" in fallen man has received ample attention in Catholic dogmatics and ethics. Such was to be expected especially in view of Catholic doctrine, which teaches that man lost the *donum superadditum*, i.e., supernatural spiritual gifts, through the Fall, but that he remained man, with his human nature and his natural morality. Essentially this teaching raises the same problem as that which came to the fore in the doctrine of common grace. But it is characteristic of Catholic doctrine that it opposes the Reformers' doctrine of total corruption, and thereby aims at honoring the remaining "natural-ness" of fallen man.[14]

Such an emphasis on "injury" as over against "corruption" does not intend to underestimate the significance of saving grace in Christ. The necessity of grace is confessed precisely because of the

14. Cf. Ch. IV of my *Conflict with Rome* (1954, 3d ed.). This "naturalness" does not mean a complete intactness of human nature, for the loss of the *donum superadditum* brought with it a wounding of nature. Aquinas indeed goes so far as to say that original sin was not merely a privation, but a *"habitus corruptus"* (*Summa Theologica*, Ia, II ae Qu. 82, art. 1, ad. 1). Man's nature is disoriented through the loss of the supernatural, and this involves vulnerability in natural things, e.g., a weakening of free will. Man lost the highest and most valuable element of his original nature. See M. M. Labourdette, *De Erfzonde en de Oorsprong van de Mens* (1956), p. 98. Thus man has not only fallen back to his "natural" state, but is "cruelly affected" by the loss. All this should be kept in mind when evaluating the simplistic summary of Catholic teaching as *"naturalia remanent integra"* — the natural remains unaffected. Cf. A. van Hove, *De Erfzonde* (1936), pp. 251ff. He regards this as the general teaching of the scholastics, and understands the vulnerability after the Fall as in comparison with the original state.

loss of original righteousness. Already in ancient times the Pelagians and Semi-Pelagians were opposed, so that no shadow might fall from "nature" on the need for grace in Christ. The Roman church still feels in duty bound to repulse all tendencies to overestimate human nature. We even get the impression from earlier decisions (e.g., that of the Council of Orange in 529) that the need of grace is stressed so strongly that apart from grace there is little room left for "natural goodness." Not only is it declared that the Holy Spirit is necessary to bend the will of man from unbelief to belief and from godlessness to piety, but equally (Council of Carthage, 418) that such grace does not enable us merely more easily to carry out God's commandments; the help of Christ is needed to carry them out at all (John 15:5). God Himself works in our hearts and thus only can holy thoughts arise and the action of a good will, so that there is no instant in which we do not need divine help. For it is nothing but pride when human nature arrogates anything to itself. What can we expect from a man who judges himself to be good and does not see the grace of God working?[15]

Thus from these earlier statements of the Church we can hardly derive the notion of natural goodness and righteousness outside the grace of Christ and the guidance of the Spirit. But this by no means disposes of the matter. The real problems involved do not become evident until Rome's attack on the Reformation doctrine of total corruption, and later its attack on the Augustinian Catholic theologian Baius.

The Council of Trent[16] indeed did state that all men lost their innocence in the Fall, and became impure, children of wrath and enslaved to sin and subject to death, from all of which neither the

15. For Orange, see Denzinger, p. 178. The context is a discussion of baptismal regeneration. It is denied that we can come to it without the gift of grace through the Spirit. For Carthage, see Denzinger, p. 105. He is opposed to the idea that grace eased the fulfillment rather than being necessary to it. For pride involved in such arrogation, see Denzinger, p. 135. He cites Eph. 6:12, Rom. 7:24, I Cor. 15:10. For the man who judges himself to be good, see Denzinger, p. 131. He says no one is good *"nisi participationem sui ille donet, qui solus est bonus,"* unless as a gift of God.

16. For Trent, see Denzinger, pp. 793, 815, 739, 817. For Trent as opposing both Pelagiansism and the Reformation, cf. the *Acta.* This preparatory agenda was read before the plenary Council June 9, 1546; the list of heresies on original sin emphasizes Pelagianism, and also mentions Luther — who is accused of following the error of Pelagius (see *Acta,* 8, 9). The Anabaptists are also condemned (11) as is Erasmus (3). See Labourdette, *op. cit.,* pp. 198-199.

heathen on the ground of their natural powers nor the Jews on the ground of the letter of the law of Moses could free themselves, but then follows the statement that free will in no sense is eradicated, though its powers are weakened. In this connection, the question of justification by works is taken up; all those who say that every work done before justification, no matter how done, is actually sin in the eyes of God, or deserves His hate, are condemned; and so also all who say that the more man through works tries to prepare himself for grace, the more he sins. Thus Trent opposes on the one hand any form of Pelagianism, and on the other hand the teaching of the Reformers. But Trent is here concerned primarily with the topic of preparation for Christ's grace, so that the subject of works done wholly without relation to Christ is not as yet clearly defined, since in such preparation God is already cooperating.

The question of natural goodness is more clearly taken up in the case of Baius,[17] a theologian who, influenced by Augustine, denied the supernatural nature of man's original state, and thus also held that man's natural life after the Fall was wholly incapable of any good. Rome then condemned as errors the propositions that "all works of the unbelievers are sins, and the virtues of the philosophers vices" and that the free will without help from God is capable only of sinning.

This is thus a much more positive declaration on the question of whether good can be done apart from grace. Moreover, the distinction between natural and supernatural is applied not only to works, but also to love; a fact evident from the condemnation of the thesis, attributed to Baius, that the positing of two sorts of love (a natural love for God as cause of nature, and a supernatural love, through grace for God as the source of salvation) is idle fancy and an insult to Scripture. Thus Rome held to a natural love of God alongside of a supernatural love. The climate of opinion evidenced in the condemnation of Baius is thus very different from that of the Council of Orange. Sometimes the very opposite of Orange's conclusions seems to be stated, e.g., when Orange says that we can do nothing without Christ and His grace, and Baius is condemned for saying that without grace man can only sin.

17. For Baius, see the documents in Denzinger, pp. 1025ff. For the two sorts of love, cf., also H. de Lubac, *Surnaturel. Etudes historiques* (1946), p. 111. Cf. also the condemnation of the ideas of the Jansen-influenced Catholic theologian Quesnel, who held similar ideas (See Denzinger, pp. 1388ff.).

It is not surprising that these later condemnations have occasioned the question whether the Council of Orange would not have confirmed and defended them as orthodox doctrine.[18] The Roman Catholic answer is a *denial* of any contradiction; involved is only a shift of emphasis to meet the change which the issue itself had undergone. Thus, the Council of Orange was concerned with holding the orthodox belief against Semi-Pelagianism, while later condemnations (e.g., Baius, Jansen, Quesnel) were concerned with holding the orthodox belief against the Reformation's doctrine of total corruption.

We can let the question of the relationship between earlier and later decrees rest at that, but it is surely clear that the later condemnations of various positions give a clear defense of the possibility of a human "nature" which remains not merely "structurally" intact and protected, but which also is judged capable of natural good and even of natural love for God. We encounter here the well-known Catholic distinction between the natural and supernatural life, and it is not surprising that the contemporary "new theology" in some Catholic circles, which seeks a more harmonious relation between nature and, grace, has concerned itself especially with the condemnations of Baius and Quesnel. One constantly receives the impression that the decisiveness of these decisions condemning the denial of natural goodness, poses a problem for the "new theology's" supporters. They are convinced that they can agree with the condemnations, but nevertheless in order to achieve a sound understanding of the decisions, they lay emphasis on the controversial situation of that time, and feel able in this manner to show that there is no contradiction between their views on the relation of nature and grace and the view implied in the condemnations of Baius and Quesnel.

Very closely related is the fact that these "new theologians" have their own view of the concept of a "pure state of nature." They see the concept arising fairly late, in the time of Jansenism, when, in reaction to Jansen's condemned views, "nature" was emphasized. And when the Reformers, and Jansen and Baius, reckoned man's praeternatural and supernatural endowments as part of man's nature before the Fall, the Church replied by distinguishing between

---

18. See E. Berbuir, *Natura humana* (1950), p. 63. His answer to this question is that the doctrinal decision of the church is directed at the conception of the complete corruption of human nature through the Fall, and its radical sinfulness. Cf. also A. van Hove, *op. cit.*, p. 17. For a fuller discussion of the "apparent" contradiction, see my *Conflict with Rome*, Ch. IV.

natural and supernatural. The concept of a "pure state of nature," they continue, was therefore delimited and strongly colored by controversy. Since that time, theologians — not the Church — have too often forgotten this fact, and have made the distinction between natural and supernatural into a separation between the two. This view of the growth of the concept of nature, which we find emphasized today by various Catholic theologians such as Balthasar and Lubac,[19] cannot, however, erase the fact that Rome in its criticism of Baius and Quesnel and in these controversies wished emphatically to confess the truth — so that merely emphasizing that the concept arises from controversies would seem to clarify the matter but little.

It is of importance to ask how such theologians, with their more harmonious relating of nature and grace, now view "natural goodness." And it is difficult to escape the impression that we are here in a different climate of opinion than that of the Church's condemnation of Baius and Quesnel. Thus the Dutch Catholic theologian Schoonenberg[20] feels that grace is necessary not only for acts directed towards salvation but also for all morally good acts. For a morally good deed is not one that merely conforms to the letter of the law, to the "content of the law," but one which has deliberate moral purpose. Conformity with the content of the law is not impossible, and so Schoonenberg concurs in the condemnation of Baius' idea that there was no distinction between acts fulfilling the substance of the law and acts directed towards salvation. No, we can make such a distinction; but, says Schoonenberg, we must not overestimate its importance. And further, even fullfillment of the letter of the law, morality between man and man, can perhaps exist without grace, but it surely cannot long be maintained by fallen man. If this fulfillment of the letter is not integrated with man's final aim and the love of God, there cannot be a harmonious existence; man's apostasy will always be a force which will affect and finally destroy these autonomous fragments of natural morality. Only in the whole of morality, and the total appropriation of it, is the letter of the law safe; and for this whole moral order, grace is necessary, says Schoonenberg. We unexpectedly encounter here a noteworthy parallel to Kuyper's common grace

19. E.g., H. Urs von Balthasar, *Karl Barth* (1951); H. de Lubac, *Surnaturel;* M. Schmaus, and others. Cf. Berbuir, *op. cit.,* p. 54.
20. For the material which follows, see the important article by P. Schoonenberg, "De Genade en de zedelijk goede Act," *Werkgemeenschap van Kath. Theologen in Nederland* (1950), pp. 221ff. For the condemned view of Baius, see Denzinger, p. 1061. Cf. also Denzinger, pp. 373, 230.

outlook; Kuyper held the necessity of grace for a good deed since it could not arise from the natural powers of fallen man as such. But Schoonenberg goes on to reject the idea (held by Baius) that man stands either under love or under cupidity; there is a middle way, that of the "acts disposed toward justification," which lead to love, though they do not arise from love; and which therefore are not sinful but good acts. Man's fallen nature still possesses freedom, and thus natural goodness and morality and love are possible — a position which, says Schoonenberg, Baius wrongly called Pelagian.

Thus there appears to be a tension in Schoonenberg's view; on the one hand, grace is necessary for a good act, because of the corruption of the heart; on the other hand, Baius is rejected. He himself, however, sees a possible solution. There is no contradiction in the Church's doctrinal decisions if we hold that the later statements against Baius and others do not deal with the total meaning of good, but only with good within the limits of nature. In the earlier statements against the Pelagians, the total view of the good act was treated, and the necessity of grace affirmed; and in this sense also the Church later denied that free will of itself can produce anything good, against the view of Abelard. Man retains psychological freedom, but nowhere does the Church deny the necessity of grace, says Schoonenberg.

We encounter here a view of the relation between nature and grace which will not admit a dualism and which, more so than earlier Catholic views, sees nature in the light of grace. And thus there is an unavoidable tension as regards the decisions of the Church against Baius and Quesnel. Baius was accused of denying any possibility of good coming from man's nature alone. But was not Baius, too, concerned with man's total apostasy, which led him to conclude that grace was necessary, and which furnished the background of his (dogmatic) exegesis of Rom. 2:14? And was not this total aspect also decisive in the controversy between Luther and Erasmus? And is Schoonenberg, on this most important issue able to rise above dilemma by means of his "totality view" — the "totality view" which the Reformers also emphasized so strongly in their doctrine of total corruption? We raise the question especially because Schoonenberg refuses to choose clearly for free choice as over against an enslaved choice, but speaks of man's freedom as "disoriented, bound, enslaved," and holds that man retains his freedom of choice only "within this bound condition." Schoonenberg considers the view which stresses the need for grace because of man's "enslaved" powers of choice, not only logical but also traditional, and in support points to the earlier decisions of the

Church, such as those of the Council of Orange; but it then becomes of importance to ask whether his outlook can be called traditional in terms of the later decisions against the Reformation, Baius, and Quesnel. And this, in my opinion, it will be extremely difficult for the "new theology" to maintain.

It is not our purpose to consider in detail all sorts of new trends. We wished only to direct attention to the fact that, universally, fallen man's acts "analogous to the law" give rise to identical problems. It is extremely interesting to compare Kuyper and Schoonenberg, and then to note that the latter holds grace to be necessary for a morally good act, and at the same time rejects the position of Baius; while Calvin and Kuyper consistently deny that such an act can find its basis in human nature as such. That Kuyper and Schoonenberg as they become more deeply involved in the problems clustering around this point approach each other is related to their common concern for the total apostasy of the heart, which plays an important role not only with Calvin and Kuyper, but also with Schoonenberg. One cannot but conclude that at least this new Catholic theology has the obligation to concern itself anew with the meaning and legitimacy of the Reformation's doctrine of total corruption, and with the question whether the fairly general Catholic view of this doctrine as implying the "annihilation" of man's nature is really justified.[21] For in this doctrine the end in view is exactly not such an annihilation, but rather accentuation of the total act of alienation from enmity toward God, which cannot be reduced and relativized by a remnant of goodness that can stand before the face of God.

It is further noteworthy that the Reformation did not at all deny the conformity of fallen man's acts "analogous to the law," but maintained the corruption of man's nature because it refused, in the light of man's alienation from God, to consider such acts in the last analysis as integral good works which could stand before God's judgment. The Reformers did not exegete Romans 2 as did Baius later; though the fear that the doctrine of total corruption would lead them in this direction was not at all illusory. That they were not so led is an evidence of the exegesis of the text, which is neither dogmatic nor a priori, which in my opinion clearly does

---

21. Such a concern seems already visible in Schoonenberg's remark elsewhere that the Protestant view of man's fallen nature needs not so much to be rejected as supplemented, and that this supplementing consists in affirming that man remains man. See Schoonenberg, "Aantekeningen over Natuur en Genade," in *Katholicisme en geestelijke Vrijheid* (1951), p. 26.

not speak of "heathens with faith" (Gentile Christians) but of plain heathen.[22] The danger doubtless existed that the Reformers might have concluded on dogmatic grounds that fulfillment of the law without faith was impossible, and, that, as Baius said, the contrary was a Pelagian view. But the Reformation saw itself placed before the problem of conformity in fallen man; and however many problems cluster around the concept of common grace, it is nevertheless true that in the form of an imperfect solution, it does center our attention on the gracious act of God in protecting man's corrupt and apostate nature from total demonization.

Men have sought in various ways to explain the acts of fallen man which are conformable to the law; by seeking to relate them to the revelation of God in all His works or to His common grace, which opens fallen man's eyes to the goodness of the commandments of God. Or, attention has been directed in a general way to the external limiting of evil, or to the organic development of the human race. It is a striking fact, however, that Scripture itself nowhere specifically addresses itself to this problem.

While Romans 2:14 plays an important role in all theological discussions of the problem, Paul himself does not here give an explanation of the fallen man's conformity to the law, nor does he take this up anywhere as a separate topic. We can only say that Paul does not wish to deny such a conformity, but views it as a possibility which sometimes becomes an actuality within the limits of a life turned away from God, without examining further how this can be reconciled with the radical apostasy of man's alienation from God. Paul does not clarify such acts in psychological or historical terms, though he is obviously convinced from his own observation of the actuality of such deeds; "they *show* the work of the law written in their hearts" (Rom. 2:15).

22. Baius' idea that Rom. 2:14 does not refer to heathens who lack faith has received new support from the exegesis of Karl Barth. See Denzinger, p. 1022. See my *De Algemene Openbaring* (1951), p. 147 (ET: General *Revelation*); and since then K. Barth, *K.D.*, IV, 2 (1955), p. 635; and extensively F. Flückiger, "Die Werke des Gesetzes bei den Heiden," *Theologische Zeitschrift* (1952), 17-42; and cf. his *Geschichte des Naturrechts* (1954), I, pp. 295-297. He says that the text does not refer to a "law of nature," since Paul has just said (2:12, 2:14) that the heathen have no law; and he refers also to Matt. 12:33 that only the good tree brings forth good fruit. In his more detailed article, he says that "being a law for themselves" means "autonomy" in its real sense, i.e., the freedom to decide without super-personal constraint. His whole exegesis is, in my opinion, too strongly influenced by a reaction against the concepts of natural law and natural right. See further on this text, Max Lackmann, *Von Geheimnis der Schöpfung* (1952), pp. 95ff., 212ff.

Theologians have often drawn various sorts of conclusions from Romans 2 which — however plausible — can hardly be deduced from the text. And Paul's theme is certainly not that of the break through or limitation of corruption. Rather, he constantly points to man's guilt, and to divine grace, which alone is able to cleanse us from this guilt. Though he observes a conformity to what the law commands, and though he sees in the lives of the heathen a "witness," an accusing and excusing, one may not at all conclude that this reference to "their conscience bearing witness" implies that Paul is on the way to an optimistic anthropology. For he knows of the apostasy of the heart, the ignorance of God, the alienation from God, and his aim in speaking of the heathen is clear enough in the context; these phenomena which are visible in the life of the heathen are used against those who boasted of their possession of the law. Paul's adoption of an optimistic theology would radically contradict his own witness regarding Jews and heathen. Paul does not posit a moral *habitus* apart from man's apostasy, in order to indicate some deep-rooted source of visible "goodness"; and every attempt to demonstrate such an idea in Paul, by way of dependence on Stoic ideas, contradicts his whole outlook.[23]

The doing of what the law commands is a doing by nature, whereby men are "a law unto themselves." This typification shows that Paul is not praising the wonderful things man can do as literally autonomous — though it is true that Paul in this context is not concerned with criticizing the heathen but uses the fact of their conformity as part of a criticism of others. And he certainly does not make of the conformity which they show a bulwark of morality. He goes on to accuse both Jew and Greek; they are all under the yoke of sin, "there is none righteous, no, not one" (Rom. 3:10; cf. Gal. 2:15; Acts 2:23; I Cor. 9:21). Thus it

23. Cf. B. Reicke, "Syneidesis in Röm. 2:15," *Theologische Zeitschrift* (1956), p. 158. In relation to the Stoics, cf. P. Barth (Goedeckemeyer), *Die Stoa* (1946, 6th ed.), p. 296 on Rom. 2. He sees in the chapter the Stoic teaching of a natural inclination to good, and sees in this concept of *syneidesis* (conscience), perhaps the most important Pauline contribution to Christian ethics, a concept which does not appear in the Old Testament and therefore must be traced to the Stoics. Cf. C. H. Dodd, *The Epistle of Paul to the Romans* (1949), p. 36. He calls it "strongly Stoic in coloring," while the "being written" of the work of the law reminds him more of Plutarch than of Jer. 31, and "the law unto themselves" reminds him of Aristotle. But cf. C. A. Pierce, *Conscience in the New Testament* (1955), Ch. I, on "the fallacy of Stoic origin"; cf. also the works of Spicq and Dupont.

is surely unacceptable to say that Christian ethics here finds one
of its most important concepts, that of a special moral organ through
which man can escape the effects of corruption and can respond
in obedience, in the whole of his existence, to God's command.[24]

It is, however, undeniable that man's conscience has taken on,
in the eyes of many, a certain aura of holiness and unassailability.
Associated with man's awareness that it may not be violated, conscience is identified with the voice of God in the heart of man.
This means there is present in every man, even in his alienation
from God, a truly transcendent element. Especially in the
Middle Ages, theologians examined the idea of conscience in great
detail. The concept of *synteresis* played an important role; it was
already used by Jerome, and refers to the moral abilities of man,
the drive toward the good conscience then being the practical
application of *synteresis* in specific cases.[25] In contrast to *synteresis*,
conscience is subject to change, and can make mistakes. In
Catholic ethics, further distinctions are made between various modes
of conscience; e.g., erroneous, doubting, perplexed, apparent, and
true conscience. But behind the possibility of errors in the conscience, there remains the figure of *synteresis*, as a "light of nature
inclining man towards good and away from evil," as the *scintilla
conscientiae*; it is *synteresis* rather than conscience (*syneidesis*)
which raises the problem of remnants of man's original nature in
acute form, since *synteresis* has a stability which cannot be ascribed
to conscience.

It was only natural that for the Reformation this distinction
would gradually lose its importance. The Reformation was acutely
conscious of the real wrath of God and of the self-accusation of

24. See L. Cerfaux, "Le monde paien vu par Saint Paul," *Studia Hellenistica*, V (1948), 155ff. He sums up the views of Paul on heathendom
but says that there are features which soften his portrayal. He sees
Paul as a theologian who passed a sharp judgment on heathendom, but
— actuality is complex — who in his "human vision" of the heathens had
a very optimistic appreciation of them: a strange tension between optimism
and pessimism.

25. For the foregoing, cf. W. J. Aalders, *Het Geweten* (1935) pp. 38ff.;
H. G. Stoker, *Das Gewissen* (1925), pp. 25ff.; W. von Loewenich, *Luthers
Theologia crucis* (1929), p. 56; *Theologisch Woordenboek* and *Dict. de
Theologica Catholique, ad loc.;* and H. Hof, *Scintilla animae. Eine Studie
zu einem Grundbegriff Eckhardts Philosophie* (Lund, 1952), pp. 198ff.,
on various attempts at a more detailed definition of the *scintilla*. Cf. the
image of the eagle, of the child who is protected against fear, and of
the spark which does not go out. We have used the generally cited
definition of *synteresis* given by Alexander of Hales.

conscience. How then could it possibly fall back on a stable *syn-teresis* as something which would relativize total corruption? The conscience was not a counter-resort against judgment, but rather the place where judgment was experienced, in order so to be led to a good conscience through the grace of God.[26] The term "terrors of conscience" is used, but always in reference to the correlation between the yet restless and anxious heart and the judgment of the holy law of God. In the Reformers' use of the term "conscience," the static condition of an inclination to good is completely dispelled by the reality of man's inclination to evil, which is experienced with fear, as the divine law is used by the Holy Spirit to tear away man's pretensions.[27]

We can never look to conscience as something which enables man to retain a relative goodness in a special organ standing outside the effects of corruption. When Paul Tillich[28] speaks of Luther's concept of conscience as "transmoral," since it is related not simply to the moral law but rather to something which exceeds the range of the moral law, then it should be realized that this "transmoral" element — if one wants to use the word — is precisely the great barrier to any reliance on the conscience to produce a diminution of man's restlessness. For conscience is then something other than an inclination to good which manifests itself in holding us to the good and warning us against evil.

In this connection, we do well to examine what the New

---

26. Cf. E. Wolf, "Vom Problem des Gewissens in reformatorischer Sicht," *Perigrinatio* (1954). He notes correctly that discussion of *synteresis* markedly fell off during the Reformation. Opposition to the concept was related to that against Semi-Pelagianism. (Cf. W. von Loewenich, *op. cit.*, p. 59). Luther specifically opposes *synteresis* as an inclination to good in his commentary on Rom. 4:7, and in radical terms. Cf. also G. Rupp, *The Righteousness of God* (1953), pp. 150ff., 227.

27. Cf. R. Prenter, *Spiritus Creator. Studien zur Luthers Theologie* (1954), pp. 213, 361; for Calvin, cf. *Institutes* III, XIX, 15. Calvin's statement that the conscience is "*medium inter Deum et hominem*" can hardly lead to misunderstanding when seen in the context of guilt, and indeed the context does not deal particularly with our set of problems on conscience, as citation of the proverb "*conscientia mille testes*" evidences — that conscience which is a watcher and perceives all man's secrets, so that nothing should remain hidden.

28. P. Tillich, *The Protestant Era* (1951), pp. 152-166. This "transmoral conscience" receives from Tillich a much more formal structure, as appears from his references to Nietzsche and Heidegger. He speaks of a dangerous road, from Luther's idea of the transmoral conscience to the ideas of Heidegger. This makes plain how little content Tillich's term really has.

Testament says about conscienc[29] We should note first of all
that the New Testament concept of *syneidesis* does not allow
an immediate and obvious identification with our "conscience." The
word is translated in different ways: "conscience" (e.g., I Pet. 3:21;
Rom. 2:15; cf. Heb. 9:14; Heb. 10:22), "consciousness of," "feeling
of," and so forth. And if we examine more closely what this "feeling
of" or "consciousness of" intends, we find that *syneidesis* is often
used in Scripture in the sense of "a good conscience." Thus Peter
speaks of a "good conscience" towards God in relation to baptism
(I Pet. 3:21), and Paul also speaks of a pure heart and good
conscience (I Tim. 1:5, 3:9, cf. 1:19; II Tim. 1:3; cf. I Pet. 2:19).[30]

Such words thus concern a *good* thing in the Christian life.
"The end of the charge" of Paul to Timothy is "a good conscience"
(I Tim. 1:5). It is a knowing that one walks in the right path;
the conscience witnesses that the relation to God's law is good.
Syneidesis involves a knowledge of conformity to God's law which
is coupled with boldness and which is restfully and assuredly
directed towards Him who is true (Heb. 10:19, 23); it is the situation in which the believer is certain that his heart is "sprinkled from
an evil conscience" (Heb. 10:22). The term *syneidesis* in these
relationships thus clearly does not at all refer to some separate
organ of moral norms, but rather to a consciousness of being in a
good relationship with God. This consciousness is closely related
to salvation, to baptism, to sanctification, to purification (Heb.
9:14). We find ourselves not in a context of an autonomous moral
organ but rather in that of practical action. The conscience is
not an organ wholly separate from the heart with which men believe.
The conscience expresses the richness of life in communion with
God and the prospect of salvation, which resonates into the deepest
regions of man's heart and life, and so leads to a godly boldness.
In any event, it surely does not mean some remnant of natural
goodness, concentrated in some special organ called conscience, but

29. Cf. W. Stacey, *The Pauline View of Man* (1956), p. 206. He says that
    the word *syneidesis* has no Old Testament equivalent. It does speak of
    the reactions of the heart to specific actions; e.g., I Sam. 25:31, "it shall
    be no grief to thee, nor offence of heart"; cf. II Sam. 24:10 and Job 27:6,
    "my heart shall not reproach me as long as I live." Cf. I Sam. 24:6,
    "David's heart smote him," and on that text, see P. Prins, *Het Geweten*,
    pp. 51ff.
30. Cf. further on this paragraph B. Reicke, "Syneidesis in Rom. 2:15,"
    Theologische Zeitschrift (1956), pp. 156ff. Cf. also Greijdanus, *Com-
    mentaar, ad. loc.* thereon, and also E. G. Selwyn, *The First Epistle of
    St. Peter* (1949), pp. 176-178.

rather an assurance of faith, by which, with an eye to the "sprinkling" in sanctification, we tread the path of life.[31]

But the New Testament use of the term does not limit itself to the concept of the good and pure conscience. We read also of a weak conscience among those who "are used until now to the idol" (I Cor. 8:7). The strong may be aware that there are no idols in the world, since there is only one God and Father and one Lord Jesus Christ, through whom all things are made, but the weak are not yet fully aware of this (I Cor. 8:6; cf. 10:25). When they eat meat sacrificed to an idol, they eat it as a sacrifice, and thus their conscience, which is weak, is defiled. Although objectively speaking their act has no connection with idols, subjectively it does, for in evaluating a concrete act we may not use a legalistic norm, but we are rather to consider the total act, and so considered, their eating of this food is a defiling of their conscience. Here *syneidesis* is not correlated with salvation and the command of God, as in the case of the good conscience, but with the still persistent suggestion of idols; these idols in one or another way still play a role in the thinking of the weaker brethren. Paul's interest is concentrated on the attitude of those who have knowledge toward those of weak conscience, toward those who are not yet inwardly free from idolatry; the knowledge and acts of the stronger can lead to sin against their brothers, unless they see in the weak brother "the brother for whose sake Christ died" (I Cor. 8:11).

Paul is here in no way implying the holiness of the consciences of the weak and of each individual — conscience can be related to idolatry! — he is simply concerned to protect the weak from a

31. For the "good conscience," see also Zahn (Wohlenberg) on I Tim. 1:15. He says, "the consciousness of the closest belonging to and friendship with God: a good conscience"; cf. also his similar remark on II Tim. 1:3, "a conscience in which no barrier stands between myself and God." Cf. Kuyper, *E. Voto*, III, 501. He refers to a good conscience as the "reconciled" conscience. For conscience as a knowledge of the faith, cf. "a conscience void of offence" (Acts 24:16); "I know [am conscious of] nothing against myself" (I Cor. 4:4); "our glory is this, the testimony of our conscience" (II Cor. 1:12), "my conscience bearing witness with me in the Holy Spirit" (Rom. 9:1). For the good conscience in general, see especially P. C. Spicq, *Saint Paul. Les épitres pastorales* (1947), pp. 29-38. He says that "requisite for the good conscience is renewal in Christ." Cf. also his "La conscience dans le Nouveau Testament," *Revue Biblique* (1938) XVII: 50-80. Cf. also C. A. Pierce, *Conscience in the New Testament* (1955), pp. 100ff., and J. Dupont, "Syneidesis aux origines de la notion chrètienne de conscience morale," *Studia Hellenistica* (1948), pp. 119-153.

way of error in connection with something which for them is still a reality and therefore still plays a role in their total relation to God. The motif of Paul's warning is not the unassailability of the conscience, but love toward the weak. Spicq speaks of "an absolutely original discovery" of Paul's, the existence of an erroneous conscience, but Dupont's remark is more correct, i.e., that the novelty here is not Paul's, but the general Christian message, in which the conscience is not the final norm for conduct, but rather love, and in love not doing that which one's conscience allows — not as a limitation but as a *manifestation* of Christian liberty.[32]

When the *Heidelberg Catechism* poses the question whence we know our sin and misery, it answers: From the law of God. The believer is not directed to another possible source of norms, the conscience, which might be the decisive and revelatory factor. There is indeed in human life, in countless variations, a negative and condemning conscience which (as *conscientia antecedens*) warns us beforehand of the sinful nature of an act. But this human phenomenon is not given the decision as to what is good or evil; it is not capable, by itself, of pointing out to us our guilt before God. In all sorts of effects of conscience we can indeed discern the unrest and disturbance of man as he takes the way of evil — how could the heart be peaceful in the way of evil? — and we can indeed say that no one can fully succeed in his flight from the holy and good commandments of God. There is even in the corrupt heart still some consciousness that the violation of what the law commands is opposed to all that which is truly good for man, and is against his own humanness, but still, the conscience does not stand above the effects of corruption. There is therefore no hidden power of regeneration in conscience, and we may not at all identify conscience and repentance. Superficially seen, perhaps, these are not far from each other. Repentance involves a turning, a distancing of the self from the evil it has practiced, by means of a confession of guilt and taking refuge in God (Heidelberg Catechism, L.D. 33) — and conscience, too, involves a certain disqualification of the self and a certain distancing of the self from evil.

32. For the foregoing, cf. also W. Gutbrod, *Die Paulinische Anthropologie* (1934), pp. 64, 166. He writes about the remnants of idolatry in the weak conscience. See Spicq, *St. Paul*, p. 30; and cf. Dupont, *op. cit.*, p. 152. For the conscience as such not forbidding the eating of such meat, cf. I Cor. 10:28-29, and Rom. 14:1; such eating is blameless unless the consciences of the weak are thereby defiled. Paul, in Titus 1:15, also mentions those whose "mind and conscience are defiled"; cf. I Tim. 4:2, "branded in their own consciences as with a hot iron."

But true repentance is not at all a mere extension of conscience. Not only can the conscience be erroneous and diffuse and subject to all sorts of influences, but it is also imprisoned in an abstraction, for the distancing from evil is abstracted from the living God. The conscience implies a protest against evil, a negative, but this does not necessarily lead to repentance, penance, and release.[33]

Conscience is thus not a limit on that corruption which alienates man from God in the very depths of his being. The reaction against evil, in the sense of protest even to the extent of self-accusation, may show that man is not withdrawn from the holiness and goodness of the ever present commandments of God, but it does not break through man's alienation from God, and presents no solution which can restore life's harmony.[34]

Conscience is thus not in the least an unassailable "light of nature," but an indication of a disharmony; of a denigration, in which the unity of life appears to be lost, and in which man — in spite of himself — accuses himself. It can err, it can be weak, and it can shift because of all sorts of changes in religious, moral or sociological areas. The conscience can, by giving a legalistic interpretation of the law, denounce as sinful something which is not at all forbidden by God's commandment (e.g., regarding the Sabbath: Matt. 23:23-24); and when seducing spirits through men forbid marriage and eating of meats (I Tim. 4:3), they form a

---

33. See Max Scheler, "Reue und Wiedergeburt," *Vom Ewigen im Menschen,* I (1923), 5-58. He views remorse as one of the emotions of conscience. It is not a symptom of inner disharmony in the soul, not a self-punishment, but a self-healing of the soul, a destruction of the power of guilt (p. 39), a counter-act, the mightiest self-regenerating power of the moral world; and this is seen as an idea not specifically Christian, though the natural functions of remorse first came to their own in the Christian church. Though many of his views are of value as over against evolutionistic explanations of repentance, the untenability of Scheler's position lies in the relations between conscience and repentance and in the ignoring of the correlation between repentance and forgiveness, despite the efforts Scheler makes to find such a relationship; e.g., "repentance annihilates that psychic quality called guilt" (p. 41). Cf. H. G. Stoker, *Das Gewissen* (1925). (He received his doctorate under Scheler.) He says that conscience as experience of guilt is only "half of a total phenomenon," since only the "counter-act by the Judge" can remove guilt. This is in my opinion an attempt at a cautious critique, which actually has far-reaching consequences, though the expression "half of a total phenomenon" is not sufficient to approximate the correlation between repentance and forgiveness. See further my *Geloof en Rechtvaardiging* (1949), pp. 190ff.

34. Herein lies the difference between the co-witnessing conscience and the conviction of sin through the Holy Spirit, "who will convict . . . the world of sin because they believe not on me."

conscience of sorts, but Timothy is told, as over against them, to recommend the good doctrine that all that God has created is good, and nothing of it is to be rejected, provided it is received with thanksgiving. And many amazing examples of conscience could be adduced to make even more clear that the voice of conscience is not to be identified with the voice of God.[35] The conscience is in all of its activities, a human reaction; a knowledge, a heart, which is and which will be restless, until man with a good and pure conscience finds rest in God. And when the believer, still conscious of the gulf that there yet exists between the old man and the new, speaks of the heart, which condemns us (I John 3:20), then only through the knowledge that God is greater than our heart can he advance to that godly boldness which presupposes the good conscience, and to rest in the unity of his life in communion with God.

Among the problems of special interest, alongside those concerning fallen man and his conscience, are those clustering around fallen's man's "conformity" to the law. It is perfectly clear throughout the whole New Testament — not only from Romans 2! — that conformity need not at all be identical with obedience. A conformity is possible which is abstracted from consideration of the Giver of the law, while the defining characteristic of obedience lies in listening to God's command. In the call to obedience we can hear the tones of "I am the Lord," the demand for a type of conformity in which man gives himself in obedience to the command of God.

This does not mean that the inclination (of obedience) is more important than the deed (of conformity), but rather that in the deed of obedience the giving of one's self is demanded. The commandment of God is not an inert law, which man can impersonally fulfill or not, but something which calls for a total and personal relationship, in the giving over of the heart, and therein of the

35. See H. Bavinck, "Het Geweten," *Kennis en Leven* (1881), pp. 17ff. He says that "it is indeed a voice of God which comes to us in conscience"; but he goes on to speak of a divine side of conscience which is infallible, but is not conscience as it reveals itself empirically in us. There is a shift of emphasis in his later *Dogmatiek,* where he sees conscience as an evidence of the derangement of man's communion with God (III, 153-154) ; before the Fall there was no gulf between what man was and what he knew he should be, and therefore no conscience. Cf. A. Kuyper, *E Voto,* III, 500ff. Judgment according to conscience was wholly foreign to Christ, who lived only to do the will of His Father; what Kuyper means by saying that Jesus "obviously" had a conscience in the sense of solidarity is not explained further, neither here nor elsewhere; cf. also H. G. Stoker, *op. cit.*

whole man, to obedience. In this relation, any abstraction is illegitimate. Obedience is always response to the divine demand, and excludes every merely legalistic understanding of the law.[36]

That such tension, indeed even conflict, can exist between conformity and true obedience, and that this fact confutes all self-righteousness and all boasting based on mere conformity, does not imply a denial of the importance of conformity. Anyone who can fail to appreciate the value of acting as the law demands surely has no eye for the darkness and terror of complete lawlessness.

Precisely in conformity — even where it remains abstracted from God's commandment and thus from Him — men have always supposed they saw God's hand acting in some manner, His hand which holds back human life from complete darkness and demonization, from self-annihilation in total alienation of man from himself and others. In various ways, and cutting through all the various motives of men, life is still preserved in the world which God has loved, and no one is capable of finding a common denominator for all the factors which play a role in this preservation.

Various attempts have been made: it is man's indissoluble relationship with God; it is His general revelation in all the works of His hand, in creation, preserving and ruling (Belgic Confession, 2); it is His general and preserving grace ("conserving" grace, to use the term of the Dutch Calvinist philosopher Dooyeweerd), which according to Calvin protects us from complete blindness; and finally, reference has been made to various sorts of conformity or legality which can arise from egoistic motives, or from fear of punishment.

Attention has repeatedly been given, and not without reason, to the fact that at issue is not some 'static' relationship between 'life' and what was called the "preserving grace" of God.

Rather, under consideration is a preserving, continuing and response-demanding act of God, under the sun of the gospel, the Sun of righteousness, which will never set. We see the message

---

36. Hence the always concrete content and reference of "obedience" in the New Testament (and likewise in the Old Testament of obedience to Jahwe). It is obedience to Christ (II Cor. 10:5), obedience to the truth (I Pet. 1:22); cf. the obedient children (I Pet. 1:14). This is in the nature of the case not at all in conflict with Rom. 6:16, "to whom ye present yourselves as servants unto obedience, his servants ye are whom you obey; whether of sin unto death or obedience unto righteousness," for Paul's purpose here is to point to true obedience as opposed to the slavery to sin, which also affects the whole man. Obedience of course excludes mere lip-service to God while the heart is far from Him (Isa. 29:13, Matt. 15:8).

of the gospel go out into a world in which the guilt of alienation throws its shadows in every direction; and precisely in the midst of these shadows we are asked to give our attention to the light. When Calvin directed attention to this light, he was — to use his example — thinking of the fairness and justice of Titus and Trajan in contrast to the cruelty of Nero. He pointed to the grace of God in the world, and even to His compassion for men in their wretchedness. That Calvin should select an example from the world of man is in the nature of the case not coincidental, for the preservation of humanness closely involves the relationships between ourselves and our fellow men. When we consider how God, the God of all grace, safeguards life through all the tension-filled moments of His judgment and grace, His love and wrath, we confront the fact that in the alienated world we encounter human love and trust, pity and compassion. There is every reason for us to reflect on just these human relationships. The preservation of humanness has often been interpreted as the preservation of understanding and will,[37] but actually it manifests itself in a much deeper and more important way in the various sorts of relations between man and fellow man.

Precisely in this relationship between man and man the preservation of humanness shows itself most clearly as preservation, for it is here that we become conscious first of all of how corruption affects and attacks the life of man; as when Cain becomes the murderer of Abel.

Thus it is understandable that various presentations of the preserving grace of God have not only pointed to the limiting power of His regulations for the individual, but have also specifically mentioned the relations between man and fellow man; which is undoubtedly related to the fact that we may not think of man's humanness in an individualistic manner. Humanness is preserved in the numberless relations between man and fellow man. Man is a creature, and this very creatureliness is as such the opposite of an individualistic autonomy; and this is understandable first of all in view of man's dependence on God, but also, in this dependence, in man's dependence on and relation to his fellow man. Already in Genesis we read of the relationship between man and woman, and that it is good for man not to be alone.

37. This emphasis can be found in many Protestant and Roman Catholic views; in the latter case in a context of the loss of the supernatural image and the preservation of the natural. Cf. F. Diekamp, *Dogmatik*, II, 93, and G. Söhngen, "Die biblische Lehre von der Gottebenbildlichkeit des Menschen," *Die Einheit in der Theologie* (1952), pp. 177ff.

He received a "help meet for him" after the creation of the animal
world, which despite all its richness could not give him such
help: "there was not found a help meet for him" (Gen. 2:20).
Thus arises, as an act of God who brought man and woman together, that wonderful relationship which binds them so closely;
"That which God has joined, let not man put asunder" (Matt.
19:6). This joining was not a mechanical addition of two individuals, but a relation, a community of wholly unique character.
And Christ refers to this divine act "in the beginning" (Matt.
19:5; cf. Eph. 5:31) to show the depth of man's rebellion against
God also in this relationship, a rebellion which shows itself in
mutual independence.[38] And human relations are not preserved
only in marriage but also in numberless other relationships.
Scripture emphasizes the importance of man's not being isolated
vis-á-vis his fellow man most clearly when it speaks of the restoration of man's humanness. The reconciling act of God in Jesus
Christ takes away our alienation from Him, and directly implicated
in the restoration of our humanness is also a new relationship to
our fellow man. The command to love our neighbor as ourselves
is the second part of the great commandment, but it can hardly
be called secondary; it is "like unto" the first (Matt. 22:39; cf.
19:19).

The holy commandment of God, with a reference to the
individual's self-centered love, lays open the way to the isolated
individual, and then shows him — by analogy — the other, his
neighbor; "thou shalt love thy neighbor as thyself."

Thus the restoration of the image is not a rehabilitation of
separate individuals, who thereafter are joined to form a community.
Our relation to others does not *follow* as a more or less important
result of this restoration, but is in the divine intention essential
to our being human.

Thus only can we understand that love of God can not be actually

---

38. The doctrine of *androgyny* fails to understand the significance of the
creation of man and woman and reaches beyond this mystery of communion, as can be clearly seen in Böhme and, in this century, in N.
Berdyaev, who says "Man is a sick, wounded and disharmonious being, especially because he is a sexual and therefore divided being, robbed of
wholeness and purity" (Berdyaev, *Von der Bestimmung des Menschen*,
1935, pp. 89-93). For the darker problems involved in the doctrine, see the
symposium on *Adam: der Mythus vom Urmenschen* (E. Benz, 1955),
e.g., on Böhme, Baader, and Berdyaev. Cf. the sharp critique of Karl
Barth, on the Word of God as over against a mythical approach (*K.D.*
III:4, pp. 177-179) and O. Piper (*Die Geschlechter*, 1954), p. 149.

present if it does not manifest itself in our relations to one another (I Joh. 3:17, 4:20).[39]

When "the earth shall be full of the knowledge of Jehovah," then "they shall not hurt or destroy in all thy holy mountain" (Isa. 11:9). Love for our neighbor is not something to be mechanically added to love for God, as a "moral" addition to a "religious" command,[40] but something which finds its origin and basis in the love of God itself: "I am the Lord thy God. . . . Thou shalt love thy neighbor as thyself" (Lev. 19:18; Matt. 22:39).

Because of this unbreakable relationship, it is clear that we do not correctly interpret the remnant of man's humanness when we see it as meaning that man retains his understanding and his will, as is so often done in individualistic views of humanness. Such a characterization completely ignores the profound significance of our creaturely relations to our fellow man.[41] When God in His grace preserves man's humanness from demonization, from a complete disintegration in mutual enmity, He does this in the relationships of society. It is and remains one of the most striking features of the actuality of fallen man that we see relationships between man and fellow man function in the midst of the corrupting power of sin, which certainly is directed especially against society and against any feeling of responsibility towards the other. Cf. Cain's question, "Am I my brother's keeper?" (Gen. 4:9). This

39. Cf. also Matt. 6:14-15, "unless you forgive others . . . ," and the suffering together of I Cor. 12:26, "whether one member suffer, all the members suffer," and the Lord's Prayer ". . . as we forgive our debtors," which the Heidelberg Catechism (L.D. 51) explains as meaning that the inclination to forgive is a *witness* of grace.

40. Cf. H. Dooyeweerd, *A New Critique of Theoretical Thought,* II (1955), 155, on the impossibility of splitting the basic command to love into two parts, a religious and a moral. Closely related is Dooyeweerd's critique of M. Buber, which, as I see it, touches primarily the danger of separating the I — thou relation from the relation of the I to the non-human. The criticism thus does not intend to relativize the uniqueness and centrality of human relationships, but rather intends to criticize a personalistic view of these relations. We shall return to this personalism in more detail in the following chapter.

41. See A. Kuyper, *E Voto,* IV, 94. He describes this social aspect in connection with the basic idea of the sixth commandment. In this connection he refers to Christ's sharp warning against anyone who calls his brother "thou fool" (Matt. 5:22). Cf. Barth, *K.D.,* IV, 2 (1955), p. 499. Note his criticisms of "private Christianity," and his remarks on doubt and the lack of assurance of faith, in which he poses the question "whether the doubter ought not just once ask himself from how many men he has turned aside, how many he has offended and harassed, how many in the sense of the Gospel he has already murdered."

social sense is not a *superadditum*, but pertains according to God's intention to the most essential components of humanness. Any separation and isolation of love of God from love of neighbor is directly opposed to the Biblical witness. In reaction against such a separation, theologians have often almost equated the love of God with love of neighbor;[42] but, although in this reaction the first great commandment, to love God, is robbed of its meaning, it remains true that the relation between love of God and love of neighbor is indestructible, and we may never lose sight of the validity and the power of the second great commandment, which is like unto the first.

In this connection, we are reminded of what has often been said about the power and the effect of sin: that it forces man into isolation, since sinful man is egoistic, concentrated in himself, and envious of the other.

But we must also consider that this isolation in sin always remains relative. While the power of sin can lead to complete isolation, in the fullness of the preserved creaturely existence the inexhaustible richness of social relations is, indeed, uncontrovertible.

Actually no one is wholly given over to self-concentration. Life itself, in the hands of God, resists, sustained by the glory of social relations, of common humanity, by helplessness and the forthcoming help, by this living in society with each other. Only this enables us to explain the fact that any complete and absolute individualizing of humanness, and resultant merciless and savage attack on the life of the other has always aroused a protest, and in many ways is viewed as un-natural and anti-natural.

Theologians have often concluded from this that the doctrine of total corruption is unreal and illusory. But such a simplistic conclusion does not take into account the fact that God preserves man, not only in the limiting power of external regulation, but also in these manifestations of a common humanity. Sin indeed disturbs the whole of man's life, but in the midst of corruption sinful man again and again escapes the isolation which threatens him and again lives in the richness of his common humanity, divinely preserved. Then even sinful man gives — through affection and sentiment — "good gifts" (Matt. 7:11) to his children, and Christ's "how much more shall your Father . . ." makes this into an analogy, however weak, of the gifts of the Father in Heaven. When Cain killed his brother — and is portrayed in his flight from God — he was nevertheless preserved in social life,

42. Cf. Barth's "anticritical digression" (*K.D.* IV, 2, 901).

and we see him follow his way with his wife, within the humanity which he retained; "and Cain knew his wife, and she conceived and bare Enoch: and he builded a city" (Gen. 4:17). And this Cain is the same Cain who is held up as a fearsome example before the community; his works were evil, and the Christian community is called to love, and not to be like Cain (I John 3:11-12).

This feeling for fellow men, this common humanity, as a gift of God operative in a human world that is never to be understood individualistically has an evident goodness and glory, and in the very corruption which threatens his humanness (his social humanness also!), man can always turn to his humanness, enticed by the mysterious light of this goodness; though he can also turn to deeds which cannot be characterized otherwise than as unnatural and anti-natural.

Common humanity: the words can be lightly used and be made into a theory which today is hardly taken seriously in actual life; but this fact does not invalidate their richness and deepest meaning. Man is — even when alienated from God — not alone. In considering the estate of fallen man, there is indeed more reason for us to reflect on this social component than on the preservation of his understanding and will. For surely this breaking through the bonds of isolation, full of continuing enrichment and responsibility, can hardly be due merely to a remnant of individual endowments. Such a "remnant" might explain a certain legality and outward conformity to the law, but not the development in the course of the life of fallen man of these truly surprising relationships. It need not therefore amaze us that this common humanity, this mutuality of relationship, has always attracted attention. Just as, also outside the Christian faith, the uniqueness of man has often been asserted, so his social relationships, his communication and community, are the subject of perennial treatment. Impressed by this common humanity, which seemed evident in so high a degree that there seemed to be no need for a religious foundation for the relation between man and fellow man, men have even attempted systems of ethics on a purely humanistic basis. Indeed, the deepest crisis of contemporary humanism arises from the fact that the obviousness of this evidence can well be called into question; though it is clear that humanism still wishes to safeguard man's humanness on the basis of this "evident" social aspect. Man's relation to his fellows is cut loose from his relation to God, and thus from its religious meaning and religious richness.

The impression meanwhile prevails — that any defection from
this humanness is basically only incidental and peripheral, and
does not at all force us in the direction of the doctrine of total
corruption. But such a view underestimates the far-reaching apostasy
of corruption, which can manifest itself in terrifying ways even in
the richness of God's gifts. This corruption affects all the social
bonds of man's common humanity. Man, in his rebellion against
God, is alienated in the very depths of his being, turned against
himself and against the other, for the harmony in which alone
man's true humanness is safe from the darkness of man's heart has
been broken. Corruption alone would make everything possible —
and indeed much, very much, does become actual. We see its
powerful effects in the man who walks in darkness and knows not
where he goes (I John 2:11).

This social component of man is not a remnant of goodness
which endures unassailable through the ages, like the Sphinx
in the desert sands of Egypt. We should not forget that corruption
is also directed against humanness, against human nature in all
of its creaturely relationships. Man can lift his hand against himself and against others; he can fall into unnatural sins (Rom. 1:26-
27) which immediately affect this social component; and we see the
power of corruption working in countless manifestations of almost
hopeless alienation, in which men are so driven by hate for each
other that they become almost unrecognizable as creatures of God
(Titus 3:3), and must be most seriously warned by divine authority against the completion of this alienation in cursing or murdering
(Gen. 9:6, Jas. 3:9). This alienation is so manifest that the
Christian congregation at Ephesus which was previously alienated
but is now made near to God, must through continuous divine and
daily "turning away" from sin, be torn away from that which
threatens the new human life in Christ. The "checks and hin-
drances in our attempts at communicating with each other"
manifest themselves everywhere, even in the least relationships,
sometimes in ways which are not particularly striking, but sometimes in ways which are catastrophic. Living in alienation from
God has far-reaching consequences for all of life. Not only are there
aliens who can become a threat when God in His judgment puts
His people in their power (see Ezek. 11:8), but there is also the
destruction of human relationships in the danger of the "strange
woman," with all the darker aspects and consequences of this
strangeness to which Proverbs refers (e.g., 6:24, 22:14, 23:27; cf.
Eccles. 7:26), including the divine judgment on it.

Anything can happen in our alienation from one another, in the state of our alienation from God's command. Outside this command, life is not safe, nor are we safe for the other, nor is the other for us. Outside this command, men are "inventors of evil things" (Rom. 1:30) and can be without heart and without pity.

The picture which Paul paints of the last days is an especially dark one; it is a time when love is indeed present, but it is a love of pleasure rather than of God; "men shall be lovers of self, lovers of money, boastful, haughty, raillers, disobedient to parents, unthankful, unholy, without natural affection, implacable, slanderers, without self-control, fierce, no lovers of good, traitors, headstrong, puffed up," (II Tim. 3:2-4), and in this all, lovelessness (cf. Matt. 24:7, 10). This all points to a ripening, a consummation of evil in the last difficult times, in which man, in his social aspect, will be severely and generally threatened, when man's alienation from fellow man will reach its high point,[43] and we know that then Christ will come, and the new heaven and the new earth in which righteousness shall dwell.

The meaning of the divine limiting of the effects of sin becomes even more clear to us when we consider those cases when and where life has been preserved from savagery, and the human society, as a gift of God in man's humanness, still spreads its light in the darkness.[44]

In their concern for the doctrine of total corruption, theologians have sometimes been ready at once to draw the conclusion that all of fallen man's humanity and social relationships were nothing but *appearance,* deception of the individual himself and of others, and that, for example, every marriage made outside the faith was nothing but sin, "moral" sin, in all its forms without any goodness. And then, naturally following, an attempt was made to unmask all love of order, every act of mercy or philanthropy, and all self-sacrifice as arising solely from impure motives, which actually did not involve the slightest concern for the welfare and enrichment of the other man. Behind this attempt (and not without reason) lay fear of a humanistic appeal to the evidence of the intrinsic nature of man's relation to his fellow men, and fear of

43. It is clear that Paul does not lose sight of the direct and actual relation to the community of his time. It is evident also that elsewhere in the New Testament this dark alienation is referred to as something contemporary (e.g., Titus 3:3; cf. Rom. 1 and Matt. 15:19). But II Tim. 3:5 in any event strongly emphasizes the general aspect.

44. On this point, cf. S. J. Ridderbos, *Rondom het Gemene Gratie-Probleem* (1949), p. 70.

thus becoming entangled in the dialectic of a remmant or reserve of goodness in man.[45]

But this concern should not lead us to interpret life in such a simplistic way, and indeed we do this only in theory, and even then rarely; we do not do it in practice, for that would undermine every bit of trust in the fellow man who does not reckon with God's commandment. Such an explanation is generally not attempted, and when it is presented, it can never be convincing. Anyone who attempts to combat humanism in this way must necessarily underestimate the actuality of God's gifts to fallen man, however much he feels he is basing his view on the doctrine of total corruption. We can be safeguarded against two extremes — a superficial optimism which deadens our alertness, or a simple pessimism which convinces no one — only when we see the divine limitation of the dark dynamic of corruption functioning not only through an external bridling of the effects of evil, but also through the endowments God has given to mankind.

Any ethic which abstracts man's social aspect from his relation to the living God does not reckon adequately with the perversion of man's humanness, with its condition of being forever threatened, nor with the self-alienation and alienation from the other, to which a man can become so accustomed that its existence hardly bothers him. And seeing that the corruptive power of evil does not manifest itself unqualifiedly in the despising of the good in the last days (II Tim. 3:1), and that life still goes on, preserved, towards the future, we shall not explain this fact in terms of our goodness, or a relativizing of our corruption, but in terms of the preservation of God, wherein is involved the social interrelatedness of man as human. Kuyper's well-known remark that the world goes better than expected, and the Church worse than expected, is more than a merely jesting phenomenology of reality. In it also lies an accusation first of all against oneself because of the depth of corruption, which continues to throw its shadow over the life of the new man in Christ. The Church confesses that we are inclined by nature to hate God and our neighbor. But this dark evil is held back from its consummation. We are reminded, in the very power of corruption, that man's humanness is saved and remains

45. A noteworthy example can be found in A. Schweitzer, "Die Kraft der Humanitätsgesinnung" (1951), *Mensch und Menschlichkeit* (1956); he speaks of the confidence that the spirit of inhumanity which had its beginnings in the nineteenth century will again be broken through by man's "disposition to humanity," appearing once again through the creative power of history.

safe only in the great reversal: formerly, "living in malice and envy, hateful, hating one another; but when the kindness of God our Savior and his love towards man appeared . . ." (Titus 3:4-5), then everything became otherwise, and a limit was placed on this wickedness and this alienation. A limit, in our renewal, in the miracle of our rebirth (Titus 3:5), in the grace of being children of God. There is no other limit.

This limit is placed on corruption through Him whom the Church confesses to be not only true God but also true man, and in whom the divine love of man found its concrete and historical embodiment. It is no coincidence that Paul places his humiliation to the likeness of a servant in a context of exhortation to the Christian community: "if any fellowship of the Spirit, if any tender mercies and compassions . . . be of the same mind, having the same love" (Phil. 2:1-2).

That disciples of this Lord can be filled less than others with humanness, this true humanity, is disturbing. Such would seem to indicate that they have misunderstood the meaning of the whole Gospel as well as of their own confession that He is "true man." "I am in the midst of you as he that serveth" (Luke 22:27). *Ecce homo!*

"Again, a new commandment write I unto you, which thing is true in him and in you, because the darkness is passing away and the true light already shineth" (I John 2:8). The light, which throws light also on the question, "What is man?"

One of the noteworthy facets of contemporary theological thought is this, that after all sorts of discussions of the series of problems surrounding the doctrine of common grace, theologians are once more, with varied terminologies, concerned with the divine preservation of human life, even in its alienation from God. It becomes increasingly apparent that we cannot explain the problem of common grace from a clearly secularizing tendency which wishes to create a common terrain alongside the terrain of grace in Christ, a common terrain which would find its characteristic feature in its autonomy. Nor can the problems be reduced to a dualistic nature-grace view, which would make nature a preparatory phase of grace. The doctrine of the general grace of God appears to be much more closely and unmistakably related to the doctrine of total corruption. This relation does not imply a relativizing of corruption, but rather deals with God's preservation of man. In view of the reality of this preservation, it becomes understandable that a new recognition of these problems has suddenly appeared, in all sorts of byways of current theological discussion.

This is the case, for example, with Van Oyen, when he speaks of the faithfulness of God, which manifests itself in the preservation of human relationships.[46] He refers, rightly, especially to inter-human relationships, and attempts to explicate these further through a distinction between *agape, philia* and *eros. Philia* is an especially basic point in his consideration, since, though it is not *agape,* he sees divine preservation manifesting itself in *philia* as a means to this preservation. He thus touches on a problem which had already concerned Calvin and Kuyper, and he endeavors to come to a sharper solution of it by considering the nature of this *philia.* In this connection, it is particularly striking to note that he does not hesitate to speak of "a necessary consciousness of 'Mitsein' which bears with it a 'Dasein' for the other" — i.e., of a coexistence which implies a being present-for-the-other.[47]

We might receive the impression from this that Van Oyen regards *philia* as exempt from dialectical development. But he goes on to speak of the "double face of *philia,*" and of its "inner tragedy" which must be resolved through *agape;* while the same sort of tensions appear — perhaps in even greater measure — with *eros,* when it is "separated from the higher elements of love." The tragedy of *philia* corresponds to the perversion of *eros.* It thus is difficult to avoid asking whether Van Oyen can then speak so comfortably of a "necessary knowledge," when that knowledge, and when *philia,* and *eros* do not seem to have escaped the set of problems arising from man's corrupt heart. But this does not take away the fact that Van Oyen (and it is not coincidental) places such a strong emphasis on these human relationships, even when abstracted from *agape.* In my opinion, it is incorrect so to distinguish *agape* and *philia* that *agape* is "existential" in character, while *philia* structurates the feeling of "we," stamped to start with by our confrontation of the world of objects; for the command to love, *agape,* is precisely the central religious commandment, and

46. Cf. H. van Oyen, *Evangelische Ethik. Grundlagen,* I (1952), 153-160, for God's "preserving grace"; which may be called His "general grace" (common grace), and in which He preserves the relationships of *philia* (feeling of responsibility for fellow man); this is an excellent term provided the agency of the Holy Spirit is recognized; through these relationships the Holy Spirit safeguards against complete chaos.
47. For the feeling of "we" as the basic form of *philia,* see, *ibid.,* pp. 160-61; for the tragedy of *philia* and the perversion of *eros,* see pp. 143, 166, 193-199.

one which makes it impossible to picture the objective world as autonomous.[48]

But the problem which Van Oyen poses is a real problem, which forces us to recognize that God's preservation of man is not the superior force of an external limitation, but preservation through the riches of His endowments to man.

And precisely for this reason, the history of this preservation of man is full of long-suffering and admonition, of comfort and of warning.[49] It is also one of admonition and warning because it shows how the corruption of sin can manifest itself even to the point where it affects the most elementary communication. Thus Cain — pointed to as a horrible example even in the New Testament church — despite his ˙other communications is still a sign, a warning symbol of an insecure humanness which has not found in *agape* its earthly and eternal safeguard.

Living his life within the limits of his common humanity, man is arraigned by Scripture as guilty before God. For he is alienated from God's glory in this humanness given him by God. The Biblical passage, "There is none righteous, no, not one; there is none that understandeth, there is none that seeketh after God; they have all turned aside" (Rom. 3:10-12), applies to man in his humanness. Fallen man can nowhere and in no respect escape the judgment of God: "Therefore thou art without excuse, O man" (Rom. 2:1). Here man stands before us with all his norms — and this man is without excuse.

He stands guilty before God in the total apostasy of his heart, in his rebellion, even though he can never wholly escape his

48. The difficulties involved in Van Oyen's description of *philia* are increased because he not only relates it to the world of legal forms in the *analogia ordinis*, with "power and compulsory obedience" as "genuine characteristics of legality," but also to "that love which characterizes ordinary life; family relationships, friendship, and every kind of liking one another." See his *Theologische Erkenntnislehre* (1955), pp. 180ff. and his *Evangelische Ethik*, I, 123. In our opinion, this makes clear one of the difficulties of Van Oyen's distinction. He himself says that such a "systematic distinction" is unknown in the New Testament (*ibid.*, p. 126), since *eros* is lacking and *philia* and *agape* are used indifferently. Our objection is not Biblicistic, but concerns the question of structure: "I — the world of 'it'; *agape* — legality." Precisely those human relations, too, that do not depend on "legality, power, compulsory obedience" deserve our attention when reflecting on God's preserving of mankind.
49. Kuyper, *Gemeene Gratie*, I, 443. This is correctly noted, in our opinion, when he deals with the history of common grace as expressed in the acts of God, and he recognizes that common grace is something which rises above a merely static relationship between God and man.

humanness in his individual and his social life, and though he lives from day to day in the midst of the richness of common humanness. This judgment on the whole man finds no limit in our nature, and thus we confess our guilt not as a partial but as a total guilt. It is a striking fact that when men of God confess their guilt in the Scriptures, they lay aside all excuse, and often speak in such terms that we can only feel ourselves confronted with the very limits of humanness. Their voice cries from the depths, when they admit their guilt without restriction and without reference to the fault of others. Thus Paul calls himself without hesitation the chief of sinners (I Tim. 1:15), and Asaph speaks of the depth of his guilt, as he remembers the bitterness of his heart, "so brutish was I and ignorant, I was as a beast before thee" (Ps. 73:21-22). But this confession, replete with the strongest kind of self-judgment, does not imply annulment of man's humanness, but rather a humanness sinful up to its very limits. Asaph's lament is a self-accusing analogy, not a metaphysical identification with the sub-human. But the very possibility of making such analogy indeed contains a deep seriousness and a frightening actuality. It excludes every attempt by fallen man to glory in his humanness ("I was like a beast"!), just as the marauding and savagery described in the Apocalypse are symbolized in the beast which is contrasted to the Lamb which is slain (Rev. 13:11, 16:13, 19:20, 20:10, 5:6). These most extreme passages in the Apocalypse concern the high point of sin as also its manifest ultimate lack of power. They concern "demonization" within the limits of humanness. "Let him that hath understanding count the number of the beast, for it is the number of a man" (Rev. 13:18).

Thus a reference to man's humanness can never be ground for self-excusing, but is rather an evidence of guilt: guilt, even when man lives within the relations of common humanity. Man sins in the midst of these endowments, with his norms, with his morality. For he goes his own way. We see also in such confessions of guilt that every abstraction suddenly vanishes, every human relationship is suddenly removed from the realm of abstraction, and the depth of the individual's alienation from God is confessed: "Against thee, thee only have I sinned" (Ps. 51:4). In this confession there is no disclaimer of David's guilt over against Bathsheba and Uriah, and no minimizing of sins, but rather, in this guilt as over against his fellow man, he confesses his guilt before God. There is no delimiting of sin here, but rather an acknowledgement of guilt in the much wider context of its relation to God. This confession rises above all limiting and localizing, and relates to the total orientation of his life: "I was brought forth in iniquity, and in sin did my mother conceive me" (Ps. 51:5).

Thus the sphere of humanness or of common humanness can never furnish a haven from the judgment on human guilt. For every guilt is human guilt, and therein lies its seriousness and its dimension, its dimension as total and irrevocable through any power of man.

In this context, we might return again to a term often used: "demonization." It is often used to refer to excesses of evil. In order to express shocked denunciation of a concrete act, we call it "inhuman" or "demonic." Such usage may lead — and the danger is not illusory — to a feeling of disinvolvement, and may tend to localize excessive evil in individuals, or in many individuals (always other people!), and we may not feel that *our* humanness is involved in these excesses of evil. We often see this sort of evil, in such excessive proportions, as something which falls outside the limits of the human, in which we share.

In such a way, the localized excess of evil will in the depths of the heart become an occasion for self-excusing; man becomes a far-off spectator of this terrible evil; it is demonic, inhuman. One might, however, at this juncture raise the question whether Scripture does not itself set the example of such excessive formulations and description of the depths of evil. Did not Christ, in reaction to Peter's "Be it far from thee, Lord; this shall never be unto thee," say *to Peter,* "Get thee behind me, Satan" (Matt. 16:23)?

Here, in the same context in which Peter has just been praised (Matt. 16:17) for his confession that Christ is the Son of God, he is now revealed and condemned as a hindrance, a *skandalon,* a stumbling block in the path of the Messiah. The masks fall away from him who used Peter's "pious" statement as an instrument. It is Satan speaking through Peter who is the subject of Christ's condemnation, and however much the power and influence of Satan are evidenced in this passage, it is clear that it does not deal with demonization and dehumanizing.

For Satan's power manifests itself exactly in this power over man's humanness. This is even clearer in Christ's sharp words, "Did I not choose you twelve, and one of you is a devil?" (John 6:70; cf. II Tim. 3:3, I Tim. 3:11, Titus 2:3). This passage also obviously concerns man, become the instrument of demonic power, turning against Christ, and thus furnishing occasion for the most extreme and bitter characterizations (John 17:12, cf.

II Thess. 2:3; cf. also John 13:18, Ps. 41:10). Such words do not deny his humanness; they do not give a metaphysical description of Judas; but they witness to the terrible nature and the extent of the demonic, which becomes manifest in the betrayal of the Son of man.[50]

Hence we must be cautious in using the terms "dehumanization" and "demonization" as general and apparently evident characterizations. They can be used to refer to excessive evil, which rebels against the nature of humanness according to God's creation and opposes and betrays true humanness to the point where it is almost unrecognizable (cf. Mark 5:5). But this terminology can also manifest a flight from the harrowing fact that sin plays its role within the limits of man's humanness, from the human element in sin: the depth of evil.

The fact that demonic powers are here at work in all their disastrous effects does not mean that the sin is no longer human; it is not accidental that the Antichrist is called the *man* of lawlessness (II Thess. 2:3).

This existent and permanent humanness, therefore, is not in itself a power in life which reduces the effects of evil. There is only one limit on the power of corruption: Christ's word of grace, which He spoke when confronting demon possession, a word which can lead only to gratitude. If we view the limiting of the power of corruption in any other way, we inevitably fall victim to a disengagement from excessive sin; we view it as falling outside the limits of the human, and ourselves as therefore innocent.

---

50. Cf. Luke 22:3, "Satan entered into Judas"; cf. John 13:2, "the devil having put into the heart of Judas . . . to betray him." See K. Schilder, *Christus in Zijn Lijden,* I (1948, 2d ed.), pp. 226ff., 247ff. He discusses the power of Satan in the "great Passion," with a warning against our having proud reactions to Judas' betrayal of Christ and our isolating of Judas. Judas has recently been discussed in detail. See K. Barth, *K.D.,* II, II, 508ff. and especially K. Lüthi, *Judas Iskariot in der Geschichte des Auslegung von der Reformation bis in die Gegenwart* (1955); and also his "Das Problem des Judas Iskariot — neu untersucht," *Evangelische Theologie* (1956), pp. 98-114. They discuss Judas in detail. Lüthi strongly underscores the demonological and eschatological tendencies and sees the former especially in John, for whom he says, Judas was the incarnation of nothingness and the actualization of original power of chaos. Despite much that is worth-while in Lüthi's views, the "kerygmatization" of Judas plays a so one-sided role that Lüthi in a certain sense is forced to play off one evangelist against another. (See "Das Problem des Judas Iskariot," p. 112.) Cf. further my remarks in "Nieuwe Beschouwingen over Judas Iskariot," *Gereformeerd Weekblad* (18 Jan. — 15 Feb., 1957).

Corruption and humanness . . . .

It has become clear to us in this chapter that the Reformation's confession of man's Fall and guilt is not in the least a doctrine of pessimism which sees his humanness as an accursed fate. The cursing of the day of birth does indeed find a place in the peripheral witness of Scripture (Job 3:1, 11; Jer. 20:14), but then as the lament of an individual who has lost understanding and is no longer able to keep his perspective amidst the tensions of life; and as a temporary lament, until the windows of understanding once more open. The only legitimate lament, according to the witness of the Scripture, is not because of man's humanness, but because of his guilt. And this lament then bears that total and radical character, in which there is the resonance of the confession of total corruption. It corresponds to the wonderful message of the Lord that there is joy among the angels of God over one sinner that repenteth (Luke 15:7, 10; cf. I Cor. 13:6, "Love . . . rejoiceth in the truth," and the dark counterpart of this text in Rom. 1:32), and with the rejoicing of the father over the prodigal son, who was dead and who became alive again, who was lost and was found again (Luke 15:32). This joy was not understood by the Pharisees, who murmured because Christ ate with sinners (Luke 15:2). But in it we see the whole gospel summed up; in the turning from death to life, in penance and conversion, in the recovery of sonship, in which the lost house of the Father is rediscovered. In this, the meaning of humanness is understood anew, as the proud are resisted and the lowly receive grace (Luke 1:51, I Pet. 5:5). It is freed from its delusions and gropes no more outside the limits of creatureliness. For it is within these limits that its meaning is found.

CHAPTER SIX

THE WHOLE MAN

I N OUR consideration of man as the image of God, there is every reason for us to devote attention specifically to the fact that in our discussion of man we are dealing with the whole man, and that we can never gain a clear understanding of the mystery of man if, in one way or another, we abstract mere components of the whole man. And as we pointed out earlier, the doctrine of the image of God has often suffered from such abstraction, especially in relation to the human body.

To gain orientation on this matter, we may perhaps begin best with what is generally called the "Biblical view of man." This is an expression which needs some explanation. The general judgment of theologians has been that the Bible gives us no scientific teaching on man, no anthropology, which should or could concur with scientific anthropological research on man in the many aspects of his existence or with philosophic anthropology. Bavinck's remark that Scripture "never intentionally concerns itself with the scientific as such" surely applies also when man is the subject of consideration; as he says, it "does not speak the exact language of science and the universities, but rather the language of perception and of daily life," and concerns itself not at all with "the scientific vocabulary of astronomy, physiology, psychology, etc."[1]

It is noteworthy that Bavinck in this quotation also makes mention of psychology, and evidently feels no need in this respect to make an exception of it; indeed, he says that it is impossible to "obtain a psychology from the Bible"; obviously he must have some different meaning in mind when he uses the term "Biblical psychology." He emphasizes that such Biblical terms as spirit, heart, soul, etc., "are borrowed from the contemporary Jewish vernacular and usually have a different meaning than is customary with us." The question might also be raised whether "Biblical psychology"

---

1. H. Bavinck, *Gereformeerde Dogmatiek,* I, 416-417 and *Bijbelsche en religieuze Psychologie,* p. 13.

can always deal with the whole man, as when, e.g., the "soul" of man is made the special object of this science.

In any case, to insure comprehension of the whole man, it is better to use the term "anthropology," keeping in mind, however, that we do not encounter in Scripture a scientific description of man.[2]

And yet . . . how surely man stands in the very center of the Biblical witness! Every page deals with man in all the rich variations of his countless facets and aspects. And thus there is every reason to inquire as to the "Biblical view of man."

We may say without much fear of contradiction that the most striking thing in the Biblical portrayal of man lies in this, that it never asks attention for man in himself, but demands our fullest attention for man in his relation to God. We can doubtless characterize this portrayal as a religious one. With this term, we do not at all mean to imply that Scripture has no interest in man's various cosmic and inter-human relationships. The opposite is unquestionably the case. This appears already in the divine command to man to "replenish the earth and subdue it" (Gen. 1:28; cf. Ps. 8:7), and further from the whole Scripture, which constantly refers to man in his countless historical relationships and his completely responsible relationship to his fellow man. What we mean by "religious" is not at all in contradiction to these facts. When we speak of the demand for full attention to man's relation to God, we do not mean to relativize all his other relations; but it appears again and again that the relation to God is of decisive and all-inclusive character in these other relationships. For man's relation to God does not exclude these other relationships as unimportant, but rather implies the utmost importance of these other relationships. There is no conflict here, except man construes a tension and then eventually arrives at either an exclusive orientation to God or an exclusive orientation to creaturely relationships. The characteristic of the Biblical view lies precisely in this, that man appears as related to God in all his creaturely relationships. The Biblical portrayal of man, as a religious portrayal, also emphasizes that this relation to God is not something added to his

2. Cf. E. Brunner, "Biblische Psychologie," in *Gott und Mensch* (1930), pp. 70ff.; H. Karpp, *Probleme altchristlicher Anthropologie* (1950), pp. 1ff. For an earlier treatment, see F. Delitzsch, *System der biblischen psychologie* (1861, 2d ed.), 10ff. He defends a scientific Biblical psychology, although he admits it is not couched in the language of the schools.

humanness; his humanness depends on this relation. This can hardly be more clearly expressed than in the words which Scripture itself uses: man as "man of God" (see, e.g., I Tim. 6:11). The man of God is man in this relation, from which we may never abstract him. This is man as he makes his way through the world, not enclosed in himself, not independent and autonomous, but as man of God.[3]

This point of view is so central and dominant for the Word of God that it never gives us a neutral independent analysis of man in order to inform us as to the components and structure of humanness in itself.

Without thereby in any sense detracting from the full creaturely reality of being human, we may say that we never encounter in the Bible an independently existing abstract, ontological, structural interest in man. In the Bible man is indeed analyzed, but in a very special sort of analysis, a basic sort, which exposes man in his evil and apostasy, in his mortality and rebellion, his sin and guilt. It deals fully with the actuality of humanness, but it is an actuality before God. And in seeing man before the countenance of God, we see him not only in the light of the wrath and judgment of God, as when He "turns man to destruction" (Ps. 90:3), or when man is "consumed in his anger and wrath," (Ps. 90:7; cf. also Gen. 6:5, 11, 13; 7:1; Ps. 39:6; Jonah 1:2), but also in the light of the goodness and mercy of God: "What is man, that thou art mindful of him?" (Ps. 8:5, 144:3). The Biblical concern for man is founded in God's concern; "What is man, that thou shouldest magnify him?" (Job 7:17). We hear this divine attention referred to as God's good will toward men (Luke 2:14), as His "love towards man" which "appeared" (Titus 3:4), and so many similar statements that prevent us from ever viewing man in himself, apart from his relation to God. Man never appears as an isolated self-contained entity, or in the pure factuality of his weakness or strength or poverty or riches, but always and exclusively in that relationship which so decisively defines man in the full actuality of his existence (cf. Ps. 84:6, Luke 12:21).

We see man so described in a striking manner in Psalm 139, where the permanence of this relation is expressed quite clearly.

3. Cf. J. A. T. Robinson, *The Body* (1955), pp. 15-16. He says regarding "this vertical dimension of man's relatedness to God," "all questions of the interrelation of it [the body's] parts and functions were entirely subordinated to the question of the relation of the whole man, as part of the solidarity of creation, to God."

The writer's attention is directed to man's life, but this does not lead him to see all sorts of human relations — propagation, birth and existence — as in themselves. Such an abstract viewpoint is completely foreign to him.

Man's conception and birth are viewed in a special light.[4] The actualities of man's humanness are not described neutrally and objectively, but always in their unbreakable relationship with the divine "Thou." "Thou didst form my inward parts: thou didst cover me in my mother's womb. I will give thanks unto thee; for I am fearfully and wonderfully made: wonderful are thy works: and that my soul knoweth right well. My frame was not hidden from thee, when I was made in secret, and curiously wrought in the lowest parts of the earth. Thine eyes did see mine unformed substance, and in thy book they were all written" (Ps. 139:13-16; cf. Job 10:8-12).

This passage is completely concerned with man, but in this relation; concerned with man's "horizontal" life, but only in and through this "vertical" dimension: God's miracle, His eyes, His book, His nearness, His knowledge and searching. "Thou hast beset me behind and before" — here is the mystery of the whole man: "such knowledge is too wonderful for me" (Ps. 139:5-6). And in all this, once more, we are not dealing with a "plus factor" which is added to man's humanness as a sort of *donum superadditum,* or with a subjective religious aspect from which we can view man, but with the full reality of man's humanness, so actual that we can even speak of the "inescapable God." The above text does not merely represent man as standing before the "searching eyes of God," but it is also "the expression of the astonishment of the man who discovers that in his ways he is involved in relationships which are not apparent to the natural eye, that he no longer belongs wholly to himself, that he no longer has his life for himself only, since his life everywhere evidences invisible relations with which he is tied in with the reality of God." Man without this relation cannot exist, he is a phantom, a creation of abstracting thought, which is no longer conscious of the relationships, the basic actuality, of humanness, which concerns itself with that which can never

---

4. We find this also in the Old Testament in regard to the birth of children. The biological fact is placed in a light, nay, seen in the light which for Israel dominated all: "Lo, children are a heritage of Jehovah, and the fruit of the womb is his reward" (Ps. 127:3). Childlessness is viewed as a misfortune and a punishment (cf. P. Schoonenberg, *Het Geloof van ons Doopsel,* I, 217, with citations of Gen. 30, I Sam. 1:6-18, Isa. 47:9, Jer. 18:21).

exist: man in himself, in isolation. This man, now, in the impossibility of his being isolated and independent, is the whole man.[5]

We have already in another chapter seen that theologians have often, in connection with man as the image of God, made various distinctions and in sometimes peculiar fashion have localized the image in man's soul in distinction from his body, which was thus not part of the image.

They asked that attention be given to the fact that Scripture appears to concern itself not merely with man in his totality, but as well with man in terms of his various aspects, and makes distinctions which appear to show a certain anthropological concentration on one or another kind of composition or structuredness of man. It is true, they said, that the whole man never vanishes from the Biblical viewpoint, but does it not also speak of man in many different ways which involve distinctions? In answer to this question, we may well say that Scripture indeed does speak of man in very differing ways. Various terms are used, such as soul, flesh, heart, spirit, innermost parts, mind, conscience; and we also read of the inner and the outer man. We do not further include the distinction between the old man and the new man, since that obviously does not concern an anthropological distinction within man's general humanness, but refers rather to man from a historical-soteriological viewpoint. But the other distinctions we have listed are enough to raise the problem whether our attention is not thereby directed to clearly defined parts of man in terms of an independent anthropological interest. This can be pinpointed by asking this question: whether Scripture directs its attention to some part of man in which his uniqueness or essence can be found, in distinction from other parts of his humanness.

5. For the use of "inescapable," see W. Eichrodt, *Theologie des Alten Testaments*, III, 146. The quote is from A. Weiser, *Die Psalmen*, II (1950), p. 535; cf. his reference to "an all-embracing synoptic view on the reality of life under God" (p. 538). Cf. on Ps. 139, H. Dooyeweerd, *A New Critique of Theoretical Thought*, I (1953), pp. 174ff. For this relation as definitive of the whole man, see G. Pidoux, "L'homme dans l'Ancien Testament," *Cahiers théologiques*, 32 (1953), and his *Anthropologie religieuse* (*Etudes publiées sous la direction de Prof. C. J. Bleeker*), (1955), pp. 155-165. Pidoux speaks of the "monistic" Hebrew outlook in contrast to "modern dualism" (p. 156); "an indissoluble unity." Cf. E. G. van Teylingen, "Dit is de gehele Mens," *Mededeelingen voor Calvinistische Wijsbegeerte* (May, 1956). He refers to Eccles. 12:13, translated by him as "this is the whole man." There are various and different translations of this text, however; e.g., "for this is the whole duty of man" (King James Version).

If so, Scripture would demand attention not so much for the whole man as for the essence of his humanness. There have been constant attempts, in this connection, to search through the Biblical conceptual material bearing on man in order to introduce system, and to deduce a clear-cut anthropology or psychology.

But these attempts have only made clear that because of the great variety of concepts used in the Bible, it is not possible to synthesize them into a systematic Biblical anthropology in which the structure and composition of man would be made clear. Robinson even speaks of a "chaotic" use of terms, and though such an expression perhaps too much implies a scientific context of fixed usage, his meaning is clear enough: the Biblical concepts cannot be systematized to yield a clear insight into the different parts of man.[6]

It is obviously not the intention of the divine revelation to give us exact information about man in himself and thus to anticipate what later scientific research on man offers. The Scriptural anthropological concepts which vary so extremely never occur in a context which is concerned with the composition of man as such, in himself. God's revelation directs our glance towards man in his totality, in his relation to God. This has been expressed by saying that the Bible speaks of man existentially, meaning thereby the dimension of Scripture's treatment of man. In this connection, Schlink refers to "the question of the psycho-physical structure of man as dogmatically relatively uninteresting," meaning thereby not that such aspects of man are not important, but that they do not in themselves come within the purview of Scripture, since its outlook is delimited by the integral unity of man. It is indeed true that various aspects of humanness are spoken of in very concrete and extremely varied ways, but the decisive question is this, whether the intent of the Biblical witness is to reveal to us something of the composition of man, or whether it makes use of this composition as an anthropological given only incidentally, in order to speak of man as a whole.[7]

6. J. A. T. Robinson, *A Study in Pauline Theology* (1955), p. 16. He says "from the standpoint of analytic psychology and physiology, the usage of the O.T. is chaotic; it is the nightmare of the anatomist, when any part can stand at any moment for the whole."

7. For this "existential" approach, cf. Karpp, *op. cit.* p. 23. For E. Schlink, see his *Der Mensch in der Verkündigung der Kirche*, p. 127. On the general point, cf. J. N. Sevenster, "Die Anthropologie des N.T.," *Anthropologie religieuse*, (1955), p. 167: He says the New Testament has very little interest in "man as such," in the "anthropologically interesting or uninteresting human data"; its "essential interest is directed very

We can say that in our times, under the influence of Biblical research, a fairly general consensus of opinion has arisen among theologians. They are increasingly conscious of the fact that the Biblical view of man shows him to us in an impressive diversity, but that it never loses sight of the unity of the whole man, but rather brings it out and accentuates it.

No part of man is emphasized as independent of other parts; not because the various parts are not important, but because the Word of God is concerned precisely with the whole man in his relation to God. Thus the various terms and concepts it makes use of give us no exactly expressed or scientifically useful definitions, but rather are related always to the same basic reality of humanness; so that despite the various shifts in terminology, we never receive the impression that we are dealing with an important shift in the portrayal of man. This has been recently emphasized strongly and with convincing argument not only for the Old but also for the New Testament.[8]

We think first of all of the impossibility of substituting our later ideas of soul for the Biblical word "soul," which holds both for the "*nefesi*" of the Old Testament and the "*psyche*" of the New Testament, since the Biblical "soul" not only can be used in very differing senses, but also in completely different relationships than the "soul" of later substantial dichotomy. Thus we encounter usages which would become completely inexplicable in the later meaning given to the term "soul": heart and flesh cry out to God (Ps. 84:3, cf. 73:26), the soul waits in silence before God (Ps. 62:2), the soul thirsts for God and the flesh hungers for Him (Ps. 63:2). The term "*nefesj*" (just as "*psyche*") often means nothing more than "life," and is thus used not to distinguish one

---

differently." For the idea that the Bible does give us data on the "composition" of man, see the older work of Delitzsch, *op. cit.*, pp. 12-13. He thinks we can obtain material on the "spiritual essence of man" and "a characteristic complex of basic psychological viewpoints." But cf. Sevenster, *loc. cit.*, and in general C. A. van Peursen, *Lichaam-ziel-geest* (1956), ch. VIII.

8. Pidoux, *op. cit.*, p. 5. For the O.T., see especially J. Pedersen, *Israel, Its Life and Its Culture* (1926). Pidoux sees this book as a "decisive turning point" in our understanding of the O.T. view of man, a "revolution comparable to that of Copernicus in astronomy." For the N.T., see J. N. Sevenster, "Het Begrip Psyche in het N.T.," *Anthropologie religieuse* (1955); W. Gutbrod, *Die Paulinische Anthropologie* (1934); H. Mehl-Koehnlein, *L'homme selon l' apôtre Paul* (1951); W. G. Kümmel, *Das Bild des Menschen im N.T.* (1948); W. C. van Unnik, "Enige Aspecten van de Anthropologie bij Paulus," *Waarheid, Wijsheid en Leven* (1956), pp. 37ff.

part of man from other parts, but rather to refer to man himself, who can be described in so many varying ways.[9]

The discussion has especially turned on this point, whether the term "soul" as used in Scripture has some special religious emphasis in the sense that we must deduce at least some sort of dichotomy. And this is more and more denied by theologians. Their denial does not mean that the soul should become "secularized," but rather that it may not be made the special seat of religion, in dichotomistic and anthropological fashion, since religion deals precisely with the relation of the whole man with God. This does not of course imply that *nefesj* always refers to the totality of man, or that Biblical usage is not deeply conscious of variation in man, of periphery and center, of the center of man — but it does mean that we may not see this variation and this centering as showing a localized religious part of man. On the contrary, the Biblical anthropological references unmistakably appear to concern the whole man. In this sense, Sevenster is certainly correct when he cites Mark 8:35, in connection with the question of whether *psyche* as such has a special religious sense: "what doth it profit a man if he lose his life" (*psyche*); the parallel passage in Luke 9:25 reads "lose or forfeit his own self."[10]

We may certainly not remove the distinctions between the various Biblical terms, as if they all (heart, flesh, reins, spirit) actually refer anthropologically to the same thing, but we must indeed deny that the religious in man is specifically related to one or another anthropological part of man as such. It is undeniable that the Bible uses various localizing expressions, as is apparent, for example, from the references to the reins or heart: "my heart [reins] instructeth me" (Ps. 16:7), "my heart [reins] is consumed within

9. For *"nefesj,"* see the dissertation of J. H. Becker, *Het Begrip Nefesj in het O.T.* (1942). He begins by noting the first impression one gains, that of a "chaos of meanings." Note the chapter headings; the term used as breath, power of life, life, seat of desire, seat of physical affections, person, "a man," "someone." Cf. also H. Wheeler Robinson, *The Christian Doctrine of Man* (1947, 3d ed.), pp. 16, 26, 78, on *"nefesj, ruach and leb"* and *"psyche, pneuma and kardia";* cf. also P. van Imschoot, *Théologie de l'Ancien Testament,* II (1956), 16-26; E. Jacob, *Théologie de l' A. T.* (1955), pp. 129ff.

10. See Becker, *op. cit.,* Stellingen III, IV. He agrees with J. Ridderbos that *nefesj* refers primarily to something in man, and states that we are not yet ready exegetically to agree with Pedersen that "man, in his total essence, is a soul," and, e.g., refer to the soul as the "seat" of various "feelings" (Stelling IV; cf. pp. 30, 105). For the point made by Sevenster, see his *Anthropologie religieuse* (1955), p. 174, and cf. Luke 21: 19.

me" (Job 19:27), "my soul was grieved and I was pricked in my heart [reins]" (Ps. 73:21). It is said of Jehovah that he "tries the minds and hearts [reins]" (Ps. 7:9; cf. also 26:2, Jer. 11:20, 12:2-3, 17:10, 26:12) — but here it becomes clear in the context that this localization is used to show God's relation to the whole man. Thus, such localization seems to concern itself with concrete examples which show man forth even in the depths as a being who is never hidden from the eyes of God, and who therefore can pray, "Examine me, O Jehovah, and prove me; try my heart [reins] and my mind" (Ps. 26:2).

The purpose of such localization, as Von Meyenfeldt points out in connection with the Biblical use of the term "heart," is to represent the whole man, and it is clear that we may not employ the auxiliary concept of a seat or center to mean that religion is localized in a dichotomistic fashion in that center. This is clearly apparent in the way in which the Old Testament speaks of the heart. In this usage we again encounter a localization, but it is immediately obvious that in this term we are dealing with the whole man, who is therefore not addressed as a loose conglomeration of functions, but in his concentrated unity. This is the man we see before us when we read: "Keep thy heart with all diligence, for out of it are the issues of life" (Prov. 4:23).

Such words have as their purpose not the shedding of light on the compositional structure of man, but rather to deal with the whole man in all his complex of functions; not to deal with a part of man in distinction from other parts, but to deal with man in his total existence, which lies open before the examining eye of God.

Jesus said that "from within, out of the heart of man, evil thoughts proceed" (Mark 7:21-23). "Blessed are the pure in heart, for they shall see God" (Matt. 5:8; cf. Ps. 51:12) — not because of a functional anthropology or a dichotomistic ethic which separates inclination and act, inner and outer (cf. Matt. 22:37), but because in the pureness of the heart, the whole man is pure (cf. John 15:3).

In the heart, man's whole life is open before God, who is the knower of hearts, of all hearts (Acts 1:24; cf. 15:8, Luke 16:15, Rom. 8:27, I Thess. 2:4, Rev. 2:23). The Old Testament writers already knew that man sees what is before his eyes, but the Lord sees the heart (I Sam. 16:7); Samuel saw only Eliab's stature and countenance, and was sure that he was the Lord's anointed, but God rejected this as a failure to appreciate man's deepest aspect. The heart shows forth the deepest aspect of the whole humanness of man, not some functional localization in a part of man which would be the most important part. The term "heart" deals with the total orientation, direction, concentration of man, his depth dimension, from which his full human existence is directed and formed. He who gives his heart to the Lord gives his full life (cf. Prov. 23:26).[11]

It appears clearly, then, that Scripture never pictures man as a dualistic, or pluralistic being, but that in all its varied expressions the whole man comes to the fore, in all his guilt and sin, his need and oppression, his longings and his nostalgia. And it is thus a priori unlikely that the Biblical view of man will distinguish a higher and a lower part in man implying that the higher part is holier than the lower and stands closer to God, the lower as such then being impure and sinful and further away from the God of life. Such a view of higher and lower in man usually forms the background for anthropological dualism and often also manifests itself in theology. The soul then comes to be thought of as closer to God than the body, which forms the lower part of man. And though the creation of the whole man is not denied, nevertheless it often becomes difficult to honor man's body as part of his full and genuine creatureliness and humanness. We shall not here analyze more closely this depreciation of man's body, which came to the fore in theology under the influence of Greek thought, and which showed itself not only in the theory of salvation from the body as from a lower form, but also in the practice of asceticism. It is clear that there is no room for such a conception of a higher and lower part in the Biblical view of man. This is especially apparent from the fact that sin, the evil and apostate in man, is never related to one or another part of man in the sense of an anthropologically distinct part, and is never localized in man, as though evil has its seat here or there — though there have often been attempts to find such localizations in the Scripture.

The fact already emerges in a striking manner when Scripture speaks about sin in relation to the heart of man. When Christ says that evil thoughts proceed from the heart (Mark 7:21-23), He calls attention to sins that lie not merely on the periphery of man's existence, but in the center of his life. On the other hand, it is

11. On the foregoing material, cf. especially F. H. von Meyenfeldt, *Het Hart (leb, lebab) in het O.T.*, (1950). Any concordance will show the immense number and varied nature of Biblical references to the heart in relation to evil, joy, reflection, etc.; cf. also Pidoux, *L'homme dans l'Ancien Testament*, pp. 24ff.

said that this heart must be preserved, and it is certainly not seen as something higher and holier in distinction from other parts of man. This can hardly be denied, once we consider what Scripture says about the possible orientations of the heart. The heart is certainly not lifted above the dark dialectic of sin. That is true only of God's heart, which is filled with holiness and glory: "For thy word's sake and according to thine own heart hast thou wrought all this greatness" (II Sam. 7:21; cf. I Kings 9:3, Ps. 33:11). But when man walks in the ways of his own heart, then danger lurks precisely there in the depths of his own heart. This heart does not always correspond with what is God's heart (cf. II Kings 2:10), but it can become proud (Ezek. 28:2, 6), evil and perverted (Gen. 8:21), obdurate (Ex. 14:17) and apostate (Prov. 14:14). There are countless references to the heart, which can lead man's whole life amiss. It can indeed through the grace of God become wise (Ps. 90:12, I Kings 3:12), understanding (Deut. 29:4), full of integrity (I Kings 9:4), faithful (Neh. 9:8); but decisions can be made in the heart which alienate the whole life from God in the hardening of the heart.[12]

Scripture does not rule out any localizing of higher and lower only in relation to the heart. The Scriptural references to spirit and flesh, *pneuma* and *sarx*, also rule out such a contrast. Theologians have often suggested that Scripture does show an anthropological ontic duality (as *dualism*) especially between these two terms. Bavinck discusses this idea in connection with the origin of sin, since the attempt has often been made to deduce man's sin from his sensual nature. *Sarx*, flesh, was then readily identified with the corporeality of man as something lower, which was essentially alien to the spiritual structure of the higher part of man. According to supporters of this view, redemption can mean nothing else than release from that which can only hinder the spiritual; release from the chains of corporeality. Such a dualism between *sarx* and *pneuma*, they say, occurs especially in Paul. He often speaks of *sarx* in a clearly bad sense, as when he says "I am carnal, sold under sin" (Rom. 7:14), or "they that are after the flesh mind the things of the flesh" (Rom. 8:5), while

12. Cf. J. H. Becker, "Het Begrip 'Hart' in het O.T.," *Gereformeerd Theologisch Tijdschrift* (1950), p. 12. In our opinion, there is no difference between Becker and Von Meyenfeldt (*op. cit.*, p. 223), since Becker does not mean what Von Meyenfeldt thinks he means. Cf. also Becker, p. 223: the heart as the "unqualified organ of thinking and feeling." The heart *in malem partem* is not hereby excluded, as is obvious in the Old Testament.

"they that are after the Spirit mind the things of the Spirit." And there are other texts: whereas there is jealousy and strife among you, are you not yet carnal?" (I Cor. 3:3); or "though we walk in the flesh, yet we do not war according to the flesh, for the weapons of our warfare are not of the flesh" (II Cor. 10:3-4). *Sarx* opposed to *pneuma*: is this actually an anthropological dichotomy of lower and higher, a localizing of sin in man's bodiliness?[13]

But over against this view a whole series of cogent counterarguments can be presented, and has been. It has been pointed out, in the first place, that the contrast between *sarx* (and *sooma*) and *pneuma* in Paul's thought is not a contrast between body and spirit. This is clear from Rom. 8:6, where Paul speaks of the mind of the flesh, and I Cor. 3:3, where carnality is associated with such spiritual matters as jealousy and envy, and Galatians 5:19ff., where the "works of the flesh" include similar spiritual things such as idolatry, sorcery, envy, and so forth. And furthermore, Paul speaks not only of *psyche* and *sooma* as needing sanctification, but also of *pneuma* (I Thess. 5:23). He exhorts the Christian community to "cleanse" themselves from "all defilement of flesh and spirit" (*sarx* and *pneuma*) (II Cor. 7:1). The contrast is thus clearly not one between the body, as the seat of sin, and the spirit, above sin. Paul does not view the body as of lesser worth; indeed, he exhorts the church to "present your *bodies* as a living sacrifice, holy, acceptable to God, which is your *spiritual* service" (Rom. 12:1). His concern is not with vilifying the body, but rather in seeing that sin is not master in the body (Rom. 6:12). His struggle is not against the body, but for the body, that it might be directed rightly: "Neither present your members unto sin as instruments of unrighteousness, but . . . as instruments of righteousness unto God" (Rom. 6:13). Thus the body is not an instrument of whoredom, but for the Lord, and our bodies are members of Christ (I Cor. 6:13, 15; cf. 19).

Further evidence of the impossibility of Paul's seeing in *sarx*, in the body, an evil and sinful bodiliness, is the fact that he also uses the term "*sooma*" for body[14] — and this is a term closely bound up with man's true humanness. Thus Paul's thought is far removed from a gnostic dualism, in which the soul is imprisoned in the body and longs for its escape.

13. See Bavinck's *Gereformeerde Dogmatiek*, III, 30ff. For *sarx*, see W. Schauf, *"Sarx," N.T. Abhandlungen*, XI (1924), and C. H. Lindyer, *Het Begrip Sarx bij Paulus* (1952). Schauf's work deals especially with *sarx* in relation to Paul's doctrine of redemption.
14. For *sooma*, see I Cor. 9:27, 13:3, Gal. 6:17; for *sarx* and *sooma* in general, see W. D. Stacey, *The Pauline View of Man* (1956), pp. 182ff.

Rudolf Bultmann, in discussing this subject,[15] holds nevertheless to the position that Paul poses so sharp a contrast that "he comes close to a gnostic dualism," evidenced by his use, on occasion, of *sooma* as synonomous with *sarx*." But Bultmann actually is here putting forth a line of argument which does not conform to Paul's usage of the terms, and which soon brings him to a striking hesitation in regard to Paul's relation to gnostic dualism. Bultmann sees the Pauline dualism as evidenced particularly in II Corinthians 5:1ff., where the *sooma* is referred to as man's earthly tent, and living in the body is "completely dualistically" opposed to leaving the life of the body, so that Bultmann sees Paul as saying that man desires to be released not only from *sarx* but from *sooma*. But Bultmann hesitates. He notes that Paul in contrast with Gnosticism pictures a "somatic" existence after death, as part of man's perfection. And he sees in II Corinthians 5 a polemic against Gnosticism, which teaches the ascension of the ego freed from the body, while Paul does not want such an unclothing of the ego but rather "to be clothed upon." Besides, Paul uses *sooma* in these passages: "who shall deliver me out of the body of this death" (Rom. 7:24), and "the redemption of our body" (Rom. 8:23); i.e., he uses the very word which Bultmann takes as an indication that Paul is not a supporter of a gnostic dualism. To separate Paul from gnostic ideas on the one hand, and to speak of "a Hellenistic and dualistic devaluation of *sooma* as bodiliness" on the other, is hardly consistent. The complicated Pauline usage of terms suggests rather this solution: that this usage radically excludes any idea that an essential anthropological dualism, an a priori ontic structure of higher and lower, dominates Paul's presentation of the Gospel.[16]

This, of course, does not solve all the difficulties involved in the varying terminological usage of Paul's letters, and many, after rejecting a gnostic dualism in Paul, have tried to answer the

---

15. R. Bultmann, *Theologie des N.T.* (1948), pp. 197-200. Bultmann also sees an even more important gnostic influence in I Cor. 7:1-7, where Paul views marriage "in the sense of dualism's ascetic emphasis" as less worthy. But he also judges it to be methodologically unjust to interpret Paul's use of *sooma* only from II Cor. 5 and I Cor. 7. It is striking to note that Bultmann holds that Paul was not acquainted with the Greek-Hellenistic view of the immortality of the soul released from the body.

16. Cf. Bavinck, *op. cit.*, III, 30. He notes that if sin is localized in the body, then asceticism is the way to salvation; but precisely the history of asceticism should once for all deliver us from the error that asceticism can conquer sin.

question why Paul so closely relates the two concepts "*sarx*" and "sin." However this question may be answered,[17] it is clear, in our opinion, that there can be no idea of an essential dualism in Paul, since this would contradict numerous Pauline statements, and would on completely insufficient grounds throw doubt on the unity of Paul's presentation of *sarx* and *pneuma*.

We come to the conclusion, then, that the great variation of Biblical usage gives us no occasion to read into this variation all sorts of scientific definitions of structure which can serve as the basis for a scientific Biblical anthropology. We might in conclusion add that Christ's words on the command to love illustrate very tellingly the constant Biblical concern, in all its types of reference, with the whole man. The difference in the terms used by the Evangelists is very instructive. Matthew says, "Thou shalt love the Lord thy God with all thy heart, and with all thy soul, and with all thy mind" (Matt. 22:37), while Mark has "heart," "soul," "mind" and "strength" (Mark 12:30) (*kardia, psyche, dianoia, ischus*). Such unsystematized and unaccentuated usage of concepts, in order to place the whole man before his total life's calling, should be all the more a warning against rash and premature conclusions regarding the Biblical view of man.[18]

It is, however, understandable that theologians, even when acknowledging the many-sided terminological usage of Scripture, have time and again raised the question whether there is not at least one important distinction which springs so clearly to the fore that we can hardly avoid the impression that we have to do with a normative Biblical distinction; namely, the dichotomy between soul and body, the duality-in-unity of two substances. Do we not here encounter a certain anthropological and structural reference in God's revelation? And may we not then rightly conclude that this dichotomy is a Biblical anthropological given?

In answer to this question, it may be stated, first of all, that the problem is not at all so simple as is sometimes set forth.

---

17. See especially the important views of Lindyer, *op. cit.*, pp. 217-222, 141. He feels that the Pauline usage of "*sarx*" cannot have originated from the Greek-Hellenistic world, nor entirely from the Jewish world, and that it is a creation of Paul's, which is related to Paul's sometimes using words for man and world in a denigratory sense which is not implied in the words themselves (Lindyer cites as examples the references to "man" and to "world" in I Pet. 4:6, I Cor. 1:20, I Cor. 2:12).

18. Cf. Deut. 6:5 and II Kings 23:25 in comparison with Matt. and Mark; in general, G. Bornkamm, "Das Doppelgebot der Liebe," in *N.T. Studiën für R. Bultmann* (1954), pp. 88ff.

Bavinck[19] already pointed out that the terms "soul" and "body" arise fairly late, and do not occur in the Old Testament, and he felt that Hebrew has no fixed term for what we today call the body. In proceeding to examine this dichotomy more closely, we are not dealing with the question whether the terms may be used — as is frequently done in the confessions of the Church — to indicate the whole man, but rather with a wholly different question, namely, whether we must accept as Biblical teaching that man is composed of two substances, soul and body; an idea which is both strongly affirmed and strongly denied. And at this point in our discussion, we may well pause to consider a previous question which arises; viz., did not the Church consciously affirm this dichotomy when it took a stand against the trichotomy of "body, soul and spirit"? This question is well worth considering.

Is it Scripture which forces us, in this dilemma, to choose for dichotomy and against trichotomy? And was this the reason that the Church viewed the trichotomous approach with so much suspicion? Or is this rejection related to other elements in the trichotomous approach which were deemed wrong, and which then made the Church suspicious of any such approach? The question arises already in Bavinck's statement that the choice between dichotomy and trichotomy is "not indifferent, but stands in close relation to the Christian doctrines of the unity of human nature, the value of the body and the meaning of the resurrection and therefore also with the doctrine of the Creation and the Incarnation." The very relations instanced by Bavinck, however, already suggest that the Church was not concerned with a formally anthropological choice between the two; it surely is not a priori evident that unity is possible in a dichotomy but not in a trichotomy. It might also be asked why Bavinck feels that trichotomy brings the value of the body into question, since it too holds to the body as an integral part of man (body, soul, spirit).

We should note, in the first place, that the idea of trichotomy does not originate in Christendom, but in Greek philosophy. It arises from the need for some intermediary between the two poles of visible and invisible things, for something which should bridge the gulf between the two worlds of body and spirit (nous). This need was met with the "soul," which so to speak formed the bond, the juncture, between two things which could actually not be united. Only in this way could a certain unity of human nature

19. Bavinck, *Bijbelsche en religieuze Psychologie*, p. 22. Bavinck views the terms themselves as allowable.

be arrived at. The idea of trichotomy thus rests not at all on a fortuitous preference for a trichotomy rather than a dichotomy, but rather finds its origin in the problem of mediating between the two worlds of Greek dualism. Consequently, injustice was done to the unity of human nature (hence Bavinck's objection), and the notion of an original and polar opposition between spirit and matter is introduced into the idea of creation. Thus Bavinck attacks trichotomy not with the argument that Scripture knows nothing of three substances, and refers to two only, but rather with the argument that it knows nothing of any original dualism between spirit and matter. And here also lies the reason why trichotomy exerted relatively little influence on the Church. The Church's aversion to trichotomy has sometimes been related to the fact that the Christology of Apollinaris, judged heretical in 381, was related to a trichotomistic view of human nature. It is certainly possible that, historically speaking, these relations may have helped the repulsion of trichotomy, but the reason for the Church's rejection surely does not lie exclusively in this Christological relation, as appears all the more from the fact that Apollinaris appears to have developed his Christology first in a dichotomistic context, which presumably should thus also have been rejected by the Church. The problem of mediation may also occur, of course, in a dichotomistic approach, though it can hardly be denied that in the trichotomist's "soul," mediating between body and spirit, it appears much more openly. Not only the relation of trichotomy to an heretical Christology, but also trichotomy itself, came into conflict with the Biblical view of the whole created man: man, in which his unity is maintained against any sort of dualistic tension in the work of God's hands, a tension which has then to be bridged by a third mediating substance in order to accommodate it to the Christian doctrine of Creation.[20]

20. See Bavinck, *op. cit.*, pp. 52-53; cf. *Gereformeerde Dogmatiek*, II, 517. He also says that trichotomy found some support among Greek theologians in the first centuries of Christendom, but was discredited by the condemnation of 381. See A. Grillmeier, *Das Konzil von Chalkedon*, I (1951), p. 106. He says that "it was secondary" to Apollinaris' synthesis of *sarx* and *pneuma* whether this was related to a trichotomistic or dichotomistic view of man's nature. He first taught a dichotomy of *sarx* and *psyche*, in which the latter was replaced by the Logos. See further Harnack, *Lehrbuch der Dogmengeschichte*, II, 326; and recently Karl Barth, *K.D.*, III, 2. See A. Kuyper, *Loci*, 3, p. 22. He calls trichotomy pantheistic and likewise speaks of "a mediating element between two antithetical elements." Cf. Hodge, *Systematic Theology*, II (1880), 47ff. His attack on trichotomy is unsatisfactory.

The Church's attack on trichotomy was carried out in spite of the fact that Scripture uses expressions which at first glance seem to leave a trichotomistic impression. Thus Hebrews 4:12 speaks of the "dividing of soul and spirit," and I Thessalonians 5:23 of the preservation of "spirit and soul and body." It is clear, however, that these texts could hardly be a compelling evidence for the Church's acceptance of trichotomy. There is no thought in these texts of a scientific description of man's structure. Hebrews 4:12 deals with the power of the two-edged sword of the Word and its deep-cutting sharpness, and this sword's cutting and separating power is related to as many terms as possible: soul and spirit, joints and marrow, the thoughts and intents of the heart. This sharp sword pierces through the whole man; no creature can hide himself before Him, for all things lie open and revealed before God's eyes (Heb. 4:13). There is nothing here of a scientific splitting of man into parts as a doctrine taught by Scripture. And the unsatisfactoriness of an appeal to Scripture in support of trichotomy is no less clear in relation to I Thessalonians 5:23, where the believers are brought into the orbit of the sanctification of spirit, soul and body, so as to be preserved blameless until the coming of Christ. This obviously concerns the universal and total aspect of sanctification, as the context makes clear enough, and this fact is now generally acknowledged; though, naturally, from this text one may in turn deduce that Paul does not deal in terms of a fixed dichotomy.[21]

---

21. The appeal to Heb. 4:12 is found, e.g., in Vilmar, *Dogmatik. Akad. Vorlesungen* (1874), pp. 334-336. He feels that we cannot speak of "dividing" unless we distinguish substantially between *pneuma* and *psyche.* He acknowledges that Plato taught a sort of trichotomy, but then merely as an "obscure and confused forerunner" of the correct Scriptural trichotomy. Kuyper holds that Vilmar was driven to trichotomy by the Lutheran doctrine of the Eucharist (*op. cit.,* p. 25). On Heb. 4:12, see also W. G. Kümmel, *Das Bild des Menschen im N.T.* (1948), p. 49; F. W. Grosheide, *Comm. op Hebr., ad loc.* In connection with I Thess. 5:23, cf. the extremely varied terminology of Scripture; "stand fast in one spirit, with one soul" (Phil. 1:27), "my soul doth magnify . . . and my spirit rejoice" (Luke 1:46), "defilement of flesh and spirit" (II Cor. 7:1), "no rest for my spirit" (II Cor. 2:12), and "our flesh had no relief" (II Cor. 7:5). For general recognition of the text's reference to the whole man, see Bavinck, *Geref. Dogmatiek,* II, 517; his *Bijbelsche en religieuze Psychologie,* p. 58); and Kümmel, *op. cit.,* p. 20; Kümmel notes that Paul used the anthropological concepts of his time in great numbers. Cf. W. Gutbrod, *Die Paulinische Anthropologie,* pp. 90ff., J. A. T. Robinson, *The Body,* p. 26, citing H. Wheeler Robinson; and W. D. Stacey, *The Pauline View of Man* (1956), p. 123, citing Deut. 6:5 as an analogy. It should also be noted that the text is a prayer. Cf. Delitzsch,

Now, however, the question arises whether, since the Church rejected trichotomy (because of its dualistic background, which broke the unity of man's nature), we do not have even more reason to reject dichotomy. Does not the dualistic tension so visible in trichotomy become even more acute in a dichotomistic view? Strasser[22] has shown that modern trialism (in distinction from dualism) replaces the dualism of Descartes with quite a different view of man. He sees this trialism as beginning with Kant and judges that it breaks up the existential unity of man even more than did Cartesian dualism, and holds that the trialism of Max Scheler, for example, neglects the evidence for man's unity. If these questions are so acute in trichotomy and trialism, are they not just as acute in dichotomy, and have not dichotomists also attempted all sorts of mediation to restore the unity of man after first breaking it? Dichotomy may be simpler than trichotomy, but it too must face the question of the unity of man. Can we reject trichotomy and still accept dichotomy? With this question we face an issue which has aroused deep and complex theological and philosophical discussion: the issue of whether dichotomy is necessarily dualistic and thus necessarily involves a dialectic of mediation which must destroy the unity of man.

It is important to make the simple observation that duality and dualism are not at all identical, and that a reference to a dual moment in cosmic reality does not necessarily imply a dualism. Trichotomy and dichotomy have this in common, that neither is to be rejected merely because it distinguishes several aspects in man – any more than we can say that the many "spheres" of the Calvinist philosopher Dooyeweerd a priori imply a splitting of man into various parts. A certain duality can be spoken of, for example, in the creation of man and woman, without this implying that God's intention was an opposition, a dualism, between the two (cf. Gen. 2:18). Duality within created reality does not exclude harmony and unity, but is exactly oriented towards it. Duality

---

op. cit., pp. 91-92. He argues quite differently from the contemporary consensus and thinks that these texts concern man's essential structure; he also cites I Cor. 15:45.

22. Strasser, *Het Zielsbegrip in de metaphysische en empirische Psychologie* (1950), pp. 32, 40, 41, 48. Cf. Klages, *Der Geist als Widersacher der Seele.* Strasser refers to him in the context of the separation of spirit and soul. He also speaks of the "dualistic splitting of the ego by Husserl" and "the total annihilation of the view of man held by the *philosophia perennis.*"

between man and fellow man, man and world, becomes a dualism only when there is a polar tension, an inner separation, which destroys the unity between the terms.

The same holds true when we consider various distinctions and aspects within man. Tension between the terms was clearly evident in the trichotomistic approach, and the question is now whether dichotomy's "soul and body" do not involve us in similar tension. If that should be the case, dichotomy should be rejected just as was trichotomy. We should know what we are doing if we choose for dichotomy and against trichotomy without having a sound basis for our choice; we are surely then not equipped to deal with the question whether the dualism we rejected in trichotomy is ruled out by the dichotomy we have accepted.

The most controversial form of dichotomy in theology is that which pictures man as a composite of two substances, body and soul. This idea, for which support is claimed in Scripture, does not in the least intend to imply a dualism, a polar tension. The attempt is rather made to show the unity of man despite — or, rather, in — this duality, by calling attention to some relation which, in whatever way it is more closely described and defined, unites soul and body.

But merely posing such a duality-in-unity does not mean that we actually have a real unity. The question always remains whether this duality-in-unity is not so construed that the tension between the two terms, the impossibility of joining them, becomes unmistakably clear; and whether, actually, the two terms which are first separated in a dualism are not illegitimately joined in a fictitious unity.

There have been sharp attacks made, from various quarters and especially in our time, against this substantial dichotomy (which is usually associated closely with Descartes). There is a widespread feeling that this theory of man does not propose a duality-in-unity but rather a tension-filled dualism, which is not at all abrogated by saying that soul and body are related to each other, in some explicable (or inexplicable) way. The argument thus concerns dualism rather than duality. When the Dutch Calvinist philosopher Dooyeweerd (and his philosophy of the Law spheres) made his sharp attack on the teaching of two substances in man, he nevertheless spoke of a distinction between "heart" and "body" ("functie-mantel") and declared more than once that he was not opposed to the idea of dual moments; he held that a substantial dichotomy implied much more than a duality, and that it dualistically destroyed the unity of human nature.

In the first period of such criticism of substance dichotomy, the question was raised whether the criticism did not also affect the confessions of the Church, since they speak of man as "composed" of body and soul, and also on one occasion speak of the two "substances," body and soul. The Council of Chalcedon (451) speaks of human nature as composed of "rational soul and body" ("ex anima rationali et corpore"), an expression which is often used in later times also.

The Reformed confessions speak of our being Christ's, with "soul and body" (Heidelberg Catechism, Q. 1; cf. Q. 57); of punishment of soul and body (Q. 11), of salvation of soul and body (Q. 37), the dire needs of soul and body (Q. 26, 125); these are all expressions in which the emphasis is on the totality of man, which is described in these terms. This emphasis comes to the fore when the completeness of Christ's human nature is confessed as over against various heresies (Belgic Confession, 18). It is said, against the Anabaptists, that Christ not only took on human nature so far as the body is concerned, but also a human soul, so that he would be true man; since the soul as well as the body was lost, this was necessary in order to save both.[23]

The decisive question here is whether the confessions in their use of anthropological concepts intend and mean thereby to give positive statements on the composition of man, or whether they make use of these concepts (as does Scripture) in a very free and imprecise manner, intending by means of them to refer to the whole man.[24] There is a great difference between non-scientific

23. For Chalcedon, see Denzinger, p. 148. An earlier edition of the Belgic Confession says that God created man composed of two parts, body and soul (Latin text, "duabus partibus, corpore et anima"; Dutch text, "twee dinghen, van lijf ende ziele"; French text, "composé de deux choses"). Cf. Bakhuizen van den Brink, De Nederlandsche Belijdenis Geschriften, (1940), pp. 82-83; and V. Hepp (Het Voortbestaan, de Onsterfelijkheid en de Substantialiteit van de Ziel (1937), p. 27. Hepp holds that if Dordt had foreseen that a misunderstanding as the present one would arise regarding the soul, it doubtless would have seen to it that this sentence was also incorporated in the standard editions.

24. Cf. the anthropological concepts in the Canons of Dordt (III, IV, XI), which say that man's understanding is powerfully enlightened through the Holy Spirit, but that the Spirit also penetrates to the innermost parts of man, opens the heart, and vivifies the will. We are not here bound to a church-imposed anthropological analysis, but rather to a confession regarding the powerful working of the Holy Spirit, who affects man to the very depths of his existence (as over against any idea of faith as merely intellectual assent).

references to a dual aspect of human nature and a thesis that man is composed of two substances, body and soul.

The criticism by Dooyeweerd and by other proponents of the recent Dutch Calvinist "Philosophy of the Law Spheres" is not directed against various confessional formulations as such, but rather against the idea of a substantial dichotomy, and it rightly denies that the Church intended to make this a confession of our faith and thereby to delimit a priori all investigations into the structure of man. It opposes the idea that all the rich variation of humanness can be forced into two substantial categories (the "psychic" and the "physic" categories of the two substances, body and soul) as two function-groups which are somehow bound together in marvelous fashion. This is clear from Vollenhoven's statement that "when we use the words 'body' and 'soul' in Scriptural fashion, we refer to a difference which God placed in the life of man. But this has nothing to do with function-groups which man arbitrarily elevates to so-called things, thereupon toiling vainly to find an answer to the insoluble riddle of how two such pseudo-things can be one." This critique emphatically denies that such a dichotomy can be justified in the light of Scripture, and rightly points to all those Scriptural passages which make it clear that the Bible does not intend to give us a revelation concerning the composition of function-groups such as the psychic and physic, but rather to present man in the totality of his existence, for which reason it refers especially to the heart. Vollenhoven and Dooyeweerd, in the nature of the case, do not mean that the heart, which occupies a central position in numerous Scriptural passages, implies some new sort of substantial dichotomy. They do not take the "body-soul" dichotomy and produce by merely terminological alterations, another and similar substantial dichotomy between heart and body (*"functie-mantel"*); they mean rather by the term "heart" to refer to the whole man as he functions in all his aspects in the midst of his created actuality. It is clear that this criticism of substantial dichotomy cannot be answered — as has been attempted — by referring to the text which is the *locus classicus* of apparent Scriptural support for such a dichotomy, "God formed man of the dust of the ground, and breathed into his nostrils the breath of life, and he became a living soul" (Gen. 2:7).[25]

25. See D. H. Th. Vollenhoven, *Het Calvinisme en de Reformatie van de Wijsbegeerte* (1933), p. 33, for the "function-groups" which are elevated into things; and cf. his remarks on the "pre-functional" aspects of the heart in "De Waarheid in de Godsdienst-Wijsbegeerte," *Vox Theologica* (1942). It is therefore understandable that Vollenhoven's

It is very generally agreed today that it is impossible to read in this text the juncture of body and soul as two substances, material and psychic; this is already evident from the fact that man becomes a living soul, living being, through this creative act, and thus Pidoux writes "to say that man in Genesis is composed of two elements, a material one represented by the dust of the earth and a spiritual represented by the breath of God is not to give the biblical interpretation, for it does not say that man *has* a soul, but that man is a soul."[26]

We may indeed call Genesis 2:7 the *locus classicus* of Old Testament anthropology, but not in the sense of showing a substantial dichotomy; but rather, as a revelation of man's complete createdness and dependence in his whole existence. Of these same characteristics with respect to the whole of creation we read in Psalm 104:29-30: "Thou sendest forth thy spirit, they are created. . . . Thou takest away their breath, they die and return to their dust." This does not imply a denial of the uniqueness of man, but shows us what can and must be said of him and of the whole creation, and we see this creatureliness and total dependence affirmed elsewhere in the Old Testament also (Job. 34:14, Isa. 42:5, 57:15, Job 33:4; cf. Gen. 7:22). Thus the appeal to Genesis 2:7 does not, for understandable reasons, impress critics of substantial dichotomy, since it is hardly permissible to impose the idea of two substances on the text, and since its reference to the act of the living God and Creator in man's created humanness is something wholly different from the problem of man's dichotomous composition[27]

Such considerations opened the way for a closer analysis of dichotomy as it had frequently been expounded. And this closer analysis clearly reveals that dichotomy had often been understood as the relation of two substances, the mortal body and the immortal soul. Once man is thought of as put together of psychic and physical components, immortality is naturally associated with

pupil, F. H. von Meyenfeldt, in *Wetenschappelijke Bijdragen door Leerlingen van Dr. D. H. Th. Vollenhoven* (1951), p. 60, in order to illustrate his own feeling, cites the words of Barth "the heart is, in a nutshell, the whole man; not only the seat of his activity, but its summary" (*K.D.* III, 2, 1951, p. 521).

26. G. Pidoux, *L'homme dans l'Ancien Testament* (1953), p. 17.
27. Cf. the rejoinder of H. Dooyeweerd in his series of articles on "De Idee der Individualiteitsstructuur en het Thomistisch Substantie-begrip," *Philosophia Reformata*, 8-10, (1943-5). He is especially against interpreting the "breath of life" as *anima rationalis*. On the psycho-creationism mentioned by Dooyeweerd, see Chapter VIII below.

the psychic; and thus arises the dialectic that earmarks dichotomy, for the psychic (the soul) is now abstracted and isolated from the concrete context of human life, and made into the definitive immortal substance in man. It can hardly be denied that such formulations played a role not only in medieval Scholasticism but also in Protestantism, and occasionally even found their way into the confessions.

This is not true of the Heidelberg Catechism and the Belgic Confession, since while they constantly speak of body and soul, the context makes clear that man's total aspect, the whole man, is continuously the dominant consideration.

We also meet with the terms "rational soul" and "substance." The former term can surely not be confined to Scholasticism, since long before the medieval period it was used in the ancient Church, and appears even in various ecumenical confessions, for example, in the Council of Rome, the Council of Chalcedon, the Athanasian Creed, and the Constantinopolitan Creed of 553; moreover the term, also after it had acquired such a marked influence in the Middle Ages, was used in later theological discussion and even occasionally in the confessions (e.g., Westminster Confession, IV:2). It is a striking fact that the expressions when used in the ecumenical symbols occur in a clearly Christological context and do not at all imply confession of a compositional anthropology. While the emphasis in the Westminster Confession is indeed anthropologically oriented, we can hardly speak of a conscious anthropological confession. Thus we certainly cannot say that the ancient Church was bound confessionally to the dialectic which later became so closely associated with the term "rational soul" (as some have claimed, with reference to the expressed agreement of the Reformed confessions with the ancient symbols.)[28]

We encounter similar, but perhaps even more complicated problems in connection with the use of the concept of substance. This term was sometimes used in a special religious context in various polemics on the Eucharist. Thus, as over against those who contended that in the Lord's Supper we have only a communion with the gifts of Christ, the Church confessed that we also have communion with Christ Himself, "with the substance of the body of Jesus Christ," and despite requests to alter the term, retained it in order to confess — in a particular situation — the reality of the

---

28. For the ecumenical symbols, see Denzinger, 65, 148, 40, 216. For the idea that these bound the early Church to a specific anthropology, see V. Hepp, *op. cit.*, p. 69.

eucharistic communion. It is of course possible, bearing in mind the history of philosophical thought, to point to dangers in the use of this term, even in a special religious situation; but we may certainly not tax the Church with all the implications of the dialectic of substance, when its intention in using the term is perfectly clear from the historical context.[29]

The real difficulty lies not so much in the word "substance" itself, but in the question of what is meant when we speak of "two substances, a mortal body and an immortal soul." The Second Helvetic Confession, article 7, for example, speaks of man as made up of "two wholly separate substances in one person (*duabus ac diversis substantiis in una persona*): of an immortal soul, which when separated from the body neither sleeps nor is interred, and of a mortal body, which shall be raised from the dead at the Last Judgment, so that thereafter the whole man, whether in life or in death, shall remain immortal."

Hepp concludes from this that the idea of two substances is so clearly expressed that any criticism of substantial dichotomy is "undeniably in conflict with the Reformed confessions." But from various angles Hepp's conclusion may be questioned. First of all, as to the structure of the confession; whether it means to be a confession regarding man's anthropological composition, supported by the binding authority of Scripture itself, or whether it is basically concerned with an affirmation regarding the future and the resurrection of the body, without assigning binding character to the particular form of anthropology and the terms ("substance") which are employed. This question, in our opinion, is not too difficult to answer, since the critics of substantial dichotomy, whom Hepp pronounces "anti-confessional," pose a further question: what is and must be understood by the substantiality of soul and body. And precisely the fact that Hepp gives no answer to this decisive question, and refers to a concept of substance which must be worked out later, is, in our opinion, an indication of the danger that the

29. For this use of "substance," cf. my *De Sacramenten* (1954), p. 304. There can hardly be disagreement on the conclusion of this paragraph if we consider other instances when the Church has also used charged terms in a context of a particular polemic situation; e.g., when the word "*homo-ousios*," which had been condemned in 268, became the hallmark of orthodoxy in the Arian controversy. Cf. also in this connection Dooyeweerd's use of the concept of *aevum*, borrowed from Scholasticism, which has various charged connotations because of its involvement in the controversies over human participation in the divine (cf. Ch. VIII below). A clarity which excludes misunderstanding is most important in the use of such charged terms.

confessions of the Church may be so interpreted as to become directly dependent on theology and philosophy.[30]

We may also say that such special formulations (substance, rational soul, and the like) which in the course of history have gained all sorts of controversial implications, need not necessarily confuse the Church's affirmations. Though the fact is more evident in the clearly Christological context of the early ecumenical councils than in the anthropological context of certain later confessions, the context even in these confessions is not primarily anthropological but — even in their anthropological form of expression — soteriological and eschatological (cf. the criticism of "soul-sleep" and the affirmation of the resurrection of the body in the *Second Helvetic Confession*). And we certainly may not conclude from the use of special anthropological terms that any later criticism of dichotomy will be in conflict with the deepest intentions of the confessions of faith; though we can surely also be grateful for the simpler and thus purer formulation of other confessions, which clearly mean with their use of "soul and body" to refer to the totality of man's lost condition and of his salvation.

It is well known that the idea of substantial dichotomy, with all sorts of philosophical results, played a role primarily in the Scholasticism of the Middle Ages. The burning question was then how man's unity could be maintained in the face of a belief in man's being created as a composition of two substances. The discussion of the legitimacy of this anthropology centered around the relation between the idea of creation and the use of the form-matter concept taken from Greek philosophy. Much more than merely the usage of the terms "soul" and "body" was at stake; the nature of the relation between the two came up for discussion in a most striking way, because of the form-matter motif.

These problems are all the more fascinating since the nature of this unity-in-duality not only played an important role in

30. See Hepp, *op. cit.*, pp. 40-41, 71, 79. One can of course attempt to remove the concept of substance from its historical complications, estimating that these after all do not affect the general church membership. But the word itself hardly lends itself easily to such an attempt at simplification, a fact evidenced in the philosophical distinctions regarding the use of the word which appear in the discussion between Dooyeweerd and Stoker as to the meaning of the terms *"systase,"* "substance," "thing," and "individual." Stoker is willing to define "substance" as "the systatic core of man, that which functions in all spheres" — at least until a better definition appears. See H. G. Stoker, *Die nuwere Wijsbegeerte aan die Vrije Universiteit* (1933), pp. 40ff.

scholastic theology and philosophy, but was also taken up in official church statements when the Council of Vienne (1311) made some attempt at defining it. This Council rejected, against the Franciscan scholastic Peter of Olivi, the idea that the "rational soul" was not the form of the human body. This statement was of great weight, and the definition is one of great importance. Vienne also said, regarding the relation of soul and body, that the soul is *"per se et essentialiter"* the form of the body.

Rome's serious concern to defend this view of the relation between soul and body appears from the fact that this definition of Vienne was renewed at the Fifth Lateran Council (1512-17) against the Italian philosopher Pomponazzi, while in the 19th century, a similar rejection was made of the ideas of Günther.[31]

The statement of Vienne on the soul as the form of the body was undoubtedly intended to emphasize the unity of man. This is clear from the ideas which Vienne condemned, those of Olivi. Olivi, too, affirmed a relation between soul and body, but held that the soul was the form of the body only through a lower form of the soul, an idea arising from his Platonic dualism, which implied that an intermediate form was necessary between the *anima intellectiva* and the body; and it was in opposition to this mediating lower form of the soul that Vienne formulated its statement that the soul is *"per se et essentialiter"* the form of the body. Though the lower aspects of the soul are not denied, they are no mediating form between soul and body, for they are led and controlled by the rational soul. Vienne felt that only through this *per se*, through this rejection of a mediating form, was a truly substantial unity of man

31. For Vienne, see Denzinger, pp. 480, 481; cf. also Pohle, *Dogmatik*, I, 377; and P. Schoonenberg, *Het Geloof van ons Doopsel*, I (1955), 152. On Olivi, see also J. Koch, "Die Verurteilung Olivis auf dem Konzil von Vienne und ihre Vorgeschichte," *Scholastik*, V (1930), pp. 489-522, and D.H. Th. Vollenhoven, *De Noodzakelijkheid eener Christelijke Logica* (1932), p. 73. Vienne's rejection of Olivi's teaching on the Incarnation has the same thought: Christ took on a human body and a rational soul, the latter informing the body *per se et essentialiter*. For Pomponazzi, see Denzinger, p. 738. Affirmed again is the idea that the soul informs the body *per se et essentialiter*. The controversy concerned the immortality of the soul, which Pomponazzi denied, and thus the question of the relation between soul and body arose also. Cf. C. Stange, *Die Unsterblichkeit der Seele* (1925), p. 82; P. Althaus, *Unsterblichkeit und ewiges Leben bei Luther* (1930), p. 51; H. Wolf, *Onsterfelijkheid als wijsgerig Probleem* (1933) p. 108. On Günther, see Denzinger, p. 1655. The condemnation repeats that the rational soul is the *"immediata corporis forma."* Cf. also *Dict. de Theologica Catholique, ad loc.*

possible, and only so could the *unio personalis* in Christ be maintained. Thus we must conclude that Vienne in its statement on the soul as the form of the body clearly did not mean to affirm dualism, but rather to reject it.[32]

The foregoing is of importance, in view of the fact that Vienne has often been referred to as a clear statement of the Church's substantial dichotomy with a dualistic background. The question arose whether the Church had not burdened its confession with a hylomorphic view of human nature, under the influence of Greek philosophy. This problem has received renewed attention in contemporary Catholic theology, for the so-called "new theology" is much concerned with the relationship between concepts used by the Catholic Church and what the Church actually meant to affirm.[33]

The question is especially asked whether the decision of Vienne implies a choice for the Aristotelian-scholastic hylomorphism of substantial form and prime matter, in which undeniable dualistic tendencies exist because of the tension between the two terms, which must be somehow bridged. This tension undoubtedly often comes to the fore in Scholasticism, and it is with this tension, especially as present in Thomas Aquinas, that Dooyeweerd is

32. This desire to emphasize the unity of man appears again when we note that Günther held a particular sort of trichotomism (Pohle, *op. cit.*, I, 375), and that Rome then rejected a dualistic view of man, emphasizing the unity of human nature. The statement of Pius IX in his *"Dolore haud mediocri"* (Denzinger, 464-465) is important: to deny that the one vital principle in man is the rational soul is to fall into an error of faith. For Olivi, see Koch, *op. cit;* cf. also Wetzer and Welter's *Kirchenlexikon, s.v.,* Olivi. Olivi held that the soul was the form of the body not according to its spiritual substance, but according to its vegetative and sensitive powers, which are really distinct from the substance and the rational part of the soul. Cf. on Vienne the *Dict. de Theologica Catholique, s.v.,* Vienne, which says that Olivi taught a form of trichotism, and that the Council, in opposition, wished to affirm that the union between soul and body could not be safeguarded if it was held (as Olivi did) that all parts of the soul do not participate equally in this union.

33. The problem was posed by H. Bouillard in connection with the use of the concept *"causa formalis"* in the doctrine of justification as affirmed at Trent. See his *Conversion et grace chez Thomas d'Aquin* (1940), pp. 219ff. In the nature of the case, the question can also become acute in the context of the relation between substance and accident employed in the doctrine of transsubstantiation. Cf. my "Nieuwe Perspectieven in de Controvers: Rome — Reformatie," *Mededeelingen van de Koninklijke Akademie van Wetenschappen* (1957).

concerned. Now, Vienne did not speak of "prime matter," but of the soul as the form of the body, so that its statement appears to imply merely a schema which is not in itself taxed with such difficulties; that is, the contrast between soul and body. It was because of the well-known background of the term "form" that the problem came inevitably to the fore. Catholic theologians have recently emphasized that Vienne's concern was, in opposition to dualism, to emphasize the unity of human nature, and thus they view Vienne as much less loaded with philosophical implication than does Dooyeweerd. It is held that the Church actually was not concerned with the form-matter schema *as such*, but that this Greek anthropology was used merely as a means of expression, without being made a dogma in any sense.[34]

According to the Dutch Catholic theologian Schoonenberg, Greek philosophical reflection led to the dualism of Plato, but this was corrected by Vienne — as over against Olivi — through the doctrine of the soul as the form of the body. The Church indeed held that the soul was higher than the body, but it also stated that it penetrated the body. The soul transcends the body (Plato), but is also included in it. In our opinion, we can well agree that the Church at Vienne was indeed concerned with maintaining the unity of human nature as against Olivi's dualism; but it also appears clear that the series of problems involved in the form-matter view can not simply be reduced to an attempt to maintain this unity. If this emphasis on unity is violently extricated from the Scholastic substantial dialectic — and this appears to be what is happening in the Catholic "new theology" -- then this is such a striking simplification that it becomes meaningful to ask whether then the whole history of the doctrinal authority of the Catholic Church, and the official use of various philosophical ideas, should not be completely rewritten.

We cannot here go into further detail on this problem, so important for the future of Catholicism; it should be noted, however, that much is at stake. In any case, the problem has been raised

34. For Dooyeweerd, see his remarks in the already cited series in *Philosophia Reformata* (1942-1945), especially 1942, pp. 85ff.; and cf. 1946, pp. 27ff. These deal with Thomas' doctrine of creation in its application to the form-matter schema (since the Christian doctrine implies that matter cannot be an independent counter-pole to form), and with the general problem of the soul as substance and as form of the body; the latter citation also has Dooyeweerd's views on Vienne, which he sees as an example of doctrine's increasing entanglement in the form-matter schema of Scholasticism, used as the basic motif in the interpretation of human nature.

in Catholic circles; there are attempts to follow the Biblical view of man; and the Biblical emphasis on man's unity is seen as primary. The "new theologians" agree wholeheartedly with the resultant criticism of dualistic dichotomy. They speak of duality, but not of dualism, and feel that thus the real intent of Vienne is being honored. As De Valk says, "not duality in composition, but separateness, is the only obstacle to unity"; and in these words we can see a summary of the simplifying tendency towards the unity of human nature which has appeared recently in Catholic circles. But it is clear that the problem is thereby not yet solved. We may be fairly generally inclined, after study of the Biblical view of human nature, to emphasize the unity of man; it is clear, however, that this unity is not a purely formal concept, but at once acquires definite content.

This is apparent, for example, when we note that Schoonenberg in this connection agrees closely with Gabriel Marcel, while De Valk holds that Marcel exactly does not give a closer description of the unity, since Marcel opposes Cartesian dualism with an appeal to the unity of man, but is not able to bring this unity into harmony with any composition or duality in man, such as . . . body and soul.[35] There is, indeed, real danger that in our reaction against dualism, we may end in a diffuse monism; and anti-dualism as such is not a guarantee of a true insight into human nature, as materialistic monism and psychic monism prove.

But this does not take away the fact that the dualism of substantial dichotomy does not do justice to the unity of human nature,[36] and that time and again it reveals its own inner tension, however veiled by the notion of some kind of unifying relation or mediating substance between soul and body. These tensions are especially revealed in relation to the idea that the substance of the soul is the "psychic" in man, accompanied by the identification of the immortal soul with the *anima rationalis*. And it can surely not be held that the Church in its confession has committed itself to a fixed dichotomy of two substances (a mortal "material" part and an immortal "psychic" part of man's nature), thus obstructing the

35. P. Schoonenberg, *Het Geloof van ons Doopsel* (1955), I, 154; Th. G. de Valk, "Ben ik mijn Lichaam of heb ik mijn Lichaam?" in the collection of essays on *Lichamelijkheid* (1955), pp. 47, 63.
36. For various problems in connection with the rejection of dualism, see J. J. Poortman, *Ochèma. Geschiedenis en Zin van het hylisch Pluralisme*, I (1955), pp. 68ff., on Thomas. Hylistic pluralism holds to more than one sort of material substance, and on this ground attacks anthropological dualism (which Poortman sees as especially represented by Thomas, Descartes and Kant; p. 71). *Ochèma* means "vehicle" (pp. 25, 149).

way to a philosophical anthropology which investigates the differences and the unities in human nature.

The crisis of the idea of substantial dichotomy has raised all
sorts of new problems, and these are especially apparent when we
consider the strong inclination on the part of contemporary theologians to emphasize the central moment of man, the center,
from which the whole man unfolds himself. Thus the Dutch Calvinist philosopher Dooyeweerd holds that the heart is the prefunctional center of man, and in contemporary Protestant and
Catholic theology today in general, the category of the "person" is
strongly stressed.

Some of the Catholic "new theologians" have seen strong affini-
ties between this centering on the "person" and Dooyeweerd's centering on the "heart," as can be seen, for example, in the contacts between Marlet and Dooyeweerd. These "new theologians" discuss such
things as the "personal structure of being" and the "depth structure
of the person," while for the "prefunctional" aspect of the person,
they, too, sometimes use the term "heart," in relation to the orientation of the whole man to God.[37]

This centering of man in his "person" is generally referred to as
"personalism," and it is of importance to us, in our reflection on
the whole man, to consider exactly what the term means. If we
investigate the senses in which the term is used, we soon receive
the impression that various sorts of motifs can play a role in it.
It is generally used to refer to "a personalistic way of thinking"
rather than to a specific theological or philosophical system.

The term is often used to refer to the personal responsibility of
man and to the personal initiative which is demanded as his unique
contribution to humanness — one which cannot be limited or defined by another. The term then stands in contrast to the orientation of the mass man, who drifts along the stream of collectivity,
without personal initiative, without blazing his own trails. Thus
Denis de Rougemont uses personalism to oppose every form of
totalitarian thought, which does not do justice to personality.

The Dutch Protestant philosopher Kohnstamm has also given an
explanation, perhaps even more profound, of his preference for
the word "personalism." He emphasizes a "Biblical personalism,"
meaning thereby that the Christian faith does not gravitate around
an intellectual acceptance of a number of "truths," but centers in

37. M. Fr. J. Marlet, *Grundlinien der Kalvinistischen "Philosophie der
Gesetzesidee" als Christelicher Transzendentalphilosophie* (1954), especially
pp. 121ff. Marlet's most characteristic expressions are those of J. B. Lotz.

the encounter with a Person, Jesus Christ, who *is* the Truth. Personalism for him is a reference to the existential character of the knowledge of faith, as over against an impersonal objectivizing view of truth in which our vision of truth is that of a mere onlooker, or that of merely intellectual or mystical contemplation. For Kohnstamm, personalism means a reference to the existence of man *"coram Deo,"* man in personal responsibility to God as Person, the called and therefore responding man, who stands as an "I" in relation to the divine "Thou."[38]

ㅅ   Such uses of the term "personalism," it would seem clear, are concerned with a protest against intellectualism and objectivizing, a protest which has its analogy in the pastorate of the Church which without underevaluating man's social aspect nevertheless calls for a personal faith, a giving of the heart, and therein of the whole life, to God. One may raise the question whether there is reason to use the word "personalism" for this necessary emphasis, but the question is merely terminological; the exhortation to genuine faith, to commitment and service with the whole heart, is central to Christianity, and may never be placed in the background by the Church without thereby endangering its very life. No matter what implications may sometimes be erroneously drawn from this personalistic "I — Thou," we may never relativize the significance for Christian life of this personal relation (cf. the many passages in the Psalms, e.g. Ps. 139, where the believer knows himself placed before the living and omnipresent God).

It is, however, clear that we have not completely described contemporary personalism when we have listed the foregoing characteristics. For personalism can also manifest a special and uniquely accented view of human personality in which the function of man's person becomes involved in the whole created reality. We can even say that the real problem of personalism faces us when we consider the relation between this human person, so strongly stressed, and the surrounding reality, with its "objective" and "ordered" structure. This tension can today be encountered in all sorts of forms. When "the personal" is made the central and uniquely important category of life, it sometimes becomes difficult then to find the way back to nature's objectivity and orderliness. Reality is not denied, but nevertheless it is experienced primarily in its unruliness. And thus the tension arises; "objective" reality

---

38. Ph. Kohnstamm, *Hoe Mijn "Bijbels Personalisme" Ontstond* (1952, 2d ed.), p. 32. Here he says that the dogma of the incarnation is the most central in his personalism. Cf. C. A. Van Peursen, *Encyclopedie van het Christendom* (Prot. section), *s.v.,* *"personalisme."*

cannot be encompassed in a "personal" encounter. This difficulty has played a fairly important role in recent theology, for example, where personal encounter is sometimes emphasized to such a degree that it is hardly possible to maintain the significance for faith of the facts of salvation; and the result is that in this personalistic approach the content of faith suffers a far-reaching diminution and contraction. It is also possible that, while there is no intention of denying the acts of God in history, obvious difficulty is experienced in attempting to harmonize the "personal" essence of faith (the encounter) with the related (but how?) "ontic" aspects.[39] This type of personalism can also appear in other fields besides theology, whenever reality is separated into that which can be approximated through the person and that which remains essentially alien to the person.

At issue in this sort of personalism is surely much more than a call to personal faith and commitment. For the whole position of man in created reality is now at stake. In this kind of personalism, man not only has a central position in reality, but assigns himself a creative place in it, in the sense that his being a person is made a normative thing; with the result that such a separation is introduced between personal and impersonal realities that man can actually no longer possibly assimilate, or integrate himself with, the real world. The diminution of God's acts in history up to and including the *eschaton*, which becomes apparent in theological

---

39. Cf. the important article by G. Gloege, "Der theologische Personalismus als dogmatisches Problem," *Kerugma und Dogma,* I (1955), 23-41. He tries on the one hand to show the value of the protest against abstraction, intellectualizing and objectivizing, and of the stress on the "personal" relation to salvation (as in Luther's "concrete" personalism in contrast to Scholasticism, and in the Augustinian emphasis of the "new theology" in Catholic circles); and on the other hand he sees a danger in contrasting too completely the personal in salvation and the ontic (the reality of salvation), since "the ontic structures" of salvation "cannot be interpreted personally." Cf. also W. Joest, "Verhängnis und Hoffnung der Neuzeitliche Kritische Gedanken zu Fr. Gogartens Buch," *Kerugma und Dogma,* I (1955), 70-83. He presents a notable critique of Gogarten's dilemma between "person" and "nature." He agrees with Gogarten's criticism of "substantial metaphysics," but sees his personalism as a "disembodying of faith." Also see P. Schoonenberg's "Het Geloof als Persoonsovergave," *Katholiek Cultureel Tijdschrift* (1952), pp. 126ff. This is an interesting article on his Catholic personalistic understanding of faith; especially in his views on the function of the Church (in relation to the Vatican's "on the authority of the revealing God," Denzinger, 1789), which he does not wish to crowd out from his personalism. Dogma, he says, is not a hindrance to a personal encounter with God, but the point at which this contact becomes possible.

personalism, here finds its analogy in the break introduced into
reality itself.

Now, it is not our intention here to discuss in detail the dialectic
and the problems encountered by modern personalism. But we
would say, after the foregoing brief comments, that anti-dualism
(whether Protestant or Catholic) does not establish its legitimacy
merely by centering its view in the heart or the person. There is
no theoretical solution which can a priori escape the dangers of
human imperfection. And we should be on our guard, now that
man is described more and more in terms of a unity, lest our
attempts at healing the break introduced by substantial dualism
result only in our introducing a break in reality in another fashion,
and thereby also a break in our own "person."[40]

Within the general attempt to reach the Biblical understanding
of the created man in the unity of his whole existence before the
eye of God, controversies on the soul-body problem have concentrated in a striking manner on the evaluation of the soul which
is expressed in the words "the infinite worth of the soul." This was
one of three terms used by Harnack as valid summaries of the
Biblical message and of the proclamation of Jesus: "the kingdom of
God and its coming, God the Father and the infinite worth of the
human soul, the higher righteousness and the command of love."
The expression actually was not used exclusively by Harnack; one
can encounter it in various relationships in theology, and also in
practice. It is certainly incorrect to think that the words themselves
imply an anthropology which contrasts higher (soul) and lower
(body), and this as such was surely not Harnack's intention. He
meant by "the infinite worth of the soul" man's being a child of
God, related to God the Father in His providence. When he
declared that "the worth of the individual soul first became ap-

40. It is obvious that personalism has points of contact with various
criticisms of an "abstract" understanding of divine Law; e.g., in our
opinion, in the "personalism" (moderate though it may be) of E.
Brunner's distinction between "Gebot" and "Gesetz." Cf. on revelation
and truth, J. Vrielink, Het Waarheidsbegrip (1956) pp. 12ff.; and A.
de Wilde, De Persoon (1950). De Wilde distinguishes two main types
of personalism: a relative personalism (the worth of the person as over
against collectivism) and an absolute personalism in which the person
is absolutized and is the basis for all our thinking about reality. Theological personalism, as with Gogarten, is not of this latter sort, but
is an attempt to find, in personalism, some way to the "historic" facts
of salvation, which, however, are in many aspects explained personal-
istically.

parent" in Jesus Christ, he meant that man "belongs on the side of God," and he cited Jesus' words (Matt. 16:26), "For what shall a man be profited, if he shall gain the whole world and forfeit his soul?"

Harnack's reference to this passage led to discussions which are intimately related to the whole view of man in the Biblical witness. The passage can easily be misunderstood in the sense of a partial theism, which considers the soul as "the higher" part of man. Sevenster said, in criticism of Harnack, that the "infinite worth of the human soul" could not be evidenced from the Gospel, since in Christ's words (Matt. 16:26) "soul" ("life") did not refer to something very precious which must be preserved inviolate at any cost, but rather to life as eschatological good; but he was attacked by Heering, who acknowledged the value of the criticism of Platonic influences and evaluations in the idea of the soul, but said that such criticism may not lead to an underestimating of the worth of man; Christendom has always honored the soul as the "highest creation of God." Heering is obviously here concerned with a specific anthropological datum, with *psyche* as the seat and bearer of life, which as the bearer of eternal life is most precious. We have here, unmistakably, an anthropological and functional localizing of the soul; at issue is the emotional life of man, which in Christianity is more important than the intellect, according to Heering.[41]

It appears to us that Heering's criticism of Sevenster misses the point. Sevenster's concern is not at all to diminish the value placed on man as a creature of God, but rather to oppose the view that the soul is a higher part of man, a view which he feels the gospel does not justify. The importance of man's relation to God is not at stake here, for what Heering calls Sevenster's attack on the "value of the soul" is at bottom an attack on the isolation of the soul as something anthropologically higher. This appears from the emphasis with which Sevenster says "man's soul as such does not in any way guarantee man's eternal welfare." For Heering, things are somewhat otherwise, for he sees the soul as an anthropological-functional datum with religious connotations, while Sevenster feels that the New Testament "does not find psyche as such important." Sevenster does not mean to deny the significance of created life but rather to point out the basic dimension of all

41. See J. N. Sevenster, *Het Begrip Psyche in het N.T.* (1946), especially pp. 8-9; G. J. Heering, *De menselijke Ziel* (1955), especially pp. 27-31. The higher status of the soul is often buttressed with the well-known summary of Augustine: "I desire to know God and the soul; nothing more? Nothing whatever" (*Soliloquia*).

New Testament references to man: the New Testament speaks of man from out of the reality of sin and grace, judgment and forgiveness. The value of the soul as such, in itself, is surely not a Biblical theme, since the Biblical view never abstracts from his relation to God. If Herring's point is that man as God's creation is never nothing or unimportant in His eyes, he is certainly correct. But there is no reason to relate this merely to the soul, since this importance also applies to man's bodiliness, which God so to speak takes so seriously that the Holy Spirit makes the body His temple (I Cor. 6:19). Thus the difference between Sevenster and Heering lies not in the former's underevaluation of God's creation, but in the latter's view of the soul as the bearer of earthly and heavenly life, which unavoidably involves him in a dualistic approach. This becomes clearly evident when he later gives a description of the soul, in which he agrees with earlier writers who draw from Greek philosophy, and teaches that the rational soul can be separated from the organic soul, since the soul as a non-spatial spiritual *subsistens* retains its status, while the soul is also (as Thomas and Melanchthon say) *separabilis*. Thus, he says, *psych*-ology can show the "possibility, indeed the probability, that the human soul as spiritual essence does not vanish with the transitory human body." Heering thus abstracts the "psychic" or (anthropologically) "pneumatic" aspect of man from the fullness of his human existence, and sets it up by itself as an immortal substance, protected by God because "nothing in His creation stands nearer to Him."[42]

We thus have a duality between "spiritual soul" and "material body" in one human essence, and Heering speaks of a "division between two components." We see one functional complex lifted out, abstracted from the whole man, and then given the qualities of the higher, the eternal, the immortal: the infinite worth of the human soul.

We stand here before a conscious choice for dichotomy. Heering goes from man's psychic or pneumatic life to an incomprehensible but nevertheless real "spiritual form of existence," and thus we need not wonder that he constantly involves himself in the context of medieval Scholasticism and its problems, such as those of Thomas. The mystery of the soul's separability leads him to refer to God: "Does our confession that God is spirit mean that we can represent or understand fully His spiritual reality?" We must, he says, uphold the "spirituality" of the soul against naturalistic or biologistic psychology, which has no place for an independent

42. See J. N. Sevenster, *Leven en Dood in de Evangeliën* (1952), pp. 12, 113, 136; and Heering, *op. cit.*, pp. 28, 141-142, 176.

psyche. And thus Heering finally proposes a psychology which honors the independence, the metaphysical origin, and the transcendental essence of the soul. Heering's adherence to this tradition arises from his liking for Erasmus and his plea for the infinite worth of the human soul. He reproaches Sevenster for not having asked himself why God seeks man; a most remarkable criticism, since according to Heering it is this question which must lead to the study of man, his spirit, his soul; thereby it will become clear why God specifically seeks man, among all his other creatures.

It is apparent that this approach to man differs from that of the Biblical witness; for the Bible tells us only of man's astonishment that God should seek him: "What is man, that thou art mindful of him?" (Ps. 8:5).

The amazement expressed in this question is incompatible with an explanation that God is mindful of man because of certain qualities of man's soul. The dichotomy of soul and body seems inevitably to produce an ontological emphasis which throws its shadows over the Scriptural witness to man as he actually is sought and found by God. In Scripture we hear no ontological explanations, but rather a religious affirmation, that Christ died for us "while we were yet sinners" (Rom. 5:8). Here all human analogies fail completely: "For scarcely for a righteous man will one die: for peradventure for the good man some one would even dare to die. But God commendeth his own love towards us, in that, while we were yet sinners, Christ died for us . . . . we were reconciled to God through the death of his Son" (Rom. 5:7-8, 10). This is a New Testament parallel to the question of Psalm 8 — "What is man . . . ?" and in such a context any answer to that question in terms of "man's soul" is completely insufficient. There is no dichotomy which could lead us to the Scriptural answer. The wonder of the divine concern for man, which Scripture speaks of as "the tender mercy of our God" (Luke 1:78), cannot be explained in terms of man's body and soul, and still less in terms of man's soul alone. But we should remember that it is the whole man who is restored and saved. Any statements about the "infinite worth of the soul" must be subordinate to this normativity. And since it is this normativity, which touches the whole man, the distinction between this soul and the body, which would serve as a basis for the worth of the soul, is excluded and made unacceptable by the gospel.

We have already remarked in passing that Scripture, to use the terms of dichotomy, takes not only the soul but also the body, very seriously. This affirmation of the body's worth has always been a *skandalon* to every dualistic theory of gradation between higher and lower elements in man. One of the most valuable possessions of the early Church was its confession of the resurrection of the body, against all tendencies to devaluate the body; this article is already present in the early form of the Apostles' Creed.[43] This eschatological affirmation is indissolubly related to the whole New Testament witness regarding the salvation of man. It is not the light of the freeing of the soul from the bonds of the body which falls on the threat of death, but the light of the resurrection of the Lord of the Church, and in Him the resurrection of all flesh (cf. Acts 4:2)[44]

And in the New Testament, we find the unmistakable prelude to this eschatological gift. The whole man is constantly called to the service of the Lord, and we read that the Holy Ghost dwells in the body (I Cor. 6:18-19), and precisely this indwelling is given as a reason against whoredom. The New Testament community is to strive towards the full reality of man: "glorify God therefore in your body" (I Cor. 6:20).

Though Scripture gives us no exposition of the nature of all the relationships in man, the whole Scriptural witness deals with the whole man in the actuality of his existence. The problems of dualism and polar tensions can only arise when man is alienated from his created fullness and his relationship to God; these problems are themselves but a reflection of the break which sin and death brought into human actuality. But we can never see man from the Biblical viewpoint as long as we abstract the "real man" from his bodily existence. Christ was concerned with the whole man in His many miracles of healing, when He took as His, and was concerned with, the need and sickness and pain in the whole man (cf. Matt. 8:17). This healing was the sign of the reconciling and victorious Kingdom which in Him and with Him came to be.[45] Because of His bodily resurrection, man is called to His service — and who else than the whole man would be called? However we

---

43. The "resurrection of the body" is found in the old Roman form of the Credo: "eternal life" is a later addition.
44. Cf. H. Schlier, "Der Mensch im Gnostizmus," *Anthropologie religieuse* (1955); especially pp. 70ff. Gnosticism held to "an escape from the unspiritual, the bodily" "a re-finding of the self"; an "inhuman abstraction from actuality," which the Church saw and rejected (pp. 73, 74, 77).
45. Cf. the valuable comments of W. Stählin, *De Betekenis van het Lichaam* (1932); also P. Schoonenberg, *op. cit.*, II, 137ff.

may view anthropologically the relation between soul and body, or inner and outer man — and Scripture gives us no scientific solution to such problems — and whatever terms we may use ("instrument," "organ," function," "expression"), it is undeniable that in this expression, in this functioning, it is man, real man, we are concerned with. This man is affected by the curse of sin in his whole existence, and the devils must be called out of him, so that an inexorable divine halt may be called to the desecration of his humanity, as God shows His concern for His people in the concreteness of their creaturely existence. And while it is true that at no time is bodily need in sickness and death abstracted from its relation to sin, and while the relation of Christ's miracles to faith and forgiveness is made unmistakably clear in the whole gospel, nevertheless, we may never justify an anthropology which would assert a special relation of sin to bodiliness, and which would separate salvation and resurrection from bodiliness. Although spiritualism, in its quest for the "real" man, the essential man, has played a role which we should not underestimate, nevertheless, the Church has always affirmed the full humanity of Christ, not only against Arius but against Docetism, and has also seen and affirmed the meaning of this confession for our humanity. And Scripture does not at all view man's bodiliness as something secondary; rather, the moment one devaluates the body, one has "deactualized" man's whole reality as a creature of God. And when man's life is restored (cf. Mark 8:25, Acts 3:21), this whole man functions anew and immediately; in the folded and uplifted hands, in song and confession, in preaching and the breaking of the bread: take, eat, and drink . . . .

Man, cutting through the shadows of sin and death, functions in the richness of community, which is filled with the mystery of love — not the darkly secretive mystery of an autonomous and hence abstract eroticism, but the "mystery of Christ" (Eph. 5:32).

The prospect of the resurrection of the dead is so basic and central for Paul that he writes "if there is no resurrection of the dead, neither has Christ been raised" (I Cor. 15:13). Anyone who wishes to view the eschatological mystery in terms of the dilemma between personalism and ontology surely misunderstands the meaning of the gospel, and has fallen, via personalism, into a no less serious spiritualism. Scripture does indeed tell us of a change from the corruptible to the incorruptible, from the mortal to the immortal (I Cor. 15:54), but this triumphant transformation is the exact opposite of spiritualism.

It is the "spiritual body" to which Paul refers (I Cor. 15:44),[46] in which he is not paying tribute to the spiritualizing so influential in his time, but rather rises above all spiritualizing, in his reference to the power and leading of the Spirit who already in this life wishes to make His temple in the body (I Cor. 6:19). We must indeed remember, here especially, John's statement that "it is not yet made manifest what we shall be" (I John 3:2), but this living and not-knowing as we wait the last revelation does not extinguish the light of the *eschaton,* and the Church can confess, from the weakness and transitoriness of the flesh, its belief in the resurrection of the body.[47]

Thus the Church, because of God's creative work and because of the eschatological mystery of the Resurrection, will always be suspicious of any view of the body which in one way or another devaluates it, and in such devaluation will always out of necessity see a detraction from the genuineness of divinely created human nature.[48] And inasmuch as the shadows of sin fall over the whole

46. Cf. H. Clavier, "Brèves remarques sur la notion de sooma pneumatikón," *The Background of the N.T. and Its Eschatology; Studies in Honor of C. H. Dodd* (1956), pp. 342-362. He sees this as in opposition to opinions at Corinth, which were influenced by the classical idea of the immortality of the soul, liberated from the body.

47. W. Bieder, "Auferstehung des Fleisches oder des Leibes?" *Theologische Zeitschrift* (1945), pp. 105ff. He wishes to correct the Latin of the Credo ("*credo resurrectionem carnis*") to show belief in the resurrection of the body, "from Biblical and Pauline witness." His argument from I Cor. 15:50 ("*flesh* and blood cannot inherit the kingdom of God") is not at all convincing, in our opinion, since there follows "neither doth corruption inherit incorruption," and yet (v. 53) "this corruption must put on corruption." Bieder's dilemma is certainly not an actual one for the Christian community, since it awaits the unfathomable miracle of the resurrection. The ancient Church used, as a point of reference, the transitory man in the flesh. Cf. also the "*credo etiam veram resurrectionem eiusdem carnis, quam nunc gesto*" of Leo IX's *Symbolum fidei* (Denzinger, 347) and the ". . . *quam gestamus*" in the profession of faith demanded of the Waldensians (*ibid.,* 427), and Lord's Day 22 of the Heidelberg Catechism, "this, my flesh. . . ."

48. This desire to avoid devaluation of the body plays a role in the recent Papal encyclical, *Munificentissimus Deus* (1950) which made the Assumption of the Blessed Virgin Mary a dogma for all Catholics. The opportuneness of promulgating the dogma is associated with the elevated goal of our soul and our body, a goal so often unappreciated in contemporary immorality and materialism (51-52); the dogma will show the value of a human life when wholly directed to the carrying out of the will of the Heavenly Father. I Cor. 15:13's reference to the clothing of mortality with immortality is here applied to Mary (49). For the connection between the worth of the body and the dogma of the

man — his soul and his body — it will always, with the signs of Christ in mind, retain the prospect of the taking away of these shadows and of the curse of sin. It will not exclude asceticism, bodily self-control (*ascese* as such is mentioned only in Acts 24:16), but such asceticism is related precisely to the body's wreath of immortality; it is not negative ·but positive and is oriented to service in the Kingdom. And therefore the Church will not oppose the contemporary anti-spiritualistic emphasis on the body so long as it does not fall into the temptation of abstracting and separating the body in theory or in practice, from its relation to the Creator of the whole man.

As we see the light of the Biblical witness, and in it the light of Christ, fall on the whole man and his God-determined destiny, we encounter a question which rises very naturally in this context: the meaning of the well-known words, "the immortality of the soul." These words have undeniably played an enormous role in the Christian thought of all times. And the passions which the question often aroused show that men were conscious that a reality was involved here which in a very existential way affected each of their lives. We must now consider the varied problems which center around the continued existence, the immortality, of man.

Assumption, see P. Schoonenberg, "Het Mysterie van ons verrezen Lichaam," *Katholiek Cultureel Tijdschrift*, N. Reeks, V (1951-1952), pp. 103ff., 314ff. He sees the dogma as "an unexpected commentary on I Cor. 1:15," notes that the encyclical speaks of a strengthening of our faith in our own resurrection, and relates the dogma directly to the recent discussion in Catholic circles on the function of bodiliness. The controversy between Rome and the Reformation does not concern the evaluation of bodiliness as a creation of God, but rather the opposition between the dogma of 1950 and the exclusiveness of the "surety" mentioned in Lord's Day 17 of the Heidelberg Catechism.

CHAPTER SEVEN

IMMORTALITY

T HE RELATION between the subject of immortality and the
Biblical witness regarding the whole man to which we have
so far devoted our attention, is certainly not an arbitrary one.
Especially through the problems surrounding the so-called dichotomy of the two substances, body and soul, one naturally arrives
in the area of this well-known term, the "immortality of the soul,"
which has played an important role, not only in theology and
philosophy, but also in the terminology of the Church. And an
important question occurs immediately: whether the term "immortality of the soul" is something which is not only compatible
with the Biblical view of the whole man, but arises from it because of inner necessity.

It strikes us immediately that the expression does not speak of
the immortality of man, but of the soul. This already seems to
point to a background of a certain duality or dichotomy, a context
within which special attention is paid to the immortality of the
soul. The expression then takes on a special color in relation to
the soul: viz., that the soul by nature cannot die, the natural
immortality of the soul. It is, however, clear that this "natural"
immortality is not necessarily implied in all statements about immortality; this is already evident from the Biblical witness on
immortality. The natural immortality rules out any historic or
eschatological approach, since immortality is implied in the very
nature of the soul as such. However, we also encounter various
statements on the immortality of man, in which historical aspects
can play a role. Bavinck, for example, in his treatment of immortality as belonging to the image of God, says that the body is the
organ of the soul and thus also originally partook of immortality.[1]
Such a statement at once involves a different context, not only

1. Bavinck, *Gereformeerde Dogmatiek,* II, 522. K. Dijk deliberately uses the
term "immortality of man," because of objections to the "immortality
of the soul" (*Over de laatste Dingen,* 1951, ch. 1, pp. 13-17).

because soul *and* body are mentioned, but also because an historic aspect is introduced. This later fact is evident in Bavinck's statement that there was originally a possibility of immortality conditioned on obedience. This "immortality" was thus not absolute but rather provisional, dependent on the fulfilling of a certain condition. Man, says Bavinck, was not created mortal, and death was not something natural which was given at the creation of man. Thus there was indeed immortality, but this was not identical with life which could not be lost; it could and in fact did change to mortality through the violation of God's command. The point of view in Bavinck's consideration of immortality is thus not the immortality of the soul, but that of man, and one which can change to mortality. We are reminded of the many Scriptural references to man's mortality, his transitoriness, as a mortal who returns to dust (Ps. 90:3, 9, 20-21; 10:18), with a length of life which is as nothing before God, a breath, a shadow (Ps. 39:5-7); who goes the way of all the earth (I Kings 2:2), with the measure of his days, to which there comes an end (Ps. 39:5), as he goes away and is no more (Ps. 39:14). The story of Paradise already mentions death, when the divine warning is given to man: "in the day that thou eatest thereof thou shalt surely die" (Gen. 2:17).

Now, all of this refers to man, who dies. It is true that we read "the *soul* that sinneth, it shall die" (Ezek. 18:20), but the reference is to man as dying. Mortality characterizes man. There is a limit to his days, and an end; "for everything there is a season . . . a time to be born and a time to die" (Eccles. 3:2); and the prayer to "teach us to number our days that we may get us a heart of wisdom" (Ps. 90:12, cf. 39:5) is a meaningful and necessary one. We can thus speak without any hesitation, in agreement with the Biblical witness, of the mortality of man, and the going away, the return to dust, of the mortal and transitory man.

The witness of the whole Bible is so clear on this point that no denial is possible. Different insights arise only when we begin to reflect on the meaning of this "death." There has been a renewed concern in theology regarding the mortality of man, and it is noteworthy that there have been objections from various sides against making the connection between death and divine judgment on sin the only relation in which death can be seen. This connection between death and divine judgment is not at all denied, but various theologians feel that we can also speak of a "natural" death, which according to God's intent at creation goes along with man's created humanness as such. Karl Barth especially has written at length on the limit (*Befristung*) of our life, our limited length

236236

236236

236236

of days, as an original given which belongs to God's good creation and thus may not be brought into connection with God's punishment and judgment.[2]

The Dutch theologian Van Leeuwen has also taken this approach;[3] he states clearly and unequivocally that "man as he was created was, and was willed and intended by God to be, a mortal being. We must deny that death is something unnatural, a break in God's creation." We may not say, says Van Leeuwen, that this mortality is the result of sin, for it is man's natural lot, something self-evident from the fact that God who gives can also take away. God has created man so that he must die. And this having to die is not without sense or meaning,[4] for it is precisely this dying which leads to the Psalmist's prayer for the wise heart (Ps. 90:12). Man's mortality is "one of the most powerful means through which God holds him attached to His leading and His communion." Van Leeuwen opposes this view to the traditional interpretation, which followed Paul's line of thought in Romans 5, and viewed death as punishment, as a curse, as something unnatural.

But we may not conclude that Van Leeuwen means that the divine giving of life is followed only by a divine taking of life, and that God meant at creation for man to return to nothingness. The most noteworthy aspect of his criticism of the traditional view is his idea that mortality acquires meaning and sense. It is a means for holding man in communion with God. When the grain dies, it brings forth fruit, and dying is necessary to reach true life, so that Van Leeuwen can say that "natural mortality finds its meaning and goal only in natural immortality," and that God has created man "with the destiny of eternal life, and actualizes this destiny through dying." Thus in man's original created state dying is implied in life, and in this state created man dies since completely

2. K. Barth, K.D., III, 2, pp. 628ff. Cf. the lengthier treatment in our *The Triumph of Grace in the Theology of Karl Barth,* chs. 6 and 12.
3. P. J. van Leeuwen, *Het Christelijk Onsterfelijkheidsgeloof,* pp. 307, 316, 323-330. He approves of Barth's *"Befristung"* (p. 307); cf. also the remarks following on Brunner and Althaus.
4. Chr. Barth, *Die Errettung vom Tode in den individuellen Klage-und Dankliedern des A. T.* (1947), p. 68. He refers to various attempts to understand death as "a meaningful unity." This applies also to Van Leeuwen, but in reference not so much to death as to dying. Chr. Barth says that the power of death "in its evil aspect" appears to militate against this, a view with which Van Leeuwen would agree, since he also speaks of two aspects.

dying is part of man's creaturely completeness. But this dying is not the complete end. Life is not given and then taken, but given and taken and then given again. And it is this second giving which discloses the meaning of natural mortality, the meaning of the "limiting" of man's life.

We encounter here a unique vision of and interpretation of "dying," and one which we can hardly say is based on Scripture. The idea that death is one of the most powerful means used by God to hold man in His communion has a strange paradoxicality, since precisely thereby the idea of the limited duration of man's life (Barth's *"Befristung"*) is once more relativized by being placed in the context of the meaning and finality of dying. The idea is indeed related to various Scriptural passages, but it is apparent that these (e.g., Ps. 39 and John 12) do not at all refer to a dying which can be called a "natural" dying.[5]

Van Leeuwen acknowledges that Scripture continually relates sin and death. That relation is not only explicitly stated in Genesis 2:17, but also recurs time and again, especially with Paul. How then can this Biblical emphasis be honored? By a distinction between natural dying and death. Paul certainly understood the message of the Old Testament correctly when he says that death entered the world through sin, and that the wages of sin is death (Rom. 5:12; 6:23); but the term "death" is not the same as the natural end of life, but it refers to destruction, corruption, damnation. This death does indeed have an evident relation to sin. Dying as such is not connected with sin, but sins leads to a way of dying which is threatening and terrible. Thus it is explicable, continues Van Leeuwen, that in the actual situation of us sinful men, dying and death are the same. But they must be distinguished in principle. The traditional view has still to be rejected, since it sets up a direct relation between sin and mortality. That the Christian faith has always seen "an immediate relation between death and dying, between death and mortality," does indeed make

---

5. Ps. 39 contains a lamentation not only for the transitoriness and brevity of human life, but also (as Van Leeuwen also notes) for vanity, while the threat of death is related to sin (cf. vss. 9, 11, 12 in connection with 13), so that from this psalm we can hardly deduce the original goodness of natural dying. John 12:24-25 relates eternity for man to dying (which dying?), but this does not at all support Van Leeuwen's position, any more than the following verse about "hating" one's life in this world and the thus keeping one's life to eternal life. Cf. his exegesis of Heb. 9:27, which is also abstracting and out of context. Nor is his finding traces of concern about the positive sense of mortality in Ps. 39 and 90 warranted.

sense; but we must distinguish. The exegesis of Vriezen, who in Genesis 3 sees mortality as a consequence of disobedience, is permissible; but in any case, says Van Leeuwen, dying as the natural end of life is not identical with "godless existence in sin," though in the concrete situation of sinful man they coincide.

But it is just in this "coinciding" that the problem lies, if we mean that there is something more than a merely accidental temporal co-existence. If natural dying actually belongs to God's original, good and meaningful creation as the ending of life, then it is most difficult to see how this end can ever be brought into any essential relation with death as destruction, corruption and damnation. The unique dialectic of Van Leeuwen (death and dying) indeed leads to incorporating natural dying as a meaningful thing into God's creation intent as the way of God with man.[6] It is oriented towards eternal life as means to an end, and to this end is meaningfully serviceable. Thus natural dying becomes a "moment," a "transition." The end becomes a new beginning. "In the life which God gives us and to which He destines us, dying is a moment, a transition, and the temporal is taken up in the eternal."

But in this very context he rejects the misunderstanding "that death as the correlate of sin may be identified with dying." Natural mortality (from our being creatures) leads to natural immortality (from our destiny).

It is clear, in our opinion, that the real problems in Van Leeuwen's approach lie in his concept of "dying" as "moment" or "transition." That which for Bavinck was the "transition" in obedience from mortality to immortality becomes for Van Leeuwen a natural mortality, a having to die, which results in a natural immortality. Now, the question of this "transition" has constantly concerned theology at least since the time of Augustine; but this transition, from "being able to die" to "not being able to die," is a different one than that of Van Leeuwen — from "dying" to "not dying." The decisive link is man's natural dying as something given by God. But the unsatisfactoriness of Van Leeuwen's solution appears precisely here; not only from the nature of his concrete appeals to Scripture, and not only from the relation drawn — without qualifications — between sin and death by Paul; but also from

6. Van Leeuwen, op. cit., p. 326. He speaks of the "strong consciousness of creatureliness which is so definitive of O.T. piety and which simply accepted mortality as grounded in God's will." Paul also, he says, has his roots in this thought-world.

the Old Testament, which does not see the ending of life[7] as a general, natural thing, as such integrated in God's creation.

In the Old Testament there is indeed a deep consciousness of the generality and finality of death, and the words of the woman of Tekoa — the wise woman — expresses this feeling well: "for we must needs die, and are as water spilt on the ground, which cannot be gathered up again" (II Sam. 14:14). But this does not make dying a natural event. We encounter death throughout the Old Testament as it stands opposed to the richness of living. Death was viewed and experienced as a transition to weakness and powerlessness, as deprivation of vitality;[8] and there is joy when life is saved from the grave and man's days are lengthened.

Why should we die? — so asked Israel as God spoke to man from the fiery mountain (Deut. 5:25; cf. Judg. 6:22-23, 13:22). There is rejoicing in not dying, as when Hezekiah saw his years lengthened and after all his anxious moments could sing his song of life: "I shall go softly all my years because of the bitterness of my soul. O Lord, by these things men live, and wholly therein is the life of my spirit: wherefore recover thou me, and make me to live," and as his life is "delivered from the pit of corruption," he says, "For Sheol cannot praise thee: death cannot celebrate thee: they that go down into the pit cannot hope for thy truth. The living, the living, he shall praise thee, as I do this day" (Isa. 38:15-19; cf. Num. 4:19).

The end of life appears again and again as the robbery of all the riches which lie in life. "Shall thy lovingkindness be declared in the grave? or thy faithfulness in destruction? Shall thy wonders be known in the dark? and thy righteousness in the land of forgetfulness?" (Ps. 88:11-13; cf. 6:6, 30:10, 49:15-16, 115:17). Now, such words have often been used to show that Israel had no

---

7. Cf. Bultmann, Kittel, *Theologisches Wörterbuch*, III, *s.v.*, *thanatos* on death as the result of, and punishment for, sin; over against the "inescapability" of death there stands only the "unique salvation through Christ." It seems to me simply impossible to interpret the clear statements of the New Testament in terms of a consistent application of a distinction between dying and death or of a "factual" coincidence of the two. Besides the words of Paul, see Heb. 5:7ff. and 2:9.

8. See Van Leeuwen, *op. cit.*, p. 30; Chr. Barth, *op. cit.*, p. 59; and R. Martin-Achard, *De la mort à la Résurrection d'après l'Ancien Testament* (1956), pp. 36ff.; E. Jacob, *Théologie de l' A.T.* (1955), pp. 240ff. On the general subject, see also H. M. Feret, "Der Tod in der biblischen Ueberlieferung" and J. Hild, "Der Tod — ein Christliches Geheimnis," both in *Das Mysterium des Todes* (1955).

eschatological expectation, no outlook which included a resurrection from the dead or a genuine living on after death; others, in turn, have emphatically rejected this conclusion; but we cite these passages here to show that the Old Testament is not to be read in terms of a distinction between death and dying (as a natural and good thing), but only in terms of the constantly recurring contrast between death and life, in which dying is brought into connection with the land of darkness and forgetfulness.

The end of life is not at all integrated with life as a natural dying, but precisely *as* end is it pictured as the removal, the deprivation of the richness of life, the loss of all "acquaintances" (Ps. 88:8), and it is in relation to this peril, that the Psalmist stretches his hands out to the God of life.

Therefore we must conclude that the distinction between "death" and "dying" has neither a terminological nor an actual basis in Scriptural witness, and that there is a profound reason for the "usage" of which Van Leeuwen speaks, the usage which does not distinguish between dying and death and which employs the terms interchangeably. In Christian belief, too, dying has never been interpreted as natural dying, but always and exclusively in the context of Christ's conquest of death. Nothing can separate us, not even death, from the love of Christ; and dying can indeed take on a completely new context (dying in the Lord), and the Heidelberg Catechism (L.D. 16) can say that death is merely a passing through to eternal life — but this all does not make death into a natural event.

The interchangeable use of the words "dying" and "death" in the Bible does not arise from a *de facto* temporal coinciding of natural dying and death in our fallen condition, but rather from that relation between the two which dominates the usage of Scripture, and which comes to very explicit expression in Genesis and in the words of Paul.[9]

---

9. See A. H. Maltha, *Theologisch Woordenboek*, I (1952), *s.v.*, *Dood*. There is a noteworthy, but superficial, parallel between him and Van Leeuwen. Maltha says that while death is actually a punishment for man, it is as such natural. But in the context it is pointed out that the idea of death as punishment is more markedly religious. Maltha says that death as such being natural was defended by Rome against Baius and the Protestants (cf. Denzinger 1006, 1078, 1517), but a closer examination will show that these statements are concerned with Baius' idea of immortality as a natural condition. And, finally, Maltha's point of view is essentially different from that of Van Leeuwen: he stresses the question of nature and supernature rather than the "necessity of dying" which Van Leeuwen accents.

In connection with Van Leeuwen's views, we have already encountered the term "natural" several times, in relation to dying as well as to immortality. And indeed, we constantly encounter the term "natural immortality" in the history of theology, especially as regards the immortality of the soul. We must now face the problem whether this expression can be reconciled with what Scripture so expressly says about man's mortality and his actual dying.

What is the relationship between this human mortality and what is called the "immortality of the soul"? It is clear that the affirmation of this immortality is not meant to deny man's dying, but rather speaks at the same time of man's death and of the immortality of the soul. That is the unique and complicated situation in which this expression places us, and which constantly gives rise to the question whether we can actually speak of the mortality of man, and whether perhaps we would not do better to speak of the mortality of a part of man. The intent is obviously to say that while man does indeed die, this "death" does not affect the whole man to such an extent that there is a transition from being to being no more. And thus in the history of the doctrine of immortality we can see coming to the fore the idea of the natural immortality of the soul, a not-being-able-to-die ("*non posse mori*") as of the very nature, or essence, of the soul, and therefore capable of proof. Bavinck speaks of a belief in immortality which we encounter in the religion and philosophy of all peoples, a belief which does not deny the notoriously obvious fact that man dies, but which in spite of this dying still postulates the immortality of the soul. We are thus brought into an area of general or at least widespread feeling which is not at all specifically or exclusively Christian.[10] Bavinck refers especially to Plato, whose teaching "had an amazingly great influence on theology and philosophy,"

10. Bavinck, *op. cit.*, IV, 567, 574, 577, 591. We should not view the belief in immortality as "generally human." Belief in the immortality of the soul was primarily a philosophical idea among intellectuals. Cf. in the New Testament, "the rest, who have no hope" (I Thess. 4:13, Eph. 2:12), "let us eat and drink, for tomorrow we die" (I Cor. 15:32), the anxiety before death (Heb. 2:15), the quarrel between the philosophers of the Areopagus (Acts 17:18), of whom the Epicureans were critical of the belief in immortality. Cf. Dijk, *op. cit., p.* 8; E. Rohde, *Psyche. Seelenkult und Unsterblichkeitsglaube der Griechen,* p. 221. Rohde emphasized theology and philosophy. Cf. also A. A. T. Ehrhardt, "Unsterblichkeitsglaube und Politik im Römerreich," *Theologische Zeitschrift* (1946), pp. 418ff., on doubt and skepticism, also in relation to the influence of Epicurus.

and who held that the soul is immortal because of its nature.[11]
Now, this widespread belief gives rise very naturally to the question whether the Christian faith should hear and follow this idea
of the immortality of the soul as an echo of the words of God,
or whether with this phrase we are on a completely different track
than that of the Biblical witness. Bavinck, in considering Plato,
makes the noteworthy acknowledgement that, under his influence,
theology "gave much more attention to the immortality of the
soul than does the Holy Scripture."

And, indeed, theologians spoke about the natural immortality of
the soul as a "truth" which was known more from reason than
from revelation, and which was already known before the light
of revelation shone through to disclose the secrets of man's existence and future. The immortality of the soul was viewed as an
articulus mixtus, and one cannot suppress the question what
Bavinck wished to suggest as he emphasized the greater attention
given to this problem by theology than by the Bible.

Bavinck says that Scripture adopts a standpoint which "at first
sight cannot but astonish."[12] However great the apparent significance of the immortality of the soul for religion and life, "Scripture
never treats of it specifically; it never announces it as a revealed
truth; it never places it in the foreground, and never makes any
attempt to argue its truth or to maintain this against its opponents."
Bavinck does indeed oppose the opinion of some, that Israel knew
nothing of a life after death, but he sees in Scripture's treatment
a wholly different dimension of meaning than that which we
usually imply in our treatment of life and death: "there is woven
into the general and natural contrast between life and death another contrast, a moral contrast, between life in the service of sin
and life in the fear of the Lord." Life as undifferentiated existence
is not true life according to Scripture, and basically is merely an
abstraction. Genuine and real life is, says Scripture, a life in
communion with God, and thus it can say of a "living" (existing)
man who is outside this communion that he is *dead* in sin and

---

11. See especially Plato's *Phaedo,* in which evidence is given for immortality
of the soul (e.g., memory, and the nature of the soul) and the idea
defended against objections. The soul is imprisoned in the body and
philosophy exhorts it to collect and concentrate itself in itself, so as not
to fear or oppose the dissolution of soul from body. On Plato, see H.
Scholz, *Der Unsterblichkeit als philosophisch Problem* (1922); H.
Wolf, *Onsterfelijkheid als wijsgerig Probleem;* G. J. de Vries, "Plato's
Beeld van de Mens," *Tijdschrift voor Wijsbegeerte,* XV (1953): 427ff.
12. Bavinck, *op. cit.,* IV, 567 (574, 577, 591, for the material which
follows).

trespasses (Eph. 2:1, Col. 2:13). And thus also, says Bavinck, Scripture does not treat the immortality of the soul as if that in itself implies some great wealth of man, his life's "natural" continuation after death. "Those who have compulsively wished to find the philosophical idea of the immortality of the soul emphasized in the Old Testament have not understood the revelation of God to Israel, and have inserted Western ideas into the religion of an Eastern people." Scripture defines the contrast between life and death not "naturally" but along religious lines. True life is that life which partakes of that sort of immortality, that immunity from death, which is brought to light in Christ. Bavinck does not deny the immortality of the soul — he refers to it as life after death — but it has a limited value in Scripture: "It does not deny, but neither does it specifically teach immortality of the soul, and it surely does not intend, as deism held, to make this immortality known to us as one of the most important truths of religion." What Scripture teaches us is that mere existence and nothing more "is no life fitting for men."

It is clear that in this discussion we encounter several things which are most important and decisive for the correct view of life and death. That the expression "immortality of the soul" does not occur in Scripture does not as such imply that we may not use it, but it does imply that there is every reason to scrutinize this expression and examine what exactly is meant by it. And there is all the more reason when we consider the way in which Scripture does speak of "immortality." The term itself occurs only twice; first in connection with God, who alone is immortal (I Tim. 6:16), and secondly in relation to mortality which must put on immortality (I Cor. 15:53). The latter reference obviously does not concern a natural immortality, but rather in a Christological-soteriological context is concerned with the eschatological salvation of God, with the dying-no-more, with complete freedom from death. Dying-no-more, as conquest of death, here stands in the full light of Jesus Christ, and we are here in a wholly different context of ideas than that of the natural immortality of the soul. It is not the light of a generally held natural immortality which takes away the sting from the contrast between life and death, but the light of Christ who has conquered sin and thereby vanquished death (I Cor. 15:55-56). And this, once more, makes it clear that Scripture directs our attention to another, a deeper, a religious contrast between life and death. Here, too, we do well to recall what we have emphasized before: that Scripture never sees man as a being enclosed in himself, an isolated "essence" which can be fathomed in terms of itself alone, but rather shows us man as a being who can never be thought of apart from his continual relationship with God. It is man in this relationship who is represented as actual man. This light which falls on man from the revelation of God is so strong that we need a long time to become used to it, and thus the words of Scripture on life and death have a strange sound to our ears, oriented as they are to a naturalistic and abstract approach to man.

Thus, consider the words of Christ in the Gospel of John: "He that believeth on the Son _hath_ eternal life, but he that obeyeth not the Son shall not see life, but the wrath of God abideth on him" (John 3:36). So decisive is the relationship to Christ that it is said that "He that heareth my word and believeth him that sent me hath eternal life, and cometh not into judgment, but hath passed out of death into life" (John 5:24; cf. I John 3:14), and the point is emphasized sharply in the further statement that "if a man keep my word, he shall never see death" (John 8:51; cf. 11:25). And this is not all merely some exaggerated form of expression, some hyperbolic mode of speaking, but deals with the actuality of life and death. These words announce a completely altered viewpoint, a decisive dimension, a different outlook on man than that which is visible in the "natural" and "obvious" view of the transition from life to death.[13]

13. In connection with the foregoing material, the following observations may be made. For God as "true life," cf. the reference to creation in the Belgic Confession (Art. 14). Abraham Kuyper noted the contrast between Scripture and deistic emphasis on immortality in his _De Leer der Onsterfelijkheid en de Staatsschool_ (1870), pp. 12ff. In connection with "putting on immortality" (I Cor. 15:53), cf. Rom. 6:9, and the comments in the book of D. H. Th. Vollenhoven, _Het Calvinisme en de Reformatie van de Wijsbegeerte_ (1933), p. 6. Art. 19 of the Belgic Confession says that Christ _gave_ immortality to His human nature through His resurrection; cf. Art. 37 also. That Scripture views life and death in another dimension than the usual, cf. the many various "modes" of dying; man can die "in the Lord" (Rev. 14:13); cf. Paul's triumphant words in I Cor. 15:55. Besides the cited passages in John, cf. the passage, "he that believeth on me, though he die, yet shall he live; and whosoever liveth and believeth on me shall never die" (John 11:25). Cf. also John 8:52, where we see the reaction of the Jews to this "never seeing death": Abraham died, and the prophets; and their conclusion is that Christ is possessed; His view of life and death was so opposed to theirs that it could be explained only from the "demonic." For comment on the general contrast we have noted, cf. also A. Kuyper, _Het Werk van den Heiligen Geest,_ p. 359, on the Scripture's "appalling contrast" between life and death, "which affects not only the body but also, definitely, the soul"; cf. Kuyper, _Van de Voleinding,_ III, 29ff.

The characteristic of this new dimension lies in this, that it is not at all a psychological reaction to feelings of anxiety, or a rejection of thoughts about death, but is rather a deep and stark realism which does not close its eyes to a single "reality," but which finds its exclusive basis in the *reality of Christ.* We surely underestimate this new and decisive dimension when we interpret the various Biblical references to life and death figuratively.[14] We do that, for example, when we take a natural view of life and death as the only real view, and consider Christ's words on life and death as not applying to so real an actuality as that which we intend with our general concepts of life and death. On the contrary, Christ's words are so penetrating, direct, and clear, that any "figurative" interpretation is a violation of His authority. It is understandable, of course, that we, with our natural view, constantly err in the direction of a "figurative" understanding of Christ's words. The impression of the decisive contrast between life and death is often still so strong in our life that we have but little eye for the light which Christ's message radiates, and this is true also as regards this transition from death to life. Who understands this "dying no more," this "not seeing death" (cf. Luke 2:26, Heb. 11:5)? But yet we are again and again placed in the light of Him who is the Resurrection and the Life (John 11:25, cf. 14:6), who has robbed death of its power and shown us eternal life (II Tim. 1:10; cf. I Cor. 15:57, Col. 3:6, Rom. 8:3, Acts 2:24). His words on life must thus be taken with complete seriousness, when He speaks of "he who believeth on me, though he die, yet shall he live" — words so earnest, so real, so wonderful for man alienated from the light that He understood full well the tendency of the heart not to believe them, and thus added the question, "Believest thou this?" (John 11:26).

This was spoken in a situation in which death had powerfully struck in the life of Lazarus, to the extent that bodily decay was already setting in (John 11:39). But now the light begins to stream into this world of death and suddenly everything becomes wholly different, culminating in the words which show and ex-

14. Cf. R. Bultmann, *Das Evangelium des Johannes* (1950, 11th ed.), p. 121; cf. p. 308, life "in the definitive sense." See Kittel, *Theologisches Wörterbuch*, II, 865. Bultmann also refers to the use of the word without an attribute; cf. his remarks there on the relation between the New Testament concept of life and the immortality of the soul. Cf. also the relation of this "life" to the divine act of salvation in Jesus Christ; e.g., II Tim. 1:1, I John 5:11, and, besides the texts from John already cited, John 4:14 and 12:25. Cf. A. A. van Ruler, "De Relativering van Leven en Dood," *Kerk en Theologie* (1954), pp. 65-67.

plain the great mystery of life. This change is already announced
in Christ's words that the sickness of Lazarus is "not unto death
but for the glory of God" (John 11:4), and further in His words
in the very face of death; "Our friend Lazarus is fallen asleep,
but I go that I may awaken him out of sleep" (John 11:11). And
when the disciples understood this as meaning a sleep from which
Lazarus would naturally awake, Christ told them plainly: "Lazarus
is dead." Now, we would reach a wholly wrong conclusion if we
viewed Christ's first words as figurative, and His later words as
"real." It is immediately apparent that Christ first spoke of
sleeping, and only after the disciples' misunderstanding spoke of
death. One might sooner think of this plain speaking as an
accommodation to the level of the disciples' understanding rather
than as a literal speaking of death after a symbolic reference to sleeping. For the things we see in the area of death appear quite differently when we look at them in the light of Christ, who is the Resurrection and the Life. We can no longer describe them adequately in
natural categories. There can be no more idea of a self-evident and
all-powerful Death. This "omnipotence" is destroyed in the peaceful and triumphant use of these words in a situation which because of Him is not dangerous: "sleeping," and "awaking."[15] This
by no means implies an optimistic relativizing of death's destructive
power. Jesus "groaned in the spirit" at the grave, and we read that
He called Lazarus from the power of death in a loud voice (John
11:43), and the dead man came forth with the clear signs of
death (John 11:44). Apart from Christ, we should indeed speak
of death rather than sleep.[16] But Christ is revealed as Resurrection
and Life in and against this power, and in Him the triumph of life
over death becomes visible. Thus, when Christ reveals to us the
actuality of life, we are dealing not with a symbolic or figurative
manner of speech but with the most realistic use of words. He
speaks then of sleep, and awakening; as when He said of the

15. Cf. Grosheide, *Commentaar,* II, 156; and Bultmann (in Kittel, *op. cit.,*
III, 13), on "sleep" and "death." Even if "sleep" is interpreted
to mean that "Lazarus is not forever away from the earth" (Grosheide),
implied already is the rest-giving and conquering power of Him
who can here use the word as Lord over death. Cf. also Grosheide on "sleep" ("an ambiguous word"). But even if we wish to be
cautious about the precise meaning of Christ's terms here, in view of
the recurrence elsewhere of the word "sleep" for death, we surely can
not deny the text's evidence of Christ's power over death.
16. Cf., e.g., Schopenhauer's view of death, and his affection for Epicurus, as
regards sleep as "the twin brother of death"; L. Muller, *De Onsterfelijk-
heidsgedachte bij Schopenhauer onder Invloed van Kant en Plato* (1956),
pp. 111ff.

daughter of Jairus, "the child is not dead, but sleepeth" (Mark 5:39, Matt. 9:24). These are no jesting words, but words in which His presence reveals actuality, the actuality of His great Messianic mystery. And thus only can the words which precede be understood, in their complete real and actual reference: "Why make ye tumult, and weep?" We feel that we are not deducing from Christ's words more than is therein implied. The words refer to reality, and were made actual in a wonderful manner as death was conquered, in the time of the Messianic salvation. Sleep — "the word was already used for death by Jews and Greeks. But what was then only a euphemism has become actuality for the Christian."[17]

But men did not understand the meaning of Christ's words, in the context of these great events which were the signs of the Kingdom: they laughed at Him (Mark 5:40) — a parallel with the Jews' explanation of Jesus' words on not seeing death, that He was possessed (John 8:52)! But all Christ's words are realistic, since He is Life, and His words on the Resurrection were an answer to Martha's witnessing her faith: "I know that he [Lazarus] shall rise again in the resurrection at the last day" (John 11:24). Christ did not deny that resurrection, but in the prospect of the future He spoke His realistic words on the present,[18] as when He said of Himself that "I am the bread of life" which "giveth life unto the world" (John 6:33-35), or when He said to the Jews that "ye will not come to me, that ye may receive life" (John 5:40). This life is eternal life (John 3:36, 5:24, 6:47, 6:54), inviolable by the power of death and corruption, and in the glory of God, which is seen by faith (John 11:40). And the Christian Church's affirmation that death, in view of the resurrection, is a sleep, is surely not meant as a natural relativizing of the power of death, but as a reference to life in the power and reality of the Resurrection.[19]

Now that we have seen how Scripture speaks of life and death, of dying and not dying, and of the change not from life to death but from death to life, there is all the more reason, in the light of this witness, to examine the "immortality of the soul." If the

---

17. J. Schniewind, *Das Evangelium nach Markus* (1949), p. 90. Cf. Oepke in Kittel, op. cit., III, 439. Oepke sees the term as a general euphemism for death rather than as a specifically Christian term, but adds that the passage has a special relationship with Matt. 9:24. Cf. other commentaries on Mark, *ad loc.*

18. Cf. C. H. Dodd, *The Interpretation of the Fourth Gospel* (1953), pp. 147ff., 364ff.

19. F. W. Grosheide, *Commentaar op Johannes*, II, 156. He cites I Thess. 4:13. Cf. Acts 7:60; 13:36, I Cor. 7:39; 15:6.

witness of Christ on life and death is the cause of that "strangeness" which strikes us, according to Bavinck, when we first compare the message of Scripture with the general belief in immortality, then the question must naturally arise whether we have in the general concept an *articulus mixtus,* and whether indeed this belief in the immortality of the soul does belong essentially to the message of Scripture. Is there a way from the radical messages of Scripture to the immortality of the soul?

We can say, in the first place, that Scripture does not call our attention to a natural immortality to be concluded from the nature and structure of the soul as an anthropological given involving essential indestructibility. And when theologians speak of a natural immortality, they indeed acknowledge that only God is essentially immortal and that the human soul has no such essential immortality. But nevertheless, some sort of natural immortality is frequently posited as somehow essential and structural, and as therefore deducible even by reason from the structure of the soul. The combination of man's creaturely dependence with the soul's natural immortality often led to an unacceptable antinomy, as Kuyper already noted: "the concept of dependence in human existence (i.e., man's creatureliness) cannot be combined with the concept of the immortality of the soul." Any complete affirmation of creaturely dependence forbids a line of reasoning which bases its conclusions on the nature of the soul.[20]

This should all be considered in attempting to understand correctly the objections raised against various views supporting natural immortality. As we shall see, such objections do not in the least necessarily imply a denial of the continued existence of man after death. This is quickly apparent when we consider, for example, that the Dutch Calvinist philosophers Vollenhoven and Dooyeweerd attacked the immortality of the soul without becoming involved in any quarrel with the church regarding eschatological statements of the Calvinist creeds (notably the *Heidelberg Catechism,* Lord's Day 22, which deals with the communion with Christ after death); objections to their ideas were made on other grounds.

20. Kuyper, *Loci,* V, p. 45; cf. K. Steur, *Onsterfelijkheid* (1941), p. 13. For theological affirmation of some sort of natural immortality, cf., e.g., A. Janssens, *God als Schepper,* p. 200. He distinguishes between the essential immortality of God, the natural immortality of the soul, and the supernatural immortality of the body; cf. also Pohle, *Dogmatik,* I, 380. Janssens (p. 205) argues that the soul, because it is spirit, cannot be resolved into parts; it is psychically simple; it is inwardly immortal; immortality "follows logically" from spirituality.

Kuyper had already in 1870 called the expression "immortality of the soul" one which could not exist for the Bible, and pointed out that no creed of the Calvinist churches used the term: "what the rationalist calls immortality is for the Christian eternal life."[21] It is clear that the decisive question here is what is meant by immortality of the soul, and whether or not the affirmation of a natural immortality is based on an "essence" abstracted from its relation to God, from which we can draw (without considering this relation) further conclusions, such as the soul's "indestructibility."[22] And it should also now be clear why criticism of the natural immortality of the soul is often most closely related to criticism of the substantial dichotomy of soul and body. At issue was not existence after death, nor an agnostic "death is death," but the problem of an anthropology which defines the "essence" of man and from it draws further conclusions. Thus it is possible, also, that a criticism of the idea of natural immortality can go hand in hand with a full acceptance of the expectation of the Catechism (Lord's Day 22) that the soul after death will at once be taken up to Christ. The fact that no objections were made against this article of faith shows that the problems are not primarily of an eschatological nature, but are rather anthropological.

Now it is clear enough that various questions could arise in and around such criticism. And it is completely understandable that the *status intermedius*, (the state of the soul after death and before judgment,) was a special issue in many of the discussions. The question was posed whether criticism of the substantial dichotomy of soul and body and of the immortality of the soul would not inevitably produce a whole set of problems in the confession and expectation of salvation after death. It is not our intention here to discuss in detail the question of the *status intermedius*, but we can hardly avoid a brief consideration of the anthropological implications of that question. We note that there has recently been sharp criticism from various quarters of the doctrine of the intermediate state, and often in unmistakable relation to criticism of the soul's immortality. Such criticism did not originate with the Dutch Calvinist philosophers Vollenhoven and Dooyeweerd, but can clearly be seen in German theology. It is noteworthy that it is connected with a sharp criticism of the substantial dichotomy

21. A. Kuyper, *De Leer der Onsterfelijkheid en de Staatsschool* (1870), p. 12.
22. Calvin (*Commentary ad* I Tim. 6:16) points out that the soul depends on God for its existence and continuance, so that "properly speaking, it does not have an immortal nature"; citing Acts 17:28.

of soul and body, which pictures man as a *compositum* of a mortal body and an immortal soul. There has been a sharp reaction against the post-Enlightenment idealistic belief in immortality, based on an optimistic view of natural immortality, as demonstrable by reason. Kant already delivered a sharp philosophical critique of the rational evidences for the immortality of the soul; in our age, all sorts of objections have come from theology itself. It is said that such an idea is in conflict with the basis of Christian belief, since it shows traces of the concept of the soul as something divine, of a partial deification of man. And along with this, there is criticism of the dichotomy of two substances (body and soul) as resulting in the soul's escaping the judgment of God, His holy judgment of death because of sin. The immortality of the soul, it is said, seems to imply that this judgment does not affect the whole man; it affects only the body, not the soul. The criticism is especially associated with Althaus; e.g., "the Christian faith knows nothing of an 'immortality of the soul' — which indeed calls death a lie and misunderstands the judgment of God — but only of a resurrection from an actual death through the power of God." And with these words, we encounter an influential dilemma which has played a more and more important part in recent eschatological discussion: immortality or resurrection.[23]

A fruitful aspect of this dilemma as it appears in recent theology lies in the fact that it occurs in a context of thought which rejects the substantial dichotomy of body and soul, and wishes to begin

23. Cf. Mozes Mendelssohn, *Phädon* (1767). He is typical of the Enlightenment; cf. H. Wolf, *De Onsterfelijkheid als wijsgerig Probleem* (1933), pp. 158ff. His "evidences" were attacked by Kant in his *Kritik der reinen Vernunft* (see I, 246, in the Renner edition); especially the idea that the simplicity of the soul implied its indestructibility. See H. Scholz, *Der Unsterblichkeitsgedanke als philosophisch Problem* (1922), pp. 38ff. For the quote from P. Althaus, see his *Die letzten Dinge* (1933, 4th ed.), p. 109; cf. *Die Christliche Wahrheit*, II (1948), 85, 475ff. The discussion on this point also had implications in the terrain of the history of dogma, and concentrated there on Luther's ideas; cf. the rewarding discussion between Althaus and C. Stange, who claimed that Luther attacked the idea of the immortality of the soul as unchristian (especially in his remarks on the Fifth Lateran Council), while Althaus held that Luther attacked only the ways in which Rome defended the idea, rather than the idea itself. See C. Stange, *Das Ende aller Dinge* (1930), pp. 122-239; "Die Unsterblichkeit der Seele," *Zeitschrift für systematische Theologie* (*ZST*) (1924); "Luther und das funfte Laterankonzil," *ZST* (1928), pp. 339-444; "Die geradezu lächerliche Torheit der päpstliche Theologie," *ZST* (1932); and Althaus, "Die Unsterblichkeit der Seele bei Luther," *ZST* (1925-26).

with the whole man, who is affected with the divine judgment
of death precisely as whole man. There can then be no idea that
death affects merely the body, as a part of man; the soul is also
affected by death, so that after man dies there remains only one
eschatological perspective: awakening from death.[24] That is a
perspective which has nothing to do with the "natural" immortality
or indestructibility of the soul, but comes exclusively from God's
future creative act in Jesus Christ.

Thus Van der Leeuw criticizes the dualistic view of man, which
he says is the source of the popular belief in immortality which
has infiltrated modern Christianity. Such a view is, he says, Greek
rather than Christian, and "in conflict with the essence of the
Christian faith." We may make no distinction between body and
soul as regards the effects of death. The whole man, according
to the Old Testament as well as the New Testament, is threatened
by death. There is nothing he can fall back on; "the soul also
dies." Only God, continues Van der Leeuw, is immortal; "He
gives man the promise of resurrection." This is to be taken in
strict seriousness; man, the whole man, has lapsed into death.
But does not the promised resurrection necessarily involve a certain continuance of existence after death, so that it is "we" who
are awakened? Yes, it would appear there must be something
which remains, which continues, and on which God builds the
new creature. That "something," says Van der Leeuw, we may
call "soul" — not in contrast to the body, but in reference to that
in us which God holds fast, the image of God which was impressed in us at creation, which is not our "deepest essence" or
"highest being" or "divine nature," but which is that nameless
thing in our life which makes it possible for God to contact us,
a point of contact for His love. There seems to be a little hesitation
here in Van der Leeuw's treatment of the problem of continuity.
He does not wish to deny all continuity, but on the other hand
wants to avoid making of this point of contact more than "a
possibility implicit in our being-created-by-God," nor may we take
it as a "personality" or "soul" in the psychological sense. The
language of faith is that which confesses that "we vanish, irrevocably,
wholly, and there is nothing left, unless God performs a miracle
of creation, and raises us up." The reason why the expression

---

24. Cf. G. van der Leeuw, *Onsterfelijkheid of Opstanding* (1936, 2d ed.), pp.
    19, 20. "Unsterblichkeit," *Eranos-Jahrbuch* XVIII, *Sonderband für C. G.
    Jung* (1950), 183-206. Cf. C. Stange, *Das Ende aller Dinge* (1930), p. 122:
    two possibilities — immortality through the immortality of the soul, or
    through the divine power which wakes from the dead.

"continuity" is so misleading, he says, is that it implies some *thing* in us which continues in existence after death. There is no continued existence of the soul as such, but a "continuation" by God of the "contact point" even through death. "God does not create out of something — our spirit or personality, for example; He does not transform something. He creates from nothing, He creates something new from our annihilated existence."[25]

We need not wonder that the idea of the intermediate state of the soul after death has also been brought into the discussion in connection with the attacks on dichotomy and on the immortality of the soul. Thus Althaus, for example, delivers a sharp criticism of this idea, in which both eschatological and anthropological motifs play a role. The idea is rejected from an eschatological point of view because of its individualism and its underevaluation of the decisive meaning of the Kingdom of God, while from an anthropological viewpoint it is rejected because it fails to appreciate the effects of death on the whole man; and therefore the idea of an intermediate state must be rejected. The problem of what happens when we die does not involve a "purely spiritual salvation" but can be answered only in a context of death and the Day of Judgment. Any other attempt at an answer always ends in a substantial dichotomy, in which death and the judgment of God are no longer understood as serious and total, but only as partial.[26]

25. Van der Leeuw, *op. cit.* (1936), pp. 19-20, 30-38. Cf. the 1950 article, in German, cited above; there is no reason at all to exclude a part of man from annihilation; the effect of death may not be so restricted or "reduced"; immortality can never mean that something of man remains; this was a Platonic idea, which dominated antiquity and early Christian anthropology; Biblical thought had its "revenge" in the Church's confession of the resurrection of the body: the "point of contact" is that "nameless" something which does not pertain to the essence of man, but which yet constitutes him.

26. Althaus, *Die letzen Dinge*, pp. 149-152. "Private salvation, without communion with the people of God" is spiritualistic and a-cosmic, and has confused our understanding of the completion of the kingdom. Cf. R. J. van der Meulen, *Het Vagevuur* (1956), p. 19. Althaus stresses the effect of death on the whole man in these pages. It is necessary to be cautious in drawing conclusions on the relation between views on the intermediate state and views on immortality; there is a direct connection between the two in Althaus and Van der Leeuw. But cf. P. J. van Leeuwen, *Het Christelijk Onsterfelijkheidsgeloof*, pp. 378-379. He holds immortality and yet rejects the intermediate state as "a projection of our limited powers of representation into eternal life," which does not do justice to "the completeness of salvation in communion with Christ," though he acknowledges that occasionally in the New Testament the thought appears that salvation will not be complete while the old world endures (e.g., Heb. 11:39).

We meet the same sharp criticism of dichotomy in H. Thielicke, who likewise stresses strongly death as judgment on the whole man, and who detects in the idea of immortality something of escapism, permitting the "real" man (the soul) to evade death; it is an attempt to disarm death. The anthropological division of man into "real" and "non-real" parts is, he says, the basic fault of all natural anthropology. Thus men have often seen in death a liberation — for the soul — since death cannot touch the core, the real essence, of man. Thus it is forgotten that death affects man, and not in the periphery of his existence, but precisely in the "region of the ego." We may not think of death in terms of the analogy of a cocoon from which the butterfly appears. There is no super-personal immortal part in man. What we encounter in Plato, Kant, Hegel and Goethe is nothing more, says Thielicke, than a "dexterity at division" in which the "reality of death" is underestimated. We may hold in idealistic fashion to some "inviolable ego region," but death is not a "passing over" but a "going under," and it leaves no room for romanticism or idealism. We may not devaluate and obscure the reality of the grave through the idea of immortality. The Christian outlook is resurrection, not the immortality of the soul. According to the Biblical standard, death is unnatural, is destruction, catastrophe, is in conflict with out original destiny. Only where God is, is there life.[27]

We need not wonder that Thielicke, at the end of his book, gives an excursus on the intermediate state. We should surely expect that his conclusion, like that of Althaus, would inevitably be that the intermediate state must be rejected; but now we read, unexpectedly, that Thielicke will not use his view of the whole man and his "going under" in death as criterion for evaluating the Scriptural reference to the intermediate state. There is, according to the New Testament, a *Daheim-Sein bei Christus,* there is a communion which is not broken off, and there is thus a certain continuity. But we must not see this continuity as related to the soul or to something in us, but to us, to the "I," to the whole man. The intermediate state can not be clarified in terms of the subjective structure of some part of man, but there is a personal communion with Christ, which does not involve partial immortality or survival of a part of the ego, but rather the "inexplicability of the subjective structure," the whole man. It does not concern some characteristic of man, but rather the faithfulness of the Lord so that we may be

27. H. Thielicke, *Tod und Leben;* pp. 30, 43, 45, 55, 87, 98, 106.

with Him, as the murderer on the cross was with Him in Paradise; but we must not ask about the precise *modus,* the form, in which this is possible and becomes actual.[28]

Thus we see that in one case (Althaus, Van der Leeuw, etc.), criticism of substantial dichotomy results in a denial of the intermediate state, while in another case (Thielicke) the idea of the intermediate state and of a certain continuity is not attacked, though it is indeed added that we can not attempt to analyze and dissect the "personal relation" with Christ anthropologically. The consensus vanishes on this important point, and we can say that the orthodox doctrine of the intermediate state has not yet been generally rejected. Nor is the reason hard to find. It lies in the New Testament witness, insofar as it refers to the "thereafter." Thus it is remarkable that Cullman recently referred to the sharp and radical difference between the Greek idea of immortality and the Christian idea of resurrection, and emphasized the new creation of God, who calls to life not merely a part of man but the whole man — but then did *not* go on to conclude that the intermediate state must be rejected, since the New Testament speaks of the "thereafter" as a "being with Christ." Cullman asks whether this does not bring him back to the Greek idea of immortality, and even speaks of an "approach to the Greek teaching," but "the difference is still a radical one," for the fact that the dead already live with Christ "does not result from the natural essence of the soul, but is conditioned on a divine act from without, through the death and resurrection of Christ."[29]

Thus the influence of the New Testament statements has brought about a breaking of the previous negative consensus on the intermediate state, and at the same time we see a shift in the conviction that the dilemma "immortality or resurrection" is in all respects an inevitable dilemma. In giving full attention to what the New Testament says on the communion with Christ after death, theologians again exhibit some hesitation in letting the "eschatological boundaries" flow together. Sevenster feels that the idea of the "interim" is to some extent self-evident, since it hangs together with the "faith in the resurrection of the dead as a unique total event," though he does add that difficult questions remain, and that Paul never specifically answers the question what

28. Thielicke, *op. cit.,* pp. 209-210.
29. O. Cullman, "Unsterblichkeit der Seele und Auferstehung der Toten," *Theologische Zeitschrift* (1956), pp. 156, 153, 154.

lives on after death, nor how we must understand "being with Christ."[30]

Now that we have seen how maintaining the criticism of the "natural" immortality of the soul has produced renewed reflection and an increasing hesitation regarding the supposed dilemma of "immortality or resurrection," it might be well to consider the attitude on this point of the Dutch Calvinist philosophers Vollenhoven and Dooyeweerd, who have also sharply criticised the substantial dichotomy of soul and body. We have already noted in Vollenhoven's case that this criticism did not in the least bring him to a denial of a "being with Christ" after death; and the same questions recur in Dooyeweerd's criticism of the idea of man as a composite of two "incomplete substances," i.e., immortal soul (*anima rationalis*) and mortal body. He rejects such a view not only because the idea of a substance centered in human reason (i.e., the soul) is in conflict with the confession of the radical corruption of human nature, but also because the separability of the soul from the body raises various problems.

Thus, for example, the dichotomy of the two substances raises difficulties in connection with man's death. When the "soul" is separated from the body, what activities is it still able to carry out? This question must indeed arise as soon as the "soul" is abstracted and separated as an *anima rationalis separata* from the complete temporal activity of man. This raised a difficult problem for the idea of substantial dichotomy, which appears with especial clarity in Thomas Aquinas. He taught that the soul needed a bodily organ to carry out its functions; and thus he had to face the problem of how the soul could know anything after being separated from the body. Thomas sought the solution for this crucial problem in the idea of divine illumination, which is superior to natural knowledge; but this answer endangered the idea of an unchanged

---

30. For this shift, see Th. L. Haitjema, *Dogmatiek als Apologie* (1948), pp. 343-345; also J. Kooy, Persoonlijke Onsterfelijkheid (1939), pp. 139ff., *Contra* Van der Leeuw; F. W. A. Korff, *Onsterfelijkheid* (1946), p. 17. Korff says "if the Christian faith does not know what more to say, then it is leaving a great deal of New Testament thought lie." The term "eschatological boundaries" is that of Haitjema, who advises caution (cf. I John 3:2), but who refuses to reject the intermediate state, relying on Rev. 14:13. For J. N. Sevenster, see his "Einige Bemerkungen über den Zwischenzustand bei Paulus," *New Testament Studies* (1955), p. 296; cf. also his *Leven en Dood in de Brieven van Paulus* (1954), pp. 122-134.

existence of the soul after death.[31] Dooyeweerd criticized this solution as nothing else than a speculative metaphysics applied to the continued existence of the soul. He held this solution to be impossible, since it did not give enough weight to the fact that the psychic functions are indissolubly connected with the total temporal — cosmic relationship of all modal functions and cannot be abstracted from this total relationship. He formulated his own view quite sharply; all temporal existence, not merely one element in the fullness of man's being, ends with death. Thus to the question of what activity remains for the soul separated from the body, the unqualified answer is obviously "nothing!"[32]

It is clear that we should not conclude from this that Dooyeweerd rejects the idea of communion with Christ after death, or wishes (and must) object to the Heidelberg Catechism (Lord's Day 22). His "nothing!" is an answer given to the problem as posed in the context of substantial dichotomy, with its *anima rationalis separata*. He rejects this approach to the problem, since it involves a dichotomy which makes a "part" of man immortal. Dooyeweerd

31. Cf. the recent reconsideration of these problems from a Catholic point of view by A. Hulsbosch, "Onsterfelijkheid en Opstanding," *Het Schild,* XXXI, 49ff. He acknowledges, with Protestant critics, that one-sidedness and attenuation have crept into the Christian consciousness regarding the soul, under the influence of Greek ideas, but he rejects the dilemma. He does this in connection with the doctrinal definition of the Fifth Lateran Council, which said that the soul was immortal because of its incorporeal nature. He acknowledges (cf. Bavinck) that Scripture never uses these precise expressions, but this truth must nevertheless be supposed if we are to hold fast to the Biblical data regarding the continued existence of the soul after death. It is clear here how much the conflict on immortality centers around the problems involved in substantial dichotomy. Cf. Ch. VI, and the remarks which follow above on the critique of Dooyeweerd. Cf. also Hulbosch's important comments on Van der Leeuw's thesis: "De Discussie rond Onsterfelijkheid en Opstanding," *Het Schild,* XXXIII, 40-46.

32. H. Dooyeweerd, "Kuypers Wetenschapsleer," *Philosophia Reformata,* IV: 199ff. Illustrative of the crucial difficulty pointed out by Dooyeweerd is C. Friethoff, *Kennen na den Dood* (1945); see especially pp. 5-8, 11, 16, 19. Friethoff speaks of a major difficulty, the relation between the immortality of the soul and the impossibility of its carrying out its normal life-functions after death. There is an "apparent contradiction" in speaking of a "living soul, which does not live," which later in his argument reappears "in all its difficulty." The solution lies, he says, in the soul's "infused images." The natural state of the soul involves obtaining knowledge through the senses, and when death takes away the senses, the soul is in a status of restraint in which the infused images play a decisive role. Thus knowing after death is only a part of our earthly knowing.

prefers to speak of another sort of "dichotomy" between soul and body: the duality of the supra-temporal religious center of man (his heart or soul) and the whole temporal "functional cloak," functional complex, to which man's psychic life also belongs. It is striking that Dooyeweerd, just as Van der Leeuw, Althaus and Stange, stresses the centralized unity of man, which cannot be split into two "parts," an immortal soul and a mortal body. If we ask how Dooyeweerd's "dichotomy" (heart — functional complex) escapes the objections against earlier dichotomies, we soon find that the "heart" or "soul" in the religious sense means something quite different for Dooyeweerd than the *anima rationalis,* man's rational soul, which is part of man's psychic modal aspect. The heart is not a *part* of man, but his full "self," or, as he says, "our egoicity as the radical unity of our existence," "the religious center of our existence," which should not be confused with "any one of the modal aspects of the temporal horizon."[33]

It is thus clear that Dooyeweerd's reference to the heart as the religious center of man is not meant as an analogy or substitute for the old dichotomy of substances, nor as a simple substantial dichotomy of center and periphery, which might still have a place for "higher" and "lower" elements in a dualistic sense. He specifically wishes not to restore, in any way, the old dichotomy, and thus lay himself open to all the objections regarding the "composite" of soul and body which he himself had raised against Aquinas and scholasticism. But this raises a question: Just what, then, are we to understand by the term "prefunctional heart" or by the "supra-temporality" of the heart? What means this term "heart," for which we can substitute "self," "I," "egoicity," or "*soul* of human existence"? Can we say anything more about it, when Dooyeweerd

33. For Dooyeweerd and this communion with Christ after death, see his "Het Tijdsprobleem in de Wijsbegeerte der Wetsidee," *Philosophia Reformata,* V, 181. The "soul," Scripture shows, is not affected by temporal death, but after the end of the body (i.e., of all the temporal aspects of man) , it continues as a form of existence with an individuality structure. As Dooyeweerd adds in a footnote, the answer "nothing!" refers to the soul in the context of substantial dichotomy, "an abstraction from the temporal function-complex of the soul, an abstraction which in scholastic psychology is raised to a substance." It is also clear enough that Dooyeweerd can not be charged with teaching "soul sleep"; he would not accept all the arguments used by Calvin (in his *Psychopanny-chia*) , but the idea of soul sleep is based precisely on a dichotomy of substances; cf. the Catholic rejection of the teachings of Rosmini (Denzinger, 1913) . For the heart as the "religious center of our existence," see Dooyeweerd, "Calvinistische Wijsbegeerte," *Scientia,* I (1956) , 144.

says that it is beyond all conceptual grasp, and pictures it as "the hidden player on the instrument of theoretical thought"?[34]

It should be noted, to begin with, that the heart is not a reduction of man to some core, from which the periphery — the body — can easily be removed. The "prefunctional heart" is not something which should be placed outside its functions, as a new substance which then is joined to the body's function-complex and which can be separated from it at death. The heart is much more man himself in all his functions; but just for that reason, it is inaccessible to scientific analysis and to substantiation. Nor is it accessible to "psychological" understanding: "the ego itself escapes every attempt to grasp it in a psychological view. The human ego expresses itself in the entire temporal human existence, but it recedes to an intangible phantom as soon as we try and localize it in our temporal existence."[35]

It has been said that the attack directed at the idea of substance by the "cosmonomic" philosophy of Dooyeweerd and Vollenhoven is based on a new form of functionalism which nearly results in a "psychology without a soul" in which man is equated with his functions, and loses unity and internal relations, and indeed loses "existence" as man. This criticism has been brought forward especially from the Catholic side. Albers, for example, accuses Dooyeweerd of ignoring ontological problems and — like the Reformation — giving no attention to man's "being" but only to his "relation," in an unscriptural "vivisection," a separating of the

34. The term "prefunctional heart" occurs in D.H. Th. Vollenhoven, "De Waarheid in de Godsdienstwijsbegeerte," *Vox Theologica*, XIII, 115. It is striking that all sorts of anthropological views use an extremely varying terminology to express the "essence" of man. Cf. besides Dooyeweerd, J. Waterink, *De Mens als religieus Wezen en de Hedendaagse Psychologie* (1954), pp. 23-24. For the "hidden player," see Dooyeweerd, *Scientia*, I (1956), 144.

35. Dooyeweerd, *A New Critique of Theoretical Thought*, II (1955), 115. Cf. Waterink, *op. cit.*, p. 24, concerning the inaccessibility to analysis of the deepest essence of man. Dooyeweerd's idea that the heart "expresses itself in" temporal existence and yet "escapes" analysis finds a striking parallel in the views of C. A. Van Peursen, *Lichaam, Ziel, Geest* (1956). See especially Chap. XI, on the "inaccessible ego," where Van Peursen speaks (as against the ego as a self-existent substance) of the mystery of the "I," on which we can never lay hold (p. 128). Cf. also the "hidden player" of Dooyeweerd and the "chessplayer" of Van Peursen (p. 136)! The parallel is all the more striking because Van Peursen rejects (as does Dooyeweerd) Rickert's impersonal subject of theoretical knowledge, since the question involves the concrete human subject (expression and escape). Van Peursen refers repeatedly to the fascinating book of G. Ryle, *The Concept of Mind* (1949).

religious-ethical sphere from the physical and ontological.[36] Typical of his misunderstanding, in our opinion, is the statement that if created reality is no more than a religious relation of dependence, the relation itself is impossible, since a relation is always between two things. This criticism makes it clear that Albers is using a different concept of essence from Dooyeweerd. Dooyeweerd holds that besides functionalism and substantialism there is a third alternative; namely, that we cannot view man's essence in itself and then place it in a relation to God, as Albers does with his concept of relation. Anyone who is attracted to the philosophy of substance will see in the idea that man's relation to God is essential to his essence, a sort of actualism which does away with man's independent existence in a relational emphasis. But this criticism is nothing else than a reaction to the dangers of real actualism and functionalism, which stress relation to the extent of ignoring reality. There is also the possibility that stressing man's relation to God does not at all threaten or obscure or dissolve reality, but rather helps us to understand the nature of this reality in its dependence on God.[37]

36. In connection with the charge of a "psychology without a soul," it should be said that, in our opinion, the views of H. de Vos on Dooyeweerd's idea of the psychic aspect of man are completely unintelligible and must rest on a basic misunderstanding. See H. de Vos, "De Wijsbegeerte der Wetsidee," *Kerk en Theologie* (1952), p. 153. He writes that Dooyeweerd holds that the psychic aspect does not exist; but cf. "the general theory of the modal spheres," Dooyeweerd, *A New Critique of Theoretical Thought*, II, 111ff., especially on the psychical sphere. Dooyeweerd himself touches on the charge; anyone who says that we hold man's existence to be only a "complex of modal temporal functions which are centered in the heart" has a "very simplistic and erroneous understanding of what we mean by anthropology" (*A New Critique of Theoretical Thought*, III, 629).

37. O. J. L. Albers, *Het Natuurrecht volgens de Wijsbegeerte der Wetsidee. Een kritische Beschouwing* (1955). For the accusation that Dooyeweerd ignores ontology, see pp. 163, 175, 188. For the charge that Dooyeweerd sees the created cosmos merely as relation, see p. 163. This has reference to his view of the created cosmos as meaning. See *A New Critique of Theoretical Thought*, I (1953), 100; II, 30. Cf. my "Identiteit of Conflict? Een Poging tot Analyse," *Philosophia Reformata* (1956), pp. 31ff. The extent of Albers' misunderstanding is shown in his charge that Dooyeweerd limits himself to the ethical and religious, ignoring the psychic, concrete, and ontological; and in his further statement that "not only the direction of the heart is changed but man in his totality, psychic and ethical" — a remark which implies that Dooyeweerd's view of the heart involves problems of delimitation. But what Christ said about that which comes forth from the heart was concretely meant, and manifests itself in full reality.

The way is now open to answer the question of what led Dooyeweerd to his emphasis on the "supratemporality" of the heart. Is this similar to the earlier substantial "immortal soul"? Surely this would seem to follow if this "supratemporality" implies a "transcendence" in the sense that theology uses in speaking of the "transcendence" of God. Perhaps the concept of transcendence which plays a role in the philosophy of Dooyeweerd does seem to imply an association with implications of "supracreatureliness." Thus he speaks of the basic unity of our existence "which essentially *transcends* the modal differentiation of the temporal aspects."[38]

It is clear, however, that we must not conclude from this terminology that Dooyeweerd has here denied his original concept of the boundary, the difference, between the Creator and created reality. The meaning of the term "transcend" is indissolubly bound to the modal complex, which is transcended, but there is no thought here of ascribing transcendence to man in the sense in which we speak of God's transcendence. If this were the meaning, then Dooyeweerd would have come back in spectacular fashion, via the criticism of the dichotomy: higher — lower, to a partial theism, which he has opposed consistently.

In this connection, it is of importance to consider a discussion within the ranks of Dooyeweerd and his followers, which has arisen over precisely this cardinal point in anthropology — Dooyeweerd's concept of the supratemporality of the heart. Although it seemed clear that this term in no sense meant supracreatureliness, the question was nevertheless raised whether humanness as a whole did not bear a temporal character and was not subject to time, and whether it was then still legitimate to speak of the *supra*temporality of the heart. Spier especially raised various questions: "Is the soul perhaps eternal? Or is there some intermediate state between time and eternity?"[39] Spier was well aware that Dooyeweerd had no intention of erasing the boundary between God and man by making the heart eternal, any more than this was implied by speaking of its transcendent character. But he

---

38. H. Dooyeweerd, *Scientia*, I (1956), 144, (italics his); cf. p. 145. The terminology is not only recent: it often occurs in the first year of *Philosophia Reformata* (e.g., p. 7 *re* modal differences, and p. 69, "our transcendent center of existence"). The term "transcendent" is used also of God. Cf. *A New Critique of Theoretical Thought*, II, 115. He says; "The human ego . . . transcends all modal functions and all temporal individuality structures of human existence referred to it."

39. J. M. Spier, *Tijd en Eeuwigheid* (1953), pp. 95f., 164f. The expression "rising above" is often used by Dooyeweerd in the sense of rising above the temporal differences of meaning in the temporal context.

raised objections against the ambiguity of the heart's "rising above" the modal spheres, and especially against the supratemporality of the heart, because the whole existence of man is temporal. And to speak of man's temporal existence and the supratemporality of man's heart is, said Spier, a contradiction.

It is noteworthy that Spier interprets this supratemporality as being (in Dooyeweerd) a gift, a supratemporal crown, added to the basis of temporality. It seems clear that a misunderstanding has entered the discussion, for such a formulation surely does not accurately portray Dooyeweerd's meaning. It suggests a sort of *donum superadditum*, and at the same time a sort of "substantiality" of the heart as a transcendent given. Spier is afraid that supratemporality will lead (unwittingly) to supracreatureliness, and the extent of his fear is evident from his remark that while man's relations with God transcend time and creatureliness, nevertheless man as *relatum* does not, and he adds that "if this should be the case, then he as creature would also be supratemporal." It is clear that Spier interprets Dooyeweerd as moving in that direction; and in this inference of supracreatureliness from supratemporality lies, in our opinion, the misunderstanding which has arisen. That a misunderstanding is involved is already apparent from the fact that Dooyeweerd speaks of the "supratemporal in a sense proper to the creature," in distinction from the eternal character of God, and further of the "*creaturely* concentration of the temporal on the eternal in the religious transcending of the time boundary."[40] Spier's argument, that man's relation to God is supratemporal and in so far bears a transcendent character but not man as such, does not hold against Dooyeweerd, whose concern is with the problem raised by the fact that we cannot speak of man outside this relation. Thus Dooyeweerd does not understand the supratemporality of the heart in the sense of an added "gift" or a "crown," nor does he wish a "relation" between God and an independent and self-enclosed and self-existing man, a relation which would be added to man's humanness.[41] Since Dooyeweerd includes man's relation to God in his delimitation of man's essence, Spier's point that supratemporality must imply supracreatureliness does not affect him.

Spier's views threaten to make man's "relation" to God a relation in which man by himself is then related to God — while Dooyeweerd (rightly, in my opinion) views such a man as already an

---

40. Dooyeweerd, *Philosophia Reformata*, I, 4 (italics mine).
41. See Dooyeweerd, *Scientia*, I, 145. The "ego" is not enclosed in itself as a windowless monad. It is only "I" in the central societal relation of "me" and the existential relation to "Thou," its divine origin.

abstraction. All this is further clarified through examining the way in which Dooyeweerd, in this connection, uses the concept of *aevum* in contrast to the *aeternitas* of God. This concept was used by the Fathers and the Scholastics to refer to a "created eternity," a state between time and eternity, and its use by Dooyeweerd was probably also responsible for the misunderstanding regarding the "supratemporality" of the heart. Though the scholastic concept of the *aevum* is related to the "intellectual soul" (*anima intellectiva*), Dooyeweerd nevertheless wishes to use the term for the supratemporality of the heart.[42]

Spier criticized Dooyeweerd on this point also, and sided with Popma, who viewed Thomas' *aevum* as implying an *aeternitas participata,* the creature sharing in the eternity of God, and held that it contained nothing which could be useful in Christian thought. Spier rejected any reference to the heart as a supratemporal *aevum.* Since man's whole existence is temporal, the unity of man cannot be maintained if soul and body are related in terms of supratemporal and temporal, and besides supratemporality might be the opening wedge for a full-fledged scholastic understanding of the *aevum.*[43]

Now, our concern here is not with the question of whether the use of the concept of the *aevum* in this connection can be commended or whether it is rather a source of misunderstanding; it is rather to understand what Dooyeweerd means by the term.[44] And we then see that he does not use the concept without fuller explanation. He does not mean to imply the scholastic idea of participation, but rather refers to man's religious relation to God. He describes the *aevum* as an "actual situation," as "nothing but the creaturely concentration of the temporal on the eternal through a religious transcendence of the time boundary," and the reference to a relationship is even clearer when he says that the "*aevum*-consciousness" can also reveal itself in an apostate direction. It is thus not a deeper layer or *Schicht* in man's being, which could become part of a "dichotomy." Spier somewhere raises the question

---

42. Dooyeweerd, "Het Tijdsprobleem en zijn Antinomieën op het Immanentiestandpunt," *Philosophia Reformata,* IV, 2ff.

43. K. J. Popma, "Tijd en Religie," *Philosophia Reformata,* XIV, 153-154; Spier, *op. cit.,* pp. 163, 142-143.

44. We might ask why the concept of substance could not also be used, freed from its scholastic contexts. Evidently Dooyeweerd views this as a more impossible task than that of the *aevum* concept. Cf. Stoker's somewhat different view of the concept of substance. For Spier's attack, see *op. cit.,* p. 143. Cf. in general, Dooyeweerd's "Het Tijdsprobleem in de Wijsbegeerte der Wetsidee," *Philosophia Reformata,* V, 180-181.

whether it means nothing that we are not conscious of any deeper
supratemporal part of ourselves, while our body clearly is subject
to time; but the very use of the term "deeper part" shows that
Dooyeweerd's use of the concept of the *aevum* is not understood
correctly. For Spier's use suggests an analogy between supratemporal
and a substantial dichotomy, while it is precisely characteristic of
the Dooyeweerdian "dichotomy" (a term he himself uses) that such
an analogy would be rejected. He does not mean to refer to
a deeper "part" of man, but rather to the whole man with all his
temporal functions in his religious concentration; i.e., in his relation
to God. And thus only is it explicable that Dooyeweerd, who
usually is extremely critical of taking over concepts from the
scholastics, here feels he is able to introduce clarification by means
of the concept of the *aevum*. He does not mean to place eternity,
aevum, and time neatly next to each other, much less to allow
man to "participate" in the eternity of God; he uses the concept
as over against assignment of independence to man, just as he
uses the terms "transcendence" and "eccentric" in the same context.
He is concerned not with a part of man, as Spier's polemic would
suggest, but rather with the whole man in all his temporal functions. After rejecting the scholastic relating of the *aevum* to the
rational soul, he relates it to the structure of our selfhood. And
though we may feel that terms such as "*aevum* state," "in-between
state" and "*aevum* consciousness" can give rise to all sorts of misunderstandings, it is in any event clear that Dooyeweerd is not
referring to a supra-creatureliness in the sense of a partial theism,
but rather to the fullness of the creaturely humanness in its indissoluble relationship with the living God.[45]

It is obvious that various problems arise at this point. But that
is always the case when theologians deal with the "essence" of
man, as is especially clear when we try to say something regarding
the communion with Christ after death. There is no one who
does not grope for words to express this mystery. Critics of the
body-soul dichotomy have often said that involved is not a "part"
of man which lives on, but something which can not be intellectually

45. Cf. Dooyeweerd, *Scientia*, I, 144. He speaks of the concentration of
theoretical thought on the "real or fancied Origin of all the relative."
This "fancied" is not happily used here, in my opinion, for man's
relation is always to the living God. This relationship can be misunderstood or perverted, and the word "fancied" is doubtless to be so
understood in this context. But it can not easily (in my opinion) be
coördinated with "actual."

approached; as Thielicke put it, (while retaining the concept of an in-between state!) "the subjective structure about which no questions can be asked." Meanwhile theologians — cf. Cullman, Sevenster, etc. — fall back on direct Biblical concepts such as, "being with Christ" and "dwelling with the Lord." It seems very evident to me that all these variations have the mystery of man in view, just as Dooyeweerd, when he rejects the "part" solution and refers to the heart, the ego, or the self. Simplistic anthropological explanation is thereby rejected. And when Dooyeweerd rejects all speculation about the *aevum*-situation, at the "separation" of soul and body, as intellectually unfruitful, he can cite Calvin (*"meteorica et vacua speculatio"*) and refer to that which is hidden from us.[46]

Such speculation is not only philosophically but also religiously unfruitful, and reference to "the hidden things" is something other than an *asylum ignorantiae*. This becomes incontrovertibly clear when we consider that Scripture itself gives us no help in a search for an analyzable anthropological solution.[47] It does speak of the reality of the communion with Christ which is not broken through death, of a "being with the Lord" in unbroken communion. We remember not only Christ's words to the thief on the cross (Luke 23:43), but also Paul's desire to leave this world to be with Christ (Phil. 1:23), on his view of the profit of dying (Phil. 1:21), and of the building of God which we have after death, "a house not made with hands, eternal in the heavens" (II Cor. 5:1-2). In this connection, Paul speaks of that mortality which shall be "swallowed up" by life, and affirms that precisely for this has God prepared us and given us the Spirit as pledge (II Cor. 5:4-5). This confidence inspires Paul with his willingness to "be absent from the body and to be present with the Lord" (II Cor. 5:8), so that he can serenely say "whether we live therefore, or die, we are the Lord's" (Rom. 14:8).

It is noteworthy in these and other references in the New Testament that we never encounter an anthropological definition or analysis of what it is that remains after death.[48] Paul speaks impartially of "me" (man) and remains, in his description of this expectation, wholly within the limits of our earthly concepts.

46. Thielicke's quote is from his *Tod und Leben*, p. 210. For Dooyeweerd, see *Philosophia Reformata*, IV, 5.
47. See P. Feine, *Das Leben nach dem Tode* (1919, 2d ed.), pp. 14ff., and Oscar Cullman in *Theologische Zeitschrift* (1956), p. 148.
48. Cf. further Luke 16:19-31 and Christ and the Sadducees (Matt. 22:32, Mark 12:27, Luke 20:38, John 14:2). See also the articles of Cullman and J. N. Sevenster in *New Testament Studies* (1956). Cullman refers (p. 153) to Rev. 6:11, 14:13.

When he wishes to refer to the "profit" of dying, he reaches for a word full of light and glory, being "with Christ" (Phil. 1:23); but we encounter this expression also in relation to our communion with Christ in this earthly life, while Christ Himself promises to be "with us" until the end of the world (Matt. 28:20).

What Paul says about the "hereafter," then, does not go beyond the forms of earthly communion with Christ as regards terminology (cf. I Thess. 4:14, 17), but in this analogical terminology he makes us sense the progress and the increase of glory.[49] By the same token, however, it is impossible for even the most intelligent analysis to go beyond what is held before us here in religious, and not in anthropological, categories. This "religious" language should not be thought of as something vague and unreal in comparison with ontological analysis, but rather as speaking to us of man before God, man in his relation to Him, who in this relationship goes forth to meet the Lord who judges all things. The New Testament believers are not oriented towards their "private bliss" so that they forget the coming Kingdom, but they do indeed await being "with Christ," for in Him they acquired a new future. And this reality, so full of comfort, surely can hardly be expressed clearly through an anthropological "division" within man; and if we are not satisfied with the New Testament description, and wish to achieve more "reality" by postulating the "substantiality" of a "part" of man, the "ego," or the "heart," or the "person," we contribute nothing to a deeper understanding of salvation. Scripture speaks continually of that in man which cannot be attacked or threatened, and thus of continuity; but it does this by underscoring the actuality of the being "with Christ." And if our life is truly oriented towards Him, then the concept of the "in-between" state will not be an individualistic threat to the expectation of the Kingdom, but the believer will listen to the words of Christ: "[Be] like unto men that wait for their lord" (Luke 12:36). The "in-between state," too, is God's mystery.[50]

It would seem to be apparent from the foregoing that much depends on what we are to understand by the "immortality of the soul." It is clear that we may not a priori interpret this termi-

49. Cf. "present in the body is absent from the Lord" (II Cor. 5:6-7) in connection with the difference between faith and seeing (5:7). Cf. J. N. Sevenster, *Leven en Dood in de Brieven van Paulus* (1954), p. 133. He holds that Paul sees the time after death as "the beginning of the whole course of events which culminate in the full glory of being always with the Lord."

50. See Ph. H. Menoud, *Le sort des trépassés* (1945), p. 46.

nology as a truly Christian article of faith. The expression can
be used in ways which are far removed from the Christian confession.
How often is not the immortality of the soul used as a plea for
the high value of man as such! Men, when faced with the
general reality of death, often fall back on the uniquely indissoluble
quality of the "soul," in which a spark of the divine is present;
and death can then be viewed not as a threat but as a liberation.[51]
The soul can be spoken of in such contexts in a psychological or
parapsychological fashion, wholly separate from any religious outlook, and quite apart from the message of sin and grace. The soul
is viewed as continuing by itself; a noteworthy analogy to the
abstract view of man which sees man as existing by himself. This
is a theory of philosophical or psychological belief in immortality,
which in the face of death falls back on that which remains after
death and which can not be touched by death. Such a theory, in
sharp contrast to the Christian belief, speculates on "the soul and
its future" quite apart from any relation to God's wrath and His
grace. Scripture is concerned with wholly different things when
it speaks to us of the eternal life which lies in communion with
Christ. It is not concerned at all with placating conclusions deduced from the nature and structure of the soul. Indeed, how
could this be possible in Scripture, which preaches that God's judgment affects the whole man, and which teaches that "it is appointed
unto man once to die, but after this the judgment" (Heb. 9:27)?
In such a text there is no trace of a pacifying conclusion because of
the "partial" nature of God's judgment, no trace of any limit which
would make the threat of death any less serious, and nothing of
a "soul" which through such a limit escapes the crisis of death.
The Scripture does indeed promise peace, but only in the perspective of the High Priest who with His power over death dethrones
the devil and frees all who throughout life were by fear of death
doomed to slavery (Heb. 2:14-15).

51. This can be seen very clearly, e.g., in A. Sparenburg, *De Ziel en haar
Toekomst* (1953), p. 174: "Ultimately it is not so bad if the body dies,
for we do not thereby lose any essential part of our being." The ground
is here laid, from the psychic life of man and the unlimitedness of the
soul, for an optimism which does not fear death. A close relation is
often set up (in this book also) with spiritism, which can point to
"thousands of contacts" with the world where the immortal souls dwell.
Immortality is thus a general and provable given for man, and this
produces courage and confidence. The amount of dying becomes "less
dramatic" than we should superficially think. Feelings of anxiety are
superfluous, for when "we find ourselves at the end of life, soul and body
part as true bosom friends."

For this reason the Christian Church has constantly turned itself against an idealistic view of immortality, i.e., one in which the continued existence and the indissolubility of the soul are viewed as inherent in man or as a supposed permanent feature of life as such. The witness of Scripture, which knows nothing of any "existence" by itself, a priori rules out any such idealism. There is, "anthropologically," no area to which man can flee to escape death as God's judgment. And there certainly is no obviousness in such an idealism, no patent evidence for it. The Church spoke out most strongly on man's continued existence and did not view death as total annihilation; but this did not at all mean that it based these views on a part of man which remained after death. Rather it referred precisely to the completely serious character of the divine judgment, of which Paul said "we must all appear before the judgment seat of God" (II Cor. 5:10). The affirmation of this continued existence was never an a priori anthropological guarantee that some essential *part* of man would not be affected by death. This continued existence was, rather, included in man's relation to the living God in the seriousness of His judgment and grace, and thus it acquires its full existential earnestness (see Eccles. 12:14). Various attempts have been made to give expression to this fact; e.g., "the immortality of the relation to God"[52] — an unsatisfactory expression, but one which intends to say that the concept of immortality does not denote an idealistic "escape" which from within himself can give man rest in the face of death, but rather the continued actuality of humanness in the coming encounter with God's judgment. Thus we should not conclude a priori from the frequency with which the immortality of the soul has been treated in the history of the Church and of theology that a philosophical and optimistic faith in immortality was at stake. It is striking that the Church's references to the immortality of the soul occur not in an idealistic context, but rather in one of warning and exhortation, amid appeals to seek life where alone it can be found.

52. So, e.g., F. W. A. Korff, *Onsterfelijkheid* (1946), pp. 18, 22. We may not attack the immortality of the soul, he says, without giving this truth its full right. In the discussion on immortality, a remark of Luther (in his commentary on Genesis) is often cited: immortality is due to God's contact with us ("*Ubi igitur et cum quocumque loquitur Deus sive in ira, sive in gratia, is certe est immortalis. Persona Dei loquentis et verbum significant, nos tales creaturas esse, cum quibus velit loqui Deus usque in aeternum et immortaliter*"). See, e.g., C. Stange, *Das Ende aller Dinge* (1930), p. 130; P. Althaus, *Unsterblichkeit und ewiges Leben bei Luther* (1930), p. 21; E. Brunner, *Das Ewige als Zukunft und Gegenwart* (1953), p. 119.

Theologians have often spoken wholly incorrectly of a "natural theology" which would deal with the relation between God and man by himself, and to which the gospel would be a later soteriological complement. For this "relation" to God is a relation to the living God, who is the God of salvation, and who (as Paul said in his Areopagus speech) "hath appointed a day, in the which he will judge the world in righteousness by that man whom he hath ordained, whereof he hath given assurance unto all men in that he hath raised him from the dead" (Acts 17:31).

Thus it is also clear why Scripture does not take up this continued existence and the "immortality of the soul" as an independent theme, a fact which impresses those who approach Scripture from a belief in general immortality as being "strange." The basic reason for this fact (which both Bavinck and Hulsbosch acknowledge, and call the religious dimension of Scripture) is, that this continued existence as such is never preached as a comfort, an immortality which man might deduce from the structure of his being, a comfort which he could seek and find against approaching death. Scripture shows us no way through which death loses its serious character, no way in which an "immortality of the soul" can take away death's character of "enemy" (I Cor. 15:26). Such a comfort is ruled out, since true comfort can lie only in the overcoming of death, in an overpowering annihilation of death in all perspectives including the ultimate: "there shall be no more death," and God "shall wipe away all tears from their eyes" (Rev. 21:4, 3). This is something radically different from the sort of escape from death which is implied in the idea of the immortality of the soul. This is God's eschatological deed where the "tabernacle of God is with men, and he shall dwell with them" (Rev. 21:3). If we take human immortality out of the context of the acts of God and the relation of man to these acts in His judgment and grace, out of the context of Him who comes again to judge the living and the dead, then we may in our plea for immortality give the appearance of having thrown up a dam against all materialism and against all *Enteschatologisierung* of human life — but this will be a different *eschaton* than that of the Biblical *kerugma*.[53]

53. See Van Leeuwen, *op. cit.*, pp. 103ff., 138-141. In his outlook, the decisive factor is his contrast between metaphysical and eschatological thought, a contrast which in various ways affects his views; e.g., of the image of God (as destiny), of the "in-between" state, and of the resurrection of the body. The contrast is related to his sympathy for Gogarten's plea for "the complete secularization of human thought." See his remarks on eschatological thought without a world-view, and on the complete independence of human knowledge. On the one hand, he

There can be no doubt that the Church from the most ancient times was convinced of continued existence after death. Not only was the resurrection of the body affirmed against spiritualistic and gnostic devaluation of the body, but because of our salvation in Christ, our "being with the Lord" was no less firmly held. The old confessions of the Church, as Kuyper already noted, speak of "eternal life" rather than "immortality of the soul." Steur even says that the Church never spoke officially of the immortality of the soul during the centuries prior to the Renaissance; the explanation of this fact he finds in the universal agreement on the subject. We can agree with this explanation if it refers to continued existence after death; provided there is no implication of general agreement that the "natural" immortality of the soul was as such a thesis in the belief of the Church. Evidently the Church was content to limit itself in the area of pneumatology to its pronouncements on eternal life and the resurrection of the body.[54]

It is striking that the Roman Catholic Church, too, has never held that the immortality of the soul is among those truths which can be proven from the nature of the soul.[55] Nor did the Fifth Lateran Council, held shortly before the Reformation, say that a natural immortality could be proved. It did say, against Pomponazzi, that the idea of a double truth was unacceptable, and that a proof from natural reason which conflicted with the immortality of the soul must be rejected. Rome thus did affirm the immortality of the

speaks of the "complete separation" between eschatological and metaphysical thought (p. 138) and, on the other, of an "underlying relationship" (p. 140) in that "all human knowledge is oriented towards the *eschaton*, God" (p. 141). In the critique of Hulsbosch (*Het Schild*, XXXIII, 42, 46), there are good points, in my opinion, though it is limited by his view of the "metaphysical anthropology" of the Bible. To that extent his criticism of the theological method which he finds in Van Leeuwen's dissertation, with which we agree, also applies vis-à-vis Catholic theology, which takes a very conscious position at this point.

54. For early statements on continued existence, see (besides the Apostles' Creed) the *Fides Damasi* (against the Priscillianists), the Athanasian Creed, and the Niceo-Constantinopolitan Creed (Denzinger, 16, 40, 86). For Steur's remark, see his *op. cit.*, p. 100.

55. In 1855, against Bonnetty, who relativized the knowing power of natural reason, the Church did maintain that the existence of God, the freedom of the will, and the spirituality of the soul could be proved — but the immortality of the soul was not included (Steur, *op. cit.*, p. 106); cf. Bautain's explanation to the bishops, which, however, was actually limited in character; he had to promise "never to teach that with reason alone it was impossible to demonstrate the spirituality and the immortality of the soul" (Denzinger, p. 453).

soul, but not its natural or provable immortality, despite the great consensus among theologians that this could be proved.[56] This provability was often assumed to be certain, but an official declaration of the Church was never made on this point.[57] This noteworthy caution on the part of the doctrinal authority of the Catholic Church, which taught that the spirituality of the soul could be proved, but not the immortality, shows (in my opinion) something of Scriptural "dimension" in relation to life and death. Scripture never takes up a natural immortality of the soul because of its inherent nature, but always concerns itself with the relationship of the whole man to God.[58]

56. Against Pomponazzi, *"Damnanus et reprobamus omnes asserentes animam intellectivam immortalem esse"* (Denzinger, p. 738). Pomponazzi wrote *De Immortalitate Animae* in 1516; see the translation in *The Renaissance Philosophy of Man*, E. Cassirer *et al.* (1945), pp. 257-381. He did not himself doubt the immortality of the soul, which was shown clearly by Scripture (p. 302), which was superior to reason; the question with which he was concerned was whether this revealed truth could be proven by reason. Reason forces us to say that the soul is dependent on the body for the carrying out of all its functions. Thus while immortality is firmly based on the words of Christ (p. 378), no natural reasons can be put forward to prove it. It remains an article of faith (p. 380), and even Plato had no certainty of it. We cannot at this point go into the important question whether Fifth Lateran did not implicitly affirm the provability of the soul as form of the body; this is often denied by Catholic authors. See A. Deneffe, "Die geradezu lächerliche Torheit der päpstlichen Theologie," *Scholastik* (1930), pp. 380ff., who denies that the immortality of the soul follows from its being a form; but he also says that the fact that the soul is a *"forma* subsistens" does involve immortality, since because of its spirituality it cannot perish, and because of its simplicity can not be decomposed into parts (p. 383). See further the bull of Benedict XII on the beatific vision (Denzinger, 530) and the *Decretum pro Graecis* of the Council of Florence (Denzinger, 693). See Pohle, *op. cit.*, I, 380. He says the Church left the question of the provability of immortality open as a concession to the Scotists.

57. See, e.g., Diekamp, *Katholische Dogmatik*, 7, II (1936), p. 101. He says that immortality is also a natural truth following from the simplicity of the soul; it cannot break up into parts; cf. also among many others, S. Strassen, "De spirituele Enkelvoudigheid van de Ziel als Bewijsgrond voor haar Onsterfelijkheid," *Studia Catholica* (1947), pp. 145-163, who speaks (p. 145) of "phenomenological evidence" for immortality. Many other examples could be given. For the lack of official pronouncements, see, e.g., A. Janssens, *God als Schepper* (1927), p. 200; and K. Steur, *Onsterfelijkheid* (1941), p. 106.

58. Though this dimension is generally acknowledged in Catholic theology, there is nevertheless a fairly strong nuancing in the consequences which are tied in with it. This appears particularly in the anthropological problems relating to the meaning of bodiliness. For a Catholic attack

The Reformation confessions show no shadow of a doubt regarding continued existence after death, as is evident from Lord's Day 22 of the Heidelberg Catechism and from numerous other places. But, equally, in these confessions, there is no mention of *natural* immortality as an independent theme. The perspective of the *eschaton* dominates them and the relation of man to God's judgment and grace, which death does not abolish. Death and man's continued existence are indeed spoken of in anthropological categories, in terms of soul and body (as in the Latin text of Lord's Day 22), but this fact does not imply a systematic anthropological analysis in the sense of substantial dichotomy or of a natural immortality therein implied; rather the main point is the expectation of salvation which, in Christ, defies death, and in which we anticipate being united with Him. In this expectation one does not think in terms of categories such as "part" and "whole," but rather in the New Testament light of conquest and comfort; and besides, it may not be ignored that this glory is spoken of in the context of the resurrection of the body, which is the real content of this affirmation. The absence of an independent treatment of the immortality of the soul is therefore no defect; there is no incompleteness in what is affirmed regarding "life eternal" and the resurrection of the body.[59]

It might be objected that the immortality of the soul surely does form an independent theme in the 1560 *Confessio Scotica,* which devotes a special article to it (Art. XVII). But here also it is apparent that the concern is not as such with the anthropological problem of soul and body or with deductions from the nature and character of the soul, but rather with the nature of continued existence according to Scripture. The Confession's intent is to affirm the joy and rest and freedom from all labors, confessed

---

on the identification of the conquest of death with the immortality of the soul, see R. Guardini, *Die letzen Dinge* (1949), p. 15: "not the soul, or the body, but man."

59. The taking up of the soul to Christ does come to expression in the *explanation* of the resurrection: "not only my soul, but also my body." Cf. Kuyper, *E Voto,* II, 196. He says that the Catechism here inserts the salvation of the "soul," but that the original meaning of the Apostles' Creed is to confess the resurrection of the body. He adds that the salvation of the soul had already been spoken of in Lord's Day 21, where it is affirmed that the child of God is a member of the Church and will remain so eternally. For the completeness of what is said in the Catechism, cf. also Lord's Day 22, Q. 58, on the explanation of eternal joy, which exists already, and the complete bliss which comes later — an explanation which does full justcie to the Biblical message.

also against the "fanatics" who say that the soul sleeps after death. We already encounter this struggle against the idea of soul-sleep, in Calvin's sharp attack, *Psychopannychia;* but though various anthropological interests play a role here, the real motif of the struggle is not primarily anthropological, but rather soteriological — eschatological in character. It is from this point of view that the concept of soul-sleep is taken up, and not in relation to a natural immortality. It is true that there sometimes appears to be a close analogy to the philosophical idea of immortality, since man's continued existence is described with the help of the "body — soul" terminology, and references are sometimes made even to "substances" and to the immortal soul which is "separated from the body."[60]

But this terminology does not involve that which is the core of the concept of immortality of the soul, i.e., the natural immortality of the soul as an independent idea.[61] That such was not the intent of the confessions is clear time after time from the fact that such expressions occur in a soteriological context, and we should never

60. The Confessio Scotica can be found in K. Müller, *Die Bekenntnisschriften der reformierten Kirche* (1903). For Calvin's *Psychopannychia,* see, e.g., *Quellenschriften zur Geschichte des Protestantismus,* ed. W. Zimmerli (1932). It has as its motto, *"Vivere apud Christum non dormire animos sanctos, qui in fide Christi decedunt."* Calvin speaks of the soul as *"bona pars hominis"* (p. 31; cf. *"nobilior pars," Institutes* I, XV, 2). It is a substance, which has sense and intelligence after death (p. 21). The soul (being celestial) is as different from the body (which is earthly) as the heavens from the earth (p. 55). This notion is related, obviously, to Calvin's idea of the soul as the image of God. The words of Gen. 1:26 cannot be applied to the body (p. 27); the body is not part of the image (p. 27). Cf. *Institutes* I, XV, 3; Zimmerli, *op. cit.,* p. 3. He correctly notes that Calvin's passionate interest in the question of soul-sleep is to affirm that the believer once united to Christ in faith can never be separated from Him, and thus can never sink back into sleep. *Psychopannychia's* fundamental structure makes this interpretation completely clear. For a Calvinist confession referring to the soul as "substance" which becomes separated from the body, see the *Confessio Helvetica Posterior.* Cf. V. Hepp, *Het Voortbestaan,* etc., p. 40. He viewed this fact as "of uncommon weight"; a judgment in which he was evidently referring to anthropological implications, for he so used it in the course of his polemic against Dooyeweerd.
61. It is obvious that the soul-body dichotomy influences all sorts of dogmatic views. Cf., e.g., Bavinck, *Gereformeerde Dogmatiek,* IV, 594. He attempts to show, in his attack on soul-sleep, that there is nothing impossible in the soul's exercising its functions without the body, since thinking and knowing are functions of the soul. Cf. "the psychic I of man." Bavinck's positive intent, however, is to show that Scripture pictures dying as "the way to closer and more intimate communion with Christ" (p. 594).

lose sight of the real motif in these imperfect attempts at formulation by the Church. The intent of the confessions is continually
evident on examining the context, which speaks of judgment and
grace, and especially of comfort in life and death. That must not
be lost sight of in an emphasis on the anthropological material
used in the formulations.[62] Even if the concepts of soul and
body, immortal soul and mortal body, are used in very definite
fashion, we should never conclude that we are thereby ecclesiastical-
ly, officially, bound to a particular philosophical-anthropological
view, any more than we should draw such a conclusion from
various anthropological expressions used in Holy Scripture.

One can indeed ask whether the use of particular expressions
may not obscure rather than clarify the light of revelation, — such
expressions as "rational animal," "substance," "reasonable and immortal soul"; but to raise this question in relation to the clarity of the
Church's pronouncements in order to sound a call for caution is
something quite different from accusing the Church, simply because
it uses such terms, of being inclined to make such an "immortality,"
separated from the gospel, into an independent theme in its confession.[63]

We may conclude that the formulations of the Church certainly
do not force us to view man's temporal existence in such a way

---

62. It seems to us that the confessions are more cautious than various
dogmatic systems, in which the "natural" immortality of the soul,
deduced from the dichotomy of soul and body, often play a role. See
the elaborations, e.g., of Turretin, *Inst. Theol. Elenct* (1734), pp.
513-534. Natural immortality "must be demonstrated" against "atheists
and libertines" (p. 531); "Scripture teaches it" and "reason confirms
it" (p. 532). Cf. his postulate *"ut bonis bonum, malis malum
rependatur"* (p. 534); "the desire for immortality," and the evidence
from the essence of the soul (spiritual and independent of the body)
(p. 534). Cf. Calvin, who says that sleep is "not unimportant" evidence
for immortality (*Institutes* I, XV, 2), while the central thought of the
Psychopannychia is religious.

63. The question of terminology is not simple, but very complicated.
It is related to the question of how the Church uses words and concepts
to confess its faith. Thus, the question as to reasonable soul is hardly to
be decided by reference to the word "reasonable" which we encounter
in Rom. 12:1; rather, the term "reasonable soul" is generally used to
typify the soul as essentially reasonable. Much depends on the context
in which the words are used. Thus the word "hypostasis," which played
so important a role in Christological and trinitarian controversy, occurs
already in the New Testament (Heb. 1:3, 11:1). Great caution is
necessary in judging, but it is likewise clear that we must beware of
ascribing to the Church a philosophical fixation because of its use of
particular terms.

as to separate the psychical and the corporeal, the psychic according to its nature being immortal and the body not.

We saw that the Catholic church made no official pronouncement on whether the natural immortality of the soul is provable. In this creedal cautiousness — I am not speaking of theology — we said we might trace the influence of the Scriptural manner of speaking, which gives us little encouragement towards an interest in a continued existence as such which could be deduced from the nature of the psychic or of the soul. It is striking that certainty regarding such a natural immortality is by no means the unassailable possession of all men in all places. Scholz[64] speaks of two things which shook this certainty; the critique of Kant and the rise of physiological psychology, which showed the dependence of the psychic on the bodily functions. The idea of immortality can then be transformed in various ways; e.g., when it is interpreted as eternal life in time, or as "posthumous fame," or as the idea of eternal recurrence. From all sides there thus appear elements of crisis in the midst of the optimistic view of immortality, often due to the progress of science, which brought into doubt various earlier conclusions of anthropology,[65] and forced the focusing of attention on the indissoluble unity of human existence.[66]

64. H. Scholz, Der Unsterblichkeitsgedanke als philosophisch Problem (1922), pp. 42, 47, 77-80. Cf. his own solution which envisages a complete separation of spirit and matter, and thus distinguishes between soul and spirit. The soul is then so closely bound to the body that it cannot be thought of without it, and for this reason we cannot speak of the immortality of the soul. The immortality of the spirit, i.e., those contents of consciousness which remain after subtraction of the body, is something different; and in these we feel more or less (sic) independent of the body (p. 79). Spirit includes the functions of will and intellect. It is something in many ways mediated by organized matter and is never encountered without it, but is not based on it and is notably independent of it.

65. See P. J. van Leeuwen, Het Christelijk Onsterfelijkheidsgeloof. Een Bijbels-dogmatische Studie, p. 246. He writes about the dogmatic use of metaphysical arguments: "such arguments, which are foreign to her nature can be used only as borrowed weapons, which can at any moment be taken away." We can agree with this statement without accepting the contrast between metaphysical and eschatological thought as this is developed by Van Leeuwen.

66. We can already see hesitation in a period when the immortality of the soul was still an unshakable truth for many. Cf., e.g., the reflections of Herder on the impossibility of conceiving of activities of the soul without the body. His critique did not imply a denial of continued existence, but rather of an existence which because of a dualism between soul and body ignored the latter. See, on Herder and various

In such situations, which are always possible, the Church may not interpret the reference to such unities in humanness as necessarily involving an attack on its faith. It should not be concerned about defending immortality by amassing evidence that the psychic life of man is unique and can exist independent of the body and therefore *can* continue its existence after death. Even apart from the fact that this would still not give evidence for the continued existence of man, the Church would give the impression, by such behavior, that its concern was directed towards the survival of man (or the soul) as such. We should inquire, in connection with attempts to prove the immortality of the soul, as to their background. For they appear again and again to be attempts to prove beyond a doubt a natural and structural immortality of a "part" of man. The evidence for the immortality of the soul is always of an abstract nature, for it deals with the soul (or man) by itself, apart from its relation to God, and it is then immaterial whether the evidence is psychological or parapsychological in nature. Nor, therefore, is immortality an *articulus mixtus*, something that we know from revelation and also could know from human reason. There is a total difference of approach between the religious affirmation of the Church and the philosophical and naturalistic belief in immortality. It would seem impossible to envisage a point of contact. We are mistaken if we think we have found it in the idea of continued existence as such. For the affirmation of the Church does not deal with survival as such, but with man before the countenance of God. The Christian faith is not a general belief in immortality with a religious relation to God added, but a faith which has an eye only for man in his relation to God and speaks only of that. And the history of the philosophical belief in immortality itself shows that this belief often led to an alienation from the Christian faith, since immortality was interpreted idealistically and optimistically.

It is thus noteworthy that Bavinck, who was so impressed by that other dimension in the language which Scripture uses when speaking of life and death, by the orientation of its witness, still says that the evidence for the immortality of the soul, while it perhaps cannot give us certain proof, is not lacking in importance.[67]

---

other appearances of crisis in the Enlightenment concept of natural immortality, H. Groos, *Der deutsche Idealismus und das Christentum*, (1927), III, 339ff. especially.
67. This discussion occurs in Bavinck, *Gereformeerde Dogmatiek*, IV, 569-71.

If we examine more closely what he meant, it becomes apparent first of all that Bavinck was not referring to scientific or philosophic evidence. He does see a general consciousness of personal survival, and views the so-called evidence as "nothing but an attempt made by this belief to give a reasoned account of itself," and it thus forms no ground for accepting the belief. And when Bavinck takes up the metaphysical proof from the nature of the soul, he refers to the creatureliness of man. The metaphysical evidence may deduce from uniquely psychical phenomena that there is a spiritual principle differing from the material, but this conclusion does not necessarily imply the immortality of the soul. Though the evidence retains its value, it is not decisive, since the soul is a created thing, limited, finite and relative, never free from change, dependent on the body, subject to all sorts of influences. It is clear that Bavinck approaches the proofs for the immortality of the soul in a psychical context, and in this limited context no strict proof is possible. And after discussing all the proofs, he speaks of the surprising character of the Scriptural standpoint, which makes no attempt to demonstrate the soul's immortality. The explanation of the fact that Bavinck maintained the relative value of the evidence will have to be sought in the situation in which the apologetes of his day found themselves, confronted as they were by all sorts of attempts to explain man in terms of a materialistic monism. No one, says Bavinck, has shown that conscious life owes its existence to the material world, and the psychic is and will remain *sui generis*. Thus Bavinck attacked materialism and monism, and related his attack to the immortality of the soul. But his real and deepest concern was directed and remained directed to the "surprising" outlook of Scripture.

Scripture is never concerned with an independent interest in immortality as such, let alone with the immortality of a part of man which defies and survives death under all circumstances, and on which we can reflect quite apart from man's relation to the living God. The Church affirms that it awaits Christ, who shall come to judge the living and the dead, and for that future it demands full attention in this world. Its concern is not with an abstract problem of continuity, but with the future, Christ's future, and thus also with man on his way to that future. In its own life it has experienced preservation in communion with Christ. If one knows that for this life "my times are in thy hand" (Ps. 31:15), then one can also through death entrust one's life into His hands. The Church, with such a view, remains in the tradition of Paul, who calmly and impartially speaks of "I" and "we" as the subject of the joy and bliss which shall come in the approaching end and in the fulfilled future of God. And no matter how much he is forced to stammer in the pictures and concepts he uses to give expression to this great mystery,[68] the prospect is not thereby limited, for our life now and in the future is hid with Christ in God (Col. 3:3).

And there is no need to be ashamed of such stammering, against the background of the New Testament message. For it is the reflection of the mystery of the divine safekeeping which extends through and beyond death. And because of the wonder of this divine protection, this "beyond death" is quite different from the "escape" in which the actuality of death is devaluated, as by an unrealistic idealism or heroism.

That death is the divine judgment on the whole man (a point often made in attacks on the immortality of the soul and on an "in-between" state after death) the Christian never thinks of denying; rather, this forms the background for rejoicing because we may dwell with the Lord. The statements of the Church on immortality are therefore not an "escape," but an acknowledgment of a wonder. And thus the Church with its confession also finds its way into the universal belief in immortality, witnessing with regard to it that life is being-with-Christ, and that whoever believes in Him shall not see death, not for all eternity. And this witness must sound forth in every age, whether the age holds the immortality of the soul on idealistic or psychological or parapsychological grounds, or whether it posits as highest wisdom that death is the end.

And in all reflections on the future, in which anthropology and eschatology touch on each other — on actual man in the future — we may not forget the affirmation, "I believe an eternal life." We cannot here enter into the question what the Church according to the historian meant by this article, a later addition to the Apostles' Creed. But it is clear in the light of the Biblical witness

68. Cf. the way in which Paul in II Cor. 5 speaks over the dissolution of our earthly house. There is a house of God, an eternal house (vs. 1); but then follows, "For in this we groan, earnestly desiring to be clothed upon with our house which is from heaven: if so be that being clothed we shall not be found naked" (vss. 2, 3). Cf. F. J. Pop, *Apostolaat in Druk en Vertroosting. De tweede Brief aan de Corinthiërs*, p. 156. He speaks of a "strange combination": being clothed with a house. Cf. Grosheide, *Commentaar*, p. 175. He speaks of the mixture of images. Cf. J. Ubbink, *Het eeuwige Leven bij Paulus* (1917), p. 14.

that when the Church confesses that this eternal life already begins in this life,[69] it does not confess too much. The expression of the communion formula, that we "lie in the midst of death" and that of the baptismal formula, that life is "nothing but a continual death" may be explained as a reference to the darkness into which the Light triumphantly shone; it should not lead us to weaken our *"Credo vitam aeternam,"* which is to be understood not futuristically, but eschatologically. For that life is life for the whole man, which found its definitive illumination in the very actualistic speaking on life and death by our Lord. To speak of and to confess this life is to grope after mysteries: life eternal and the resurrection of the body. It is an immortality from which all *hybris* is removed, because the meaning and the explanation of the immortality stand before us fully revealed in the light of the eschatological actuality: "Death is swallowed up in victory" (I Cor. 15:54).

II COR, 12=3

---

69. Heidelberg Catechism, Lord's Day 22.

CHAPTER EIGHT

CREATIONISM AND TRADUCIANISM — *Neither!*
soul is not a sep. substance

ATTEMPTS at getting at the mysterious nature of man have through the centuries continually encountered, not only the problem of the immortality of the soul, but also various questions relating to its origin. We noted the rather striking fact that generally it was not the immortality of man which was discussed, but rather that of the soul; and likewise in this context, we shall see that attention has usually been given to the origin of the soul.

It is indeed true that both the Church and theology have been interested in the origin of man, in a sense; but this interest was always directed to the origin of the human race. Thus Bavinck takes up the "origin of man" as a subdivision of his treatment of creation. But this is a different context; we are immediately involved in the problems of the "ancestry" of man, and Darwinism and evolution are discussed at length, as is the problem of the age of the human race.[1] It is clear that in this context one is dealing with a different question of origin than when one speaks of the origin of the soul, which is taken up in connection with the apparent dilemma involving creationism and traducianism. It can hardly be denied that the formulation of the two "questions of origin" is quite different, and that this very fact suggests the question as to how justified the usual treatment in dogmatics is; in how far the dogmatician may legitimately speak of a duality of origin.

We do not plan here to take up the problems regarding the creation of man and of the human race, since these problems would soon involve us in a discussion of the meaning of creation and of the unity of the human race, and also of the fall of man. But before we begin treating the apparent dilemma of creationism or traducianism, we should note that this duality of the question of origins immediately puts us in contact with questions which in the history of Christian thought have always been closely related to one another. This is apparent already from the fact that traducianism has always appealed, in its fight against creationism, to the

1. H. Bavinck, *Gereformeerde Dogmatiek*, II, 471-483.

unity of the human race. This was done against a common background of belief in the "organic" unity of man, to which creationism also held fast in one way or another. Both held to the unity of the human race in Adam (in which not only the story of creation but especially Paul's statement in Rom. 5, and the text of Acts 17:26, played a role); and this was true in Catholicism (e.g., at Trent) as well as in Protestantism. While there were occasional denials of this unity, the resultant discussion was of an incidental and peripheral nature until recently.[2]

The change has been due to developments in the biological sciences, which for many gave much more actual meaning to the related problem of monogenism or polygenism; and since then the question has come more and more to the fore. It is striking that the question has until now been most actual in Roman Catholic theology, as appears, e.g., from the fact that the 1950 encyclical *Humani Generis* makes a pronouncement regarding it, and apparently thought this necessary in view of the contemporary encounter between theology and science. Schoonenberg notes that the Vatican Council in 1870 prepared a canon positing monogenism, in relation to the biological science of the time, but the issue was not brought up before the adjournment of the council, so that monogenism never became a dogma.[3]

Schoonenberg thus considers *Humani Generis* as the first document which explicitly takes up the problem, and most Catholic scholars deny that monogenism as such is implicitly taught in various statements of the Council of Trent (e.g., "one in origin"). It is true that a papal committee on the Bible, composed of scholars and theologians, had delivered a statement in 1909 regarding the historicity of the Bible; it held that in any event the first three

2. See *ibid.*, II, 471, 550, 544, for the duality of the question of origins and on creationism and the organic unity of man. Cf. also J. Lever, *Creatie en Evolutie* (1956), p. 146. For Trent, see the documents in Denzinger (788, 789, 790). For occasional denials of this unity in the post-Renaissance period, and for the pre-Adamite speculations of Isaac de la Peyrère, see Bavinck, *op. cit.*, II, 484ff.
3. P. Schoonenberg, *Het Geloof van ons Doopsel*, I (1955), pp. 143-144. Cf. also J. de Fraine, *De Bijbel en het Ontstaan van de Mens* (1953), p. 62. The canon affirmed belief in the common origin of the human race in Adam, and condemned those who denied it, holding that such denial would involve the dogma of original sin and the salvation of all men in Christ. It was prepared because of the denial of monogenism by some "geologists and ethnographers." Cf. K. Rahner, "Theologisches zum Monogenismus," *Schriften zur Theologie* I (1954), 271-275. The canon makes use of Acts 17:26 and of the connection between original sin and the dogmas relating to salvation.

chapters of Genesis must be regarded as historical, since they touch upon the fundamental beliefs of Christian faith, among which was reckoned the unity of the human race. Monogenism was unquestionably intended here, and this human "unity" was reckoned as part of the "literal historical sense" of Genesis. But the statement of a committee of this sort is in no sense the official teaching of the Catholic Church. Thus we can understand that *Humani Generis* (even though encyclicals do not have the authority of a dogmatic decision either!) greatly stimulated the discussion.[4]

The striking thing about the pronouncement of *Humani Generis* is the fact that it occurs specifically in the context of a discussion of the teaching of evolution. The Church is said to have no objection to a treatment of evolution which accords with the present-day position of human science and theology, so long as the theory deals with the origin of the human body from already existing and living material. But Catholic faith, it continues, compels us to hold that the souls are created immediately by God.

Here, in connection with the question of evolution, and in relation to the question of the origin of man, an unmistakable creationism suddenly emerges. A division, or at least a distinction, turns up, one might say, in connection with the approach to the origin of the body and of the soul. It is in this connection that polygenism is discussed. It is conceded that polygenism is an hypothesis in the case of the soul — just as polygenism in relation to the body's origin from already existing organic life — but one is not free to accept the hypothesis with reference to the soul, for, says the encyclical, it is utterly impossible to see how it could be reconciled with divine revelation and with the doctrinal teaching of the Church on original sin which issues from an actually committed sin by a *single* Adam.[5]

There is no unanimity as to the precise meaning of the encyclical. There are those who hold that it expresses itself with the utmost caution, and does not say that polygenism and the doctrine of original sin are necessarily in conflict, but rather says merely that it cannot be seen how the two can be reconciled; and that therefore

---

4. For the 1909 statement, see Rahner, *ibid.* The document can be found in Denzinger, 2123.
5. The encyclical's remarks were occasioned by the opinion of some Catholics that polygenism was an allowable position (see Rahner, *op. cit.*, p. 262). The encyclical condemns polygenism in relation to man's soul; it neither affirms nor condemns an evolutionary development of man's body. It specifically holds that such an idea is an hypothesis, not a proven fact, however (*Humani Generis,* no. 36).

it is not impossible that the reconciliation may later be made clear, and that thus the possibility of a new statement of the Church is not ruled out.[6]

It appears from the discussion on *Humani Generis* as it deals with polygenism and evolution that Catholic theologians on the one hand wish to be concerned, cautiously, with the results of modern science, and on the other hand wish to place limits which cannot be transgressed. We can pass over the question of whether the broad interpretation stressing the present impossibility of reconciling polygenism and the doctrine of original sin is the actual intention of the encyclical. It makes all the more striking the clearness, on which there can be no disagreement, with which the possibility of evolution as regards man's body is acknowledged, and the strong accentuation of the instant or immediate creation of the soul.

In all this we can plainly see a dual aspect to the question of origins, against a background of a dichotomy between soul and body. Insofar as there is talk of accommodation to and confrontation with the results of science, as one possible direction Catholic thought might take in the question of origins, this is restricted to the origin of man's body; while as regards the soul there is a clear condemnation of polygenism because of the doctrine of original sin, and the instant creation of the soul is emphasized. Though the evolution of man's body from existing organic life would not endanger the doctrine of original sin, polygenism appears to do so, and the creation of the soul is part of the Catholic faith. And thus we arrive again, via evolution, and monogenism versus polygenism, at a striking formulation of a certain duality — clear evidence of the fact that a distinction between soul and body when taking up the question of origins is felt to be not at all dualistic. We should remember this actual situation in Catholic theology

6. Schoonenberg, *op. cit.*, I, 145; cf. Rahner, *op. cit.*, p. 261. He also stresses the present impossibility of reconciling the two, and further states that Trent's formulations do not formally imply monogenism (the encyclical would have used other words if it had wished to say this). Cf. further: de Fraine, *op. cit.*, p. 63; M. M. Labourdette, *De Erfzonde en de Oorsprong van de Mens* (1956), pp. 155-167; and H. Renckens, *Israëls Visie op het Verleden* (1956), pp. 190ff. The views of Renckens had much influence on Schoonenberg, as the latter himself says (*op. cit.*, I, 61). According to Renckens (*op. cit.*, p. 192), the question of polygenism and monogenism is outside of the viewpoint of the writer of Genesis. For a general evaluation of the encyclical, cf. *The New York Times* correspondent Arnaldo Cortesi (Nov. 23, 1951), who called it "the most important pronouncement the present pope ever made," and speaks of "some concessions to modern science."

as we concern ourselves with the well-known dilemma of creationism and traducianism. Clearly apparent is the fact that the doctrine of original sin has for Catholics powerfully directed the course of the argument.

It is also an undeniable fact that the Protestant discussion of the "origin" of the soul has likewise often been closely connected with the confession of original sin. In the nature of the case, the situation on the Protestant side could not be the same as that on the Catholic. For *Humani Generis*, the infallible dogma of original sin, and the instant creation of the soul is emphasized. Though the decisive starting point as the limit to which Catholic thought must conform. And evidence from Scripture played a different role against such a background than it did in the Reformation, which took a very different view of the relation between dogma and Scripture.[7] There is a far-reaching methodological difference in approach, and a line of thought and argument such as we encounter in *Humani Generis* would be difficult to conceive in the Reformation. In connection with the encyclical, we think of "concessions" made in relation to the doctrinal limit; e.g., the distinction between the origin of the body and that of the soul.

Now that we have gained some appreciation of the duality regarding origins which characterizes *Humani Generis* and which allows for a certain accommodation to the results of science (albeit within clearly defined limits), we must turn our attention to the problems as they appear in Protestant thought. For here, too, the danger that dogmatic presuppositions — though they be within another view of the relation between dogma and Scripture — may influence and dominate the portrayal of man, and his origins, is by no means merely imaginary. This danger should be considered especially because also in Protestant discussion of these problems the confession of original sin was frequently introduced. Protestant discussion did not center on the dilemma of monogenism or polygenism, which played no role in the controversy between creationism and traducianism, but rather on the other question of the "inheritance" of sin. As is well known, the doctrine of original sin was unceasingly brought up by the problem of traducianism against creationism. Creationism, it was charged, could never rise above an individualistic

7. See Rahner, *op. cit.*, p. 260. He says that *Humani Generis* did not call on the relevant Scripture texts and then go on to give an authentic interpretation, but gave only indirect arguments, such as that from original sin. Cf. also Renckens, *op. cit.*, pp. 190ff.; and *L'encyclique "Humani Generis" Commentaire*, J. Levie *et al.* (1951), p. 87. It says the decision was not based on "simple exegesis of the Genesis story."

formulation. Against this charge the defenders of creationism replied by affirming that it was not at all in conflict with the doctrine of original sin. Now, though we are not going to discuss these relations here, it is nevertheless of the greatest importance to ask — with our eyes on these relations — how in the dilemma of creationism versus traducianism we come out with the Reformation principle that dogma can only be founded on Scripture. And this compelling question can be concentrated in our asking about the legitimacy of the Protestant parallel to the dualism of *Humani Generis* — the Protestant special concern for the origin of the soul.

This question as to legitimacy is surely reasonable, since there is something strange about this special concern for the soul when examined in the light of Scripture, especially when we consider that Scripture in its account of man's origin emphasizes so strongly his total creaturely dependence on the great Creator of all things. Why have we then become so concerned with the problem of the origin of the soul? Is there a special reason to seek, besides a viewpoint on the origin of man's humanness, a viewpoint on the origin of his soul?

An important role in this controversy, especially as regards those who chose creationism, has been played by the idea of the mystery of man in his relation to God. Though there are other motifs, it would seem that it was also the consciousness of this mystery which theologians wished to express by teaching that there was a separate creation involved in the origin of each individual, the creation of an immortal soul. Creationism, which directed attention to the vertical-creative aspects of each man, was opposed by traducianism, which judged it not at all necessary for expressing the mystery of humanness to hold to a separate creation of each individual soul. The two views have stood opposed to each other through the history of theology, after the Church had rejected (with well-nigh unanimous agreement) the idea of the pre-existence of the soul.[8]

8. Origen, under the influence of Plato, taught the pre-existence of the soul, coupled with an explanation of the origin of sin through a pre-existent Fall. This was condemned in A.D. 543, in the *Canons against Origen* (see Denzinger, 203), and in A.D. 561 as part of the condemnation of the Priscillianists, who followed Origen on this point (see Denzinger, 236). The idea has occurred again in modern times, e.g., in Julius Müller, *Die Lehre von der Sünde.* See J. F. Bruch, *Die Lehre von der Präexistenz der menschlichen Seelen* (1859).

If we examine the history of the controversy at all closely, we encounter so many unsolved problems that the question arises whether there must not be some basic reason for all this opposition of views, and for the frequently visible hesitation and doubt. Think of Augustine, whose own hesitation afterward restrained many others from a decisive choice for one side or the other. And this question is confirmed when we note the various attempts at compromise between creationism and traducianism, in the endeavor to avoid the difficulties of both, urging, e.g., "necessary change in the representation of creationism," without being willing to accept traducianism.[9]

But this question as to the legitimacy of formulation of the question into a dilemma arises especially when we consider that the clarity with which the Church, on Scriptural grounds, condemned pre-existentialism[10] does not appear in the same measure as concerns creationism and traducianism. Supporters of both sides indeed cite various texts and attempt to show that Scripture forces us in a certain direction or at least points to the path we should take. Such cautious phraseology poses the compelling question whether Scripture, which speaks so clearly regarding the origin of the whole man, is so unclear here; or whether the solution lies in another direction, namely, that the way of stating the problem in this influential dilemma is illegitimate. What does it mean when Bavinck feels that the texts adduced by both sides are roughly equal in value, and that a satisfactory solution cannot be gained from them? Or when Kuyper speaks of mere "guideposts" and "glimmerings"? Or that Augustine throughout his life hesitates

9. S. Greijdanus, *Toerekeningsgrond van het Peccatum Originans* (1905), p. 49. He speaks of an anthropology which would go beyond simple creationism or simple traducianism. Cf. J. Waterink, *De Oorsprong en het Wezen der Ziel* (1930), and H. Bavinck, *op. cit.*, II, 546. He speaks of "an important creational moment" along with and in relation to the truth of traducianism. Cf. K. Schilder, *Heidelbergse Catechismus*, II, 144; IV, 91. He also asks whether the apparent dilemma is inescapable, and refers to Greijdanus; he also notes those who "refuse to make a choice between the two, or wish to correct both."

10. This clarity is related to the clarity of Scripture, which gives no support to the idea (Bruch, *op. cit.*, p. 13). For various attempts by Origen to find support in Scripture (e.g., Rom. 9:11, Jacob and Esau), see Bruch, pp. 129ff.; Julius Müller, *op. cit.*, II, 548. Müller admits that pre-existence cannot be immediately demonstrated from Scripture; he explains this by saying Scripture's task is not to expound speculative doctrines. He denies the validity of Origen's appeal to Rom. 9:11. Cf. also F. Delitzsch, *System der biblischen Psychologie*, p. 22.

between the two, since various texts could be cited by both sides, and that, for example, he felt that a classic text for creationism (Eccles. 12:7) tended more to support traducianism, and that neither the Creation account nor other texts could bring him to a decision, and that his hesitation regarding creationism was tied in particularly with the doctrine of original sin as in Romans 5:12 (Augustine: *"in whom* all have sinned"*) — a hesitation which influenced later theologians for a long time?[11]

This relation to the doctrine of original sin already indicates that the question as to Scriptural evidence can easily rise above incidental appeals to texts and become imbedded in structural understandings of the whole Scripture.[12] Such would indeed appear to be the case when we note in Lutheran theology a fairly general sympathy for traducianism, while in Catholic and Calvinist theology preference is given to creationism.

Reflections such as the foregoing raise the question whether we actually are called to make a choice in this dilemma, which has so often, as a question of origins regarding the soul, troubled Christian thought.

11. Bavinck, *op. cit.,* II, 542; Kuyper, "Locus de homine," *Loci II,* pp. 60-63; Augustine, *Epistle ad Hieronymus* (Ep. 166, in the 1807 Benedictine *Opera Omnia*) ; *De Anima et eius Origine* (Vol. XIII) ; and especially *De Genesi ad litt.* (Vol. III), e.g., for the traducianist argument from Rom. 5:12 (the "in whom" implies propagation of the original human soul). See H. Karpp, *Probleme altchristlicher Anthropologie* (1950), p. 245. He sees Augustine as certainly leaning towards creationism, but cf. Kuyper's noteworthy statement that the Reformed theologians, favoring creationism, steadfastly opposed Augustine's traducianism (Kuyper, *De Gemeene Gratie,* II, II, 438). For Augustine's definite rejection of pre-existence, see Karpp, p. 243, and Diekamp, *Katholische Dogmatik,* II, 113. See Pohle, *Dogmatik* I (1920), p. 387. He says that it is an historical fact that such hesitation continued for eight centuries, till the time of Peter Lombard. For modern Catholic views, see Pohle, *op. cit.,* I, 388. He sees some Scriptural evidence for creationism, though nothing certain can be deduced; so also Diekamp, *op. cit.,* II, 115. See the Calvinist theologian A. G. Honig, *Creatianisme of traducianisme* (1906), p. 50. He held that creationism was clearly and directly taught, and opposed also Van Leeuwen, who held that the problem went beyond what Scripture taught.
12. Especially of the doctrine of original sin, which throughout the controversy — not only with Augustine — has played a major role. The creationists replied to the charge that the doctrine could be combined only with traducianism by saying that the traducianist could not explain original sin, either.

For purposes of orientation, let us begin with the views of Bavinck and Kuyper, passing over earlier Calvinist theologians.[13] Bavinck tries to explain the preference of Calvinist and Catholic theologians for creationism, in contrast to the Lutheran sympathy for traducianism, in terms of a different insight into the essence and the destiny of man. Lutherans saw the image of God primarily in the spiritual attributes of man (*justitia originalis*) and thus had little interest in what distinguishes man from animal after the fall, since the (lost) *justitia originalis* was for them the one thing that mattered. Calvinists and Catholics wished to concern themselves with "the wholly unique essence of man," and thus with what remained human also after the Fall. That man remains man "and insofar as this is so, remains always and eternally God's image" can, according to Bavinck, be maintained adequately only by creationism, which holds firmly to the "specific uniqueness of man" and "rejects both pantheism and materialism, and honors the limit between man and animal," while the Lutheran theologians are largely indifferent to the question of man's origin. Once man's original righteousness has vanished, Lutheran theology has little independent interest in a separate creative act of God with each new human individual, and thus, says Bavinck, it is held that what men possess is transmitted in the same manner as is the case with animals. Thus creationism is for Bavinck inseparably connected with what he calls the image of God in the wider sense, the humanness of man, including fallen man. Thus he can also say that creationism honors the mystery of individual personality. In Bavinck's judgment, creationism can also do justice to and maintain the organic unity of the human race; and this judgment that creationism does not lead to humanity as a sum of separate individuals, is tied in with the way in which Bavinck describes the creation of the soul. He sees therein a secret, a mystery, of which science knows nothing and about which theology has only speculated. But the creative activity of God, he is convinced, does dovetail as intimately as possible with the given material; in other words, there is not a creation of the soul apart from the body, a soul which is as it were imported into the body. God "raises the existing psychic life, in due time and in a way we cannot understand, to a higher human and spiritual life." Bavinck answers the constant traducianist objection regard-

13. For earlier Reformed theologians, see H. Heppe, *Dogmatik* (1861), p. 168; e.g., Mastricht, "the Reformers taught with Jerome and the common opinion of the Church of his time that new souls were daily created by God from nothing. . . ." Cf. the *Synopsis*, Disp. XIII, LIII, "common opinion," "instantly created." Scriptural evidence is not given.

ing the origin and existence of original sin in the newly created soul by saying we must understand the inheritance of sin thus: though the soul *qua* rational and spiritual soul is called into existence by the creative act of God, nevertheless in the "psychic life of the foetus, it was preformed in the life of parents and grandparents, and thus receives its existence not above and outside the burden of original sin which oppresses all mankind, but rather under and in it."[14]

Kuyper treated the question of the origin of the soul much more extensively than Bavinck. We should note, in this connection, that he was strongly influenced by the idea of the unity and organic relationship of the human race. There is no thought of the constant birth of isolated and independent individuals, but "through this alone, that God differentiates between man and woman, and causes the child to be born of both of them, all has become one life, one whole, one organism." The wonderful unity of the human race rests on the union of body and soul.

We have to do with a unity and continuity in the race which is not only physical in nature. It is also psychic, since the bodily stands in relation to the psychic. Kuyper does not wish to pose a simple dichotomy between body and soul, then going on to teach a "psycho-creationism"; he sees body and soul, *sooma* and *psyche*, in relation. But we should be mistaken were we to conclude that Kuyper chose traducianism. He acknowledged that each man receives his human nature "not directly from God, but from God through Adam," but he will have nothing to do with traducianism. For it does not explain the inheritance of sin; and also, sin is something spiritual, and the soul is not divisible so as to be inheritable. He views traducianism as a realistic and indeed almost materialistic view and consciously chooses creationism, which affirms that the soul originates "not through procreation, but through a creative act of God."

Though Scripture gives no completely definite answer, says Kuyper, Calvinist theologians, with an occasional exception, have

14. The above is from Bavinck, *op. cit.*, II, 545-550. For God's use of existing psychic life (p. 546), Bavinck approvingly cites Peter Lombard's *"creando infundit eas Deus et infundendo creat,"* a statement continually cited also by Catholic theologians. For his answer to the traducianist objection (*ibid.*), cf. also Honig's treatment of the same problem (*op. cit.*, pp. 75ff.); he speaks of a withholding of original righteousness, a thought that he holds present in Ursinus and taken over by Voetius, Mastricht and Moor. He speaks in this connection of a mystery relating to God as Judge.

favored creationism. Though Scripture gave only "indications," nevertheless creationism won out and for this fact there was a special reason: "man's soul is something independent, something which in its deepest essence may never stand in dependence on another man." Kuyper goes on to develop his anthropology, proceeding from the idea that soul and body are two separate substances, not two aspects of the same substance. They can be separated from each other, and thus with the development of the individual soul God creates the soul in the embryo, which has a predisposition towards a soul predestined for it. Thus the soul originates not *per traducem* but *per creationem*, and human personality originates in the unity of body and soul. Thus what is perhaps implied in Scripture is worked out by Kuyper into a positive creationism. Though he posits the relations between psychic and somatic (the unity of the human race), the soul is nevertheless something wholly distinct, and this means concretely that nothing may intervene as a medium between God and the soul. Here precisely lies the objection against traducianism; it introduces a series of intermediaries between God and man; and thus for Kuyper the choice for creationism is a religious choice. Traducianism would mean concretely that we are still far distanced from God. In such distancing, says Kuyper, a pious spirit cannot find rest, for "it wishes a future with God; but also to be directly from Him; a religious spirit wants both its goal and its beginning to be directly in God."[15]

We thus encounter in Kuyper, on the one hand, a strong emphasis on the organic bonds uniting the human race because of the relation between body and soul and, on the other hand, a decisive choice for creationism in connection with the two substances of which man is composed. His whole dialectic is carried on between these two poles, while the two outlooks (the organic and the

---

15. The above is from various places in Kuyper. For the family and the unity of the human race, see *E Voto*, IV, 132-133; cf. I, 49. For somatic and psychic, see *Locus de homine* (in *Loci*), p. 51; for psycho-creationism, *Locus de peccato*, p. 86; Kuyper sees the question in direct relationship to the doctrine of original sin; to answer the question of how original sin is propagated, he turns to the organic bond implied in generation. For God creating souls through Adam, and the denial of traducianism in the same breath, see *E Voto*, I, 49. For his evaluation of traducianism, cf. also *De Gemeene Gratie*, II, II, 438ff., where he sees it as lowering human nature; the accent on creationism, curiously, is in a chapter aiming to emphasize that nearly all works of God are mediate! For the "indications" of Scripture, see *Locus de homine*, p. 63. For the remaining material, see *Locus de peccato*, pp. 86-87, and *Locus de homine*, pp. 60-65.

creative) are then joined through the noteworthy ideas of "organic creation" and of the pre-ordained soul. The soul is indeed directly and instantly created by God, but this does not happen arbitrarily, but rather so that the soul is created in this man, at this time, in this country, in this family, with the characteristics which are suitable.[16]

It can not be denied, in our opinion, that Kuyper's solution by way of an "organic creation" evinces a peculiar tension and can hardly be considered a decisive argument for creationism. He explains that the soul takes on character traits from contact with the body, so that the parents give to the child the outline for the soul, the portrait of the "I,"[17] and here we see the organic idea of an intermediary; but we then immediately face the dichotomy of the pre-ordination of the soul and the soul's direct creation. On the one hand, the idea of organic unity directs our attention to the intermediaries while, on the other hand, all intermediaries are denied as in conflict with piety, which calls for a direct relation to God. The idea of "organic creation" does not solve the antinomy, but merely formulates it.

The decisive factor in this dialectic, in our opinion, is the fact that the motif of piety (calling for a direct relationship to God) can give the idea of creationism no support. The motif is related, for Kuyper, to the distinction between the direct and indirect acts of God; he feels that the direct acts stand closer to the religious than do the indirect. They bring us closer to God, while mediation means a certain distancing. The curious thing about such a foundation for creationism is that Kuyper elsewhere attacked such a religious preference for the direct acts of God, and stated beautifully the majesty and glory of the "indirect" acts of God. And precisely in these mediated acts he insists that God acts no less directly; so that our faith has the fullest right to say that God does things directly, in spite of all intermediaries; so that we may say, for example, that God causes rain, snow and hail directly. The dislike of intermediaries comes, he says, from a fault in our confessing; we mean to say that God expresses Himself more gloriously in direct action; but the truth is rather that "God's majesty in His organic creation is shown precisely in this, that He does not simply repeat Himself in endlessly creating, but that He has wonderfully and

16. Kuyper, *Locus de homine,* p. 65; cf. *Locus de peccato,* p. 90; the soul is accommodated to the type of the parents.
17. Kuyper, *E Voto,* I, 49.

majestically hidden in the first-created all that serves Him as means to continue created nature in all her richness."[18]

It is clear that Kuyper is not consistent with this outlook when he takes up the origin of the soul. Here the preference for direct action, which was attacked in the sphere of nature, takes on power, religious power. Were we to accept intermediaries in the origin of the soul, he feels, we should be accepting a "distancing" between us and God, and this the religious man cannot tolerate. In our opinion, the arguments Kuyper elsewhere brings up against the preference for direct acts are so strong that they should not be rejected in the case of the origin of the soul, and in any event we can hardly borrow arguments for creationism from this preference for the direct and immediate act. The "mediate" acts of God demand no other sort of dependence on Him than do the "immediate," nor can we draw from our distinction between the two any conclusions regarding the majesty and glory of His creative work.[19] Kuyper's use of this argument for creationism would have force only when directed against any view of man's origin which would separate him from the living and acting God. Any such view piety does indeed decisively protest as contrary to Scripture. But it is never permitted — nor does man's creation afford an exception to the principle — to distinguish in rank between the various works of God and to draw conclusions therefrom regarding the origin of the soul. Kuyper himself destroyed the reason for such ranking when he spoke of the direct acts of God through intermediaries and exhorted us to attend to the living God in all the works of His hand. The question remains whether there are other arguments to be given in support of creationism besides this manifest — "religious" — argument of direct creation.[20]

18. Kuyper, *Gemeene Gratie*, II, II, 440, 443.
19. Cf. the motif of speaking of Providence in terms of "continual creation"; see our *De Voorzienigheid Gods*, p. 69.
20. We find a parallel to Kuyper's outlook in Th. L. Haitjema, *Dogmatiek als Apologie* (1949), p. 187. He finds traducianism a "more biological" teaching than creationism, which treats the mysterious origin of the human soul, and views each human individual more paradoxically as a direct creative miracle of God, and thereby emphasizes the individual's personal ethico-religious responsibility towards God more strongly. Especially this use of "direct" in relation to responsibility reminds us of Kuyper. This "directness" suggests, along with the mysteriousness of man's origin, that creationism can be denied only at the cost of a "horizontal" tarnishing of the mystery of our origin. But such a dilemma is also untenable. Cf. Waterink, *op. cit.*, p. 57. He remarks, in connection with his modification of creationism, that we must consider

It cannot be denied that practically all the arguments for creationism are related to this argument of Kuyper's, which prefers the immediate — vertical to the mediate — horizontal and holds that the mystery of human individuality can be preserved only in an immediate relation with God. Not only Kuyper but also Bavinck sees the mystery of the human person in this light. And in the controversy this tension between vertical and horizontal has often played a role which should not be underestimated. Thus traducianists sometimes accused creationists of moving in the direction of "deifying" the soul, while creationists attacked traducianists for moving toward materialism or toward a complete horizontal secularizing of man's origin. We should however note not so much these excessive formulations as rather the underlying motifs which played a role. In creationism we see a strong accent on the vertical nature of the acts of God and therein on the mystery of man's origin and existence, and from this vertical emphasis a relation to the organic unity of the human race was sought by taking procreation into account. Traducianism accented the horizontal aspect in the origin of man, the organic relationship of all men, but immediately added that it had no intention of denying the vertical character of the divine acts in and through this horizontal aspect.

And here we face the real background of what is, in our opinion, an unfruitful controversy. The words "creationism" and "traducianism" suggest that the issue as regards the origin of man is that of horizontal *or* vertical relations — but such a way of putting it is far too feeble an attempt to render adequately the greatness of the work of God, both in general and in this specific case. For the controversy places in opposition to each other, by way of emphases and accents, two things which can only form a *unity* in the works of God. Whenever our view of the works of God is split, even to some extent, in two directions, then naturally one of the two will be emphasized over the other, and thus in creationism the vertical aspect is accented, and in traducianism the horizontal. Any dilemma which does not do justice to both aspects is to be rejected, for it lies wholly outside the Biblical witness regarding the origin

---

whether we must make an exception for the soul when we note that in all of nature God's working is an organic and mediate way of action. Thus Waterink does not use the argument from piety (mediate — immediate), but does agree with Kuyper's other line of thought (direct — mediate) — an important perspective for closer reflection regarding the grounds for creationism.

of man.[21] This is evident in the belief of Israel, as an echo of God's mighty works of revelation, whenever God is confessed as *Creator*. Then we hear, in directly religious and creaturely expression, of man's total dependence on God, even in the deepest sources of life. Thus says Job: "Thine hands have made me and fashioned me together round about; yet thou dost destroy me" (Job 10:8); and, "The spirit of God hath made me, and the breath of the Almighty hath given me life" (33:4). *Man* in the whole of his origin and his existence. And thus the Psalmist knows that we are "fearfully and wonderfully made," (139:14), and that there is the work of God's hands in human life: "Thou hast covered me in my mother's womb" (139:13). Thus according to the religious insight of Israel, we have not to do with an un-mysterious "natural" succession of generations, not with a self-perpetuating dynamic stream of life, an *élan vital* which can be comprehended in terms of natural categories, but with the God who wills and calls and therein creates. Jahwe, the God of Israel, is the Creator in every (real) dynamic process. Israel does not think of God as Creator in terms only of the distant past, but also of the present. It considers the Creator active in man's history and in human life itself and directs its worship and adoration to Him in the stream of events. He is the Creator in every horizontal relationship, and in those relationships we see the mystery of the incomparable works of Jahwe, and the mystery enclosed therein, of human life itself.

There is no thought (cf. Ps. 139) of an over-reaching vertical aspect which threatens the horizontal; rather, the creating and calling word of God sounds forth in the horizontal, and He does what pleases Him (Ps. 135:6), in a "wondrous and powerful and actual work of God."[22] Only so is justice done to the overwhelming thoughts of God. There is no divine activity "alone," annihilating all else and ruling out all other factors; no abstract transcendence without immanence or actual presence; but powerful and creative works in every horizontal relationship.

Thus Isaiah (44:24): "Thus saith the Lord, thy redeemer, and he that formed thee from the womb, I am the Lord that maketh all things." And thus Proverbs speaks of the Creator in the present:

21. Cf. L. Verduin, "Towards a Theistic Creationism," *Geloof en Wetenschap* (1956), pp. 183-196. He, regarding the dilemma of creationism and traducianism, speaks of an "irruptive" and of a "processional" dimension, and feels that "it is best to refuse to make this a matter of either − or" (p. 191).

22. Kittel, *Theologisches Wörterbuch*, III, 1007. The whole article on the Old Testament belief in creation is important.

"whoso mocketh the poor reproacheth his Maker" (17:5). And so elsewhere (cf. Ps. 139:13, 16).[23] The objections against creationism cannot be directed against such reference to the powerful works of God in all things, including the origin of man, but only against the manner in which creationism worked out the Biblical view of the creative power of God into a thesis which applied this power only to the soul of man. But anyone starting with such an idea cannot escape seeing the soul as having its origin in another dimension than the other "part" of man, which finds its "origin" — even though involving a general "concourse" of God's power — from its parents. And though creationism does not wish to doubt God's providential action in the horizontal aspects of life, a fairly sharp distinction is nevertheless made between direct and indirect acts; and it is this partial character of creationism which has always aroused opposition or hesitation. In spite of the intentions of the basic motifs of creationism (creation, total dependence, the mystery of humanness and individuality), other and indeed foreign elements soon were added almost of necessity, deriving from the insistence on classifying the works of God (direct and indirect acts). Just as in *Humani Generis* there was an attempt at accommodation to the results of science as regards the origin of the body, so also in creationism elements of duality could make their appearance, sometimes to the extent of setting up a dichotomy between higher and lower in which the higher aspect of man (the soul) stood closer to God, the latter fact receiving expression in the direct creation of the soul.

There was no intention of devaluating the body, and this fact was constantly reiterated against the charges leveled by traducianism; but the fear of such devaluation was awakened, and it was no longer possible to explain why the origin of man then had this dual dimension corresponding to a dualistic anthropology. And no matter how well the religious depth of Psalm 139 was understood and appreciated, when it came to conceptual formulation, this religious depth remained as a foreign element, since in the Psalm the depth refers unequivocally to the totality of man who has his origin in the Creator. And thus any criticism of creationism can be legitimate only when it arises from a feeling for this "depth,"

23. There is a consciousness of mystery in the horizontal. "As thou knowest not what is the way of the spirit, nor how the bones do grow in the womb of her that is with child: even so thou knowest not the works of God who makest all" (Eccles. 11:5). Recalling Ps. 139, we may speak of a reference from one mystery to the other.

and completely separates itself from any attempt to secularize the origin of man's life and to abstract it from the God of life.

In this connection, it should not surprise us that nowhere in Scripture is the origin of the soul spoken of as a separate theme. And this fact is undoubtedly the most basic reason for the uncertainty and hesitation regarding the Scriptural evidence which we constantly encounter in the history of this controversy. It is precisely at that point where many have reservations regarding the supposed dichotomy of substances in man in its relation to the Biblical picture of man. It is plain that we cannot be satisfied with "intimations" or "guideposts"; for if the question of the origin of the soul is a legitimate religious question, then we can speak positively only when the Word of God shows us the way clearly and irrefutably. We cannot, therefore, avoid the question whether the uncertainty in various appeals to Scripture does not give us an unmistakable indication of the illegitimate nature of the way in which the problem is posed in this dilemma, especially in view of the fact that there is no such uncertainty as to the origin of man. And this indication is confirmed when we consider that the posing of the problem is closely related to certain anthropological conceptions and that after the hesitation displayed by Augustine, certainty returned — despite his authority — when the idea of dichotomy gained such a firm place in the thinking of the Scholastics. It is thus most instructive to examine how theologians in earlier and later times dealt with the Scriptural evidence, and what was meant by the "indications" of Scripture. Reformation thinking sought never to draw conclusions from "dogma" regarding the origin of the soul, but rather to find a basis in Scripture.

Creationism has called especially on four texts. First, on Genesis 2:7 (as the creation of the "soul" of Adam); then, on Ecclesiastes 12:7, where old age and death are described and it is then said that the "spirit returns to God," who gave it to man; on Zechariah 12:1, "the Lord, which stretcheth forth the heavens, and layeth the foundation of the earth, and formeth the spirit of man within him"; and finally on Hebrews 12:9, which contrasts the fathers according to the flesh with the Father of spirits. It was thought that such texts showed that there was a separate creative act of God, which was related not to the body but to the soul or spirit of man. Though the substance of the body was formed by generation, the substance of the soul arose through creation. It is curious that, given this situation, men spoke only of Scriptural "indications" which "afford no decisive conclusion";

for, once it is assumed that a dichotomy of two substances is a definite part of the Biblical picture of man, such hesitancy no longer makes sense; for the conclusion would necessarily follow that these texts do not merely "indicate creationism, but rather clearly teach it. That most theologians nevertheless maintained certain hesitation can be explained only in one way: they realized that the dichotomy of substance in man was an idea which was most difficult to adjust to the way in which the Bible speaks of man. That is doubtless the reason why Bavinck, for example, cites a number of texts but does not examine them closely, and quickly passes on to the dogmatic problems and relations involved in creationism and traducianism.[24]

Traducianism occasions the same sort of questions. Here the texts appealed to were Genesis 2:21 (the creation of Eve from Adam; cf. I Cor. 11:8), Hebrews 7:9-10 (the "existence" of children in the loins of their fathers), and Genesis 2:2 (the termination of creation) — texts which according to traducianism prove that the soul of man does not come from a separate act of creation but rather through generation.[25]

So the arguments went, pro and con, with occasional hesitation or attempts to modify by creationists, and with varying nuances on the side of the traducianists. And given the dualistic conceptions both shared, it was impossible for either to convince the other, particularly since appeals were made to various Scriptural texts which did not at all refer to the origin of the "soul" in the sense of a psychic substance in contrast to a material substance, the two forming (in Tertullian's words) two "sister substances."[26]

24. Bavinck, *op. cit.*, II, 542.
25. Bavinck adds Gen. 46:26 to Heb. 7:9-10. For the "so to say" of Heb. 7:9, see commentaries *ad loc.* Cf. Greijdanus, *Toerekeningsgrond*, p. 50. He tries to give a version of creationism which will allow this and other texts a proper place. Cf. further Schilder, *op. cit.*, I, 345; and Delitzsch, *op. cit.* p. 110.
26. We can hardly speak of hesitation on the part of traducianists. There were indeed attempts to emphasize that traducianism did not imply materialism. Such attempts on the part of Tertullian are related to his teaching of the "bodily soul," through which he tried to uphold the complete unity of man as over against gnostic dualism. Cf. Karpp, *op. cit.*, p. 60; and F. E. Daubanton, *Het Voortbestaan van het menselijk Geslacht* (1902), pp. 157ff. He speaks of Tertullian's "paradoxical" psychology and defends him against the charge of materialism. Cf. Tertullian, "Corporalitas Dei," *De Carne Christi*, cap. II. For his traducianism, see his *De Anima*, ed. Waszink (1933), p. 104, on Gen. 1:28 ("increase and multiply"). The term "sister substances" is used by him in the same work, c. 52.

Theologians read the Scriptures with this presupposition and sought an answer to the question of the origin of one part of man, the soul, in contrast with the other part, the body, which came into being through generation. Thus the question of the Biblical witness regarding the origin of man was not done justice; or, better, the one problem was split in two separate problems in the framework of this twofold origin. In creationism one can discern the motif of depicting man in his direct and complete dependence on God, surely a motif which deserves to be honored.[27] But this motif appeared in the *form* of a dialectic concerning the dual origin of body and soul, in generation and creation. Various creationist theologians indeed have opposed the idea that the problem is actually the origin of two "parts" of man and have seen something of its unique dimension; for example, Augustine, when he in his hesitation on the problem considers Isaiah 57:16, "For I will not contend for ever, neither will I be always wroth; for the spirit should fail before me, and the souls which I have made"). He then says that no matter how men think about creationism or traducianism, it remains undoubtedly true that the basic origin of the "souls" lies in God.[28]

This sort of groping towards the question of the origin of the whole man occurs elsewhere in creationism also, but it can hardly be brought to full expression within that outlook; for there is no readiness to rise above the dilemma in terms of basic approach, and thus the dialectic of the dual origin of the "parts" of man constantly recurs.[29] And the presupposition of this dual origin, of creation and generation, then obviously controls the understanding of Scriptural passages. Thus creationists have often cited, as a very clear bit of evidence, Hebrews 12:9; Delitzsch, for example, calls it

27. O. Weber, *Grundlagen der Dogmatik*, I (1955), 526. He asks whether the point of the old debate was not really something else, and then relates this to the "I" in the *credo* and to the new creation. It appears clear to me, however, that this was not the real motif of creationism, since the concern is not with the new creation but rather with the origin of every individual soul; thus what Weber says (p. 527) about the Holy Ghost which makes the soul live lies outside the creationist-traducianist discussion.

28. Augustine, *De Gen. ad Litt.*, Book X, VI, 9.

29. G. Ch. Aalders, *Het Boek De Prediker* (1948), p. 252. He does not discuss this problem when he examines another text often cited by creationists, Eccles. 12:7; though he does speak of "the separation through which the material part of man returns to the earth, while the spiritual part, the soul, goes to God."

the classic citation of the creationists.[30] In this text, the "fathers of
our flesh" are contrasted with the "Father of spirits," and the
conclusion was drawn that this taught almost expressly and literally
the creationist position: God as Father of spirits (souls). It was
generally agreed that the theme of this pericope is not the origin
of souls, but the chastisement to which the believers must submit;
nevertheless, so it was said, the argument of the writer rests on
the difference between the fathers of flesh and the Father of spirits;
seeing that we submit to the fleshly fathers, should we not all the
more submit to the Father of spirits? But from this passage one
can actually deduce the creationist position only if one interprets
the expression "Father of spirits" in the light of a supposed
dichotomy of soul and body and a supposed separate act of creation.
And we should note in this connection that the same sort of
expression occurs already in the Old Testament (Num. 16:22),
when Moses and Aaron fell upon their faces before God and
prayed to "the God of the spirits of all flesh."

It appears to us that God is here confessed as the deepest and
unique Origin of all living creatures, as Giver of, and Ruler over,
all of life.[31] It is precisely at this point that the difference lies
between God as Father and all earthly fathers in the creaturely
and dependent fatherhood. God is the source and the Origin which
gives spirit to all of life and who is also the source of human life.
The point of difference is not that God is the source of one "part"
of man, and earthly fathers the source of another "part," but

30. Delitzsch, *System der Biblischen Psychologie*, p. 114; also cited by Bavinck,
op. cit., II: 542-543. It appears, however, that Delitzsch himself did not feel
at all that Heb. 12:9 afforded such support, for when viewed in the
context of other passages of Scripture, "the matter presents itself in a
somewhat different light." Cf. his reference to Heb. 7:5 (Levi and
Abraham!) ; therefore, he concludes, Heb. 12:9 is not creationist! Bavinck
cites Calvin's *Commentary* on Heb. 12:9 as evidence for Calvin's creationism. Calvin speaks of God as Father of body and soul, though *"in
creandis animabus non adhibet hominum operam"*; and see further
Institutes II, I, 7 on the problem which, he says, vexed the ancient
fathers not a little, and cf. the formulation with which Calvin would
be content.

31. A. Noordtzij, *Numeri* (K.V.), p. 181. Cf. Num. 27:16, "the God of
the spirits of all flesh." The Septuagint translation (in Num. 16:22 and
27:16) introduces a shift of meaning when it translates "God of the
spirits and of all flesh." Michel (*Der Brief an die Hebraër*, p. 299)
as well as Riggenbach speak of a creationist emphasis, but the question
then is whether we mean creative or creating; this is the real point at
issue. Cf. for Heb. 12:9, H. van Oyen, *Christus de Hogepriester*
(1939), p. 253. On the creative power of God, cf. also Ps. 104:30 and
Jer. 32:27.

rather that God is the Creator of life in His incomparable glory and majesty.

This is just as true of Zechariah 12:1, which shows us God as the Lord who made heaven and earth and is also the source of all human life, a passage parallel to Isaiah 42:5, "God the Lord, he that created the heavens and stretched them out; he that spread forth the earth and that which cometh out of it; he that giveth breath unto the people upon it, and spirit to them that walk therein."[32]

It would seem to be undeniable that the Scriptural evidence called on to support creationism is interpreted in terms of particular anthropological presuppositions, and the question now arises whether we must evaluate the traducianist appeal to Scripture as something basically different. But before we examine the solution offered by traducianism, let us first turn our attention briefly to what is sometimes called a "corrected" creationism, and which in any event is intended to be such.

It can readily be made out that attempts at correcting, or at least broadening, the older creationism are related to a modified anthropological point of view in which the unbreakable unity of man is emphasized. In earlier times creationists felt no need to correct the traditional creationist view, but only to emphasize that creationism was not to be understood "mechanically." But more recently, theologians have entertained the idea of correction, and this is true not only among Protestants but also among Catholics, though in the latter instance the situation is complicated by the existence of various pronouncements by the Church. The attention paid by Catholics to the possibility of correction is all the more remarkable in view of the fact that Humani Generis, strengthening earlier pronouncements,[33] stated that the Catholic

---

32. Cf. P. Volz, Der Geist Gottes und die verwandten Erscheinungen im A.T. und im anschlieszenden Judentum (1910), pp. 156-157 on Ps. 104:29 and Eccles. 12:7 (ruach, spirit, as the power of life: "Jahwe disposes of it, He takes it back and doubtless also gives it"); cf. his remarks on Job 33:4.

33. E.g., the statement of Anastasius II on original sin and the origin of souls, directed against the heretics in Gaul: "quod ille (Deus) indat animas, qui vocat ea, quae non sunt, tamquam sint" (with a reference to John 5:17). The pope recommends creationism as "sound doctrine" (see, Denzinger, 170). Leo IX said the soul is "created from nothing" (Denzinger, 348). In A.D. 553, the Armenian patriarch Mechitriz was condemned by the pope for teaching traducianism (Denzinger, 533). The Fifth Lateran Council spoke of the body in which the soul anima intellectiva "infunditur" (Denzinger, 738).

faith must hold to the "immediate" creation of the soul by God. It is striking that Schoonenberg — although the encyclical would seem to be unequivocal, especially because its pronouncement is made in the context of the origin of the body — denies that a simple creationism is demanded. He speaks of the expression "immediate" creation as one aspect of the truth, which can later be expanded through other pronouncements.[34] He explains the ecclesiastical statements in terms of the Church's concern not to attribute the origin of the soul exclusively to generation by the parents. The phrase "not exclusively" is rather striking, since it would seem more accurate to say that the encyclical's purpose was to state that the soul's origin is exclusively due to God's creative act. But Schoonenberg, because of his strong emphasis on the unity of man — in accordance with the Biblical view — is on the road to a "corrected" creationism. He indeed avoids speaking of a "correction" of the creationist teaching of the Church, but he does wish to correct "the idea of two separate actions regarding soul and body." "Correction," as one can see, raises problems for a Catholic theologian. The "expansion" of the words of *Humani Generis* discloses the difficulties of such a correction; it is said that we can speak of an immediate creation of the soul "included in generation from the parents" so that "the whole child comes from the parents and from God" — but such expressions must be reinterpreted in view of the encyclical, so that we hear of an "immediate" creation "of the body by the parents, with God's cooperation, or rather of the body by God through cooperation, and of the soul through direct creation." It would seem evident, in our opinion, that attempts at correction of the idea of two separate actions regarding soul and body must either break through the Church's creationism or else return ultimately to a dichotomistic version of creationism, with its problem of a dual origin of soul and body, involving a "division" within man: and this would seem a clear indication of the undeniable fact that creationism intrinsically cannot be "corrected." For a "correction" involves giving up the anthropological basis of creationism.

The context is different on the Protestant side, since there are no definitive ecclesiastical pronouncements on the creation of the "soul." So it is understandable that Protestant theologians have spoken more freely of a correction of the older creationism. As

34. See Schoonenberg, *Het Geloof van ons Doopsel,* I, 162-163, for the following material also.

Waterink has shown,[35] such "correction" has produced various attempts to explain the phenomena of heredity in spiritual or psychic life; but these always result in "giving up the hereditary character of these appearances," and this makes it impossible to escape a mechanical explanation. Waterink himself concludes that a "psychic" solidarity between men must be accepted, and that the various attempts to integrate this fact with the older creationist view must be rejected as untenable. The question then arises whether we must turn to traducianism. This Waterink denies, and he goes on to deal with "body" and "soul," and with the "spirit" as the immortal principle "through which man becomes human." There is, he says, a much greater complexity in creatures, including man, than can be explained in terms of "soul" and "body."

The decisive question here would seem to be what we are to understand by Waterink's term "person" or "spirit." He has been attacked[36] on the ground that he actually proposes, or logically must propose, a *trichotomism* (body-soul-spirit: *sooma, psyche, pneuma*); thus Hoekstra has said that Waterink's concept is that of Apollinaris, and therefore as regards Christology is in conflict with Article 19 of the Belgic Confession. Hoekstra inferred trichotomism because he viewed Waterink as holding that spirit is "a metaphysical substance." Waterink, in reply, denied any

35. See Waterink, *De Oorsprong en het Wezen der Ziel* (1930); the citations here are from pp. 35-36, 66, 73, 80. He notes as an example of a "mechanical" approach the idea that God gives the child a soul which "harmonizes with the body." Cf. Diekamp, *Katholische Dogmatik*, 7th ed., II (1936), p. 116. He says the soul is created and joined with the body, so that each soul has its special characteristics, and God is the "*causa unica*" of the soul while the parents are "parents of the whole child." Note also Waterink's criticism of Kuyper's idea that temperament lies in the body. He says (pp. 66, 73) that creationism "in its exclusive form" cannot be accepted under any conditions.

36. T. Hoekstra's attack is in his "De Oorsprong der Ziel," *Gereformeerd Theologisch Tijdschrift* (1930), especially pp. 240-243. Waterink answered in the same periodical, "De Oorsprong der Ziel," *G.T.T.* (1933), especially pp. 449-451. For his use of a "personal center," see Waterink (1933), p. 449; cf. (1930), p. 112, defined as "that which must complement nature to enable an individual sharing in human nature to exist," and "something coupled with nature." For his remarks on Greijdanus, see (1933), p. 144, and for his rejection of three coordinate principia (1930), p. 92; he rightly notes that the distinction between dichotomy and trichotomy is foreign to the Bible, though the Bible does express itself dichotomistically. For the "organization" of the soul in the body, see (1930), p. 126. The meaning of "creation" in Waterink's context is taken up in (1933), p. 447, and the stress on man as a religious being in (1930), pp. 117, 119. Waterink's most recent work is his *De Mens als religieus Wezen en de hedendaagse Psychologie* (1954); see p. 23.

similarity to Apollinaris. The question is important not only for
anthropology but also for the creationist-traducianist controversy. The argument centers, in our opinion, around the term
"*complementum existentiae,*" a term used by Greijdanus in connection with the human nature of Christ. Hoekstra holds that
the term was used by Greijdanus as "the formal delimitation that
complements soul and body," but, says he, Waterink goes beyond
this and makes spirit or person a substance, so that trichotomy
cannot be avoided. The question is thus whether Waterink, in his
criticism of the older creationism, has not fallen into a trichotomy
of three substances — soul, body and spirit (or person). Now,
Waterink's emphatic rejection of any similarity to Apollinaris must
be related to the nature of his conception; in this conception, in
our opinion, there is no idea of a third "substance" added to two
other substances; the reference is rather to the concentration of
the whole human being in the person, or the "I." It is evident that
misunderstandings can easily arise in connection with such gropings
towards formulations in this difficult field of problems relating to
the nature of man. Thus the idea of a third substance might
occasionally seem to be implied by Waterink, as when he speaks
of the "I" as the "core of personality" or says that the complement
necessary for the existence of human nature in each individual is
that necessary for "the created human person."

Viewed superficially, this might seem to imply a simple trichotomy,
especially since Waterink (rightly, in our opinion) says he finds
it impossible to understand what Greijdanus means by using
"*complementum existentiae*" as a *formal* definition along with body
and soul. Nevertheless, upon closer examination the situation
appears more complicated, and there need be no talk of heresy
because someone speaks of the different aspects of the unified
being of man in more varied terms than a simple dichotomy.
Waterink specifically rejects the idea of body-soul-spirit as "three
coordinated principia." He does speak of the creation of the person,
but rejects a mechanistic interpretation; and this leads him to
reject an exclusive creationism, and thus the creation of the person
does not add a new "substance" to soul and body. Thus, in our
opinion, it would appear that Waterink's concern here, and also in
what he says about the "person," differs from that of the older
creationism. His concern is with the totality of man's humanness
as it is concentrated in man's creaturely dependence on God, the
basic component of the "I." Anyone who deals with such a
concept can hardly escape using spatial and functional terms and
concepts, as indeed Scripture itself does when it speaks of the

"forming" of the spirit in man, and so Waterink speaks of the "organizing" of the spirit "within a living body." If we ask what the term "creation" means in relation to the spirit or "I," it would appear that it refers to man's religious bond with God: man is religious essentially. And here we encounter the real problem of creationism. Waterink's references to "person" or "I" should not be interpreted, any more than should Dooyeweerd's to the "heart," as a new substantialism.

Waterink is dealing, rather, with a view of man — the whole man — in his relation to God the Creator. A confirmation of this interpretation can be seen in Waterink's later work (1954), in which he deals with the development of personalistic anthropologies attempting to find a "*centrum*" of human nature. He does not criticize such attempts, but feels that the important point is whether or not it is realized that this "center" is religious in nature. "The beginning point is not the center as center, but is rather the religious function." Obviously we are not here dealing with a new (additional) concept of substance, but rather with the whole man as a religious being, a being whose deepest essence is religious, and who apart from this religious essence will never be comprehended.

It seems to me that once this idea of man's religious relationship to his Creator is adopted, creationism no longer makes sense. Creationism, in the historical meaning of the term, presupposed the notion of dual origin, and given this presupposition it became possible to speak of a separate origin of the soul. This possibility is built into the very structure of creationism, as is evident in *Humani Generis,* and quite apart from the specific concern of this encyclical with the theory of evolution, inasmuch as in it the decisive factor is the unmediated or direct creation of the soul. But in the perspective of this notion of dual origin, the relationship to the living God necessarily becomes an *additum,* something added to the "essentially human," which latter is defined independently as "soul" and "body." Both soul and body can then be viewed in different "causal" relationships without reference to some intrinsic non-causal relationship to God. If, however, it is impossible to speak of the "essence" of man except in this latter religious relationship, then it also becomes impossible to introduce duality into the origin of soul and of body within the unitary human individual; every attempt at introducing it will run foul of the religious dimension of Psalm 139. And one who, like Waterink, can no longer "under any conditions" accept creationism in its older "exclusive" form has, it seems to me, in principle broken with creationism, because creationism *intrinsically* is exclusive and is determined to remain exclusive.

We should now return again to the fact that in the history of the creationist-traducianist controversy the Calvinist and Catholic theologians have stood together against the traducianist Lutherans. It is conceivable that this alliance reveals a far-reaching agreement between the two, without basic differences on this point. This was indeed the position of Bavinck, when he noted that the opposition between Calvinist, Catholic, and Greek views on the one hand and Lutheran on the other could not be coincidental; he saw the reason for the difference between the two groups in their different views of the nature and destiny of man. This analysis is rather curious, since Bavinck elsewhere notes that Catholic and Calvinist differ with each other on this latter issue, and Waterink also speaks of "a not unimportant difference" between the two.[37] Bavinck ignores this difference as it affects creationism, but there is every reason to consider it in that connection, as indeed Waterink does. The question then arises whether the agreement on creationism between Calvinist and Catholic has any religious value or basis, and the answer would seem to be that the divergence between the two on the nature and destiny of man did not lead to a divergence on creationism precisely because other factors determined the view of the origin of the soul. And once the divergence on the nature and destiny of man is brought into consideration on this question, as is done by Waterink, there is no turning back. Thus we are interested, in reading *Humani Generis*, not only in the way Rome deals with the question of evolution, but also in the way in which this problem is related to the "immediate" creation of the soul. Meanwhile there need be no lessening of one's appreciation of the fact that the motif of creationism — if not always, then usually — lies in the intent to stress the majestic character of the divine works in all of creation, including the mysterious area of human individuality: just as the Preacher calls on us in the dynamic life of youth to remember our Creator.

But one may not conclude that this motif, this intention, legitimatizes the creationist thesis. For the motif of man's religious relationship to and total dependence on his Creator can be rightly understood, according to the clear witness of Scripture, only when we give up the idea of a dualism between generation and creation as related to the two "parts" of man.

37. Bavinck, *op. cit.*, II, 547; Waterink, *op. cit.* (1954), p. 14.

We can perhaps view the function of the creationist motif — provided it is not further qualified — as a warning against every sort of secularizing of the question of origins, as a protest against the denigration of the mystery of man's nature, of each individual man's nature; but this motif can attain full value only when it rises above the creationist thesis and becomes an expression of the wonder and amazement of Psalm 139 — something which was never denied by creationism, but which could never come to full expression within the limits of the older creationist concept.

We must now deal with the question of whether the critique of the older creationism must necessarily lead to an acceptance of traducianism. Is the dilemma so stated a real dilemma? Must we choose for one or the other standpoint, with no third possibility open before us? We might be tempted to think so, since traducianism has always strongly stressed the *unity* of man as over against dualism — and are not the objections to creationism, including "corrected" creationism, closely related precisely to this insistence?

It should first be noted that traducianism can very easily take various forms, in relation to the way in which *"per traducem"* is understood. This might well a priori give us pause before accepting traducianism as a simple conclusion to the criticism of creationism. But the main point here is that a closer examination of traducianism reveals that it actually starts from the same presuppositions as does creationism, as is apparent from the fact that traducianism, as well as creationism, was interested in the origin of the soul, and thus presupposed, as did its opponent, the duality or dualism of the body and the soul. Dooyeweerd rightly points out[38] that criticism of creationism by no means leads automatically to acceptance of traducianism, since the latter also presupposes the idea of two substances in man, and then goes on to postulate that the origin of one of these substances, the soul, is *per traducem*.

It is, of course, unfair to charge traducianism with allowing man and also man's soul to originate through autonomous evolution apart from God as Creator, for traducianists have often acknowledged that all things, including those *per traducem*, are wholly dependent on God, and that thus the intent is not at all to secularize the origin of man in a sort of "horizontal" leveling. But traducianism does say that the whole man, as a being combining the psychic and the material, comes from the parents; as Daubanton puts it in his

38. H. Dooyeweerd, "Kuyper's Wetenschapsleer," *Philosophia Reformata* (1939), pp. 193ff., esp. p. 202; cf. also his "De Idee der Individualiteits-structuur en het Thomistisch Substantie-begrip," ibid. (1943/5), p. 29.

summary of traducianism, both the "material and spiritual con-
stituents of man."[39] This dichotomy continually plays a decisive
role and results in the appearance of various complicated problems
in connection with generation. For if we presuppose that the
material and spiritual are two very different sorts of things, it
becomes a real question how the soul can be "passed on" to the
child in generation. This sort of problem is especially present in
that form of traducianism known as generationism. The term is
not especially clarifying, since per traducem itself obviously implies generation; but what is meant is that man by analogy with
the Creator is given a creative power, which enables us to explain
the per traducem. As Daubanton puts it, "By the Creator's will,
the soul has the power to posit itself — as potential soul — in the
material product of generation from the organism which it controls,
and still remain itself." Generationism holds that there is a reflection of the Creator in the creature, man. As the Father generates
the Son, so man generates man, and thus "there arises through
generation and procession, soul from soul, just as body from body."
The former is especially wonderful: the non-material soul from
the non-material soul, which happens "according to a law, not
yet unveiled for us, governing the generation of spiritual things
from spiritual things." This especially shows how much traducianism presupposes a particular anthropological view regarding material
and spiritual "parts" in man. Traducianism may wish to posit
the unity of man, even in procreation, but more than a positing of
such a unity is difficult to discern in such a passage. One of the
reasons for the great influence of traducianism was, of course,
that it claimed to hold to the unity of man; it appeared to remove
the necessity for a dualistic split between creation and generation;
but actually, the dualism reappears at a different level, within
generation. And therefore creationism was rarely convinced by
traducianism's arguments, nor by its emphasis on the unity of

39. F. E. Daubanton, *Het Voortbestaan van het menselijk Geslacht* (1902),
p. 194 for the first and second quotes, p. 241 for the third. Cf. in
general Rijk Kramer, "Creatianisme of Generatianisme," *Orgaan van de
Christelijk Vereeniging voor Natuur- en Geneeskunde* (1906-1907), in
criticism of A. G. Honig. For generationism, cf. J. H. A. Ebrard,
Christliche Dogmatik, 2d ed., I (1862), pp. 330, 431; he speaks of a "metaphysical" generationism, since the energy of the inter-directed psychic
centers (father and mother) has the metaphysical power to allow a
new psychic center to develop from them. This power is analogous to
the procession of the Holy Spirit and comes from the non-material and
super-material contact of the immortal centers of personality, which
does not happen without the *concursus Dei*.

man. Creationism and traducianism indeed stood in many respects closer together than was once thought. Perhaps it was for just that reason that each found it so difficult to convince the other. They could not find the way to each other's position because they both viewed the problem of the origin of the soul from the same point of view: the origin of the soul as a spiritual substance.

In both theoretical views, the starting point was a description of the "essence" or "being" of man as soul and body, a description in which the relationship to God was not yet regarded as essential. This appears to be more clearly evident in traducianism, since creationism placed so strong an accent on a separate creative act. But in the final analysis, creationism also followed the same path, and viewed man as originating in the union between the created soul and the generated body. Thus man was a composite; both the view of man and the question of his origin showed a dualism in relation to the whole man, similar to that which appeared in traducianism within generation.

This all points the way, in our opinion, to a clarification of this apparently hopeless controversy. Any attempts to reach clarification from Scriptural evidence remained, for understandable reasons, a very dubious task, as was indeed admitted by many; but also in attempts to elaborate the two views, theologians on both sides faced insoluble problems. It is to be regretted that the dubiousness of the Scriptural evidence did not cause earnest questioning whether or not we actually did have a Scriptural witness here which would evoke an echo in the heart; for it is precisely the emphasis on the authority of Scripture which should have led to the recognition of the limit of the type of reflection in which the problem of the origin of man is replaced by the problem of the origin of the soul. And we need not be surprised that in the measure that the Scriptural witness regarding the origin of the whole man is appreciated, the importance of the apparent dilemma seems to fade, and that consciousness of the whole man in his mysterious relationship to God opens the way for us to rise above this historic dilemma. In this light the continuing hesitation of Augustine becomes a meaningful sign in the history of Christian thought.

The change from hesitation regarding the dilemma to rejection of the dilemma is not loss but gain. The gain could be nullified only through a renewed secularizing of our view of man's being.

It is possible that theologians by way of the criticism of creationism will again arrive at a view of man as some sort of autonomous and independent being. But such a course would show a misunderstanding of the nature of this criticism. For it rises not out of a limitation of man's creatureliness and dependence, but from an accentuation of them. And indeed, each one of us will have always to remain acutely aware of this mystery of man's being whenever we speak of man's religious relationship to God. All words and terms that are used are insufficient to unveil for us this secret. We can speak of relationship and dependence and creatureliness; but ever again it will become clear why we find the most meaningful words about this mystery in the words of God, or, as an echo, in words of prayer: "Thy hands have made and fashioned me" (Ps. 119:39). When Schleiermacher chose man's "feeling of absolute dependence" as the phrase which summarized his dogmatic reflections, and proceeded to build his system, his fault did not lie in accepting the idea of dependence as such. Man stands, in this dependence, with all of creation, and thus Jahwe can say, in a text which speaks powerfully about all of creation, "I have made the earth, man, and the beast that are upon the ground, by my great power and by my outstretched arm, and have given it unto whom it seemed meet unto me" (Jer. 27:5).[40]

But this universal dependence on Him who gives breath and spirit to all that lives does not imply a leveling of all creaturely differentiation. Man is more than an incidental and more or less accidental illustration of this universal creatureliness. Such leveling is found only in man himself, who in his alienation no longer understands the meaning of his humanness, and who in this darkness opens the way towards the shadows of fallen Babylon; the merchants of the earth weep and mourn over the fallen city, where the "souls of men" are put on the same level as beasts and sheep and horses (Rev. 18:11-13). This leveling and its results, in which nothing is safe, not even man, is the perversion of the mystery of man in his unique relationship to God, in a dependence which is not a simple "causal" relationship but rather an all-embracing "plus," full of responsibility and accusation, just as in Christ it becomes filled with new promise and a new vocation.

40. Cf. in connection with heaven and earth, Jer. 32:17. For Jeremiah such thoughts had concrete meaning, for he concluded that God had given "all these lands" into the hand of Nebuchadnezzar: see 27:8. Cf. 27:8 and H. A. Brongers, *De Scheppingstradities bij de Profeten* (1945), pp. 83ff.

There is no science, and no theology, which can unveil for us this mystery of man. This does not mean an underevaluation of science and theology, but rather an understanding of their meaning and their limits. Man, who no longer understands himself, can again understand this mystery only from the viewpoint of the divine revelation in Jesus Christ. It is the mystery which is unveiled for us in both law and gospel. And even in our increasing appreciation of this mystery, we find it too wonderful to comprehend, and we cannot do so (Ps. 139:6). But this inability to comprehend does not rule out, but rather occurs in, our knowledge of God's hands, of His eyes and His book, of His way with man (Ps. 139:13, 16, 24).

It is the knowledge of our origin, the origin of the deepest sources of our life, and it is the knowledge of our destiny, the *eschaton*: "How precious also are thy thoughts unto me, O God! How great is the sum of them! If I should count them, they are more in number than the sand: when I awake, I am still with thee" (Ps. 139:17-18).

CHAPTER NINE

HUMAN FREEDOM

O NE OF THE most important problems with which we have to
deal in our reflections on man, and one which constantly
recurs, is the problem of man's freedom. The problem has aroused
innumerable discussions, not only among philosophers but also
among theologians, and the passion with which controversy was
often carried on is an indication of the fact that in this problem
we deal not with some unimportant aspect of man's nature, but
rather with the whole man in his total life. Though this freedom
usually was thought of in terms of freedom of the will, nevertheless
it was man's freedom which was under discussion, the freedom of
the human being who chooses and acts and who follows his way
through life in "freedom."

There was of course no intent on the part of those who held this
human freedom to deny that there are various factors which limit
freedom. This "unfreedom" is so evident and frequent in the
history of mankind that we must all be impressed by it, by the
impressive evidence of dictatorships, deportations, and all sorts
of destruction of freedom; and, besides, an individual may feel his
freedom cramped by physical or psychical weakness, which hinders
expression of man's full nature. But all this does not alter the fact
that human freedom has always been glorified, and its suppression
never viewed as an accomplished fact in which man can rest satisfied. The more freedom is endangered, the more it is valued and
held as an ideal, and, sometimes, brought forward as a program,
and embodied in various institutions as a preventive against those
things which can endanger freedom.[1]

1. See Benedetto Croce, *History as the Story of Liberty* (New York, 1955),
pp. 58-59 especially. He speaks of "secular and ecclesiastical tyrannies,
wars between peoples, persecutions, exiles and gallows" as evidences of
unfreedom; "with this project in view, the statement that history is
the history of liberty sounds like irony, or, if it is serously maintained,
like stupidity." But he goes on to speak of the "thirst for liberty."
Liberty must be gained through a "perilous and fighting life." Therein,
he says, lies its exhilarating aspect. A world of freedom "without obstacles,
without menaces and without oppressions" would be "worse than death,
an infinite boredom."

The discussion on man's freedom was not confined to external
limiting factors; it also specifically considered the question
of whether man was truly free even without external constraints;
whether he was not completely determined by factors within himself, or by his own being. Is not what appears to be on superficial
examination a free act not actually, upon closer analysis, an act
which "necessarily" arises from what man is, and from which he
cannot escape, no matter how he tries? Does not a bit of reflection
dispose of the naive notion that man is free? Determinism has
always given an affirmative answer to this question, while indeterminism has held that the naive consciousness of freedom is
not an illusion, and points out that all of our concepts of merit,
guilt, responsibility, and the like, presuppose it, and without a basis
in freedom lose all meaning. Even within the deterministic framework, some have been influenced by this argument, and have tried
to make some room within determinism for human freedom —
which effort H. Groos calls "backsliding toward indeterminism."
"Only a few," he says, "have thought determinism through, have
defended it consistently, and have held back from any mediating
concessions.② Some returned, under the influence of the popular
belief in freedom, to indeterminism; some have tried to reach a
solution by distinguishing between the determined and the un-
determined so that, for example, as over against the determined world
of nature there remains room for freedom to play its role within the
human personality, which can escape from the grip of the
determined.[3]

The controversy between determinism and indeterminism shows

2. H. Groos, *Die Konsequenzen und Inkonsequenzen des Determinismus*
(1931), pp. 41, 126. Groos speaks of the "halfway and inconsequent
determinism" which arises because of this popular belief (p. 127). How
long this belief will continue to dominate is not predictable, he says, but
the time will come when it will give way to philosophical determinism;
and once this happens and, for example, the implications of heredity are
understood, then determinism will also find support in the popular mind
(p. 155). There is an inescapable and necessary logic in determinism,
and we can, he says, speak of fatalism, in contrast to various halfway
determinisms, as the "world-outlook of the future" (p. 157). Fatalism
is to determinism as steel is to iron.
3. Cf. H. Dooyeweerd, *Reformatie en Scholastiek in de Wijsbegeerte*, I
(1949), 37ff.; especially on Kant for the "fourth motif" in the history of
philosophy nature vs. freedom. Cf. H. I. Iwand, "Studien zum Problem des
unfreien Willens," *Zeitschrift für systematische Theologie* (1930), pp.
225ff. He makes a similar attack on Kant's antinomy between freedom and
causality. Iwand speaks of a theoretical irrefutable "illusionary self-
understanding."

us how constantly man's thought has been occupied with the problem of human freedom, of spontaneity and choice. There is little reason for Groos to conclude that the popular idea of freedom will finally be stamped out by determinism. On the contrary, in and despite all sorts of determination and massive restraint, the sense of freedom continually manifests itself, and not only in a pre-intellectual popular intuition, but also in intellectual circles, which proclaim human freedom though this freedom is indeed surrounded by all sorts of threats from unfreedom.[4]

We can see again and again, that the discussion of the concept of freedom, especially in the controversy between determinism and indeterminism, takes place against a background of religiously neutral anthropological analysis. Determinism rules out freedom because of internal or external determination, while indeterminism wishes to break through such determination by relying on man's nature. Both views rest on a humanistically oriented analysis of man and the surrounding world, in which the central problem is always whether man is free from determination or is in bondage.

The whole dilemma thus is obscured by assuming a purely formal concept of freedom, which leaves the real and central problem of freedom untouched. The problem cannot be solved formalistically by examining what man is "free from." Such a viewpoint, expressed, e.g., in the definition of freedom as being free from all restrictions, throws no light at all on the nature of human freedom.

And even when men prize freedom as the *summum bonum* of human personality, there is still the possibility of a degeneration of freedom. And when we raise this possibility, we also bring to the fore the problem of a norm for freedom. Even those who do not relate the degeneration of freedom to what Leo XIII called "the total rejection of the sovereignty of the almighty God" (in his encyclical *Libertas*) often nevertheless speak of a "perversion"

---

4. Cf. H. Redeker, *Existentialisme* (1949), pp. 319-321; on Sartre as the philosopher of freedom, who, however, opposes both determinism and indeterminism. Even unconditional freedom, says Sartre, is saturated with necessity and facticity, so that Redeker concludes that the ontologic basis is not free, and the dialectic fails at the final point. Cf. S. U. Zuidema, "Sartre," *Denkers van deze Tijd*, I, 279-283; R. Mehl, "Het Vraagstuk der Ethiek in het Franse Existentialisme," *Wending* (1956), and the final chapter (on liberty) of M. Merleau-Ponty, *Phénoménologie de la perception* (1945), on the dilemma of total freedom and no freedom, and his comment that we are inextricably involved with the world and with others: man's "situation" excludes absolute liberty even at the outset of our actions (p. 518).

of freedom, as is shown, e.g., in the term "true freedom," which is then distinguished from false or illusory freedom. This usage already shows us that a merely formal treatment of what man is "free from" says little or nothing. For the moment that freedom is posited, one is confronted by the question of the limits of freedom, and the problem reaches formidable complexity as soon as we intuitively reject the completely individualistic and norm-less concept of freedom which the purely formal "free from" approach seeks to realize.

Nevertheless, we gain the impression that men are often little conscious of this complexity in their manifold use of the concept of freedom. In everyday practical life, all sorts of restrictions play so great a role, restrictions experienced as essentially alien and as threatening, that we are sometimes inclined without further thought to proclaim "free from" as the essence of freedom. And this definition often finds expression in everyday life. Thus we speak of liberalism in the political and social area, meaning that the state should allow man's life to keep its "freedom"; and we speak of freedom of religion and conscience, freedom of expression, academic freedom, and so forth. In this all a protest is registered against restrictions on human life which cannot be tolerated, as, for example, when during a period of occupation by a foreign power a people undergoes an experience of unfreedom, and the "free from" approach can then be the basis for a blazing enthusiasm when the conquerors are driven out and the people regain their freedom.

But this apparently clear and lucid concept of freedom is never able by itself to bring about a solution of the real and deepest problem of human freedom. For in every situation the "free from" approach immediately poses numerous problems as to the nature and the meaning of freedom, and its limits.

In theological reflection on human freedom one continually faces a much deeper question than that posed by the usual controversy between determinism and indeterminism. For when theologians discussed human freedom, they were not concerned with the freedom of a self-sufficient "being" but rather with the freedom of the man of God. Thus we need not be surprised that in this approach the problem of the relationship between human freedom and the sovereignty of God continually came to the fore. And it is also true that the determinism – indeterminism controversy was often incorporated in theological reflection on this problem. We often encounter these terms in the history of dogma, and this religiously neutral anthropological controversy was then grafted on to the religious questions. We can observe "deterministic" tendencies which because of the (determining) sovereignty of God reserved no freedom for man, while indeterminism, in reaction, often relativized the sovereignty of God to preserve the freedom of man. And thus theology fell into a most regrettable controversy, since an apparent dilemma was raised which is really non-religious in nature, and which is wholly outside of the Biblical witness. It may be stated, and happily so, that this false approach was often recognized, and that attempts were made to banish it from the theological tradition; as, for example, when the absence of human freedom was expounded not in terms of a general determinism, but rather in terms of sin: the slavery of fallen and lost man, who because of the fall was a slave to the dark powers of apostasy, which overpowered and ruled him in all his ways.

This view of man's slavery constantly comes to the fore in the history of theology in connection with the question of whether or not man had "freedom" to accept divine grace. Was it actually so that on the one hand there was a divine offer of grace, and on the other a free man, who could respond to this grace negatively as well as positively, so that the decision as to salvation lay in man's own hands only? Can the distinction between "objective" grace and "subjective" free decision be so simple? That was the question at issue in the struggle between Pelagius and Augustine, and in later forms of this controversy between, for example, Erasmus and Luther, in their argument *de libero arbitrio or de servo arbitrio.*

When as over against Rome the Reformation denied the freedom of the will, rejected the subject – object separation, and spoke of an enslaved will, most Catholic and humanist thinkers saw this as nothing less than an attack on, and indeed an annihilation of, human nature, of man's essence, which was presumed to be inconceivable without freedom as part of it.

They saw in the denial of freedom of the will a proclamation of a divine grace which was overwhelming and which could affect human life only in irruptive and mechanical fashion, overpowering defenseless and enslaved man. The Reformers' teaching on the will of man was interpreted as *coactio,* as *necessitas,* and over against this the so-called physical freedom of the will was stressed, a freedom not destroyed through the power of sin because it belonged to the essential structure of man's nature.[5] According

5. On this "physical" (or natural) freedom, cf. Leo XIII's encyclical *Libertas;* "the ability to choose the means proper to the desired goal" (pp. 17-18). Free choice (*liberum arbitrium*) is a property of the will, something proper to the will, *seu potius ipsa voluntas.* It is noteworthy that despite the supposed indestructibility of this freedom, the encyclical

to Rome, we can speak of a saving and restoring divine power only if we postulate an organic connection between grace and freedom. The point was one, Rome felt, of essential importance, and it is not coincidental that as early as 1520 Rome denounced as one of Luther's errors his denial of free will, just as it was not coincidental that the controversy between Luther and Erasmus broke out over exactly this point.[6] For the controversy was on whether man was or was not "open" to divine grace, able to accept it "freely." When Luther (and after him Calvin) denied this so-called freedom of the will, this was seen by many as an erroneous view of human nature. And therein lies the reason that Catholic theologians in various polemics against the Reformation stress so strongly the inalienable and essential and evident anthropological structure of human freedom.

Actually, it is clear enough that the Reformation's intention was not at all to posit compulsion as over against freedom. There was no suggestion that its critique of the freedom of the will meant to hold, in deterministic fashion, that only God acted, and that man was powerless, deprived of will, and driven.[7] Such an approach to the problem was definitely not the background of the real controversy. It was readily acknowledged that man followed his own way in "free," not compulsive, acts, in a self-willed activity and spontaneity from day to day. The denial of the freedom of the will posited, rather, that it was precisely this active and willing human being in his willing and acting who was alienated from God and enslaved to sin; and in no sense a man who stood like a *tabula rasa* before continually new possibilities

---

goes on to say that the "power to sin is not freedom" (p. 19), with a citation of John 8:34 ("Whosoever committeth sin is the servant of sin"). On the concept of freedom in this encyclical, and problems surrounding it, see B. van Beyen, "De Opvatting van de menselijke Wilsvrijheid in de Neo-Scholastiek," *Studia Catholica* (1956), pp. 213-215. For the organic relation between grace and freedom in Catholic thought, see ch. 2 of my *Divine Election* (1955).

6. The condemnation of Luther is in *Exsurge Domine* (Denzinger, 776). For Luther and Erasmus, cf. further my *Conflict met Rome*, ch. 4.

7. Iwand, *op. cit.*, p. 241. He sees the equation of the idea of the unfree will with the idea of determinism as the most common misunderstanding of the former. For man's enslaved will, cf. I Pet. 2:16 warning against "using your liberty for a cloke of maliciousness": this refers to an enslaved will, not to an annihilated will.

Thus we speak of a *"servum arbitrium"* in the *"privatio actuosa"* — a term which stresses the dynamic and active character of sin. The enslaved will manifests itself in this alarming dynamism.

of choosing between good and evil. The problem with which the Reformation was concerned was not first of all a psychological or anthropological problem, and still less was it taught that man did not will or act or choose: attention was directed to man as active and willing! The problem was then the condition, the state of "being" of sinful and lost mankind, the being with which he willed and acted and chose in all his activities. Thus it was primarily the central religious question which was raised. Is the "being" of fallen man of such a sort that he is "free" in each new situation of his life, in each new decisive turning point of his existence, free in the sense that the possibility of doing good, of obeying God's commands, of being "open" to divine grace, is always there? Or is he enslaved to his sinful past and to the corruption of his heart, to his alienation from God? The Reformation did not hesitate as to the answer to these questions. And its answer did not arise from a deterministic view of the acts of God or from an annihilation of man's will, but rather from its belief in man's lostness, his fallen state. The criticism of free will was not based on the assumption of a universal necessitarianism, but on the confession of man's guileful, stony heart, which — mightily active — pushed man forward on a way of sin and corruption which he is no longer able to abandon by means of the "freedom" presumed to be essentially and anthropologically his.[8]

It is thus of importance, for purposes of orientation regarding the problem of freedom, to know how and on what grounds freedom of the will is attacked. This can be done from the vantage point of determinism or fatalism, which allows no place for any freedom: but it is also possible to reject such a vantage point, and to see the affirmation of the enslavement of the will as a corollary of an affirmation of guilt. And when Rome supported the physical freedom of the will and from this viewpoint disqualified the Reformation, a horrible misunderstanding had arisen in the Church, a misunderstanding whose effects can still be felt. The difficulty of removing this misunderstanding becomes apparent even today in rather spectacular fashion when we consider Erich Przywara, who views Luther as replacing the *All-wirksamkeit* of God by an *Allein-wirksamkeit* so that the creature is completely and totally moved by the divine will, and who then concludes that Luther's

8. Cf. *Realencyklopädie für protestantische Theologie und Kirche* (s.v., *Willensfreiheit*), XXI, 317.

view is the same as Spinoza's.[9] And when the first phase of Neo-Orthodoxy stressed the infinite qualitative distinction between man and God, Catholic theologians took this as showing once again that the basic idea of the Reformation was a "deterministic" view of the will — apparently having no notion of the fact that the Reformation actually was concerned with something wholly different from a metaphysical conclusion regarding absolute transcendence as over against immanence, or from exclusive activity as over against inclusive. We shall be able to gain perspective on this point insofar as it occurs in the Protestant — Catholic controversy only when this still influential interpretation of the denial of freedom of the will becomes past history, and the religious meaning of the Reformation's belief on this point at least begins again to be understood.[10]

And that we are not here giving a more recent interpretation, arising after the Reformation because of the ever more clearly noted dangers of determinism, is apparent if one but refers, for example, to Calvin (*Institutes*, II, II).[11] He says that man has been deprived

9. E. Przywara, "Gott in uns und Gott über uns," *Ringen der Gegenwart*, II (1929), 550ff. He is followed by many Catholics in this view; recently by Marlet, *Grundlinien der Kalvinistischen Philosophie der Gesetzesidee als Christlicher Transzendentalphilosophie* (1954), pp. 129ff.

10. Marlet, *op. cit.*, p. 131. He refers to Calvin in support of his position. He says that Calvin stresses exclusively the *Allein-wirksamkeit* of God, so that both in the individual and the areas of life — all bound immediately to Him — all independence is denied; and Marlet sees this as meaning that secondary causes are completely absorbed in the original causality of God. Cf. his reference to J. L. Witte, *Het Probleem Individu-gemeenschap in Calvijns Geloofsnorm* (1949). Witte views Calvin as stressing transcendence at the cost of immanence. It would seem that there is some conflict between exclusive divine transcendence on the one hand, and a unique and complete divine activity in every creaturely act on the other — but Marlet uses both as characteristic of Calvinism. His expression *"Allein-wirksamkeit"* is unsatisfactory, since Calvin's protest against man's independence is a protest against man's supposed autonomy, and has nothing to do with a depreciation of the meaning and worth of creaturely activity. And thus Marlet's reference in this connection to the difference between Dooyeweerd and Stoker hardly indicates a flaw in the "structure" of Calvinism!

11. The discussion following is based on the *Institutes*, II, II. The introductory mention of the loss of free will is from the heading of II, II. For the Latin fathers, *ibid.*, 4, 9. For the Greek fathers, *ibid.*, 4; the word Calvin sees used by them is *autexousion*. Niesel refers to Clement, Origen, Chrysostom (cf. Calvin's remarks) and to Gregory Nazianzus, *Op. Sel.* IV, 246. For Calvin's stress on will rather than compulsion, see II, II, 7, 8.

of his freedom of will and as a result has been subjected to a
miserable enslavement. Calvin asks what it means that the fathers
so often dealt with the question of free will; he sees in them — with
the exception of Augustine — a good deal of uncertainty and confusion, and concludes that they, though disciples of Christ, treated
the problem too much in the manner of philosophers. The Latin
Fathers usually treated free will as though man was still pure and
undefiled, but the Greek writers used a much more presumptuous
approach and said that man was autonomous. Calvin then asks what
we are to understand by free will. He is not concerned to extinguish man's will. He emphasizes that man does evil with his
will and not through compulsion. One might here speak of
a psychological freedom which Calvin would fully acknowledge.
But he holds that to call this "free will" is not at all justified, and
is most confusing terminology. If "free will" means merely such
psychological freedom, fine; but, he says, why give such an unimportant thing so proud a title? On the one hand, he says, it is an
excellent thing that man is not compelled to sin; but on the
other hand, it is of limited importance, since man is still a sinner
in this psychological freedom, this spontaneous action. He is a
"willing" servant of sin, and his will is fettered with the shackles
of sin. Thus Calvin's opposition to freedom of the will becomes
evident. He cites Augustine, who called the will the slave of
sin, and said that the will has been used badly and is now
imprisoned. And the decisive argument for Calvin, as for Augustine,
is that man was created with the great powers of a free will, but
lost these through sin. It is very clear here — in this loss of the
free will — that the concern is not with a metaphysical interpretation of an enslaved will. If Calvin's opposition to free will had
been based on a deterministic causality, it would have been
impossible for him to distinguish the situations before and after
the fall: freedom would never have existed. But this is precisely
not the case. Calvin views free will as something which has
been lost; man has been deprived of it. The fall marks a basic
change, for man lost what he once possessed.[12]

12. On this point see also the *Canons of Dordt*, III, IV, Rejection of
    Errors. Here freedom of the will is rejected, and the elevation of the
    powers of the free will (III, IV, III), with a reference to the guile-
    fullness of the heart. Cf. the *Confessio Scotiana*, art. 2, on the original
    libertas arbitrii (Müller, *Die Bekenntnisschriften der Reformierten
    Kirche*, p. 250); *Confessio Helvetica Posterior*, art. IX, the will has
    been made enslaved, *"voluntas vero ex libera facta est voluntas serva"*
    (*ibid.*, p. 179); cf. the further remark *"servit peccato non nolens, sed
    volens. Etenim voluntas, non noluntas dicitur"* (*ibid.*).

And this distinction also marks Calvin's judgment of the term. If freedom of the will means that man sins with his will and not through compulsion, then Calvin has no objection; but he considers that the term must be used with great caution, and would prefer that it not be used at all (*Institutes*, II, II, 8). For, he says, he has found that the usual connotation of the term is not merely that the will is not externally compelled but also includes the idea that man can freely determine his own path and the direction of his whole life in autonomy, as if the man who wills is not a fallen and falling man, whose life's direction is already decided because of the fall.

And so our conclusion must be that Calvin took up the problem of the freedom of the will as an historical and religious problem, and that in this approach his own deepest interests revealed themselves.[13] And thus he can ask (II, II, 8) why men boast of their free will, when they are actually slaves to sin; and as for freedom, he can cite the words of Scripture, "and where the Spirit of the Lord is, there is liberty" (II Cor. 3:17).

Man, then, according to Calvin, was free before the fall, and lost this freedom through sin. As fallen man he does indeed will and act, but in this activity he walks on a path he cannot leave through his own powers. It is the path of alienation and rebellion. And once on this path, man's conversion, his return, by his own power — is ruled out. This is man's enslaved will, his *servum arbitrium*.[14]

Before the fall, freedom; and after the fall, enslavement. When the Reformation so speaks, it implies the breaking through of every form of determinism. Anyone who should wish to oppose

13. When Calvin distinguishes between necessity and compulsion (*necessitas* and *coactio*), necessity refers to a *necessitas* arising from the corruption of human nature. Cf. J. Bohatec, "Calvins Vorsehungslehre," in his *Calvinstudien* (1909), p. 365. For the distinction, see *Institutes*, II, III, 5. Calvin there says the will is deprived of its freedom and necessarily follows evil (with citations of Augustine and Bernard). Man sins with his will and not against his will; through inclination, not compulsion; through desire, not through external compulsion.

14. The point can be sharpened by saying that we are not dealing with determinism, but with the accusation of Jeremiah: "Can the Ethiopian change his skin, or the leopard his spots? then may ye also do good, that are accustomed to do evil" (Jer. 13:23). Cf. Aalders, *Commentaar, ad loc.* He says that this text is often cited in connection with the corruptness of human nature, but wrongly, since it deals with a hardening of the heart through continual living in sin. But this does not rule out the fact that the impossible is here spoken of in connection with an existing situation in which man moves and in which he is powerless.

this formulation from the standpoint of divine omnipotence and sovereignty so as to deny man any freedom a priori — apart, that is, from the question of before or after the fall — would be introducing a most unbiblical view of freedom, and at the same time a very inexact concept of God. He might perhaps from such a concept reach the conclusion that man "naturally" is not free; but it is clear that with such an approach he must develop an idea of freedom as autonomy and arbitrary choice. And this implies a line of thought which makes it finally impossible to catch the Biblical light on freedom. And it certainly must then sound strange to hear life restored through the grace of God described as a free life. No, it is precisely the clarity of the Biblical witness regarding freedom which should make us very cautious of any abstract concept of freedom. A determinist may view all actual freedom — apart from the concrete situation. however disposed — as contraband; but from Scripture it is evident that there is room for an important historical variation, and it is apparently possible to speak of human freedom once again released from restrictions. It is obvious that this freedom, which is held before us as awe-inspiring wealth, has nothing to do with autonomy or arbitrariness, and that it does not stand opposed to submission to God. We can not even say that freedom and submission are two aspects of the Christian life. There is, according to the Bible, only one solution which gives the gospel message its full due: when we refer not merely to aspects, nor to a dialectical relation between submission and freedom, but to their identity.[15]

We must then speak without any hesitation of human freedom as a creaturely freedom given by God. No misuse of the desire for freedom, not even complete anarchy, should tempt us to stop speaking boldly and emphatically of freedom. The anxiety regarding the use of the term which we find in Christian circles is indeed historically and psychologically understandable, since life has often been shaken to its foundations through an appeal to "freedom."

15. In my *Divine Election* (1955), p. 327, I noted Otto Ritschl's idea that some Calvinists when they took up man before the fall suddenly returned to an "indeterministic" outlook, and accepted free will. This is a typical misunderstanding; if Ritschl had been logical, he should then have been amazed at the "illogicality" of the Calvinists when they went on to speak of *Christian* freedom! Determinism has no room, either protologically or eschatologically, for freedom. Ritschl's astonishment thus does not correspond to the actual situation among Calvinist theologians, who evidently were completely aware of historical and eschatological perspectives on the problem.

Freedom is often understood as autonomy and arbitrary power, as a purely formal power of man to go his own way. Thus man can be "liberated" from many restrictions, and thus Cain can "free" himself from Abel — "Am I my brother's keeper?" — and thus freedom can become an idol, a myth, which fills the heart and passions of man. Such practices can bring into the open the hidden and demonic motivations that lurk beneath what is often misunderstood as "freedom," and they who have been made aware of these hidden forces tend to talk freedom only in whispers and certainly without emphasis. It is clear, however, that such an approach to the problem arises from a perverted and secularized concept of freedom, within which it becomes increasingly difficult to keep in mind the Biblical witness regarding the Christian's freedom in Christ. Speaking Biblically, we can only say that sin enslaves man, just as it originally robbed him of his freedom and made him a man bound in the fetters of sin, as Calvin says (*Institutes*, II, III, 5). The Bible never embarks on a crusade against true human freedom; it is not so that, for example, divine omnipotence and providence rule out human freedom or annihilate it. The perspective is wholly different: the Scriptural witness on freedom is limited to man's relation to God. Man's enslaved will (*servum arbitrium*) does not mean impotence in the face of divine omnipotence, but rather sin, guilt, alienation, rebellion. Man's sin is not a manifestation of his freedom, but its perversion. And it is thus of great importance to give our full attention to, and not in reaction ignore, the fact that divine grace forgives this perversion of freedom, this rebellion, and annihilates its effects, and so renders man once again truly free.

Calvin remarks with reference to the characteristics of the image of God in man that we can know it in no better way than through the restoration of man's corrupt nature (*Institutes* I, XV, 4); and the same is true of human freedom. The New Testament pictures it with great emphasis as freedom in and through Christ. There is obviously no reference here to an abstract concept of freedom, but rather freedom is spoken of in a completely relational sense.[16] This becomes perhaps most clear when we consider that there is no tension or competition between the freedom of the believer

16. In spite of the Catholic emphasis on "physical freedom," evidences of this relational nature of freedom break through again and again even in Catholic theologians; cf., e.g., "what freedom ultimately means . . . really becomes actualized before God." R. Guardini, *Freiheit, Gnade, Schicksal. Drei Kapitel zur Deutung des Daseins* (1949), p. 99.

and his submission to Christ. Indeed, it is precisely that man who stands in community with Him and who submits fully to Him who is referred to as free. The restoration in Christ, the new man, refers to our restoration from the enslaved will (*servum arbitrium*) to the free will (*libera voluntas*): One of Jesus' talks with the Jews dealt with the liberating power of the truth (John 8:32-36). When they protested that they had never been in bondage, Jesus spoke of the enslavement to sin, and told them that "if the Son therefore shall make you free, ye shall be free indeed." Jesus contrasts, in this sharp polemic, actual freedom with the slavery of sin, with that miserable servility and enslavement. (Compare the similar evaluations of this enslavement in Rom. 6:6, Rom. 6:19, Gal. 4:3, Titus 3:3.) It is the same outlook which is given us elsewhere: "Stand fast therefore in the liberty wherewith Christ has made us free" (Gal. 5:1); this is the richness of freedom, which must be protected against threats to it; "be not entangled again with the yoke of bondage."

Freedom in the New Testament is not a formal possibility or a formal power which enables the believer to choose either of two ways. On the contrary: it is no possibility but rather an actuality, the actuality of being free (cf. Gal. 3:13, 4:4). It is materially qualified and made concrete through the relation to Christ, and is identical with coming into the service of God (Rom. 6:22), with all the wealth that is implied therein. Thus the depth and completeness of this freedom become visible. It does not compete with or limit the acts of God, as if the more powerfully God's acts affect our lives, the narrower our freedom becomes! Or, as if the accentuation of our freedom should limit the power of the grace of God! Anyone who thinks in such categories should realize that the New Testament knows no such opposition. The New Testament pictures it in precisely the opposite way: the more communion with God fills our life, the more free our life becomes.[17] If

17. Cf. R. Bultmann, "Gnade und, Freiheit," *Glauben und Verstehen*, II (1952), p. 161. He says "thus our dependence on the grace of God, our surrender to it — far from limiting our freedom! — precisely makes us in the true sense free" — this is, he says, a genuine summary of the freedom of the New Testament. Cf. K. Barth, *K. D.*, IV, II, 855. He opposes the idea of competition. The denial of such competition has nothing to do with a reciprocal dependence or with one or another form of correlationism. Competition is something other than radical dependence, to which the New Testament time and again refers in connection with fatherhood, freedom and love. See I John 4:10 on divine and human love, and on which is prior. Cf. on this point Barth, *K. D.* IV, II, 855, on the ground of love; this ground is also the ground of freedom, and thus any dialectic of competition is excluded.

we place divine power and human freedom in a relation of opposition — even if we refer to a mystery in connection therewith — we
are actually operating with a secularized and autonomous concept
of freedom. When such a concept, which implies some sort of
competition in the relation between God and human freedom,[18]
is held consistently, one cannot but conclude that the divine greatness and power rob man of his due, and threaten man in his true
humanity. But such a concept actually involves a serious misapprehension of freedom, a misapprehension that really presupposes
the idea of the jealousy of a God who begrudges man his proper
nature, viewing it as a threat to His own power.

We must remember in this connection that the Bible does indeed
refer to the jealousy of God, but everything depends on what we
must understand by the term. Does the Bible speak of a jealousy
of God toward man, which could in any sense be analogous to the
impure jealousy of humans? The answer to this question is not
difficult to give. Whenever Scripture speaks of divine jealousy, it is
in a context of relationships so clear that there is no room for
misunderstanding. Consider first of all the second commandment,
in which a divine warning and threat is added to the forbidding
of the worship of images; "for I the Lord thy God am a jealous God,
visiting the iniquity of the fathers upon the children" (Ex. 20:5;
cf. Deut. 5:9), and the text in which the fierceness of God's
"jealousy" in judgment is referred to: "I will give thee blood in
fury and jealousy" (Ezek. 16:38). While we may not detract in
the least from the terrible power of such words, they are nevertheless
far removed from the "jealousy" of God toward a human race to
which he begrudges a place under the sun. The "jealousy" of which
Scripture speaks is not directed against man as such, but only
against the man who violates the only right relationship to God.
Such violation occurs in the worship of images, as stated in the
second commandment, but also, as stated in Ezekiel, when the
people are no longer faithful to the God of the Covenant. For
this is an intolerable rebellion, an attack on the mystery of God's
love for Israel, and thus the jealousy of Jahwe in all its fierceness

18. In this connection we might well reflect on Jer. 10:23: "O Lord, I
know that the way of man is not in himself: it is not in man that walketh
to direct his steps." The remarkable thing about these words (a prayer) is
that they are spoken without the slightest consciousness of any violation of
freedom; rather only with a sense of standing before the divine countenance. If we read "determinism" into this text, we do not understand it
at all; read the passionate context and the unique view of the God of
Israel. Cf. the language of Prov. 16:9.

is a revelation of a love which cannot bear that this love is disdained with impunity (cf. the whole of Ezek. 16, especially verses 8, 15 and 32). Thus the jealousy of Jahwe is not directed against man, but against the adultery of His people, against the failure to appreciate His love. Jahwe's jealousy can only be aroused because of illegitimate religion: "They have moved me to jealousy with that which is not God; they have provoked me to anger with their vanities" (Deut. 32:21).[19]

In this "jealousy" there is nothing of the illegitimate jealousy of man, who begrudges his fellow man that which is his;[20] rather, it is the revelation of God's holiness and love, with which He watches over the steadfastness of His covenant, the covenant of love.

The divine jealousy is not directed against man as such, but against the perversion of human nature in supposed autonomy, in which man's relation to God becomes troubled and endangered. Another sort of jealousy may be found in Greek mythology, but not in the Word of God. Scripture presents precisely the opposite of any idea of competition; first in creation, and then in salvation, man receives his status in wealth and communion and freedom, and he is affected by God's jealousy only when this communion and freedom are violated. Therefore, too, Scripture never speaks of a jealous attitude of God towards human "freedom," since all His acts are directed towards this freedom. His concern is with a freedom which is the freedom of sonship, not the "freedom" of arbitrary choice.

There can be tension between "free" autonomous man and God only when man wants to defend this "freedom" against God, and then makes room for it in theory or in practice. But this "freedom"

---

19. Jean Daniélou, "La jalousie de Dieu," *Dieu Vivant*, XVI, 53ff. In a fine article on this subject, he refers to Elijah as a great representative of the jealousy of God (p. 68) and refers also to Ps. 69:10 in connection with the zeal of Christ in the purification of the temple (John 2:17). Cf. also Hosea as regards jealousy and adultery (Hos. 2:5, 8, 12). It is understandable that when the image of married love is used, the thought of God's jealousy comes to the fore.

20. This is not to say that there is no legitimate jealousy possible among men. Thus, as Daniélou (*op. cit.*, p. 63) points out, we read that Paul watches "with a godly jealousy" over the Corinthians, for "I have espoused you to one husband, that I may present you as a chaste virgin to Christ" (II Cor. 11:1-2). We see here, in Paul's concern, essentially the same sort of jealousy over the children of God. And indeed not all ordinary jealousy among men is illegitimate if only it arises from respect for unique relations, as in marriage, though even this legitimate jealousy can become perverted and distorted because of man's sinful heart.

is not honored with that name in the New Testament, but is rather rejected and unmasked. This "freedom" as autonomous self-determination and self-destining is certainly not the "essence" of man, and the supposition that it is or promises to be true freedom, is pictured in the New Testament as completely illusory. Of false teachers it is said: "While they promise liberty, they themselves are the servants of corruption; for of whom a man is overcome, of the same he is brought into bondage" (II Pet. 2:18-19). Were we to begin with an abstract idea of freedom, we should find the terminology of the New Testament indeed strange, bizarre and intolerable, when it speaks of servants, slaves of Christ, and submission in every area of life. We should then see all such things as a threat to freedom, as an abolition of freedom. But the New Testament recognizes no conflict here because it holds that true freedom becomes actualized precisely in this submission. And this is no mere metaphor, no "aspect" which can be relativized through other "aspects," but it rather concerns the actual nature of freedom.[21] Often the saying that true freedom is true submission sounds somewhat trivial; the reason is the often oversimplified use of these terms. They can be used in a very general sense, as when, for example, Jacques Perk says that true freedom has regard for the laws. But we should reflect that the New Testament is not merely repeating a general truth: it is designating this identity essential for true humanness. And we shall have to admit that Scripture reveals something of the deep mystery of our humanness when it pictures the position of man not as submission in contrast with freedom, but shows in very real and penetrating fashion man's freedom precisely in his submission. Schlier expresses this in striking fashion when he says that the New Testament does not tell us that man is enslaved because he is not able sufficiently to order his own way, but rather tells us that he is enslaved just because he does so do, and to the extent that he does so do.[22]

The enslaved will (*servum arbitrium*) is according to the New Testament found precisely in attempted autonomy, in taking one's life in one's own hands, in autarchy, in controlling one own's destiny. As over against that, we see the light of true freedom.

---

21. Herman Ridderbos, *Arcana revelata,* pp. 102-103. He correctly warns against speaking of a dialectic between freedom and law. We must accept what is said on these two "in complete seriousness, but without attempting to discover in these apparent oppositions a dialectic which attempts to approximate the truth by way of clashing statements."

22. H. Schlier, in Kittel, *Theologisches Wörterbuch, s.v., eleutheros,* p. 492.

To quote Schlier again[23] "man attains control over himself only by letting himself be controlled." The words in which the New Testament concept of freedom is paraphrased often take such "paradoxical" form, but basically there are no opposing poles here, any more than for Paul when he speaks of love as the fulfilling of the law.

There is rather the miracle of the gift of freedom, which consists of this, as Paul puts it characteristically, that we are no longer our own, and therefore we rediscover ourselves in our true humanness and our true destiny. This "paradoxical" truth (as, e.g., Bultmann[24] calls it) is the great mystery of man's life, as it is revealed in the restoration to true humanness. This restoration is not at all an "annihilation," for the man who is no longer his own is, in this situation, called to glorify God, "glorify God in your body, and your spirit, which are God's" (I Cor. 6:20). The fact that we are not our own does not cast shadows over human freedom, but evidences it as a joyful reality: "For whether we live, we live unto the Lord; and whether we die, we die unto the Lord; whether we live, therefore, or die, we are the Lord's" (Rom. 14:8). Here freedom is fully revealed, for here man recovers his status, and is freed from the delusion of his autonomy to serve God. Believers must be reminded of this again and again, for they must learn so to be true man and truly free. And in the text which Bultmann calls "the most powerful expression of freedom," this reminder is expressed sharply, so that freedom will not be misunderstood: "For all things are yours . . . the world, or life, or death, or things present, or things to come; all are yours but ye are Christ's" (I Cor. 3:21-23). Though this insight does not originate first of all in Paul's experience, it does correspond well with it, for he in his encounter with Christ did not go from "freedom" to slavery, but from slavery to freedom. "I live; yet not I, but Christ liveth in me" (Gal. 2:20). And from this "not I" comes forth the powerful and seething activity which is the sign of true freedom. Thus Paul speaks (Gal. 5:13, 4:4-7) of being truly free and of being called to freedom as a very joyful thing, through which man's nature is not destroyed but rather restored.

23. Schlier as cited in the footnote above. Cf. *Heidelberg Catechism,* Lord's Day 1. It says we are no longer our own, but Christ's. And thus also man finds his own life back in being willing and ready to obey.
24. Bultmann, *Theologie des N.T.* (1948), p. 328. The context shows his insistence that freedom in Christ is not a freeing from all norms, but is a new serving (Rom. 7:6). "A paradoxical servitude! For the servant of Christ is of course at the same time one who is the Lord's freeman" (I Cor. 7:22). Cf. the "serving one another by love" (Gal. 5:13).

The New Testament revelation regarding freedom thus articulates a deeply religious verdict. Every concept of freedom which would describe man's essence ontologically, apart from his relation to God, must end with the "freedom" of autonomy and self-determination. Such an abstract ontology of essences can give no true perspective on freedom; it must always designate as the earmark of freedom, being "free from" — however the concept is then further elaborated. This freedom, this being "free from," is then seen as of the "essence" of man, a self-sufficient inwardness which protests all threats to it or limits on it, all conquest and compulsion. Freedom is then defined by man's dignity and by his inner nature. This freedom leaves man to himself, and he chooses so to be, as over against the world of the other, which limits him and threatens him. Freedom is then "the being left to oneself in the sense of pure self-limitation to oneself as one's incontestably own,"[25] so that man himself is the absolute subject who dictates the law. Freedom is thus formally qualified, and from this point of view any limit or responsibility will be seen as a relativizing of absolute freedom. But this makes clear the meaningless and subjectivistic character of such a "freedom from." All variations within this absolute freedom become purely relative. When Schlier discusses the transition from the concept of freedom as political freedom to the idealistic notion of freedom, he adds that the "formal definition of freedom remains the same": the idea of "free from" as the essence of freedom is a negative qualification and implies ultimately the breaking of all bonds with another. Thus, says Schlier, it stands in direct contrast with the New Testament idea of freedom, which is pictured as true freedom up to and including its eschatological fulfillment, a freedom in which men share and stand through the faith to which men are called, and in which men must be protected.[26] This freedom cannot be formally defined through a "free from" approach, but always stands in a material context; one can almost speak of a New Testament definition of freedom when Paul writes, "where the Spirit of the Lord is, there is liberty" (II Cor. 3:17).

This freedom is not taken for granted in the New Testament Church. It is rather surrounded by constant warnings to remain in freedom.

If the Church turns away from the path that has been shown

25. H. Jonas, *Augustin und das Paulinische Freiheitsproblem* (1930), p. 11.
26. H. Schlier, in Kittel, *Theologisches Wörterbuch*, II, 489, and in his *Der Brief an die Galater* (1949), p. 175, referring to I Thess. 4:7, "a call to stand in and by freedom."

her, she does it not in freedom; rather, the turning away endangers freedom. That is Paul's concern for the Church; that she not become again enslaved, but stand fast in her freedom.[27] The freedom of the believer in Christ is also a "freedom from," a freedom from the law, but freedom is referred to here in a polemic and antithetical sense, and refers in turn to being in Christ, because He has bought our freedom, "redeemed us from the curse of the law" (Gal. 3:13). This "freedom from" the law is thus not a standing above the law (see I Cor. 9:21), and Paul can call us to the fulfilling of the law of Christ (Gal. 6:2; cf. Rom. 13:8) in the same context as his "if ye be led of the Spirit, ye are not under the law" (Gal. 5:18; cf. Rom. 6:14).

James has often been placed in opposition to Paul, not only as regards the relation between faith and works[28] but also as regards the law. It is, however, striking that it is James who speaks of the complete royal law of freedom and calls absorption therein and practice thereof a blessed thing (Jas. 1:25, 2:8, 12).[29] This is possible only through the richness and the actuality of freedom in Christ. And this in turn, here as everywhere in the New Testament, is a matter not of appropriating an abstract philosophy but of directing attention to the meaning and the reality of freedom as the increated mystery of man's humanness.

It is obvious from the nature of this freedom that it has nothing

---

27. Cf. H. N. Ridderbos, "Vrijheid en Wet volgens Paulus' Brief aan de Galaten," *Arcana Revelata* (1951), pp. 100ff., on the threat to freedom and on freedom as a gift and its steadfast certainty and the responsibility implied therein (p. 101).

28. See my *Geloof en Rechtvaardiging* (1949); E.T., *Faith and Justification* (1954), pp. 130ff.

29. Dibelius, *Der Brief des Jakobus* (1956, 8th ed.), p. 112. He sees here an evidence that Paul did not influence all the streams of original Christianity, and that there were churches which did not view salvation as resting exclusively on faith (as did Paul) nor reject all reliance on works. Dibelius warns against identifying James's "law of freedom" with Paul's "law of the Spirit of life" (Rom. 8:2) and standing "under the law of Christ" (I Cor. 9:21). But he is forced to acknowledge — which his thesis forbids him to do — that Paul "occasionally" follows the usage of these churches and speaks of a possible fulfilling of the law (Gal. 6:2, 5:14, 23). The unsatisfactory nature of Dibelius' thesis thus becomes evident. Cf. also H. Schammberger, *Die Einheitlichkeit des Jakobusbriefes im antignostischen Kampf* (1936), p. 63. He contrasts Paul (freedom) with James (law of freedom); he sees the latter as on the way towards future Catholicism, towards moralistic teachings, etc. He finds the best parallel (p. 64) in Barn. 2:6; he finds a Judaistic legalizing tendency reappearing strongly in James. This is a misunderstanding of the whole context in which James speaks about the law.

in common with an individualistic perversion of freedom, but reveals its true meaning precisely also in the love of the other, the neighbor. This freedom fulfills the law in that way: "he that loveth another hath fulfilled the law" (Rom. 13:8)[30] The mystery of man's humanness reveals itself here, in this fulfilling of the law. It does not reveal itself in an obscure "free from," but in a love-filled "free for" and fulfills also the following of the law of Christ.

We might ask whether the New Testament concept of freedom refers only to a freedom of a specific character, to Christian freedom, and whether we can derive any conclusions from this freedom as to freedom in general, which can play such a powerful role in the heart of men. Were we to answer that the New Testament is concerned only with an isolated "freedom," that of those who have become the servants of the Lord, and that this opens no perspectives on freedom in human life in general, we should fail to recognize that freedom in Christ is the true freedom of man's humanness. This true nature, not "supernatural" but increated, does throw light on human life, which in its manifold variations is in all sorts of ways enslaved to the powers of darkness. Man's nature, as God meant it to be and as He restores it and will restore it, stands before us in Jesus Christ — in the freedom in Christ -- full of the rich perspectives of "freedom from" as well as "freedom for."

We see this already in the Old Testament, as the prayers for freedom and the songs of freedom rise to heaven from out of the need of the individual and of Israel. Liberation from that which harasses and threatens man's humanity — in general and particularly in Israel, the people of God — is viewed as the work and the blessing of God; and so also creaturely freedom, in which man can fulfill his calling and bring to expression the meaning of his humanity. The New Testament presents the freedom of man's nature not as a vague and distant ideal, but as something actually before us in the life of the Church, which in its whole existence is and must be a sign of this freedom. It has often been noted that the New Testament shows a marvelous consciousness of self, a powerful experience of freedom. Now, consciousness of self is a term which easily awakens bad associations; e.g., when we think of the sort of life (actually unaccustomed to freedom) which abstracts the "self" from its Maker and thus falls into a perverted self-consciousness. But there is a consciousness of self, in being a

30. See Schlier, *op. cit.*, p. 176: "the real and right completion of freedom is found in the mutual service of love." Cf. Paul's "I have made myself servant to all" (I Cor. 9:19); cf. also Gal. 5:13, I Pet. 4:10-11.

child of God, which can arise in a context that enables it to carry out its healing function. This is the context of freedom in Christ, which also has important implications in the area of "free from." Then we no longer deal with an abstract self-consciousness of the self-oriented man, but rather with a knowledge of the self which is structured from the freedom to which man is called through grace; the call to leave the darkness for the light of freedom. And then this consciousness sounds forth against all opposing powers, as in the triumphant words of Paul (Rom. 8:39) that nothing can separate him from the love of God in Jesus Christ; and then there is a glorying which has nothing to do with false pride: "let no man trouble me; for I bear in my body the marks of the Lord Jesus."[31]

Here — and elsewhere — there is a consciousness of impregnability, of legitimacy, of the true nature of man which is revealed in its freedom as a "being free for" and therein also as a "being free from." This concept of freedom can no longer be called formal, for it is completely concretized in actual life.

And from this now unveiled meaning of true human nature, which begins to show forth the image of God as a child of God, and from this freedom, we also gain a sharper perspective on the world. Schlier writes, and rightly so, that "in the Christian idea of freedom the breakthrough to real freedom occurs. If we comprehend what freedom is in its Christian meaning, then we have also grasped the source of every freedom."[32] In other words, the Christian idea does not imply an underevaluation of the desire for freedom found in individuals and in peoples — often so terribly outraged or threatened in their humanness — rather, it takes them very seriously, as seriously as did Paul when he speaks of the groping attempts to find God "though he be not far from every one of us" (Acts 17:27). The call for freedom, which can be heard in all ages, can be of different sorts. There can be a demand for freedom which is nothing but the lust for lawlessness, a reflection of the longing for "freedom" portrayed in Psalm 2:3, "Let us break their bands asunder, and cast their cords from us." Or, again, we can hope for a "freedom" which in actuality is slavery: "promising liberty, they themselves are the servants of corruption" (II Pet. 2:19). But

31. The "warning request" (Gal. 6:17), which arises from Paul's being a servant of the one Lord, which materializes itself in the stigmata, the need in the apostolic service, in the following of Christ (see Schlier, *op. cit.,* p. 210).

32. H. Schlier, "Das vollkommene Gesetz der Freiheit," *Die Zeit der Kirche* (1956), p. 195.

the fervid longing for freedom, in contrast to the perverting of man's humanity, is legitimate when viewed in the perspective of the human nature God intended, though its real meaning and origin may not be fully understood. The message of the Church to the world therefore lies not in the preaching of a general concept of freedom, of a concept into which each man can pour his own content, but rather in the proclamation of the gospel of Christ, in which is unveiled what being human in freedom means. And from the standpoint of the gospel it is completely clear that in every situation and against every threat liberation is never the end but it is rather the beginning: it is a renewed appeal arising from the regained — general — human nature and demanding fulfillment of human nature in this liberation. And it is certainly conceivable that such a newly contested "free from" should degenerate, and should not find true freedom in the meaning of a man or a people in the service of God and of one's neighbor, in the "free for" of true community. None the less, the light of freedom streams into the world from Christ alone, and it shows us true humanness. It is the light of the bound Christ, who fulfilled the prophecies of the Old Covenant in the coming of the Messianic Kingdom. He read Isaiah's prophecy of the bruised who should be delivered in freedom, and then said, "This day is this scripture fulfilled in your ears" (Luke 4:17-21; Isa. 61:1-2). In that day, too, men did not realize the scope of this fulfillment. The eyes of all those in the synagogue were fastened on Him, and all "wondered at the gracious words which proceeded from his mouth," but they were soon filled with wrath and sought to kill Him (Luke 4:28). But the prophecy of freedom is fulfilled and the signs of liberation are spread over the land, signs full of the richness of "free from" in the liberation from sin and guilt, from need and death, from bodily misery and demonic possession. It is the revelation of the kingdom of Christ and of that true humanness which He referred to in His statement, "ye shall be free indeed" (John 8:36). This freedom is the content of the gospel and with its immeasurable force cuts through every bond which threatens to relativize and ravage man's humanness. For over these threats — which do not honor man as the divine creation — there hangs the threat of the judgment, the judgment of the gospel of liberation as the fulfillment of the prophecy of the psalmist: "For he shall deliver the needy when he crieth; the poor also, and him that hath no helper. He shall spare the poor and needy, and shall save the souls of the needy. He shall redeem their soul from deceit and violence; and precious. shall their blood be in his sight" (Ps. 72:12-14).

And thus the light of freedom shines forth even into the eschatological perspective; the Church is directed to the ultimate revelation of freedom, until the whole creation is liberated (free from!) from its servitude to impermanence into the freedom of the glory of the children of God.[33]

We have seen that the positive insight into the true freedom of man starts from another point than many popular concepts of freedom, which begin with the idea of "free from" and see man as having power over himself and as able to make all his own decisions. In such a view, freedom is more closely defined as the possibility of man's choosing different ways, more particularly two ways, that of good or of evil, which thus lie open as juxtaposed possibilities. In the history of theology, this sort of outlook on freedom occurs in connection with the fall of man. It is here, especially when we view the freedom of the will as lost through sin and thus can speak of creaturely freedom before the fall, that the question arises whether we can speak of another freedom besides the positive richness of freedom in communion with God, the freedom of sonship: that is, whether we should not also speak of a certain formal freedom of choice in man, a freedom *utriusque partis*. Is there not, besides a material concrete freedom, a formal freedom which stands "open" before what occurs? And does not this formal freedom undeniably raise a series of problems? While true freedom may be bound up with glory now and to the *eschaton,* does there not fall over this formal freedom the shadow of this dual possibility of choice and thus also the threatening possibility of evil?

Such a formal freedom has often been posited alongside true freedom, and as an illustration thereof reference is often made to the situation before the fall and especially to the "probationary command" given to man in paradise. Does not this "test command" clearly imply formal freedom? And how must we then view the relation between the positive nature of true freedom and this "uncertain" freedom, with which man faced a choice? For we can hardly describe true freedom in terms of standing at a crossroad; it means, rather, walking along one road, and being continually reminded thereof by way of the gospel of freedom. And how is this to be understood when we see next to it freedom as choice,

33. Note the connection between glory and freedom (Luther: *"herrliche Freiheit"*) ; see O. Michel, *Der Brief an die Römer* (1955), p. 174.

as a power not to sin (*posse non peccare*) but also as the power
to sin (*posse peccare*)? Do we not face here a dual concept of
freedom, implying an unmistakable antinomy?

These questions as to the nature of human freedom arise especially when we turn our attention to the question of the origin of
sin. Only consider how many times the origin of sin has been
ascribed to this human freedom of choice, implying this twofold
power of man's nature and of his creaturely existence: to sin or not
to sin; a good part and an evil part of his nature.

Theologians have tried in various ways to incorporate this formal
freedom, and the power to choose between good and evil which
it implies, into the intention of God's work at creation. Thus it is
said that God loves freedom and thus respects this freedom of
man. "God takes delight in the unrestricted freedoms of the
desert animals" says Stauffer[34] in an attempt to show the dynamic
of human freedom. God wants a free man, not a mechanical tool
or a marionette or a pawn that can be moved at His pleasure. And
with this principle of freedom, continues Stauffer, "the possibility
of rebellion of this will, created free, is in principle given."

This idea can be carried still further, and we can speak of
a risk taken by God, or of an inner dialectic of freedom, or of the
tragedy of freedom.[35] Though all such views derive from an
initial contrast between freedom and compulsion, they seek to find
the origin of sin via human freedom and thus in a sense to make
it rationally understandable. Such views seek to include both the
"material" and "formal" freedom of man under the one aspect of
the rich endowments and the goodness of created man. It was
indeed realized that the wealth of the freedom of sonship (even into
the *eschaton*) was an unshadowed wealth which did not fall in
the category of "possibility" but could be grasped only as reality;
but nevertheless the attempt at synthesis was not given up, with
the result that in many views of freedom we can see an inner
antinomy. Men tried, within this antinomy, not so much to
explain the origin of sin as to indicate the sphere within which
it could arise, the sphere of human freedom of choice. This formal
freedom was thus generally so defined that man was created free
to choose for himself between good or evil, placed before a cross-

---

34. E. Stauffer, *Die Theologie des Neuen Testaments* (1941), p. 46. See
    Job 39:5; "Who hath sent out the wild ass free? or who hath loosed the
    bands of the wild ass?"
35. Cf. N. Berdyaev, *Vrijheid en Geest,* pp. 155ff.

road, in a situation which was still open. Against the background of the contrast between freedom and compulsion, a further idea was often added, that man was necessarily created with this freedom of choice because God did not wish compulsion and desired this kind of freedom.

It is undeniable, in my opinion, that if we take this line of approach we can very quickly wander into an impassable and tangled forest of unbiblical thoughts and speculations. The simple way in which human freedom is often defined as a double possibility, as freedom of choice, arises from an abstract and irreligious and neutral anthropological analysis of human freedom. The analysis sees this "freedom" to choose either of two directions as belonging to the essence of man as created "good." Freedom is then the possibility of choice, the open choice, and the choice of sin is then the demonstration, the manifestation of human freedom. Further thought on this formal freedom sometimes provoked a certain hesitation in relation to the essential goodness of man as originally created by God — a hesitation which is understandable in view of the Belgic Confession's definition (Art. 14) of this goodness as lying in the fact that God is man's true life. The Confession speaks of man created by God as "good, righteous and holy, able with his will to accord with the will of God in all things." It is clear enough that this "ability" does not refer to a formal and still un-fulfilled possibility without actuality, an abstract ability to choose. This is clear from the fact that "good, righteous and holy" precedes "able." In the original draft of the Confession, these three words were followed by "wholly perfect in all things," words which were later replaced by "able to accord . . . ." According to Bavinck, the reason for this change is not completely certain, though he rejects as completely without basis the suggestion that the "wholly perfect" of the original draft was turned down as exaggerated.[36]

Calvinist theologians, says Bavinck, indeed acknowledged that the first man had not reached the highest possible state in all things, and their view of the *status integritatis* was a sober one, but this did not affect their affirmation of man's original goodness: "good, righteous and holy" (Belgic Confession, Art. 14); "good . . . created in true righteousness and holiness" (Heidelberg Catechism, Lord's Day 3). And because of this it was difficult to ascribe without hesitation the possibility of a choice in either direction to the

36. Bavinck, *op. cit.*, II, 529; III, 44.

essence of man because of God's "love of freedom."[37] For to do this would be to ignore the fact that a choice for evil as an arbitrary choice would be in conflict with and a perversion of true creaturely freedom. It is thus impossible to combine the material freedom of the child of God and the formal freedom of choice in a satisfying and meaningful synthesis, since in such a synthesis we must always eventually incorporate arbitrariness into the idea of "freedom" rather than excluding it. The choice for sin then immediately becomes a manifestation of human freedom — though we go on to speak of sin as actually being slavery. Thus too, with such a view of freedom the depth of the fall can never be made intelligible, for in the fall the opposite of human freedom becomes evident; namely, man's arbitrary choice, the enslaved will (*servum arbitrium*). Man's freedom and the fall are not related as possibility and realization. We often hear of the enigmatic aspects of the fall, since the fall is that of a man created good; but this does not refer to a psychological riddle (namely, how man could be tempted) but rather to the unfathomable nature of the freedom of man which is lost in becoming arbitrary choice.[38]

37. Bavinck, *op. cit.*, II, 534-535. It is striking, in this context, that Bavinck speaks of the *posse stare* and *posse non errare, peccare, mori* and then says of the possibility of sinning and dying that it "forms no part, no piece, no content of the image of God, but was its boundary, the limit, the circumference." He refers to Wendelinus (as cited by Heppe, *Dogmatik,* p. 181) who said that before the fall the ability not to sin (*posse non peccare*) did belong, but the ability to sin did not belong, to the image of God. We can see here a wrestling with the concept of freedom similar to Bavinck's. The complete image of God was to be fully revealed in the ability not to sin. The image was to be completed, and the possibility of sinning and dying conquered and annihilated.

38. The impossibility of a rational synthesis between true freedom and formal freedom can be seen in K. Rahner, who attempts to clarify the problem through the idea of the "sphere" of freedom. "An unqualified withdrawal of the possibility of a factual and morally wrong choice would have been equivalent to the abolishment of the sphere of freedom" (K. Rahner, "Würde und Freiheit des Menschen," *Schriften zur Theologie,* II (1955), 261-262). The eschatological freedom of the *beati* is, he says, no evidence against this argument: "they have completely achieved their freedom" — an answer which does little to solve the problem of the hypothecated "sphere" of freedom to choose evil! Nor does his statement that a compulsory abolition of moral evil in this world is Utopian. There is a noteworthy parallel between the outlook of Rahner on the sphere of freedom and that of A. Kuyper, who in connection with this sphere wrote that "God cannot hinder the rational creature from rejecting in his heart or in his deed the good and choosing evil. That must be left free" (*E Voto,* I, 65). Cf. also K. Schilder, *Heidelbergse*

It is furthermore clear that we may never use such a "formal freedom" in connection with the image of God. As if man could ever show the likeness of God in the possibility of choosing evil — *possibilitas utriusque partis, in bonam et malam partem!* The only adequate basis is that of the affirmation of man's good and creaturely freedom in his communion with God. The freedom of man can be adequately described only in this context. If we begin with the positive character of the good creation of God, we must say of man's freedom, with Brunner, "thus the maximum of man's dependence on God is also the maximum of his freedom, and his freedom diminishes as he moves further from his source and origin, from God." And a hesitation to combine a formal freedom with the true freedom of man in the richness of communion with God, in some sort of dualistic concept of freedom, gives evidence of a realization of the problems involved in such a synthesis.[39]

It is not difficult to point to the characteristic problems of a dualistic concept of freedom. We might begin with the formulation of Julius Müller, who distinguished between real and formal freedom.[40]

"Real freedom" is freedom in which man is truly free. It is the freedom which according to the New Testament is the possession of the believers, who have been liberated through Christ, a freedom which does not rule out their obedience and submission but which rather coincides fully with these. With this

---

Catechismus, I, 324. He says our freedom is "hedged about, but not determined." Concerning what Adam could do, he says "for that was his freedom." We should consider, as over against this, the "free" eating of all the trees in the garden (Gen. 2:16).

39. E. Brunner, *Der Mensch in Widerspruch*, pp. 267, 269. In this connection, the views of H. Heidegger, writing in 1700, are striking (*Corpus theologiae Christianae*, Loci VI, XCVIII, p. 227). He says that liberty or freedom of the will is not the ability to sin or not to sin, and says of it *"id occupandum ante omnia est,"* for *"sic enim nec Deo, nec coelitibus immutabiliter bonis competeret,"* citing Rom. 6:20 ("when ye were the servants of sin, ye were free from righteousness") and John 8:36. His meaning is clear from his approving citation of Seneca: *"Deo parere vera libertas est."* Cf. his opposition to the idea of Adam being created indifferent to good and evil (p. 228); such indifference is *"imperfectio, vitium, prima peccati origo et defectio a Deo. Liber, non indifferens, a Deo creatus est."*

40. J. Müller, *Die Chr. Lehre von der Sünde*, II, (3d ed., 1849). The page references in the material which follows are: 6ff., 13, 15, 17-18, 20-21, 36. See also for the distinction between real and formal freedom, J. M. Hasselaar, *Erfzonde en Vrijheid* (1953), p. 82, and Karl Barth, *Kirchliche Dogmatik*, III, 3, 355.

view of freedom, Müller gets into difficulty in his chapter on the "possibility" of sin. For this rich and positive freedom can not be related to evil. It is precisely the being free from sin; it is freedom in Christ, the freedom of the child of God as the true and divinely intended humanness of man. Though this freedom is to be fully realized only in the future, in the freedom of the glory of the children of God, when creation itself will be delivered from its servitude to corruption (Rom. 8:21), nevertheless Scripture speaks of this freedom as in principle present in this dispensation: true liberty. It is liberation from all that which hinders true humanness, and it has nothing to do with a formal freedom as a "possibility" of choosing either good or evil. But it is to this formal freedom that Müller turns his attention, as he postulates another freedom besides actual freedom, namely freedom as the power to choose either good or evil. This power, man's formal freedom, is not at all a product of fantasy, he says, but rather is the necessary presupposition of man's consciousness of guilt.

This consciousness of guilt can operate only when it presupposes that we could have done otherwise than we did, and thus presupposes our freedom. Now it is a priori evident that we face a series of problems with these two juxtaposed concepts of freedom; this is already plain in the terms themselves, for making real freedom and formal freedom coordinate is wholly artificial. "Real" freedom is actually nothing more than a tautology, while the concept "formal freedom" offers no substantial contribution to clarity. Müller subsumes the two different things under the one concept of "freedom," and thus his very terminology reveals the tensions inherent in this dual concept of freedom. He himself is occasionally conscious that this dual concept leads him into great difficulty since each term appears to exclude the other. For does not actual freedom in the richness of being a child of God exclude formal freedom, and does not formal freedom throw deep shadows over true freedom? Nevertheless Müller tries to arrive at a solution by pointing to a certain harmony, for true freedom, "the full determination of man for the good, which excludes every possibility of evil" would be inconceivable if it "did not develop from formal freedom."

There are indeed not two concepts of freedom, he says, but rather two moments in one and the same concept of freedom. Formal freedom does indeed imply the ability to do otherwise, and hence appears to be in conflict with true freedom, but it is precisely the intention of formal freedom to become the true freedom of the child of God.

Müller thus tries to rise above the apparent conflict between the two concepts by making formal freedom a presupposition of true freedom, a means to reach the goal of true freedom. It is clear, however, that this is no solution since the conflict can not be removed by such means. For we still have to do with two differing concepts of freedom. Müller says that when man's free will has taken on its true content, then it no longer is formal freedom. And besides, we confront the fact that this road from formal to true freedom was not the road man followed, and it becomes clear from Müller's more detailed account of the origin of sin that it is impossible to combine true and formal freedom in a synthesis.[41]

As Müller distinguishes between formal and real freedom, so Emil Brunner distinguishes between formal and material freedom.[42] It is something obvious for him, long since well-known to theologians and philosophers. Material freedom can be lost, formal freedom not, since the latter is characteristic of man and may be called an aspect of God's image. Brunner means by material freedom the same that Müller meant by real freedom. It is the characteristic freedom which exists where the Spirit of the Lord is, freedom in dependence on God, freedom which is of complete stature only when man remains in this dependence. Sin stands over against this freedom, so that freedom and love are related as "freedom in and through love." But there is also, besides this material freedom, another sort of freedom, formal freedom. Brunner does not wish to have it relativize the loss of material (real) freedom; this was "completely and unconditionally lost."

Since material freedom is true freedom, "everything yet remaining to freedom counts as nothing compared to the loss of this true freedom," and thus we speak of formal freedom, "and deny its essential importance." For the essential thing in man's nature is

----

41. Müller, *op. cit.*, II, 97-108. He speaks of an "original self-decision" which we can point to only by going beyond the realm of time and seeking the origin of our freedom of the will in the extra-temporal, in a fatal decision that precedes all our temporal sinful decisions. The primary decision falls in "a self-decision lying beyond the sphere of earthly life." The reference to "intelligible" freedom reveals the antinomy in Müller's concept of freedom by first placing formal freedom next to true freedom. Müller cites Philo, Plotinus and Origen as supporting his outlook. The development of theology followed other ways, and only recently could reflection on the concept of freedom lead to a new understanding of this idea (p. 108).

42. E. Brunner, *Das Gebot* and *Der Mensch im Widerspruch*. The page citations for the material which follows are: *Das Gebot*, 65, 472, and *Widerspruch*, 259-272. Cf. also *Dogmatik*, II, 142.

his relation to God, and even if man still retains his formal freedom, this protects him not at all against disaster. We might remind ourselves, in considering this view of Brunner, of Calvin's somewhat similar outlook (*Institutes* II, II, 7). He also acknowledged that man on the road of sin chooses through free will and not through compulsion, but then asks what importance this has in the context. But Brunner suddenly gives this formal freedom such an accent that without it the problems of "reason and revelation" and "faith and culture" become irredeemably confused. This importance of formal freedom is related to the fact that it is concerned with being-a-subject, (*Sein-in-Entscheidung*). It is noteworthy that Brunner first speaks of the lost true freedom (material freedom) and now goes on to refer to free will as "the presupposition and the essence of man's humanness." And precisely here, on the point of the essence of man, the problem of the dual concept of freedom again comes to the fore. For Brunner's concern for formal freedom as "essence" of man raises the question of how he can harmonize this freedom with what he has previously called true freedom. If formal freedom means that man is not compelled to act and freely chooses his own way, we must consider that Scripture refers to precisely this active and freely willing man as the slave of sin. Brunner may call formal freedom the essential characteristic of reason, but he is then dealing with another "essence" than that with which he was concerned when he placed so much emphasis on true freedom. Brunner himself says that true freedom does not mean *liberum arbitrium indifferentiae*, freedom to choose regardless of good or evil, since such freedom of choice would be a perversion of freedom. What remains in Brunner's concept of formal freedom is the ontic structure of man's nature in distinction from that of the animal, the form of human nature, which leads man to art and science, civilization and culture. But it thus becomes impossible to bring the concepts of formal and material freedom together under the common denominator "freedom." How can we place true freedom next to a "freedom" in which man can say yes or no to evil? And can we say that the Bible fixes our attention on such a dual concept of freedom?

In spite of the undeniable problems which in this manner are always revived, theologians have time and again asked the question whether when we examine man's originally good nature we do not encounter *de facto* an ability to sin, a *posse peccare*, and if so whether we should not honor this *possibilitas* with the name of freedom. Can we escape postulating a formal concept of freedom — an ability to choose at the crossroads — along with true freedom? As answer to such questions, it has often been said that God created the "possibility" of sin, that He created man so that he could fall and then let man choose, freely, whether he would follow God's way or his own way. Herman Bavinck especially devoted much attention to this problem.[34]

It was not God's will, said Bavinck, instantly to lift man above the possibility of sin and death through some act of power (we should note that the word "possibility" plays an important role in Bavinck's approach). The *possibilitas peccandi*, the possibility of sinning, is from God. It was an "objective possibility," in accordance with which God created the angels and men so that they could sin and fall. This possibility is, he says, without a doubt willed by God. Bavinck then brings man's freedom into context when he writes that man did not yet possess the highest and unlosable freedom, that of not being able to sin. The image of God still had its limit, in the possibility of sin. Man was good, but he might change; he walked on the right road, but he might yet turn away from it. Bavinck even says that this could not be otherwise, for whatever is formed can become deformed, and thus a creature naturally incapable of sin is a contradiction in terms. The possibility thus lies in the nature of created things, and Bavinck goes on to analyze this possibility more closely. It is not simply implied in the reality of sin, for Bavinck calls attention to other factors, to man's imagination as a power, so that the breaking of God's command was proposed as becoming like God, to man's being body (*sarx*), to his susceptibility to temptation. Bavinck does not, with all this, intend to give an explanation of the origin of sin. Reference to the possibility willed by God is all that can be said on the subject. "How this possibility became actuality is a mystery, and will doubtless remain such." He rejects every rational explanation, since it would not do justice to the irrationality and lawlessness of sin. Bavinck wrestles with what he himself calls "the greatest riddle and cross of reason"; namely, the actuality of sin in a world created good. But he discusses it nevertheless. He considers the "not yet" of man's created nature, the not yet possessing the highest good, and discusses the good but changeable status of the first man and the unchangeable eschatological glory of the child of God. At this point in his reflections, Paul's words in I Corinthians 15:45-47 play an important role; the apostle distinguishes between the first man, who was earthy and of the

43. Bavinck, *Gereformeerde Dogmatiek*, III, 2, 27, 44-48, 53.

earth, and Christ, the Lord from heaven, who has become a quickening spirit. According to Bavinck, this comparison and contrast between Adam and Christ has great importance also for our understanding of the fall. He relates the possibility of sin and man's being "of the earth, earthy." There is a difference between the origin and nature of sin in angels and in man. Man was not spirit but earthy, "weaker and more fragilely organized," and as such gave Satan a fitting opportunity for temptation. It is thus that Bavinck explains Paul's placing a close relation between man's material nature and his sin. In man's being flesh, earthy, lies the possibility of sin. This does not imply the explanation of sin through the flesh, as many have thought, for then sin is implicit in creation and ultimately in the Creator. Materiality is in itself no sin, but it is the occasion and stimulus for sin, so that Bavinck thinks he can speak of the "inducement" for Satan, man's susceptibility to temptation, in his nature as a material, psychic being.

We have here an attempt to clarify sin, if not in its actuality then in its possibility, by way of the anthropological structure of man as creature. We do indeed arrive at some insight into the fall of man through this concept of the "inducement" to temptation which lay in the weak and fragile human structure.[44] But it is clear that we can not in this way designate the possibility of sinning as a necessity, for we would then be unable to escape attributing the actuality of sin to man's fragile and weak material nature. With this approach, in other words, possibility and actuality can not be separated.[45] Nor can we base this approach on 1 Corinthians 15. Paul is not there concerned with an explanation of the origin and the possibility of sin. He refers to the overflowing richness of Christ and His salvation, even into the *eschaton* and the resurrection of the dead.

In order to show the richness and glory of Christ, he compares Christ and Adam, the first man. He refers back to Genesis 2:7, where we read of the divine act through which man became a living being. The first man is earthy, from the earth, in contrast to Christ, who is from heaven (I Cor. 15:47; cf. 48-49).

---

44. We could more rightly say that the "inducement" to temptation lay in man's innocence. Cf. D. Bonhoeffer, *Verzoeking* (1953), p. 17.
45. Bavinck, *op. cit.*, II, 417. It is noteworthy that he mentions the distinction between men and angels (as spirits). One could conclude that the "possibility" of the fall of the angels becomes all the more impenetrable to the understanding, since in them the "inducement" to sin because of flesh would be wholly absent, they being spirits. Bavinck does not refer to the problem of "possibility" in regard to the angels at all.

But this contrast does not entitle us to draw conclusions regarding a "possibility" which lies in this earthy nature, and especially in man's material nature. The origin of the first man is contrasted with that of the last Adam who is the quickening spirit (I Cor. 15:45; cf. 15:22), and in this there is also an eschatological aspect: "as we have borne the image of the earthy, we shall also bear the image of the heavenly" (I Cor. 15:49). Paul does refer to the creaturely aspect of the first man, but there is no reason at all to feel that he was here concerned with the problem of the origin of sin (and its possibility), and indeed it is precisely the creatureliness, the createdness, of man which is his glory and his essence in his total existence.[46] And that is no humiliation of man. It becomes an humiliation only when man no longer understands the meaning of his createdness and dependence and rebels against it. And thus this createdness, this earthy nature, can never be a means to clarifying the origin of sin. Evidently I Corinthians 15 has been related to the origin (and possibility) of sin because theologians were concerned with the problems of the changeable and the unchanging, of freedom perverted in the fall and the definitive and eschatological freedom in Christ, of the transition from immortality to death and that immortality which Christ brought in the transition from death to life.[47]

And with such problems we do indeed encounter the deepest mysteries of the whole Biblical witness, those which Bavinck called not only a riddle but also the heaviest cross of reason. We can clearly see that all these problems center in the essence of creaturely freedom. At the same time we understand that the actuality of the perversion of freedom, against the will of God, can not and may not be explained from other component factors, but can only be confessed as guilt. The outlines of freedom become visible only from within the full Messianic actuality. The light of grace shines on true freedom on our way of deep shame and guilt. We understand through salvation in Christ that the perspective which we see through the windows of Holy Scripture is not that of eternal recurrence but rather that of eschatological freedom. This recovery of the disdained sonship, this coming to one's true self, as the prodigal son found himself and the way to his father's house — these we may not obscure through our terminology, through

---

46. Grosheide, *Commentaar*, p. 543. He refers to "man," from which it appears "earthy" does not refer merely to the body. Cf. Kittel, *Theologisches Wörterbuch*, VI, 417, s.v., *pneuma*.
47. See K. Schilder, *Wat is de Hemel?* (1935), p. 125.

talk of a *felix culpa,* and surely not through an attempted explanation of sin.

The riddle of sin of which Bavinck speaks[48] can not be elucidated by appeal to man's weakness because of his material and fragile nature, but according to the light of Scripture can only be seen as an enigma of man created good who became bad through his fall, his rebellion, which alienated him from the glory and from the friendship of God. It brought him on a self-chosen way of inner and far-reaching unfreedom, and thus became the enduring rebellion of his life. Of this transition there is no elucidation, now or in the future, to be given which would make this step towards alienation psychologically or anthropologically understandable. Every attempt in this direction — and there have been several attempts made — every attempt to explain the possibility of sin through man's createdness has always led to attempting to explain sin itself, to place it within causal and explanatory relationships, and thus to take away or at least to relativize its character of guilt. Now, theologians have often spoken of the *possibilitas peccandi* and of the potentially alterable goodness of created man,[49] but it is clear that these terms and references often mean no more than to point out, beginning with the actuality of sin, that the fall of man was not "impossible" but "possible." But it is further clear that we then can not speak of this ability as an ordinary "possibility" like other possibilities, which always throw some light on their actualization. If we speak in such fashion of the possibility of sinning, we throw no light on the matter, — just as it seems impossible to understand what Bavinck actually meant when he wrote that God created the possibility of sin.[50]

When Barth speaks of the "ontological" impossibility of sin, he means that it is impossible for man to fall out of the grace of God. No matter how much sin as an actual power has loaded

---

48. Bavinck, *op. cit.*, III, 29.
49. See Heidegger, *Corpus theologiae*, p. 228.
50. Bavinck, *op. cit.*, III, 2. See also Th. L. Haitjema, *Dogmatiek als Apologie* (1948), p. 192. He writes about man as "indeed created in the image of God, but nevertheless an earthy and material being" who presented Satan with "a suitable opportunity for temptation." The problem lies in the words "but" and "suitable opportunity," though Haitjema calls sin "the mystery of the evil will, the great riddle." Cf. Schilder, *Heidelbergse Catechismus*, I, 325-326. He speaks also of the "possibility of temptation" — which is something else again — which God held before man, and of the "possibility" of abandonment. Cf. H. Vogel, *Gott in Christo* (1952), p. 469. He warns against the danger of trying to understand the possibility of sin because of the *posse peccare.*

man with guilt and shame, his essence — his relation to God — could not be affected, since God's grace triumphed over this choice and excluded it ontologically.[51] But in the problem of the *possibilitas peccandi* which has concerned theologians since Augustine, the question is somewhat different; namely, whether sin as actuality can or cannot be explained. In order to clarify to some extent man's "arbitrariness" through this "sphere of action," man's "freedom" to choose either way has often been simplistically incorporated in this "possibility," so that sin is derived from the freedom given man by God.

But sin can never be elucidated from the goodness of the creation of God. This does not at all imply an excusing of sin because of the "mysteriousness" of evil. We certainly may not speak of the "riddle" of sin if we mean thereby that sin cannot be understood, in the same sense that many other things cannot be understood. "Riddle" — that oft used word[52] — can be justifiably used only when it refers to the guilt of sin, precisely in the light of God's good creation, in which man could find no "inducement" to rebel against his Maker. Scripture also speaks of this guilt, which can never be causally explained: "Lo, this only have I found, that God hath made man upright, but they have sought out many inventions" (Eccles. 7:29) *(DEVICES, EXCUSES)*

Man — the man of God — must seek inventions because they are not there, because he does not see them before him, neither in communion with God nor in his own good life. Thus sin is the senselessness of unjustified rebellion clashing with God's own work, clashing with the richness and goodness of the human nature created by Him. In that sense, sin is a riddle. This riddling character occurs again in every sin, as in Israel, where it led to the question of divine concern for His sinful people: "O my people, what have I done unto thee? and wherein have I wearied thee? testify against me" (Micah 6:3, and see 4, 5). That is more than simple unintelligibility or simple riddle.

The depth of man's guilt is here revealed, which Christ Himself with respect to the sin against Him described thus: "They hated me without a cause" (John 15:25. See Ps. 35:19 and 69:5, and John 15:22: "If I had not come and spoken to them, they had not had sin: but now they have no cloke for their sin"). This is a different description of the "riddle" of sin than that given when men try

51. See Chaps. III and IX of my *The Triumph of Grace in the Theology of Karl Barth.*
52. Besides Bavinck, see also, e.g., Schilder, *op. cit.,* I, 324.

to escape its force in the "tragedy" of evil or the "fatality" of freedom or in an ineluctable dualism.

The darkness of this "without cause," this *contra voluntatem Dei,* can only be understood and confessed in the light of the love of God, which is not an answer to our love but to our enmity: "God, who is rich in mercy, for his great love wherewith he loved us even when we were dead in sins . . ." (Eph. 2:4-5).

These fatiguing cogitations on the origin of sin, on *unde malum,* can never find rest except at the point where there is vision — without reason — that penetrates sin in all its riddling character; and this vision is from within the freedom of the sons of God. This freedom in its fullness is an eschatological fruit of salvation. It is the fruit of the Holy Spirit in the power of the "once" of Hebrews, of the revealed *mysterion* (Rom. 16:25) and the deep content of the profession of the perseverance of the saints.

We have already noted in passing that the so-called probationary command has often been referred to in support of the concept of formal freedom, since it is held that this implies a possibility of choice of good or evil, and a choice which the Creator Himself gave to man. Does this command not imply that God placed man at the crossroads of good and evil, with a free will, before a choice of two paths, a choice presupposed and pointed out by God Himself?

But there is reason to question whether the term "probationary command" is actually a correct expression of that which Scripture means to tell us in the Genesis account. We must first of all note that Genesis does not say that man was placed before a neutral and indifferent choice. We read of a command that was given man: "Of every tree of the garden thou mayest freely eat: but of the tree of the knowledge of good and evil, thou shalt not eat of it: for in the day that thou eatest thereof thou shalt surely die" (Gen. 2:16-17). It is in any event not so that God gave man the "freedom" to choose his own way according to his own will, to choose between two possibilities, for only one way is shown him on which he may walk. As the Belgic Confession (Art. 14) says, this was the command of life. The other "way" was emphatically placed under the threat of the judgment of death, and it is the serpent who later interprets the command in another way than as this most serious warning: "Ye shall not surely die: for God doth know that in the day ye eat thereof, then your eyes shall be opened, and ye shall be as gods, knowing good and evil" (Gen. 3:4, 5). It is from this side that the dialectic of freedom is called up, that the two ways are presented to man as "possibilities" open to his "free will," and that the choice for evil (*in malam partem*) is seen as a meaningful choice to be seriously considered. But God's command is a command of life, which does not leave man to a choice, nor compel him to a choice between two ways, but rather shows him with the utmost emphasis one way, the way of freedom, the way of obedience. As Humbert says, "the command is absolute and unconditional; it does not propose a choice for man, but it imposes a single attitude, that of obedience and faith. The solemn menace of Genesis 2:17 is not prelude to a "test," but is meant to prevent any willing of disobedience."[53] We might then well ask whether the description of the command of God as a "probationary" command does not awaken the misunderstanding that God presented man with "freedom" to go left or right, to choose good or evil. Man is, rather, called to obedience in this command. And thus this "command of life" can hardly be used to support a formal concept of freedom, namely, the freedom to choose evil.

We can also consider later texts which have been brought in to support this concept of formal freedom. Thus, for example, Deuteronomy 30:15: "I have set before thee life and good, and death and evil." But it is clear that this does not at all refer to an abstract secularized free will, or to an autarchic choice which is calmly recognized as a "possibility" of man, of Israel. Consider the verses which follow. "I command thee this day to love the Lord thy God, to walk in his ways" (v. 16). The other way is rejected and the threat of judgment placed over it, if the heart should turn to it (v. 17). As Jahwe once again holds before the people "life and death, blessing and cursing," we hear again the command of life: "therefore, choose life, that both thou and thy seed shall live" (v. 19). This command is a command to life and to freedom. The "either — or" of Israel's history, even as Elijah's call for the people to choose on Mt. Carmel (I Kings 18:21), is not at all the proclamation of a self-directing and autonomous free will, but rather the outstretched finger of God, pointing to a single way. And all the warnings and threats which surround this "either — or" make sense only as emphatic underlinings of the message regarding this one way. If Israel does not heed the command to life, or if Israel "chooses" for Baal, that is not a manifestation of its freedom, not an ontological freedom of the will, but an endangering of freedom and the acceptance of an enslaved will (cf. Deut. 30:18, 20). There is never a trace of the two choices as in balance, as two ways which are placed on an equal footing. The threats against disobedience can sometimes be strongly emphasized, for example in Deuteronomy 28, where verses 1 to 14 speak of blessings and 15 to 68 of curses, so that Noth can note that the emphasis in the chapter is one-sidedly ·on the curses; but he also adds that obedience and disobedience, blessings and curses, are not on the same level, and seen from the law's standpoint are not two choices placed before man in the same way as two possibilities.[54]

For precisely this abundance of threats is a very strong indication of the one way shown Israel, the way in which it can walk in truth and share in freedom: "they shall come out against thee one way, and flee before thee seven ways" (Deut. 28:7).

There are other places where a similar choice is given Israel, for example: "if it seem evil unto you to serve the Lord, choose you this day whom ye shall serve" — preceded by "serve ye the Lord" (Josh. 24:14, 15). And the same point could be repeated. It is also surely true that the point which holds for Israel holds all the more when man was originally placed, in the goodness of his creation, before the command of life. And if we there seek a synthesis between the freedom given by God and a formal freedom, the freedom to choose evil, we shall inevitably fail in this dualistic concept of freedom, for the choice for sin perverts and does not reveal a free will. And our unsuccessful striving for such a synthesis can be based only on a concept of a neutral "freedom" as part of the essence of man. If we do not abstract man's essence, and thus also his creaturely freedom, from God, if we do not see freedom as a release for arbitrary choice, then we shall not wish nor be able to combine true freedom and the *servum arbitrium*, the enslaved will. That is doubtless the basic reason for the protest of Luther and Calvin against the natural freedom of the will. That protest was not an expression of disdain for the ontic structure of human nature, but it was concerned to protect our view of genuine humanness, which has no connection with arbitrary choice. We can never see freedom as a gift of God if we begin with such an arbitrary "free" will. Our understanding of this true freedom is an exclusive fruit of divine revelation,

54. M. Noth, *Gesammelte Aufsätze zum Alten Testament* (1957), p. 160; cf. pp. 168-169. Cf. also W. H. Gispen, *Leviticus*, p. 370, on the similar situation in Lev. 16.

since fallen man can be made aware only of his own unfreedom. And man is so completely under delusion of this arbitrary free will that it takes a lifetime to become accustomed to the light of genuine freedom. It needs to be continually preached, and in such a way that our treatment of the law and the gospel takes up the enslaved will as well as the truly free will. For the law and the gospel take man away from the illusion of the crossroads at which he supposes he can choose either way arbitrarily. They break through the darkness of the "indifferent will," and the delusion which continually obsesses man on the path of sin. The light of the holy command breaks forth: "He hath shewed thee, O man, what is good; and what doth the Lord require of thee, but to do justly, and to love mercy, and to walk humbly with thy God?" (Mic. 6:8). It is knowing and practicing this good, this humility in the walk with God, which shape freedom — that freedom which in new responsibility[55] is understood and experienced more and more as true freedom. And when the actuality of evil — not only its possibility — manifests itself, then we hear the command of life: "But thou, O man of God, flee these things..." (I Tim. 6:11).

It is not without a very deep meaning that Jesus Christ called His yoke easy and His burden light (Matt. 11:30). And John speaks of the richness of freedom and conquest, in the context of the child of God, thus: "his commandments are not grievous" and this truth becomes revealed in the reality of the new freedom, in the reality of sonship: "For whatsoever is born of God overcometh the world" (I John 5:3-4).

55. See D. Bonhoeffer, *Ethik* (1949), p. 196: "freedom has open eyes."

CHAPTER TEN

THE MAN OF GOD

Now that we have seen again and again, in various contexts, how much the relation of man to God dominates the whole Biblical picture of man and the message to us contained therein, we wish in this summary chapter to examine the meaning of a unique expression which occurs twice in the New Testament, namely the term "man of God." We hear it used in the call to flee those things through which men err from the faith and thus pierce themselves through with sorrows: "But thou, O man of God, flee these things . . ." (I Tim. 6:11). And we encounter it again in another context, in which the power and usefulness of Scripture are referred to: "All scripture is given by inspiration of God, and is profitable for doctrine, for reproof, for correction, for instruction in righteousness, that the man of God may be perfect, thoroughly furnished unto all good works" (II Tim. 3:16, 17).

It is striking that these two Scriptural passages on the man of God speak of a flight and of the preparation for a task. Nor are these two specifications to be taken in isolation from each other. Consider that the "flee these things" is directly followed by "fight the good fight of faith, lay hold on eternal life," and that the preparation through Scripture mentioned in II Timothy 3:16 and 17 is in a context of earnest warnings. Thus the picture of the man of God in his unity which rises before us in one of a fleeing which at the same time implies a total preparation for the future. The man of God becomes visible in the sanctifying of all of life. The expression "man of God" is taken over from the Old Testament and refers to a close relationship to God; it is used (e.g., as applied to Moses, David, Elijah) with reference to their calling, their special commission, by which they act and speak in God's name. But it is evident that Paul uses the term in a more general sense to refer to the believer. In the first passage (I Tim. 6:11) there might still be a reference to Timothy's special commission and qualification, but in the second (II Tim. 3:17) the general nature of the reference is obvious. Bouma suspects that the term was an

antiquated one which went out of fashion in later Old Testament
days but "which was preserved in religious usage through the
special care of God and was revived by Paul." However that may
be, this expression does point to a special relation of belonging in
which the believer is placed through his freely given salvation, and
which decisively directs and completes his life in a new responsibility
which is not partial but total.[1]

— The man of God — that is surely the complete opposite of an
abstract and neutral view of man. It is man drawn out of the
darkness to the light, therein being man, the man of God, fully
prepared for every good work, placed in the midst of the world,
actively and dynamically there to fulfill his calling. His life receives
a new importance and becomes a meaningful and goal-conscious
life, a life that is really of some use. It is evidently not so that
man fades away as the glory of divine grace manifests itself. The
opposite is much more the case: the blessing of God illuminates
his every feature. The rebirth in sonship, the becoming man of
God, is the direct opposite of annihilation. All attempts to weaken
the force of Scripture on this point through a false religiosity are
the opposite of the *soli Deo gloria*. This glory does not mean that
man must be denigrated or despised, for that is precisely not
the intent of God. The *gloria Dei* is bound up with Immanuel, God
with us, always, into the *eschaton*: "the tabernacle of God is with
men, and he shall dwell with them" (Rev. 21:3).

It is the grace of God which restores life, which takes human
nature into His service and gives it a place in the Kingdom. True
human nature does not become obscured on the road of divine
activity but is made luminous in all the contexts of the divine
redemption. But this is accompanied with an earnest warning
against any misunderstanding. When the great light shines forth,
then this new humanness which occupies so much of the Bible's
attention is revealed as the opposite of every illusion of greatness
wherein man glorifies and honors himself. In the importance of
this new human nature which now appears, man's guilt is not
forgotten, but remains in knowledge as the darkness into which

1. C. Bouma, *Commentaar*, p. 215. For other examples of Old Testament
usage, see *ibid., ad loc.;* and Kittel, *Theologisches Wörterbuch*, *s.v.,
anthropos tou theou*. For the relation of belonging, see Zahn (Wohlenberg) , p. 209. Note that Jesus Christ was called the "Holy One of God"
by the demons (Mark 1:24, Luke 4:34) ; cf. John 6:69 and Septuagint
translation of Ps. 105:26, on Aaron. For the total nature of this
responsibility, see II Tim. 3:17.

the light of grace with all its blessings shone.[2] The last book of
the Bible is full of adulation for the Lamb (Rev. 5, etc.), and
when the twenty-four elders stand before the throne they "cast
their crowns before the throne" (Rev. 4:10-11). As man is
revealed in his true nature, the light is that of grace, and man's
humanness is then clearly delineated in all its importance. Thus
the point of difference is not whether man is important or great,
but rather as to the origin, meaning and orientation of this importance. Man's "greatness" is immediately surrounded with ob-
scurity whenever we approach him in the abstract, apart from
his relation to God. But once the man of God comes into focus,
it becomes clear that we may never withdraw from the perspective
on man which we are then given, if we wish to honor the work of
God and the intention of His acts. There is a self-humiliation of
man, of man's nature, which has nothing to do with Biblical
humility; we can hear it in every protest (whether secular or religious) directed against man's nature rather than against the
guilt which the perversion of this nature brought about. Then
crowns may fall, but they are not the crowns of the Apocalypse.
Such self-humiliation is nothing but hidden pride, which will not
accept grace, and which does not understand the language of
Scripture when it says that God crowns man with lovingkindness
and tender mercies (Ps. 103:4) and that He will give the believer
a crown of righteousness (II Tim. 4:8).

And we may not ignore the fact that the Bible itself speaks
of man's greatness, in certain contexts. It does so with reference
not only to the original creation of man, not incorrectly often
referred to as the "crown of creation," but also with reference to
the restoration of fallen man, who in spite of and in the gifts of
God to him is immeasurably small in his great guilt. But in that
restoration things again change. Then we see perspectives of a
new order which manifests itself. Thus John the Baptist is judged
worthy of greatness in the story of salvation: "he shall be great
in the sight of the Lord" (Luke 1:15).

This greatness casts no shadow on the greatness of Christ, but
rather stands indissolubly connected with it, so that we read in
the same chapter, and with no feeling of tension, that Christ "shall
be great" (Luke 1:32). Nor should we, in abstraction, misunderstand this greatness as casting a shadow over John's life; John's
life is fulfilled in Him who is stronger (Matt. 3:11) and more

---

2. There is indeed a divine "forgetting" of guilt (Isa. 43:25, Jer. 31:34),
   as in Isa. 38:17: "thou hast cast all my sins behind thy back." But there
   is a remembering of the (forgiven) guilt in Rev. 5:9.

(Matt. 3:14) than he. The whole aim of John's preaching is directed to the end that Christ shall increase and John decrease (John 3:30); and this has nothing to do with an acute dialectic, in which one word replaces the other, but rather is the revelation of a wholly unique greatness which bears the stamp of the Kingdom of God. And this stamp is retained in all evangelical mention of the importance and greatness of man, so that no shadow falls over the greatness of God (cf. Luke 1:46, 49 and Titus 2:13). It is true that Scripture speaks explicitly of the greatness of man only rarely, and we might be inclined to feel a certain reticence in the terms of Scripture, addressed as they are to man, who is always inclined to change even this light into darkness and who — the "man of God" also — must be constantly warned against again falling into illusion through a false interpretation of his own "greatness." A concordance enables us to see quickly how references to the greatness of God dominate in Scripture, and also references to the great evil of man (Ps. 25:11, Eccles. 10:4, etc.). But this does not alter the fact that a light shines which makes it possible to use the word in a context which excludes all misunderstanding: "thy greatness has made me great" (II Sam. 22:36; cf. the context also), or "thy gentleness has made me great" (Ps. 18:35). And anyone who would nevertheless again be tempted to misinterpret this greatness in an abstract or secularizing fashion, in his waywardness sees this misunderstanding rebuked by Christ's explicit words: "whosoever will be great among you, let him be your minister; and whosoever will be chief among you, let him be your servant" (Matt. 20:26, Mark 10:43; cf. Mark 10:37, 42). If a door is closed here, a gate is opened, a gate to the Kingdom in which John the Baptist — at the threshold — may be great, but "he that is least in the kingdom of heaven is greater than he" (Matt. 11:11; Luke 7:28). The *magnalia Dei* do not exclude this greatness, but call it forth and form its exclusive source. It is always an echo, a reflex of another greatness and of great mercy (Dan. 9:18); "Behold, what manner of love the Father has bestowed upon us, that we should be called the sons of God" (I John 3:1).

Any attempt at greatness outside sonship is a perverted attempt by man who may perhaps win the world thereby, but at the loss of his own life (Matt. 16:26; Mark 8:36). Man rediscovers his destiny only in sonship, in which the following of God restores the image of God. And in that destiny there is a unique greatness, which goes beyond all worldly measure: "Whosoever therefore shall humble himself as this little child, the same is the greatest in the kingdom of heaven" (Matt. 18:4),[3] just as "whosoever therefore shall do and teach them [i.e., these commandments] shall be called great in the kingdom of heaven" (Matt. 5:19). This greatness is removed from misunderstanding only when related to sonship and service.[4] And all secularized greatness is from the viewpoint of the Kingdom of God ridiculous because it is a wishing to be great without true service (cf. Acts 8:9ff.). But in sonship and the service implied therein, greatness is Biblically legitimate, and can be denied only because of misanthropy or a confused religiosity. Such a religiosity pays attention to "everyone that exalteth himself shall be abased" (Luke 18:14; cf. 14:11), but does not understand the promise at the end of the parable — precisely of the Pharisee and the publican — that "he that humbleth himself shall be exalted." Anyone who thinks that the proper greatness of man diminishes the greatness of God has not understood the decisive relationships of the kingdom of God; he may perhaps be convinced by the marvelous words of the Lord Himself, evincing an outlook which is astonishing and which also rules out all misunderstanding: "if any man serve me, him will my Father honor" (John 12:26; cf. I Pet. 1:7, I Sam. 2:30).

' In this connection we may well devote a word to the well-known contrast between anthropocentric and theocentric. It is possible to use the term "anthropocentric" in various contexts, but its basic meaning is always that man places himself in a "central" position. From this center all the other "givens" are evaluated, in terms of the extent to which they can serve man as center. Thus the surroundings of man, the environment, can be devaluated to serve as mere "periphery," in a serious over-evaluation of man, which also can effect everyday life by producing a proud egoism. It should be clear that any such anthropocentrism can only be branded as illegitimate from the Biblical view of man. The process by which man was forced to give up his idea of a central position in the cosmos has often been portrayed, and the ideas

3. The occasion for this teaching of Jesus lay in the disciples' question as to who would be the greatest in the Kingdom. Cf. the division, at the Last Supper, over the question of priority and Christ's answer (Luke 22:24-27); it is in this connection that we read of Christ's prophecy about their sitting on thrones and judging the twelve tribes of Israel (Luke 22:30).

4. Cf. Schlatter, in Kittel, *Theologisches Wörterbuch*, IV, 539, *s.v.*, *megas*. He says "the meaning of the greatness to which Jesus raised the disciples is service."

of Copernicus and Darwin have then been seen as important factors in the process, threatening the complete precedence of man;[5] but it is clear that anthropocentrism was already exposed as an illusion by the witness of the Bible.

This witness is more serious and more penetrating than any other relativizing of man and, while it does not denigrate man as man, it does warn him against all overevaluation of himself, and there is no sharper protest against any form of anthropocentrism conceivable than the word of God to Job: "Where wast thou when I laid the foundations of the earth?" (Job 38:4). And many, many questions meet only with the divine irony of "Knowest thou it because thou wast then born? or because the number of thy days is great?" (Job 38:21). One of the marvelous things about the Biblical picture of man is that God gives to man a central place in created reality and that nevertheless no pretension can flow from this; indeed, all pretension results from a misunderstanding of this central creatureliness. We must also conclude that anthropocentrism never shows an original character; it appears to be nothing but a perversion of the true "central" position of man according to the intent of God. Only thus can the tidal wave of practical and theoretical anthropocentrism be understood. The dynamic around this *centrum* is so strong that it does not halt at the boundary of religion, not even that of the Christian religion; indeed it has often triumphantly manifested itself within the terrain of Christian theology.

The New Testament shows us (e.g., Phil. 2:4) how anthropocentrism manifested itself in the realm of Christian faith so that men put not "man" but themselves at the center, and that even the believers had to be admonished that we must not only be concerned about our own interests but also that of others. Also in theology the drive to arrive at an anthropocentric interpretation of the revelation of God can be observed. The evident illegitimacy of this method then sometimes produces a passionate protest, pleading for a "theocentric" theology in contrast to an "anthropocentric" theology that places man, the believing man, so much in the center of concern that a subjectivistic stamp is given to the whole structure of the theology. Thus Erich Schaeder opposed his theocentric theology to the theology of the nineteenth century, which (especially under the influence of Schleiermacher) in his estimate hardly seemed to realize the priority and sovereignty of

5. See, e.g., M. Landmann, *Philosophische Anthropologie* (1955), p. 85.

God and which narrowed and limited the content of the divine
revelation on the basis of religious need and religious experience.[6]

Such an anthropocentrism is always a serious danger, and if
for no other reason, the protest of a theocentric theology is sensible
and necessary. Theological anthropocentrism is always a more serious
danger than secular anthropocentrism, since we, from the very
meaning of *theology*, might expect that it would not misunderstand man as *centrum*. Though we might well judge that the
reference to God as *centrum* is faulty terminology,[7] the intention
of the theocentric protest is plain enough. It is a protest against the
priority of the religious subject, against the idea that this centrum
is normative; and it realizes full well that such an anthropocentric
theology is grist for the mill of those who, like Feuerbach, explained the idea of God as a projection of religious man, the
projection of human needs and wishes in need and danger. Was
it not implied, if not explicitly stated, in such an anthropocentric
theology that religion in general and Christianity in particular
was nothing more than a projection?[8]

It is especially the normative subject as *centrum*, the critical-
correlative element in this theology, which determines the structure
of the theology and eliminates from the gospel whatever is judged
not "according to man."[9] Thus it could happen that Xenophanes'
criticism of polytheistic religion as a projection of human con-
structs was applied, with an appearance of legitimacy, as a universal
explanation of all religion.[10] Anthropocentric theology can only

6. E. Schaeder, *Theozentrische Theologie*, I, II, (1928, 2nd ed.).
7. Even though the term is faulty, we can perhaps detect a reference
   to the richer and manifold imagery of Scripture: the Lamb in the
   midst of the throne (Rev. 7:17); God "that sitteth on the throne shall
   dwell among them" (Rev. 7:15) and shall wipe away their tears (Rev.
   7:17); the Lamb shall lead them to living fountains of waters (Rev.
   7:17; cf. Rev. 21:6). And finally, on the communion which is the aim
   of God's actions: "I will be his God, and he shall be my son (Rev.
   21:7; cf. Rev. 3:20).
8. Cf. K. Leese, *Die Prinzipienlehre der neueren systematischen Theologie
   im Lichte der Kritik Ludwig Feuerbachs* (1912). He writes about the
   defenselessness of this anthropocentric theology against Feuerbach's
   religious analysis. For the religious a priori, see my *Geloof en Openbaring
   in de nieuwere Duitse Theologie* (1932), p. 174.
9. Cf. Gal. 1:11, which says that the gospel is not according to man.
   Cf. the crisis in Christology in nineteenth-century theology, parallel with
   the crisis in the doctrine of atonement.
10. See F. Sierksma, *De religieuze Projectie* (1956), pp. 1, 2; and see further
    S. Freud, *Die Zukunft einer Illusion* (1928); S. Vestdijk, *De Toekomst der
    Religie* (1947; for F. Sierksma's review of criticisms thereof, *Tussen
    twee Vuren* (1952).

strengthen this sort of criticism in its conviction, because the correlation between religious subject and revelation is in this theology so arranged that the revelation of God — *mirabile dictu!* — appears to correspond precisely to a general natural wish-object and the "object" of religion thus becomes precisely one which is "according to man."[11]

It is understandable that, in reaction against this notion of projection, one would be tempted to go so far as to deny or misunderstand the "central" position of man in created reality, despite the Biblical emphasis on man and his salvation. None the less such an apologetic against "projection" would fall wide of its mark. It is precisely when we realize that an anthropocentric theology is a very serious danger that we must speak of another correlation, that of which anthropocentrism is a perversion; namely, that of God's plan of salvation and man's guilt, the need and the lost condition of man. Now, this context, the gospel of salvation, is the central concern of the "projectionist" critique, and it is seen as an obvious support for the idea that revelation corresponds to human desires. But we may not attack this critique by neglecting the mystery of the evangel as though this were to play a trump card! We may not be ashamed of the mystery of the gospel, even if many view it as a point of contact with the "projectionist" theory; and besides, to do so would be to ignore the fact that the "projectionist" theory can attach itself not only to religion and to faith and to (anthropocentric) theology, but it must also attach itself to the central message of the gospel, as, for example, to Paul's words regarding the *philanthropia* of God. Every projection theory that operates with the correlation of need and salvation battens on the refused light of a God who loves man, and who, as the Nicene-Constantinopolitan Creed has it, comes down to men from heaven.

Nourished by this refusal in its critique and in its antithesis, it therefore manifests one of the most serious symptoms of the modern critique of Christianity. For it attempts to clarify pro-

---

11. Thus Freud explains the general occurrence of religion in terms of the general occurrence of need and a feeling of being threatened. Cf. especially L. Feuerbach, *Das Wesen der Religion* (1851), — based on *Das Wesen des Christentums* (1841), in the Deutsche Bibl. edition of 1913, pp. 27, 17, 22. See his psychological explanation of religion; he cites the Roman saying that *"primus in orbe Deos fecit timor"* — roughly: Fear produces religion; and sums up his view in the oft cited words: *"Die Theologie ist Anthropologie"* (cf. p. 22; *"und Physiologie"*).

jection anthropologically and thus to unmask theology as anthropology. A successful refutation of the projectionist theory can not arise from a misanthropic or obscure view of the nature of man, but only from a belief in the reality of the gospel, which promises to give rest for unrest, certainty for doubt, and life for death. We are here involuntarily reminded of the restoration of Job after his long wrestling with doubt, when God, in the divine irony of Job 42, shows the relation between the service of Him and the glory of life in the ending of Job's ordeal (Job 42:10). The criticism which views Job 42 as not a genuine part of the book because it contrasts with the prologue of Job 1, where Job's piety is denounced as self-seeking, has a parallel in the projectionist critique[12] which has no slightest surmise of how gracious and good God is, and how He places man in the center of created reality, in such a central position that man turns his eyes with praise and adoration to Him who dwells in inaccessible light.

Precisely from the standpoint of divine salvation, we can understand the projectionist theory as an interpretation which is not the fruit of intellectual reflection, but rather of pre-reflective faith, of presuppositions, viewing the soteriological correlation itself as a projection, because the gospel (which is not "according to men" and thus arouses such strong opposition — as Luke 2:34 says, it is the "sign which shall be spoken against") lies outside this phenomenological or psychological analysis of the "essence" of man as he "actually" is.

Thus we must reject the attempt of anthropocentric theology and religion to reduce and simplify the gospel, but in spite of the projectionist theory (and indeed, if we wish to fight it effectively), we must never give up our perspective on the divine care for man, which was sung of in Israel (which had seen its "projected" idols fall): "Lord, what is man, that thou takest knowledge of him! or the son of man, that thou makest account of him!" (Ps. 144:3).

We can effectively oppose the projectionist theory only when we see man as important in another manner, see him in another greatness, as the man of God fully prepared for all good works. Then anthropocentrism is cancelled; as it is in one of the most profound words of the gospel, "Let your light so shine before men, that they may see your good works, and glorify your Father

---

12. The prologue of Job (piety and self-seeking) is especially instructive for exposing Feuerbach's ideas. A moderation of this sharp judgment of Feuerbach is not, I feel, possible.

which is in heaven" (Matt. 5:16). For so the man of God is truly the central point of creation.[13]

Scripture speaks about man with unmistakable evidence. This is already the case when it takes up creation, and we read of the creation of man in the image of God. We read of the uniqueness of man, and his dominance over the rest of creation, and the sovereign arrangement of his dominion over all things (Gen. 1:28; cf. Ps. 8:6).

It is clear that this does not at all open the way to man's self-glorification, since his uniqueness is indissolubly bound with his service of God in the world. This uniqueness stands so emphatically in man's relation to God that Scripture nowhere gives us an analysis of man's essence through which by way of anthropological categories the difference between man and animal would be explained and clarified. The two can be spoken of together, as in Ps. 36:6, 7: "thou preservest man and beast. How excellent is thy loving kindness, O God"; or the emphasis can fall on man, who has the glory and responsibility of showing forth the image of God in created reality. And then we hear the difference between man and animal expressed — without further analysis [14] namely,

13. See Sierksma, *De Religieuze Projectie*, pp. 19, 21, 24, 163, 179. The extent to which the theory of projection rests on non-intellectual presuppositions is evident in Sierksma's interpretation of the "eccentric" structure of man. It is especially noticeable when he pretends to give a scientific treatment of religious projection (p. 3) and when he says that Vestdijk "posits and proves" his scientific hypothesis of religious projection (p. 197). In relation to Buddhism, "that unique moment in human history" (p. 227; cf. projection and Buddhism), he makes the striking statement that "there is only one possible way to reject Buddhism in this area: through the existential voluntaristic explanation that man accepts a life with its suffering because he finds it, suffering and all, worth living nevertheless." It is evident that there is some discordance between this possibility and the scientifically proven (according to Sierksma) theory of projection. Cf. Sierksma's strong convictions on man's "essence" and the decisive difference between man and animal (p. 23). Here is the a priori which dominates the whole book. It is so strong that he judges his interpretation of man's eccentric structure to be the only possible explanation of religion.

14. No matter how many riddles man faces as he views non-human reality, the analysis of it is emphatically part of his task. It is meaningful that today, when once again especial attention is being given to the uniqueness of man, a strong concern is also being directed towards the animal world. Cf. the worth-while collection of essays edited by F. L. R. Sassen, *Mens en Dier* (1954), from which it appears that this concern was also alive in earlier days as well, in many respects. Cf. the essay of L. Raeymaker, "De cosmische Betekenis van het Dier naar het

that man is higher than the sparrows, the birds of the air, and the lilies of the field. This in no sense implies a devaluation of the non-human world; for it is said of the lilies that Solomon in all his glory was not arrayed as they are, and of the sparrows that not one of them is forgotten by God.[15]

There is a divine concern for all the works of His hand, and this New Testament remembrance of the animals finds its parallel when Isaiah, in a call to Israel, is reminded that God made the stars and "he calleth them all by names . . . not one faileth" (Isa. 40:26; cf. Job 38:4-7). In such passages, we see every false anthropocentrism broken through by the light of the concern of God, so shaming to man, who so often passes by the works of God's hand heedlessly.

It is so easy to take man's uniqueness out of its relationships and to make it a proud "primary" thing, with the non-human world taking a "secondary" and unimportant place. The Biblical "higher" and "much more" is then unrecognizably distorted, since it is no longer in the context of service and responsibility, and of man's destiny within the plan of God. Man then becomes alienated from the non-human world, not only from the animals but from all of non-human reality, in a confused and not theoretical but practical solipsism. If we emphasize the person so much that we destroy the unity of reality and devaluate the non-human world in one way or another, we misunderstand the bonds uniting man and

---

Wereldbeeld van de H. Thomas van Aquino," pp. 120ff. It concludes — without devaluation — that "man is the end of all creation" (p. 137). Cf. also, in relation to Pascal's view of man (misery and grandeur), the essay of C. A. van Peursen, "Mens en Dier in het Denken van Michel de Montaigne en Blaise Pascal," pp. 161ff. All analysis of created being encounters the reality of the "higher" of Scripture, which is there presupposed without analysis.

15. When we mention the "incidental" nature of many of the Scriptural references, we do not at all mean to underevaluate the impressiveness of these references. Cf. the citations, in many ways revealing, collected by G. Nieuwenhuysen, *Kerk en Dierenwereld,* in which the many references to animals made by Scripture are collected and commented on (e.g., Ps. 36:7, Prov. 12:10, Job 12:7, Matt. 12:11, Jonah 4:11, etc.). The incidental way of speaking in Scripture does not imply a devaluation of non-human reality, but points rather to man and his unique place in this reality, also in his guilt and salvation. See further Barth, *Kirkliche Dogmatik,* III, 4, especially pp. 376, 396. He appeals for an attention to, and a consciousness of, responsibility and at the same time a warning against relativizing (e.g., Schweitzer's "respect for life"); Schweitzer himself took on the service of mankind (p. 398), an immanent criticism of his own position.

the whole creation and misunderstand the meaning of his humanness, and so open the way to our alienation from that which God
called good. And here is hidden (or revealed!) that pride which
busies itself in separating what God has put together. Such alienation is broken through when we see man as man of God in the
world, in God's world, and become concerned with all that with
which God is concerned; just as the eyes of Israel, which were
lifted to Jehovah, were also opened to all the works of His hand.[16]
  And at the same time we can then understand how the uniqueness and centrality of man does not pave the way toward self-
glorification. For in our reflection we may never abstract from the
revealing context of Romans 8, in which man's central position
is seen in connection with the curse and the corruption to which
the whole of creation is subjected (Rom. 8:20; cf. Gen. 3:17).
  It is God Himself who has so subjected it. "The history of
man's relation to God is the beating heart of the whole cosmos."[17]
But at the same time this uniqueness and centrality of man is
related to the creation's hope, and we see it clearly delineated
when we read that the creation "shall be delivered from the
bondage of corruption into the glorious liberty of the children
of God" (Rom. 8:21) and that it "waiteth for the manifestation
of the sons of God" (Rom. 8:19).

  In connection with the uniqueness and centrality of man, which
becomes revealed in greater glory in its restoration through Christ,
let us turn our attention briefly to what Scripture says of this
humanness in relation to the world of the angels. We are clearly
warned away from all speculation on the subject, which has led
to all sorts of conclusions, some of them fantastic indeed.[18] We
should note first of all that Scripture does not speak systematically
when it speaks of angels in relation to man. This is clear when

16. See Chap. VI of my *General Revelation*.
17. P. Althaus, *Der Brief an die Römer* (1949), p. 78; cf. O. Michel,
   Römerbrief, p. 173. The "him" of Rom. 8:20 who subjected creation to
   vanity is generally taken to mean God but cf. Zahn, *Commentaar*, p. 402,
   who takes it to be man, become sinful. There seems to be no disagreement on relating this "subjection" to man's guilt.
18. See A. Vonier, *De Engelen* (1951), pp. 113-14. Concerning men as
   taking the places in the angelic hierarchy left open by the fallen angels,
   he claims this as a Catholic tradition. See also his twelve analytical
   propositions regarding the essence of angels, in spite of the fact that
   in his opinion Scripture never explicitly instructs us regarding the
   spirits from the invisible world. Not less speculative is C. Friethoff,
   Engelen en Duivelen (1940), e.g., on "nature and grace" as regards the
   angels (p. 10).

we read, for example, "Are they not all ministering spirits, sent forth to minister unto them who shall be heirs of salvation?" (Heb. 1:14; cf. Rev. 19:10). Here, in what we may almost call a Biblical "definition" of the angels, their relation to man is set forth, and no more. This "definition" certainly does not detract from the glory of the angels; in relation to the world of the angels, we must manifestly use other measurements than we usually do; their glory and this service coincide completely. We also hear, incidentally, of the angels in relation to the glory of man's conversion from darkness to light: "there is joy in the presence of the angels of God over one sinner that repenteth" (Luke 15:10; cf. 15:7). And Paul· speaks of man's wonderful "higher" position: "Know ye not that we shall judge angels?" (I Cor. 6:3; cf. 6:2). It is clear that this text does not refer to a measureless self-elevation of man, a human *hybris,* but to the wealth and glory of the believer which has been given by God, from which Paul draws conclusions for the concrete practical life of the believer, on which falls the light of the eschatological judgment (I Cor. 6:4, 2).[19]

Anyone who dares "go to law before the unjust, and not before the saints" (I Cor. 6:1) shows that he has no idea of the perspectives proper to the Church; he finds no "authority" in it now, and yet the Church has the prospect in the future of an especial "competence"; as Zahn says, this shows[20] "a disregard for the brothers, whose authority is rejected, in sharp contradiction to the dignity which God has in store for them."

If one nevertheless views this placing of humanness above the angels in man's judging them as an overevaluation of human worth, one should consider that this judging which attests the dignity of restored humanity is a judging by the same Church through which "unto the principalities and powers in heavenly places might be made known the manifold wisdom of God" (Eph. 3:10)[21] Make no mistake: the whole relation between

19. It is the light of the future thrown on judgment in the Church regarding everyday differences (6:4). Cf. "the smallest matters" (6:2). See J. Blauw, *Gezanten van den Hemel,* pp. 151ff.; E. Schick, *Die Botschaft der Engel im Neuem Testament* (1946), p. 281.
20. Zahn, *Commentaar, ad loc.,* p. 231.
21. See Grundmann, in Kittel, *Theologisches Wörterbuch,* I, 84-85, *s.v., aggelos.* He is in error when he says that Paul has a special tendency to stress the inferiority of the angels, corresponding to "the complete overshadowing of the angels through the fact of Christ." His use of *"Geringwertigkeit"* and *"Abwertung"* for Paul's evaluation is completely misplaced. Cf. further I Thess. 4:16, II Thess. 1:7. On Eph. 3:10, see

angels and men is quite different from that of the ordinary view of higher-lower, greater-lesser. Everything is centered around the great mystery of the gospel, "which things the angels desire to look upon" (I Pet. 1:12). This "distance" between man and angels can only be understood in the context of the wonder of atonement (the light in the darkness); man's greater dignity therein, his uniqueness, his greater nearness, are all undeniable — but are in this context correlated with the guilt, from which humanness is saved.[22]

Everything that Scripture tells us in this connection is completely removed from any comparison or competition between angels as higher and men as lower. Paul speaks — in the speech of the Kingdom and the communion with Christ — of the apostles as set in the lowest place: "God hath set forth us the apostles last, as it were appointed to death, for we are made a spectacle unto the world, and to angels, and to men" (I Cor. 4:9). But the uniqueness of humanness in the plan of God is not thereby affected, and the perspective remains, the perspective which comes from man's reconciliation and peace after his enmity. Then man's true greatness is again revealed, through an unearned reconciliation, and the angels are the messengers of this new joy amidst the fields of Bethlehem: "on earth peace, toward men of good will" (Luke 2:14). The unique mystery of man evidently does not threaten the glory of the serving angels, for they sing praises and cry, "Holy, holy, holy, is the Lord of hosts: the whole earth is full of his glory" (Isa. 6:3).

The greatness, the "higher" place, of man is misunderstood only when man no longer wishes to be completely the man of God and no longer understands the meaning and the calling of this greatness as being a man of God fully prepared for every good work (II Tim. 3:17), doing God's will "on earth, as it is in heaven."

When this Biblical relationship is broken, the perspective falls away, and man stands in a "center" where he has placed himself,

---

S. F. H. J. Berkelbach van der Sprenkel, "De Brief aan de Efeziërs," *De Kerk* (1941-1947). He speaks of the perspective "which man has hardly suspected."

22. Cf. Heb. 2:16, "he [Christ] took not on him the nature of angels; but he took on him the seed of Abraham." Grosheide says it is now generally accepted as referring not to the taking on of human nature, but to concern with it. See K. Schilder, *Heidelbergse Catechismus*, II, 43ff. He paraphrases the text as "not the nature of the *fallen* angels" — an addition which does not occur in the text.

and in which he is alienated from true humanness, from being the man of God; and is then finally alienated from the world and from himself. We are called away from such a "center" by the light which shows us another order and another relationship: the mystery of a reconciliation, of an order in which "greater" and "lesser" are overarched by service and praise and thankfulness. And we shall not apply to this order, in the *magnalia Dei*, the measurements of the corrupt human heart, which has no understanding of what is great in the eyes of God.

It is by that standard that man now and later is measured. Considering how constantly greatness is misunderstood, it is not far-fetched to speak of a divine unmasking, a total exposure of the whole life of man, then, when human life passes through the completely righteous Judgment. It is that Judgment which found an unmistakable prelude in the judgment which Mary saw unfold in her vision when the Messiah should come: "he hath scattered the proud in the imagination of their hearts. He hath put down the mighty from their seats, and exalted them of low degree. He hath filled the hungry with good things; and the rich he hath sent empty away" (Luke 1:51-53).

In contrast with this scattering of the proud the gospel of grace summons to return. It is the call to true humanness. For in Mary's song of praise, the Judgment is humbly related to what now is happening; it is the song of praise that "his mercy is on them that fear him from generation to generation" (Luke 1:50).

This divine mercy leads the man of God to a small or a great task, with many or with few talents. But the demonic attraction of human greatness has been broken through, and the question of who is first in the kingdom of heaven vanishes. Being prepared for every good work leaves no room for that question, for the time is short. Time for service, for fighting the good fight, for laying hold of eternal life (I Tim. 6:11).

Until victory comes: "To him that overcometh will I grant to sit with me in my throne, even as I also overcame, and am set down with my Father in his throne. He that hath an ear, let him hear what the Spirit saith unto the churches" (Rev. 3:21-22).

Index

INDEX OF AUTHORS

INDEX OF SCRIPTURES